Cyprus: a conflict at the crossroads

MANCHESTER 1824

Manchester University Press

Cyprus: a conflict at the crossroads

edited by Thomas Diez and Nathalie Tocci

Manchester University Press

Manchester and New York

distributed in the United States exclusively
by Palgrave Macmillan

Published by Manchester University Press
Oxford Road, Manchester M13 9NR, UK
and Room 400, 175 Fifth Avenue, New York, NY 10010, USA
www.manchesteruniversitypress.co.uk

Distributed in the United States exclusively by
Palgrave Macmillan, 175 Fifth Avenue,
New York, NY 10010, USA

Distributed in Canada exclusively by
UBC Press, University of British Columbia, 2029 West Mall,
Vancouver, BC, Canada V6T 1Z2

British Library Cataloguing-in-Publication Data is available

Library of Congress Cataloging-in-Publication Data is available

ISBN 978 0 7190 9116 2 paperback

First published by Manchester University Press in hardback 2009

This paperback edition first published 2013

Printed by Lightning Source

Contents

Tables

Contributors

Emel Akçali is Honorary Research Fellow at the Department of Political Science and International Studies, University of Birmingham. She holds a PhD in Political Geography from Paris IV–Sorbonne, and an MA and a BA in International Relations, respectively from Galatasaray University and the American University of Paris. She currently works on the role of territoriality and ethno-territorial conflicts in Europe and European Union policy towards their resolution.

Bekir Azgin teaches at the Eastern Mediterranean University. He has published widely on the Cyprus problem, media and culture in both English and Turkish. Among his publications are: 'The Cyprus Conflict: A Case Study for the EU or a Headache?', in T. Giegerich (ed.), *The EU Accession of Cyprus* (Nomos, 2006); 'Nationalism and Interest in the "Other Side's" Literature', in M. Yaşin (ed.), *Step-Mothertongue* (Middlesex University Press, 2000); and 'The Turkish Cypriot Mass Media', in K.-D. Grothusen, W. Steffani and P. Zervakis (eds), *Zypern Südosteuropa – Handbuch, Vol. VIII* (Vandenhoeck & Ruprecht, 1998).

Mashoed Bailie teaches communication and media studies at Eastern Mediterranean University (EMU) in northern Cyprus. He is the editor of the *Global Media Journal: Mediterranean Edition* and the director of the Center for Communication and Peace Studies at EMU. His research areas include communication, social justice and peace studies and media, gender and democracy. Among his publications are the book *Democratizing Communication: Comparative Perspectives in Information and Power* (Hampton Press, 1997), co-edited with Dwayne Winseck, and, more recently, the article 'Women and the Media in Northern Cyprus: A Political Economy of Communication and Gender', *Journal of Cyprus Studies*, 12: 71–92 (2007).

Canan Balkır is Professor of Economics at Dokuz Eylul University, Turkey. She is the head of the European Studies Graduate Programme, and holds the Jean Monnet Chair in European Economic Integration. She has published widely on relations between Turkey and the European Union, including *Turkey and Europe*, co-edited with A. M. Williams (Pinter, 1993). She has lectured in northern Cyprus and has analysed economic issues, including in the article 'The Turkish Cypriot Business Community as a Politico-Economic Actor Searching For a Solution', *Turkish Policy Quarterly*, winter: 127–47 (2005), and *The Economic Evaluation of the Annan Plan* (TOBB, 2003).

Eiki Berg is Professor of International Relations at the University of Tartu. He is co-editor, with Henk van Houtum, of *Routing Borders Between Territories, Discourses and Practices* (Ashgate, 2003) and author of several articles published in the *Journal of Baltic Studies*, *Geopolitics*, *Political Geography*, *Cooperation and Conflict*, *Global Society*, *Space and Polity*, *Europe–Asia Studies*, *Regional and Federal Studies*, *Tijdschrift voor economische en sociale geografie*, and the *Journal of Communist Studies and Transition Politics*.

Thomas Diez is Professor of International Relations at the University of Birmingham. He was coordinator of the EUBorderConf project (www.euborderconf.bham.ac.uk) and has published widely on the intersection of international relations theory and European integration, as well as on relations between Turkey and the European Union and Cyprus and the European Union. Among his recent publications are *The European Union and Border Conflicts*, co-edited with Mathias Albert and Stephan Stetter (Cambridge University Press, 2008) and 'Expanding Europe: The Ethics of EU–Turkey Relations', *Ethics and International Affairs*, 21: 615–22 (2007).

Elise Féron is a Senior Lecturer at the Institute of Political Studies in Lille and a researcher at the Centre de Politique Comparée in Louvain. Her research deals with community conflicts and issues of identity. She was coordinator of the PEACE-COM project (http://peacecom.spri.ucl.ac.be). Among her recent publications are *L'imaginaire des conflits communautaires*, co-edited with Michel Hastings (L'Harmattan, 2002), and 'Paths to Reconversion Taken by Northern Irish Paramilitaries', *International Social Science Journal*, 189: 447–56 (2007).

Ayla Gürel is a researcher and consultant working for the International Peace Research Institute, Oslo (PRIO). At present she is leading a research and information project examining property-related issues within the context of the Cyprus problem. She studied electrical engineering and has held several academic posts at the Eastern Mediterranean University in Famagusta and at the University of Texas in Arlington. She has numerous publications, mostly in her former field, and more recently on the Cyprus problem. She is a co-author, with Kudret Özersay, of *The Politics of Property in Cyprus* (PRIO, 2006).

Fatma Güven Lisaniler is Professor of Economics at Eastern Mediterranean University. She was the North Cyprus team coordinator of the PEACE-COM project (http://peacecom.spri.ucl.ac.be) and has published on the Cyprus conflict and the northern Cyprus labour market. Among her recent publications are 'Labor Mobility and Labor Market Convergence in Cyprus', *Turkish Studies*, 8: 41–67 (2007), 'Gender Equality in North Cyprus (Turkish Republic of Northern Cyprus)', *Quaderns de la Mediterrania*, 7: 133–40 (2007), 'Determinant of Labor Force Participation: A Case of Cyprus', *Review of Social, Economic and Business Studies*, 5(6): 209–26 (2006), and 'Migrant Sex Workers and State Regulations in North Cyprus', *Women's Studies International Forum*, 28: 79–91 (2005).

Maria Hadjipavlou is an Assistant Professor at the Department of Social and Political Sciences, University of Cyprus. She teaches on comparative politics, gender studies, conflict resolution, international organisations and the Cyprus conflict from a multidisciplinary perspective. She has facilitated and designed numerous conflict resolution workshops among different social groups from both Cypriot communities. She is a founding member and president of the Cyprus Peace Center and a founding member of the first Cypriot women's non-governmental organisation, Hands Across the Divide (2001). She has published widely in the areas of conflict resolution, the Cyprus conflict, women and peace, and ethnic stereotypes. She coordinated a pioneer research project on 'Women in All Cypriot Communities', on which a book is due to be published by I. B. Tauris in 2009.

Alper Kaliber is a Research Fellow at the Department of Political Science and International Studies, University of Birmingham. He is currently conducting a research project entitled 'De-securitising Foreign Policy Unpacking the Impact of Europeanisation: The Cyprus Case'. His areas of interest include critical security studies, European security, the process of Europeanisation, Turkish politics and modernisation, and the Cyprus conflict. He has mainly published on Turkey's security discourses on Cyprus and the Europeanisation and modernisation of Turkey, in both English and Turkish.

Erol Kaymak is Assistant Professor of International Relations at the Eastern Mediterranean University based in Famagusta. His research interests include identity politics in Cyprus. Among his recent publications are 'Does Cyprus Need a Truth and Reconciliation Commission?', *Cyprus Review*, 19: 71–89 (2007), and co-authorship of 'An Assessment of Civil Society in Cyprus: A Map for the Future' (Civil Society Index Report, CIVICUS, 2005).

Tobias Kelly is Senior Lecturer in Social Anthropology at the University of Edinburgh. His research interests include the Israeli–Palestinian conflict and the anthropology of international law. His publications include *Law, Violence and Sovereignty Among West Bank Palestinians* (Cambridge University Press, 2006) and *Paths to International Justice: Social and Legal Perspectives*, co-edited with Marie-Bénédicte Dembour (Cambridge University Press, 2007).

James Ker-Lindsay is a Senior Research Fellow in European Studies at Kingston University, London, and IAA Defence Analysis Institute Senior Research Fellow at the Hellenic Observatory, European Institute, London School of Economics (2008–09). His main publications include *The Government and Politics of Cyprus* (Peter Lang, 2008), *Crisis and Conciliation: A Year of Rapprochement Between Greece and Turkey* (I. B. Tauris, 2007) and *EU Accession and UN Peacemaking in Cyprus* (Palgrave Macmillan, 2005). He is also a co-editor of the *Cyprus Review*.

Peter Loizos has been teaching at the London School of Economics since 1969. He has authored or co-authored *The Greek Gift: Politics in a Changing Cypriot Village* (Blackwell, 1975), *The Heart Grown Bitter: A Chronicle of Cypriot War Refugees* (Cambridge University Press, 1981), *Contested Identities: Gender and Kinship in Modern Greece* (with E. Papataxiarchis) (Princeton University Press, 1991), *Innovation in Ethnographic Film: From Innovation to Self-consciousness* (University of Chicago Press, 1993), *Conceiving Persons: Ethnographies of Procreation, Fertility and Growth* (with Patrick Heady) (Athlone Press, 1999), *Unofficial Views: Cyprus – Society and Politics* (Intercollege Press, 2001), and *Iron in the Soul: Displacement, Livelihood and Health in Cyprus* (Berghahn Books, 2008). He has also directed a number of documentary films.

Alexandros Lordos is the Director of the Cyprus Institute for Policy Analysis. In the years since the 2004 referendum, he has undertaken a number of inter-communal polls in Cyprus with the aim of discovering consensus-based grass-roots solutions to the issues still blocking a comprehensive settlement. The results of his surveys, reported in *Options for Peace: Mapping the Possibilities for a Comprehensive Settlement in Cyprus* (May 2005) and *Building Trust: An*

Inter-communal Analysis of Public Opinion in Cyprus (April 2006), among others, are available online from www.CyprusPolls.org. He has also served as consultant to the United Nations Peacekeeping Force in Cyprus (UNFICYP) in the first ever inter-communal survey of public opinion that the United Nations conducted in Cyprus in spring 2007, available at www.unficyp.org.

Kudret Özersay is Assistant Professor at the Department of International Relations, Eastern Mediterranean University in northern Cyprus, of which he is presently the Chair. He is working in a research and information project team investigating the problem of property in Cyprus for the International Peace Research Institute, Oslo (PRIO). He received his BA, MA and PhD in international relations and international law. He has a book and several articles on the legal dimensions of the Cyprus problem, and is the co-author, with Ayla Gürel, of *The Politics of Property in Cyprus* (PRIO, 2006).

Nathalie Tocci is a Senior Fellow at the Istituto Affari Internazionali and an Associate Fellow at the Centre for European Policy Studies. She has a long-standing interest in European foreign policy, conflict resolution, the Middle East and the Mediterranean. She has written two books, numerous peer-reviewed articles, academic and policy papers, and chapters in edited volumes. Her recent publications include 'The EU and Conflict Resolution in Turkey and Georgia: Hindering EU Potential Through the Political Management of Contractual Relations', *Journal of Common Market Studies*, 46: 875–97 (2008), and *The EU and Conflict Resolution: Promoting Peace in the Backyard* (Routledge, 2007). She is the 2008 winner of the Anna Lindh Prize for the Study of European Foreign Policy, awarded by the Compagnia di San Paolo, the Riksbankens Jubileumsfond and the Volkswagenstiftung.

Susannah Verney is Lecturer in International and European Studies and Coordinator of the Postgraduate Programme in Southeast European Studies at the University of Athens. She is editor of the journal *South European Society and Politics*, and a former associate editor of the *Journal of Modern Greek Studies*. Her previous work has focused primarily on relations between Greece and the European Union. Recent publications include two edited volumes, *Turkey's Road to European Union Membership: National Identity and Political Change*, co-edited with Kostas Ifantis (Routledge, 2008), and *Euroscepticism in Southern Europe* (Routledge, 2009).

Yücel Vural is Assistant Professor of Political Science at the Eastern Mediterranean University. His main academic interest is identity politics and Cyprus politics. Among his recent publications are (with N. Peristianis)

'Beyond Ethno-Nationalism: Emerging Trends in Cypriot Politics After the Annan Plan', *Nations and Nationalism*, 14(1): 39–60 (2008), and (with A. Rustemli) 'Identity Fluctuations in the Turkish Cypriot Community', *Mediterranean Politics*, 11: 329–48 (2006).

Max Watson is Economic Adviser to the Director-General of DG ECFIN at the European Commission, a Fellow of Wolfson College, Oxford, and an Associate Fellow of Chatham House. He served as an economic adviser to the United Nations team during the Annan Plan negotiations in Cyprus. Previously, he was a Deputy Director of the International Monetary Fund, where his work was concerned with international capital market and debt issues, and the transition in eastern Europe. He has published mainly on financial market topics, on the functioning of the euro area and on the Cyprus issue.

Galip L. Yalman is Assistant Professor of Political Science and Chair of the European Studies Graduate Programme at the Middle East Technical University. He is currently the President of the Turkish Social Sciences Association. Among his recent publications are: 'The Turkish State and the Bourgeoisie in a Historical Perspective: A Relativist Paradigm or Panoply of Hegemonic Strategies?', in N. Balkan and S. Savran (eds), *The Politics of Permanent Crisis: Class, Ideology and State in Turkey* (Nova Science, 2002), and 'Rethinking the Nature of the Beast: The Turkish State and the Process of Europeanization', in A. H. Köse, F. Şenses and E. Yeldan (eds), *Globalisation as New Imperialism: Reconstruction of the Periphery* (Nova Science, 2008).

Acknowledgements

This book has its origin in a workshop on Cyprus at the Joint Session of Workshops of the European Consortium for Political Research (ECPR), Nicosia, in April 2006. We would like to thank the ECPR for making it possible for us to meet and discuss the Cyprus conflict across political and disciplinary divides, and all the participants of the workshop, including those not included in this book, for the stimulating discussions we had during that week. Thanks are also due to Laurence Cooley, who made sure that the final manuscript was in a reasonable shape before submission, and to the referees of Manchester University Press for helping us to sharpen the arguments in this book. Our apologies go to our families and friends, who have once again suffered from us getting involved in a project they could have done without.

This book is for all those who have travelled with us over the last decade or so in our search for a fresh perspective on what people describe as a protracted conflict.

Thomas Diez and Nathalie Tocci
Birmingham and Rome

Abbreviations

AKEL	Progressive Workers' Party (Greek-Cypriot)
AKP	Justice and Development Party (Turkey)
ALDE	Group of the Alliance of Liberals and Democrats for Europe (European Parliament)
BDH	Peace and Democracy Movement (Turkish-Cypriot)
BiH	Bosnia and Herzegovina
BKP	United Cyprus Party (Turkish-Cypriot)
CARDS	Community Assistance and Reconstruction Development and Stabilisation
CFSP	Common Foreign and Security Policy
CoE	Council of Europe
CSCE	Conference for Security and Co-operation in Europe
CTP	Republican Turkish Party (Turkish-Cypriot)
CY	Cyprus
CYP	Cypriot pound
DA	Denmark
DE	Germany
DIKO	Democratic Party (Greek-Cypriot)
DISY	Democratic Rally (Greek-Cypriot)
DP	Democratic Party (Turkish-Cypriot)
EC	European Community
ECHR	European Court of Human Rights
ECJ	European Court of Justice
ECPR	European Consortium for Political Research
ECSC	European Coal and Steel Community

EDEK	Movement for Social Democracy (Greek-Cypriot)
EDN	Europe of Nations Group (European Parliament, 1994–96)
EL	Greece
EOKA	National Organisation of Cypriot Fighters
EP	European Parliament
ESDP	European Security and Defence Policy
EU	European Union
FR	France
FSP	foreign and security policy
FYROM	Former Yugoslav Republic of Macedonia
GDP	gross domestic product
GNP	gross national product
GUE/NGL	Confederal Group of the European United Left – Nordic Green Left (European Parliament)
ICJ	International Court of Justice
IDP	internally displaced person
IMF	International Monetary Fund
IND/DEM	Independence/Democracy Group (European Parliament)
IR	international relations
IR	Ireland
İŞAD	Businessmen Association in Northern Cyprus (Turkish-Cypriot)
IT	Italy
KAB	Cyprus EU Association
KLA	Kosovo Liberation Army
KTOS	Cyprus Turkish Primary School Teachers Union
KTTO	Turkish-Cypriot Chamber of Commerce
MEP	Member of the European Parliament
MP	Member of Parliament
NATO	North Atlantic Treaty Organization
NGO	non-governmental organisation
NI	independent MEPs
NL	Netherlands
NLA	National Liberation Army (Kosovo)
NPE	normative power Europe
OHR	Office of the High Representative
ORP	Freedom and Reform Party (Turkish-Cypriot)
OSCE	Organization for Security and Co-operation in Europe
PCPSR	Palestinian Center for Policy and Survey Research
PLO	Palestinian Liberation Organization
PNA	Palestinian National Authority

PPE-DE	Group of the European People's Party (Christian Democrats) and European Democrats (European Parliament)
PPP	purchasing power parity
PSE	Socialist Group (European Parliament)
PT	Portugal
RoC	Republic of Cyprus
RRF	Rapid Reaction Forces
RRM	Rapid Reaction Mechanism
RS	Republika Srpska
RSC	regional security complex
RSCT	regional security complex theory
SAA	Stabilisation and Association Agreement
SAP	Stabilisation and Association Process
SBiH	Party for Bosnia and Herzegovina
SMEs	small and medium-sized enterprises
SPSEE	Stability Pact for South-Eastern Europe
SV	Sweden
TDP	Communal Democracy Party (Turkish-Cypriot)
TKP	Communal Liberation Party (Turkish-Cypriot)
TMR	Transnistrian Moldovan Republic
TMT	Turkish Resistance Organisation
TRNC	Turkish Republic of Northern Cyprus
UBP	National Unity Party (Turkish-Cypriot)
UEN	Union for Europe of the Nations Group (European Parliament, successor to UPE, 1999–present)
UK	United Kingdom
UN	United Nations
UNDP	United National Development Programme
UNFICYP	United Nations Peacekeeping Force in Cyprus
UNICEF	United Nations Children's Fund
UNSG	United Nations Secretary-General
UNWRA	United Nations Relief and Works Agency for Palestine Refugees in the Near East
UPE	Union for Europe Group (European Parliament, 1995–99)
US	United States
USSR	Union of Soviet Socialist Republics
Verts/ALE	Group of the Greens/European Free Alliance (European Parliament)
YBH	Patriotic Unity Movement (Turkish-Cypriot)
YKP	New Cyprus Party (Turkish-Cypriot)
YTL	New Turkish Lira

1

Introduction

Nathalie Tocci and Thomas Diez

Cyprus at the crossroads

Cyprus is a conflict at the crossroads in more than one sense. It has been the site of one of the most long-standing and protracted conflicts in international politics, bedevilled by a complex interplay of actors and factors at the local, regional, European and international levels. Yet it finds itself at a particularly crucial moment in its historical evolution. After the failure in April 2004 of the 'Annan Plan', sponsored by the United Nations (UN), the ensuing entry into the European Union (EU) of the divided island in May that year, and the opening of the EU's accession negotiations with Turkey, the conflict has been propelled to a new crossroads. The rejection of the Annan Plan by the Greek-Cypriot community marked in many ways the end of an era in UN-mediated negotiations on a bizonal and bicommunal federation, notwithstanding the relaunch of the peace process under the leaderships of the newly elected Greek Cypriot President Dimitris Christofias and his Turkish-Cypriot counterpart, Mehmet Ali Talat, in spring 2008. The EU accession of a divided island has generated new incentives and opportunities for all parties to the conflict, yet it has also created new tensions and lines of division on the island and in the eastern Mediterranean. The opening of Turkey's accession talks, riddled with obstacles and uncertainties, has concomitantly opened new avenues for conflict resolution in Cyprus and raised the danger that EU–Turkey relations may become the next victim of the protracted Cyprus conflict.

More poignantly, however, the Cyprus conflict stands at the crossroads of a series of core questions in the analysis of conflict addressed in different disciplines, not only political science and international relations. This makes

Cyprus a rich empirical case study for the elucidation of theoretical and conceptual debates. The 1960 constitution of the Republic of Cyprus (RoC) is, and has been analysed as, an example of early consociationalism, and its history exemplifies the problems associated with that concept (Kyriakides, 1968; Polyviou, 1976). Inter-communal negotiations since 1974, centred on federalism, confederalism and power-sharing, illustrate the prospects and limits of attempting to square the circle between claims to self-determination and revendications of sovereignty and territorial integrity (Chrysostomides, 2000). The representation of the conflict as a bicommunal one brings to the fore questions of identity, territory and political representation addressed in many constructivist and post-structuralist works (Diez, 2002d). Cyprus was one of the first locales of UN peace-keeping and mediation, and the UN experience there illustrates a series of tensions in such operations, including the one between keeping the peace and extending the conflict (Hannay, 2005; Mirbagheri, 1998; Richmond, 1998). More broadly, the role of the UN in Cyprus has raised wider questions concerning the effectiveness and modalities of international mediation and negotiation. The EU's involvement in Cyprus has challenged widely held beliefs about the connection between European integration and peace (Brewin, 2000; Tocci, 2004a,b, 2007). We could add many other examples and questions to this list. They all demonstrate the empirical interest in studying the case of Cyprus as a laboratory where central general questions of the discipline are played out.

Yet not only does Cyprus provide interesting empirical material to substantiate research into particular theories and disciplines. Its rich and complex history, when analysed from particular angles, can also provide new insights to be translated into broader theoretical and conceptual terms. As Watson notes in chapter 14, the economics of the Cyprus question tells us much about how living standards, within and between communities in conflict, can sustain and fuel conflict dynamics, while at the same time representing an indispensable component in conflict settlement, resolution and transformation. Perhaps even more importantly, the perceptions and misperceptions of the economics of conflict, if manipulated, mismanaged or neglected, can act as formidable obstacles to peaceful resolution. A focus on law and conflict, adopted by Özersay and Gürel in chapter 15, sheds light on the complex relationship between human rights, justice and conflict, while also emphasising the complex interplay between negotiation, mediation and arbitration in conflict situations. Studying instead the changing regional dynamics of the eastern Mediterranean illustrates how and why the very definition of a region may change in response to changing domestic actors and interests, exemplifying how regions are far from static and fixed political constructs. Again, many more examples could follow. Suffice it to say that analysing Cyprus from these various perspectives offers new and critical insights for our wider understanding of conflict research in its broadest sense.

Structure and rationale of the book

The book is divided into four main parts. In the first, we focus on the internal actors and units of analysis within conflict contexts, and illustrate how and why delving into the dynamics within conflict parties, as well as the relationship between them, can offer a richer and more comprehensive understanding of the existence, persistence and evolution of conflict. In the second, we turn to external actors and factors in conflict, and assess how the regional, European and wider international dimensions of the Cyprus conflict have influenced conflict dynamics, in interaction with its internal determinants. While all the chapters in the first and second parts of the book are concerned exclusively with Cyprus, they provide a set of general approaches to the analysis of conflict, by focusing on its multiple actors and levels of analysis, thereby putting together a much more complex picture than is often found in the traditional literature. The third part broadens this set of approaches by involving the case of Cyprus in comparative analysis, be this on the constitutional features of future solutions (Berg, chapter 9), on the role of one internal actor in conflict, such as the refugees (Loizos and Kelly, chapter 12), or on the role of an external actor involved in conflict resolution (i.e., the EU) (Akçali, and Féron and Güven Lisaniler, chapters 10 and 11). In all four chapters, the authors tackle the case of Cyprus alongside other conflicts both within the EU and in the wider European neighbourhood. The last substantive part of the book broadens out beyond conflict studies strictly defined. Its chapters provide insightful analyses of how economics, law and gender studies can illuminate dimensions of conflict, which tend to be neglected or obscured in political science and international relations (IR) studies. Crucially, they do so in a language that resonates with political science and IR, thus opening the space for constructive and intelligible interdisciplinary research. In what follows, we elaborate on the chapters and parts of the book, highlighting the interconnections between them.

The internal actors in conflict: micro-, meso- and macro-units of analysis

Part I analyses the different domestic actors and their role in shaping the Cyprus conflict and its possible resolution. We unpack what are often viewed as monolithic conflict parties by assessing who the actors and stakeholders within each party are, and how their positions and actions shape the overall evolution of conflict. We do so by focusing on three principal levels of analysis: the micro-, meso- and macro-levels.

From a micro-perspective, in chapter 2 Alexandros Lordos takes the individual citizen as a unit of analysis, and examines the positions, views and calculus of Cypriot citizens regarding the 2004 Annan Plan and a future solution in Cyprus. The individual and thus the general public represent a fundamental – if not the primary – unit of analysis in conflict situations, as well as the ultimate repository of a solution. The latter is true not only in the narrow sense of achieving a positive referendum result to ratify an agreement, as was dramatically illustrated by the case of Cyprus in 2004. It is also true in the wider and more long-term sense of ensuring that a solution brokered by political leaders can be made to work on the ground. In other words, the public is the key agent in ensuring that conflict situations move beyond mere settlement and achieve a veritable shift towards conflict resolution and transformation, in which the antagonistic identities at the heart of conflicts are redefined. More specifically, Lordos's chapter uses extensive survey data collected in 2005 with a sample of 1,000 Greek Cypriots and 1,000 Turkish Cypriots, and by applying these data to two separate logistic regression models (one for the Greek Cypriots and one for the Turkish Cypriots), the author explains the choices of voters in the April 2004 referenda. Interestingly, and confirming the importance of focusing on the individual, Lordos's analysis forcefully reveals how much individuals and their specific views, attitudes and preferences matter. While party affiliation was undoubtedly one key factor shaping voters' choices, equally if not more important were underlying attitudes towards reunification, as well as specific views on details of the Annan Plan. In particular, for Greek Cypriots, the evaluation of provisions relating to security, property and settlers was critical, and those provisions were largely viewed as unsatisfactory. For Turkish Cypriots, in contrast, the overall positive tipping factors were security and power-sharing. Demographic variables were also important in shaping results, with low-income, university-educated and female Greek Cypriots often resisting reunification, while low-income and young Turkish Cypriots tended to favour the Plan.

Moving to a second level of analysis, we examine the role of meso-level actors in the Cyprus conflict. Here we focus on two cases. Balkır and Yalman focus on business actors in generating incentives and dynamics in favour of conflict resolution, focusing their attention on the Turkish-Cypriot side. Bailie and Azgin analyse the role played by the Greek-Cypriot and Turkish-Cypriot media in sustaining conflict and opening avenues for resolution. Other mid-level actors could have been chosen here, including for example non-governmental organisations (NGOs) and other civil society actors (Marchetti and Tocci, 2007). Yet what both these chapters illustrate is the critical role played by mid-level players in providing the crucial link between political elites and the public.

In chapter 3, Balkır and Yalman concentrate on the role played by business actors in the Turkish-Cypriot community. This chapter reveals how, while inherently embedded within the conflict, business actors can and have played a critical role in altering political incentives and trends in northern Cyprus. Business elites can help alter the economic structures of conflict, as pointed out by Watson in chapter 14. Yet more critical in chapter 3 is the fact that economic agents, driven primarily by economic interests, can and have played an explicitly political role in favour of peace. The Turkish-Cypriot business community is analysed as a rising political force in Turkish-Cypriot domestic dynamics, striving for the resolution of the conflict between the EU's Helsinki European Council in December 1999 when Turkey was granted candidate status and the Cyprus referenda in April 2004. The entry of the EU as a new factor in the Cyprus equation – analysed also in chapters by Verney, Akçali, and Féron and Güven Lisaniler – radically altered the calculus of Turkish-Cypriot business actors, by raising the economic stakes in resolution and highlighting the problem of Turkey as the only source of Turkish-Cypriot economic support. In other words, the Turkish-Cypriot business community in the 1999–2004 period transcended its exclusive business role within civil society, by transforming itself into an explicitly 'political society' in favour of reunification. However, the reasons for this role are rooted in the specific interests and incentives of the business community *qua* business community. Lobbying in favour of peace was, at a specific point in time, functional to the goals and interests of this specific group. This possibly explains why in the post-referenda period, which projected Cyprus at a new crossroads, the reunification impetus of the Turkish-Cypriot business community appears to have somewhat subsided.

In chapter 4, Bailie and Azgin examine the role and responsibility of the media in presenting, representing and reproducing the Cyprus conflict, and conclude that they failed to move the dominant discourses within each community from competition, confrontation and enmity to cooperation, dialogue and empathy. To illustrate their argument, the authors select a specific case study: the media coverage in the two communities of the opening of the Ledra/Lokmacı gate in Nicosia. Through a detailed analysis of this news story, media operators in both communities are depicted as strongly – and perhaps inevitably – embedded actors in the conflict, articulating rather than challenging conflict-enhancing discourses. There are several reasons for this. On the one hand, media operators are driven by the specific political and economic incentives underpinning the media industry, which prioritises immediacy, simplicity and sensationalism over incrementalism, complexity and moments of cooperation. Journalists are not peace activists with a professional 'peace mandate' and as such their discourse and actions are driven by different logics and incentives. On the other hand, the media and especially the local media in conflict situations are part and parcel of the existing structures sustaining conflict. In other words, while the agency of specific journalists is recognised – and critical-communications scholarship should rightfully seek avenues to enhance the prospects for peace journalism – the media are themselves derived from existing conflict structures and thus tend to reproduce these rather than transcend them.

A third and final unit of analysis is set at the macro-level: political elites and leaders. Kaymak and Vural in chapter 5 analyse the changes within the Turkish-Cypriot political landscape before and after the failed referenda in 2004. They do so by concentrating on political elite discourses and their public legitimisation. Mirroring the chapter on business elites, this chapter illustrates how and why changes might occur within political elites in favour of or against conflict resolution. What is striking in this case is the radical change that appears to have set in in the post-referenda period or, put differently, the 'abnormal' situation that marked the pre-referenda years. In the pre-referenda period, Turkish-Cypriot politics witnessed an unprecedented level of polarisation and divide. The nationalist right, in power and represented principally by former Turkish-Cypriot leader Rauf Denktaş, vehemently opposed the Annan Plan, EU membership and any form of EU conditionality associated with the Cyprus conflict. These actors viewed the EU as part of the problem and not part of the solution, thus reducing further their incentives to negotiate and accept a federal settlement, which would have embedded a reunited Cyprus in the EU. The left and liberal opposition took a diametrically opposite stance, actively pressing in favour of reunification based on the Annan Plan, also – if not primarily – because of the prospects of EU membership that a settlement entailed. Since the failed referenda and the EU accession of the divided island, the discourse among Turkish-Cypriot political elites has changed, and become far more differentiated and nuanced. The EU is no longer perceived unambiguously as a force for good or evil and, beyond the nationalist right and liberal left, a third current appears to be in the making, dubbed by the authors the 'neo-official stance' and personified primarily by former opposition leader and current Turkish-Cypriot President, Mehmet Ali Talat. What emerges from this analysis is that the positions of a particular party to the conflict are the result of the complex interaction and competition between different political actors with different interests, values and beliefs, whose relative strength and weakness result from the changing structural conditions at the domestic, regional and wider international levels.

All three internal units of analysis tackled in part I are closely interlinked. The relationship between the public and political elites is twofold. On the one hand, Cypriot citizens have not simply acted as 'unthinking followers' (Lordos) by blindly taking the cue from their political leaders without formulating their own views on the Annan Plan. On the contrary, the public and its mobilisation, aided also by the active participation of the Turkish-Cypriot business community, was a *sine qua non* for the turnover in the political leadership of northern Cyprus in the 2002–05 period. On the other hand, however, Cypriots have been strongly influenced by their leaders, and political party affiliation did play a critical role in shaping voting decisions in 2004, as noted by Lordos. In the post-referenda period, the vote of the Greek-Cypriot public has been used to justify and legitimise the rejectionist stance of its leadership regarding a resumption of UN-mediated negotiations. Mid-level players provide the link and conduit of communication between the leadership and the public, shaping the views and positions of leaders and publics alike. In particular, media operators, while in principle providing the necessary information to allow citizens to form independent views, in practice often reproduce dominant discourses in conflicts and provide decision-makers with the necessary images and language to justify their stances.

The external actors in conflict: regional, European and international units of analysis

Part II of the book complements the focus in part I, on the internal actors, by turning to the external dimensions of conflict, focusing on three different themes at the regional (eastern Mediterranean), European (European Parliament) and wider international (UN) levels. Cyprus as a post-colonial, semi-sovereign state with heavy EU and UN involvement is not the only case, but certainly a prime one, for such a complex relationship, tying internal actors and factors to a set of external determinants.

The role of Greece and Turkey has cast Cyprus at the centre of the changing politics of the eastern Mediterranean, concomitantly acting as the principal obstacle to the nascent Greek–Turkish *rapprochement* and inducing both Ankara and Athens to make progress on Cyprus in order to entrench the normalisation of their relations. In this context, in chapter 6 Kaliber analyses the changing politics of the eastern Mediterranean by assessing the way in which one player – Turkey – has transformed its understanding of regional politics by articulating a different security discourse regarding Cyprus. In past decades, the Turkish body politic had consistently presented Cyprus as an invaluable defence asset. At the same time, Cyprus was portrayed as an imminent security threat to the Turkish state and nation, in view of its geographical proximity to southern Anatolia, which potentially might allow a hostile Greece, in collusion with the Greek Cypriots, to access and attack Turkey's southern coastline.

Cyprus thus played into and fed Turkey's Sèvres syndrome, that is, the fear that, in the legacy of the 1920 Treaty of Sèvres, external enemies would collaborate with hostile elements within Turkey to threaten the Republic, its territory and values. In recent years, this discourse appears to have somewhat changed, with the Turkish leadership presenting and discussing Cyprus in a far more regional – eastern Mediterranean – context. Yet changing security precepts cannot explain this shift alone, given the persistence of the Cyprus conflict, fuelled in many respects by the EU accession of the divided island. This discursive shift is explained partly by Turkey's changing foreign policy role in the post-Cold War period, as it now lies at the epicentre of new dynamics between Europe and Asia. It is also partly explained by the specific role of the Justice and Development Party in government in Ankara, which is aiming to reposition Turkey as a regional hub in political, economic, security and energy terms. Kaliber's chapter thus highlights not only how regions and regionalism are socially constructed but also how their articulation and re-articulation vary alongside changes in actors, with their different interests and world-views.

Moving up a level, in chapter 7 Verney focuses on the role of the EU in the Cyprus conflict. More specifically, and not least because of the attention paid to the EU's role in Cyprus in recent literature (Brewin, 2000; Diez, 2002c,d; Tocci, 2004a,b), this chapter focuses on the positions and policies of one EU actor: the European Parliament (EP). Verney assesses the discursive shifts in the EP's positions on Cyprus before and after the 2004 enlargement. Interestingly, up until 2003 the Cyprus conflict was addressed almost exclusively in terms of its potential impact on EU enlargement and EU–Turkey relations, rather than as a stand-alone issue involving a conflict between two communities. Parliamentary debates did repeatedly refer to the catalytic role that EU accession might play in the reunification of the island, but, much like other EU actors, the Parliament was vague in articulating how and why this would come about. The EP's positions can in fact be evaluated in the context of the EU's general disengagement from direct conflict resolution in Cyprus, ostensibly justified on the grounds of the UN's involvement in peace mediation (Tocci, 2004b: 38).

The UN and its involvement in mediation and peace-keeping in Cyprus represent the final level of analysis in the examination of the external determinants of the conflict. In chapter 8, Ker-Lindsay examines the history of UN peace-making in Cyprus, and explores the way in which it evolved from a mediating mission in the 1960s into an attempt at direct arbitration in 2004. He suggests that, in moving away from the more neutral roles of good offices and mediation, the UN Secretary-General (UNSG) lost the trust of the Greek Cypriots, who came to view him as being unduly influenced by the United Kingdom and the United States and, by extension, Turkey. However, legitimate concerns were also coupled with less honourable and transparent intentions. The philosophy of the Plan presented by the Secretary-General stood against the principles of the Greek-Cypriot leadership in power at the time, despite the fact that it represented the most articulate version of a bizonal and bi-communal federal solution, ostensibly endorsed by the two communities since 1977. The chapter concludes that, at the time of the referendum campaign, a deliberate effort was mounted to discredit the UNSG in southern Cyprus because of the association of his name with the Plan, in order to ensure that the proposed agreement was rejected by the electorate. In a broader context, Annan's decision to develop an arbitration role, and the way this approach was ultimately rejected by the Greek Cypriots, has thrown up interesting questions regarding the ability of the UN to take a more robust approach towards peace-making, and indeed the desirability of it doing so. A neutral and non-coercive mediating role, such as that of the UN, has often been criticised from a realist perspective for failing to offer tangible incentives to conflict parties (Touval and Zartman, 1985). However, as chapter 8 argues, the Cyprus experience seems to cast doubt on the desirability of an upgraded role of the UNSG, that is, beyond offering ideas and a channel of communication between parties. The UNSG's shift towards 'arbitrated mediation' appears to have backfired in the case of Cyprus, raising wider doubts about the efficacy, legitimacy and credibility of 'power mediation' applied in other cases, such as the Kosovo negotiations in 2007.

As in the case of the internal variables, the external determinants of the Cyprus conflict are also closely interlinked. Turkey's transformed understanding of Cyprus set within the eastern Mediterranean is partly explained by the inclusion of the Greece–Cyprus–Turkey triangle in the EU orbit, the EU incentive in the Greek–Turkish *rapprochement* and the EU's foreign policy projection in its south-eastern neighbourhood. The EU dimension, however, has also had polarising and disincentivising effects on the conflict. The Greek-Cypriot public's rejection of the Annan Plan was certainly linked to the specific evaluation of the Plan in Greek-Cypriot eyes, yet it was also connected to the awareness that Cyprus, reunited or otherwise, would have entered the EU. The emergence of a Turkish-Cypriot post-referendum 'neo-official' position is explained partly by the Turkish-Cypriot disillusionment with their Greek-Cypriot counterparts, but also by their disappointment with the EU and its unfulfilled promises. Finally, the EU dimension also influenced the UN's mediation role in Cyprus in the 2002–04 period. Ker-Lindsay's apt depiction of the UN's role in these years as 'arbitrated mediation' was fundamentally linked to and explained by the EU and the approaching deadline of Cyprus's accession. The 2004 deadline meant not only that key incentives in the peace process had to be reaped before that date, but also that the actors involved became increasingly aware of the negative consequences stemming from the entry of a divided Cyprus into the EU (UN Secretary-General, 2004). The UN's arbitrated mediation, coupled with the EU's sticks and carrots, did reap results for the Turkish Cypriots, as examined in chapters by Lordos, Balkır and Yalman, and Kaymak and Vural. Yet they also bolstered Greek-Cypriot rejectionism couched in a popular/populist anti-colonial discourse.

Cyprus in comparative perspective

In part III, we broaden the scope of analysis beyond the empirical case of Cyprus, with four chapters comparing different approaches to conflict resolution. Berg in chapter 9 focuses on comparative trends in conflict resolution and in particular on federal models as proposed solutions to square the circle between majority claims to sovereignty and territorial integrity, and minority claims to self-determination. Berg puts forth a conundrum: we are increasingly presented with the reality of juridical states lacking the practical attributes of sovereignty, and *de facto* territorial entities lacking international legal legitimacy. To square this circle and seek compromise between norms and facts, the international community has often supported federalism. Yet in doing so it has also consistently reaffirmed the importance of statehood as the ultimate expression of sovereignty and self-determination, thus doing little to dissuade minority communities from seeking secession. In other words, internationally sponsored federal power-sharing solutions often legitimise and fuel the modern attributes of ethno-political conflicts, while claiming to diffuse them. To illustrate his argument, Berg compares two unsettled conflicts in Europe – Cyprus and Moldova – and one conflict – Bosnia and Herzegovina – in which the international community has imposed a loose federal settlement on the parties. Yet the Bosnian case illustrates that an imposed federal solution (the Dayton agreement) actually encouraged internal *de facto* states to legitimise their existence and discouraged them from renouncing claims to sovereignty and territory. In so doing, international mediators have contributed to setting a strong precedent and sending mixed signals to other conflicts in the wider neighbourhood.

Akçali in chapter 10 and Féron and Güven Lisaniler in chapter 11 focus on the role of the EU in conflict resolution (see also Diez et al., 2006; Tocci, 2007). Akçali concentrates on three case studies: one in the EU – Cyprus; one in the process of accession to the EU – Macedonia; and one in the Stabilisation and Association Process – Bosnia. Akçali notes how, in order to induce conflict transformation, third-party mediators must devote attention not only to security and constitutional issues, but also to rights, justice and socio-economic development. They must also do so without taking sides with one of the conflict parties (Young, 1968). The EU's accession process is well placed to play such a role, in particular by devoting attention to issues of rights and development, which are often neglected by traditional mediators. Paradoxically, however, the cases of Cyprus and Macedonia suggest that the potential of the EU's integration incentives in conflict resolution are not matched in practice, thus setting a poor precedent for Bosnia, which is still in the pre-accession waiting room. This chapter argues that EU weakness in conflict transformation lies principally and perhaps surprisingly in its deficiency to tackle socio-economic inequalities in conflict areas and foster an impartial approach towards adversaries.

Similarly critical of the EU's role, in chapter 11 Féron and Güven Lisaniler tackle a wider selection of conflict case studies both within the EU (Cyprus, the Basque country and Northern Ireland) and outside it (Kosovo and Bosnia). Interestingly, this chapter unpacks the idea of third-party impact on conflict resolution, and analyses the EU's impact on the different dimensions of conflict. These dimensions relate both to the root causes of conflict and to their present symptoms. In particular, the authors concentrate on four dimensions of conflict: identity factors (including ethnicity, religion and language), socio-economic and territorial factors (including modernisation, socio-economic inequalities, demography and migration), political factors (including power-sharing, political representation, citizenship and security) and external factors (including globalisation and decolonisation). They assess the EU's impact on these dimensions by applying two models (Coppieters et al., 2004; Diez et al., 2006). As pointed out by Akçali, in principle the EU should help diffuse the socio-economic and political dimensions of conflict. Far more arduous is the EU's potential to transform the identity-related aspects of ethno-political conflicts. In fact, the case of Cyprus demonstrates that the Union can actually exacerbate identity divisions, particularly if one or more conflict parties (i.e., the Turkish Cypriots and Turkey) remain *de facto* excluded from the EU. But the case of Cyprus also shows that the Union often punches below its weight in terms of offering socio-economic and political advantages to conflict parties. Indeed, in the case of Cyprus, the authors note, accession has reduced the appeal of reunification and power-sharing among the wealthier Greek Cypriots and has hardened the border between the two communities. In other words, the EU integration of one conflict party and the exclusion of the other in practice empty the EU's potential to offer tangible incentives for conflict resolution.

Finally, comparative analysis can be used to examine a specific aspect, actor or dimension of conflict. Loizos and Kelly in chapter 12 focus on one critical issue in the Cyprus and Israeli–Palestinian conflicts: the refugees. Through a political anthropology perspective, this chapter assesses the role and experience of the refugees in these two conflicts. Through a different lens from that adopted by Berg, this chapter also highlights the importance of statehood.

Indeed, the authors explain how Greek-Cypriot refugees, an impoverished and displaced community in 1974, thrived alongside the reconstruction and development of their state, the Republic of Cyprus, in the thirty years that followed. While in their eyes displacement and the lack of full integration remain salient issues, they understand that, in most ways, their children feel fully integrated. Moreover, and because of this, they consider armed struggle an irrational option, alongside the rest of their community. This is not least because their state, the RoC, has treated them as full citizens and provided them with useful compensatory housing and economic rights. By contrast, after 1948, Palestinian refugees were displaced across the states of the region. Many have remained poor and most are denied citizenship and wider civil, political and socio-economic rights in their host countries. Lacking a representative state or political authority, the refugees have been largely neglected in peace talks between the Palestinian Liberation Organization (PLO) and Israel. As such, and in sharp contrast to the Greek-Cypriot case, the temptation among displaced Palestinians, alongside other Palestinians, has been to seek redress from Israel, through violent action if necessary. The lessons for political anthropology and conflict resolution are structural, geopolitical and historically specific: anthropology is not, alone, equipped to tackle problems of international relations, but it can illuminate the mind-sets of ordinary actors and thus cast a different light on issues of integration and alienation for collectivities in conflict contexts.

Cyprus beyond political science: gender, economics and law

The political anthropology perspective discussed above offers the lead into part IV of the book, where we depart from strictly defined political science, and bring perspectives from gender studies, economics and law to the analysis of the Cyprus conflict. By approaching the study of Cyprus through different disciplines, part IV offers alternative views on the factors fuelling conflict, as well as on those contributing to its potential resolution or transformation.

The use of gender as an analytical tool opens up both a theoretical and a practical debate among academics, activists and policy-makers in conflict contexts. Listening to women's voices, studying women's writings and learning from women's experiences have been crucial to the feminist reconstruction of our understanding of the world. In chapter 13, Hadjipavlou analyses Cypriot women's experiences, voices and desires in all communities: Greek, Turkish, Armenian, Maronite and Latin. The chapter unravels the complexity of these voices, which most poignantly challenge the 'bicommunality' discourse used by traditional conflict actors as well as by peace practitioners, scholars and analysts alike. In a conflict society, as is Cyprus, the 'national problem' historically overshadows and downplays other forms of identification and in particular women's issues, voices and experiences; the conflict tends to be presented as being essentially 'genderless' (Hadjipavlou, 2006; Sharoni, 1995). Yet the predominance of official masculine discourses has led Greek-Cypriot and Turkish-Cypriot women to internalise their ethnic and national duty roles, while displacing their perspectives as women (Anthias, 1989). Thus many women adopt the roles imposed on them by their communities, and so are denied the right to be full participants or social agents in the public sphere. Beyond the general social, political and economic distortions this has generated, straight-jacketing women's roles has also foreclosed avenues to move beyond traditional conflict divides in Cyprus, as in other conflict contexts.

Economics can offer a different and equally enlightening lens to analyse conflict and conflict resolution. As discussed by Watson in chapter 14, if addressed creatively, economics can help clear obstacles to a political settlement and build constituencies in support of it. But the case of Cyprus also shows that countervailing economic risks are all too real and may hinder the search for peace. Indeed, economic issues were a sticking point in the 2004 referenda. Notably, voters in the south seem to have entertained unduly negative expectations about the economic future under reunification; all of those involved made wrong assumptions about the income gap between north and south; and there was no consensus on fiscal federalism or on strategies for economic convergence. Since then, economic changes have affected the chances of a settlement in unexpected ways; in fact, they have threatened to strengthen vested interests in the status quo. Moreover, an unsustainable boom in the north and the looming economic crisis this presents are raising the costs of – and fall-out from – reunification. There are, however, tangible potential synergies between the two economies that stand to be unlocked, and which could help revitalise the economies on both sides and galvanise real incentives for conflict resolution. Yet to reap these benefits, the two economies both face reform challenges (though of differing degrees); and there is a need to overcome physical and psychological barriers to intra-island trade – which, if left untackled, will simply entrench the dynamics of division prevalent in Cyprus today. In other words, Cyprus stands at a crossroads in economic terms as well. Potential synergies are considerable, but realising them will require a concerted effort on both sides.

Finally, by analysing the role played by law in conflict, Özersay and Gürel, in chapter 15, examine how the parties in conflict have attempted to bolster their bargaining positions and relative strengths over one of the most salient issues on the conflict-resolution agenda: property. The property issue is undoubtedly a key aspect of the Cyprus problem. More than any other, perhaps, it concerns the rights and interests of individual Cypriot citizens, and helps to explain why, as noted by Lordos, property was a critical aspect in shaping voters' opinions in the 2004 referenda. Property is also inextricably linked to the economic considerations surrounding future reunification and, as discussed by Watson, it strongly influenced the (unsustainable) economic boom in post-2004 northern Cyprus. More broadly, property (alongside power-sharing and political representation) is crucial in determining the geopolitical character of any future settlement in Cyprus. Because of its salience, the Cypriot parties have thus pursued, in parallel with UN-sponsored negotiations, unilateral actions through the law to position and reposition themselves on the property issue. Indeed, that issue has been the subject of numerous proceedings at the European Court of Human Rights (ECHR). A remarkable aspect of these cases is the way they have been treated by the leaderships in the conflict as yet another political instrument for seeking endorsement of their fundamental positions and ambitions in the Cyprus problem. Chapter 15 highlights how a clear separation between politics and law is not only difficult to make but also obscures our understanding of complex issues and developments in conflict contexts. To exemplify this argument, this chapter, based on a study of ECHR judgements delivered on property-related applications, examines how Cyprus has become a critical arena for the complex interplay between politics and law.

This book is thus an attempt to cast and analyse Cyprus as a conflict at the crossroads of different issues, disciplines and approaches. As an empirical case study, the Cyprus conflict lends itself well to such an exercise. As the first two parts of the book highlight, the myriad of actors and factors that have shaped the history and evolution of this protracted conflict encourage scholars to examine it in a variety of different lights. Yet beyond this, our attempt in this book is to show how one case study, when analysed from different perspectives, can provide a rich variety of diverse yet equally fascinating stories, which can in turn illuminate and be illuminated by different approaches in the social sciences, a theme we will return to in the Conclusion.

Part I

The domestic determinants of conflict and resolution

2

Rational agent or unthinking follower? A survey-based profile analysis of Greek-Cypriot and Turkish-Cypriot referenda voters

Alexandros Lordos

Introduction

Ever since the failed reunification referenda of April 2004, various commentators and analysts have sought to explain why the Greek Cypriots and Turkish Cypriots voted the way they did. Beyond the various academic papers and books that have been published on this matter (Attalides, 2004; Bahcheli, 2004; Coufoudakis, 2004; Heraclides, 2004; Jakobsson Hatay, 2004a,b; Palley, 2005) many journalists, politicians and diplomats have also declared their views about the motivations underpinning the referenda votes. The most common 'bones of contention' in this ongoing debate have been whether the Greek-Cypriot 'no' was a rational decision on behalf of the voters based on a personal evaluation of the Anan Plan, or whether voters were misled into voting 'no' by their leadership. Was the Greek-Cypriot vote a 'no' to the specific Plan or to the concept of reunification? And was the Turkish-Cypriot 'yes' a vote in favour of coexistence or merely in support of European Union (EU) membership and economic development? Unsurprisingly, most political declarations have tended to present the 'other' community in the most unflattering light possible (i.e., Greek Cypriots are against reunification and were misled by their leaders; Turkish Cypriots do not care about reunification and voted 'yes' for the sake of EU membership), while academic analyses have tended to be more balanced and sophisticated. Yet what all these analyses – academic and political – have in common is a lack of empirical backing: almost all of the literature published on the subject hinges upon the personal opinion of the author.

While some first forays into an empirical understanding of the April 2004 referenda have been made (Lordos, 2004a,b, 2005; Webster, 2005a,b), the literature still lacks a comprehensive statistical model that can explain how various factors interacted to create the final results. Based on extensive public opinion data collected in mid-2005, this chapter presents such a model.

The surveys and construction of the model

For the purposes of this research, two public opinion surveys were conducted in May 2005.[1] In each community the sample consisted of 1,000 voting adults, and all responses were collected via face-to-face interviews with a single structured questionnaire, translated into Greek and Turkish. The sample was selected according to the methodology of multi-stage random stratified sampling. Breakdown by district and by urban/rural area was designed to mirror the actual population, while accurate representation in age and gender was sought through the birthday rule.[2] The interviews lasted forty-five minutes on average. The questions covered underlying attitudes towards the other community, motives for desiring a solution, views on the acceptability of specific provisions of the Annan Plan, views on the acceptability of alternative provisions in a revised Plan, and various standard demographics – such as age, level of income and education, and voting patterns in recent elections.

The dependent variable in both the Greek-Cypriot and the Turkish-Cypriot regression models was 'Vote in April 2004 referendum'. In both models, a declared 'yes' vote was coded with a dummy variable (value = 1), whereas a declared 'no' vote was denoted with a null value. Those who declared that they did not vote, or those who did not wish to reveal their vote, were excluded from the analysis. In total, 10.4 per cent of the Greek-Cypriot sample and 3.1 per cent of the Turkish-Cypriot sample were excluded from the analysis for this reason.

The independent 'predictor' variables that were used in the construction of the model can be classified in four major categories: underlying attitudes, political allegiance, views on specific aspects of the Annan Plan, and demographics. A complete list of all the predictor variables that were included in the model can be found in the appendix to this chapter. It should be noted here that, while the surveys on which the analysis was based provided a rich foundation of possible predictor variables, there were some limitations too. Not every potential predictor variable that we would have wished to include in hindsight was represented in the survey; for instance, there were no variables to represent values such as social conservatism or risk aversion, level of social or economic despair, or expectations at the time of voting regarding future options, scenarios and dangers in the event of acceptance or rejection of the Annan Plan. This notwithstanding, the model was, as illustrated below, substantially successful in predicting the referenda votes in the two communities.

Because the dependent variable is dichotomous (i.e., either 'yes' or 'no'), the standard linear regression model was not appropriate for the analysis – since one of its prerequisites is that the dependent variable should be continuous. Instead, the binary logistic model was used, which posits a hypothetical dependent variable, denoted z, which is used to estimate the probability of a certain individual voting 'yes' or 'no'.[3] Having calculated this hypothetical z variable, the probability of having voted 'yes' is then calculated as follows:

$$p = \exp(z) / (1 + \exp(z))$$

If $p > 0.5$, then the model allocates the case as a 'yes' vote. If, however, $p < 0.5$, then the model allocates a 'no' vote.

The model was created in accordance with a forward step-wise approach. Variables were added successively to the model, with the most significant being added first, until there were no more significant variables to add. The criterion of significance was the Wald statistic, which is defined as the square of the ratio between the variable's model coefficient (B) and the standard error (SE) of the coefficient. The higher the Wald statistic, the more certain we can be that the specific variable is a reliable predictor. Variables were included in the model only if the probability of them being significant predictors was greater than 95 per cent (i.e., $p < 0.05$).

Model findings: Greek Cypriots

With these introductory comments in mind, we can now proceed to the first regression model, relating to the Greek Cypriots, as shown in table 2.1.

The model proves substantially able to predict whether a Greek Cypriot voted 'yes' or 'no' at the April 2004 referendum. More specifically, it correctly allocated 85.3 per cent of the sample cases, as shown in table 2.2.

In interpreting the findings of the model, the most important value is the variable coefficient (B). The higher the B coefficient, the stronger is the predictor effect of a particular variable. A negative B coefficient means the particular variable is inversely related to a 'yes' referendum vote. 'Sample score' is also important for interpretation of the model: quite simply, 'sample score' is the proportion of the respondents who exhibited the characteristic in question. For instance, the 'DISY supporter' score of 0.29 means that 29 per cent of the respondents declared themselves to have voted in favour of the Democratic Rally Party (DISY) at the 2001 parliamentary elections; similarly, the 'Annan Plan settler provisions' score of 0.14 means that 14 per cent of the respondents

Table 2.1 Predictors of a 'yes' vote in the April 2004 referendum: Greek Cypriots

	B	SE	Wald	Sig.	Sample score
DISY supporter	1.96	0.22	83.35	0.00	0.29
Annan Plan security provisions	1.30	0.24	29.76	0.00	0.33
Annan Plan property rights	0.64	0.25	6.76	0.01	0.32
Annan Plan settler provisions	0.60	0.30	3.93	0.05	0.14
Annan Plan legal status	0.52	0.26	3.90	0.05	0.47
'I would not mind having Turkish-Cypriot neighbours'	0.77	0.23	11.37	0.00	0.57
'Our side is also to blame for the current situation of the Cyprus problem'	0.75	0.33	5.12	0.02	0.79
'The two communities should go their separate ways from now on'	−0.68	0.30	5.21	0.02	0.22
Famagusta district resident	1.58	0.40	15.34	0.00	0.05
Refugee status	0.51	0.21	5.68	0.02	0.31
Higher education (college+)	−0.60	0.25	5.60	0.02	0.25
Low family income (less than CYP750)	−0.66	0.25	7.08	0.01	0.30
Female gender	−0.70	0.21	10.85	0.00	0.50
Constant	−3.94	0.60	81.23	0.00	

Table 2.2 Predictions of the Greek-Cypriot vote

	Predicted		% correct
	No	Yes	
Observed			
No	677	35	95.1
Yes	97	87	47.3
			85.3

found the relevant Annan Plan provisions acceptable. We now turn to examining the parameters of the model in detail.

DISY supporter, B = 1.96

A very strong predictor of whether respondents voted 'yes' was whether they were DISY supporters. It would seem that, all else being equal, a DISY supporter experienced a stronger urge to vote 'yes' – presumably because this was the official party line, expounded both by its historic leader, Glafkos Clerides, and its current chairman, Nicos Anastasiades.

In this sample, the sample score for 'DISY supporter' was 0.29, which means that 29 per cent of the sample declared themselves to be DISY supporters. In a more generalised predictive version of this model, 'DISY supporter' could be substituted with 'political party support of the proposed Plan', since we have every reason to assume that the dynamics of 'conformity with the party line' would work in a similar way for supporters of other political parties and their respective stances on the Annan Plan.

Annan Plan security provisions, B = 1.30

An almost equally strong predictor of the vote was the view of the security provisions of the Annan Plan. Much more than any other aspect of the Plan, the vote largely reflected the 'partial vote' that Greek Cypriots gave to the Plan's security provisions. If an individual viewed the security provisions as unacceptable, then that person was likely, all else being equal, to vote 'no'. If alternatively the security provisions were felt to be tolerable, then that individual was more likely to vote 'yes', all else being equal. The sample score for the Annan Plan security provisions was 0.33, which means that only one in three Greek Cypriots viewed these provisions as tolerable: some 67 per cent were not convinced of the adequacy of the security arrangements of the Plan, and this contributed greatly to the overall 'no' result.

We can thus begin to observe how the interplay between political party discipline and private evaluations of the Plan led to the referendum result. It is known from exit polls (but also from data derived through the survey on which this chapter is based) that about 10 per cent of the supporters of the Democratic Party (DIKO) voted in favour of the Plan, while 60 per cent of DISY supporters voted against the Plan – both groups defying the official party line. It is reasonable to assume that many of these dissenting voters were, respectively, DIKO supporters who found the security provisions of the Plan tolerable, and DISY supporters who found the security provisions of the Plan unacceptable.

Annan Plan property rights, B = 0.64

The property provisions of the Annan Plan were also an important predictor of the vote among Greek Cypriots, though nowhere near as important as the security provisions: where $B = 1.30$ for the security provisions, we have $B = 0.64$ for the property provisions. The relation between approval of the Plan's property provisions and final vote is present, but it is less absolute than is the case with the security provisions. Many citizens may thus have been 'pushed over the edge' into voting 'no' by the perceived inadequacy of the Plan's property provisions, but this generally worked in combination with other factors, having an overall cumulative effect. The sample score for the Annan Plan property provisions was 0.32, meaning that only 32 per cent of Greek Cypriots found these provisions of the Plan to be a tolerable compromise.

Annan Plan settler provisions, B = 0.60

Of similar importance to property were the provisions relating to the fate of the settlers from Turkey. Again, this factor had a cumulative effect, which for many voters worked in combination with a disapproval of the security and property provisions of the Plan, creating a strong undercurrent in favour of 'no'. It should be noted, in fact, that these three factors put together – security, property and settlers – had a cumulative effect that was much greater than the effect of 'discipline to the party line'. According to the model, a citizen whose party was in favour of the plan (e.g. a DISY supporter) but who found the security, property and settler provisions unacceptable, was more likely to vote 'no' (*p*{Yes} = 0.38), all else being equal. Alternatively, a citizen whose party was against the plan (e.g. a DIKO supporter), but who found the security, property and settler provisions tolerable, was more likely to vote 'yes' (*p*{Yes} = 0.54), all else being equal. Of course, it was quite unusual for a Greek-Cypriot citizen to find all these provisions tolerable. In the case of the settler provisions, for example, the sample score is only 0.14 – meaning that a mere 14 per cent approved of these provisions of the Annan Plan.

Annan Plan legal status, B = 0.52

The Annan Plan's hallmark was the 'constructively ambiguous' way in which it dealt with the opposing views of the two communities regarding the legal status of the new state. In the Plan, the issue of history was bypassed, the long-standing arguments between legal continuity and legal succession were glossed over; both sides were given just enough supporting evidence to assume that the new state of affairs would come about in accordance with their own historical and legal thesis. This devious or ingenious approach – depending on how one evaluated it – was an important predictor of the vote, carrying about the same predictive strength as the property and settler provisions. The difference is that the legal status aspect of the Plan was less unacceptable than the other aspects. With a sample score of 0.47, we can estimate that about half the Greek Cypriots felt they could live with the Annan Plan's 'virgin birth approach'. Those, however, who did not approve of this specific aspect tended to consider it an important reason to reject the Plan altogether.

'I would not mind having Turkish-Cypriot neighbours', B = 0.77

Beyond party politics and the specifics of the Annan Plan, a number of attitudinal factors also contributed to determine the vote. The most important attitudinal predictor among Greek Cypriots was whether someone felt that 'coexistence on the ground' was desirable or not. On the whole, this factor worked in favour of a 'yes' vote. With a sample score 0.57, a clear majority of Greek Cypriots would not mind having Turkish-Cypriot neighbours, and this factor predisposed them to vote 'yes', all else being equal.

'Our side is also to blame for the current situation of the Cyprus problem', B = 0.75

Interestingly, the extent to which a Greek-Cypriot voter accepted Greek-Cypriot responsibility for the historical course of the Cyprus problem was an important predictor of the vote. In hindsight, it is natural that accepting historical responsibility would be correlated with a willingness to accept the painful compromises proposed by the Annan Plan. The reasoning would be: 'we also made mistakes, therefore we now have to accept a less than ideal solution'. Given the very high sample score, 0.79, this attitudinal factor was a strong predictor of a 'yes' vote among the Greek Cypriots, all else being equal. Nearly four in five Greek Cypriots seem willing to accept a share of the responsibility for the conflict, and this bodes well for future efforts to achieve a settlement.

'The two communities should go their separate ways from now on', B = –0.68

The extent to which a Greek-Cypriot citizen had lost faith in the concept of reunification was also an important negative predictor of the vote. Having said this, the sample score is low (0.22): only one in five Greek Cypriots was willing to support partition at the time of the survey, meaning that the desire for partition does not have strong explanatory power of the 'no' vote. As we will see below, however, this factor could become more relevant and cause serious difficulties in future if pro-partition attitudes among Greek Cypriots gain strength.

Famagusta district resident, B = 1.58

Current residents of the Famagusta district were far more likely to vote 'yes' at the referendum than residents of other districts, all else being equal. By 'Famagusta district resident' we mean the Greek-Cypriot residents of the villages just south and west of the town of Famagusta, under Turkish-Cypriot control – we do not mean 'refugees from Famagusta'. This group of individuals would have been strongly and directly affected by the Annan Plan, given that within three months they would have regained the capital city of their district, and the whole region would have been upgraded economically, socially and culturally. These tangible benefits were felt strongly by these respondents, who were more likely to push aside contrary party lines and other considerations. This finding also tends to support the 'rational agent' hypothesis of referendum voting patterns.

Refugee status, B = 0.51

Refugee status was also a factor in favour of a 'yes' vote. Refugees have a greater emotional and practical stake in efforts to reunify the island, making this result predictable. The coefficient is, however, comparatively low ($B = 0.51$) when compared with the coefficient for 'Famagusta district resident' ($B = 1.58$), for example. If refugees could expect substantial and tangible gains from the Annan Plan, why is this coefficient not very high? A possible explanation is that the refugees as a whole did not believe they had much to gain from the Plan. This leads us back to the low popularity of the Plan's property provisions, and in particular the widespread Greek-Cypriot suspicion that the proposed compensation scheme would not have lived up to its promise of guaranteed and fair compensation for the loss of property.

Higher education (college+), B = –0.60

Among Greek Cypriots, respondents with college or university education were more likely to vote 'no', all else being equal. One possible explanation for this intriguing finding is that the more educated could understand the subtler arguments used by the 'no' camp – such as concerns regarding the administrative functionality and economic viability of the solution, or fears that bipolar ethnic federations have centrifugal tendencies to break down. Further research is needed here.

Low family income, B = -0.66

Greek Cypriots with a low family income (less than CYP750 a month) experienced a stronger urge to reject the Annan Plan, all else being equal. This is an important finding insofar as it confirms the role of economic concerns in the rejection of the Annan Plan. Although there were widespread fears in the south that the Annan Plan would have proven economically costly for the Greek Cypriots, as funds would be transferred to the Turkish Cypriots, in practice these fears influenced the vote only of the less wealthy Greek Cypriots. The wealthier, while accepting these arguments, may have felt the luxury to accept the risks of an economic downturn for the sake of reunification, a risk that was deemed intolerable to those closer to the poverty line.

Female gender, B = -0.70

The strongest demographic factor that predisposed Greek Cypriots to vote 'no' was female gender. All else being equal, women felt they had more reasons to reject the Annan Plan. A working hypothesis to explain this finding is that women are more risk-averse than men, mostly because their parental role leads them to put a premium on social stability, and the Annan Plan represented a risk to social stability that they were less willing to take than were men. Again, this finding calls for further research to understand the concerns of Greek-Cypriot women regarding reunification.

Overall evaluation

The overall picture emerging from this explanatory model of the Greek-Cypriot vote is interesting and multifaceted. Political party discipline had a strong role to play; but a stronger role was played by each citizen's personal evaluation of the Plan – especially of the security aspect, but also of the provisions concerning property, settlers and legal status. Underlying attitudes towards reunification also mattered, though these attitudes served more to restrain than to enhance the 'no' vote. Finally, demographics also played a role. Future research into public concerns *vis-à-vis* the prospect of a comprehensive settlement should specifically focus on the concerns of refugees, of the more educated, of the less wealthy and of women.

From explanatory model to predictive model: Greek Cypriots

We now proceed to test several 'what if' scenarios. In the same way as the model can be used to predict the probability of an individual voting 'yes' (e.g. $p = 0.58$ means that a particular individual has a 58 per cent chance of voting 'yes'), it can also be used to predict the overall percentage 'yes' vote of the population (e.g. $p = 0.58$ means that 58 per cent of the population can be expected to vote 'yes'). We now attempt to use the model to make overall predictions for alternative scenarios.

For the purposes of this predictive model, the variable 'DISY supporter' has been renamed 'political party support for the revised Plan', while the variables 'Annan Plan security provisions', 'Annan Plan property rights', 'Annan Plan settler provisions' and 'Annan Plan legal status' have been renamed, respectively, 'revised Plan security provisions', 'revised Plan property rights', 'revised Plan settler provisions' and 'revised Plan legal status'. The underlying assumptions are that voters would be equally influenced by a 'yes' stance of their political party regardless of which party this is, and that they would give similar weight to the evaluation of the specific provisions of the 'revised Plan', as they did to the evaluation of the provisions of the original Annan Plan. Finally, the constant has been adjusted in such a way that, with the starting parameters of the April 2004 referendum (which we assume are correctly represented in the survey results), the model correctly yields the actual 24 per cent 'yes' vote of the referendum. This can be viewed as a calibration of the predictive model.

Before presenting the model, a disclaimer is in order. The use of this model for predictive purposes is a daring undertaking, since the circumstances of a new referendum may be very different from those prevailing in April 2004. Furthermore, other hidden factors may come into play that are not included in this model. Disclaimer aside, using a statistical model is a better predictive strategy than relying on purely subjective evaluations, and in this spirit we may proceed to examine five alternative scenarios (A–E). The results are presented in table 2.3.

Scenario A – Annan Plan as before, but with AKEL support

The first scenario foresees an unrevised Annan Plan receiving the support of the Progressive Workers' Party (AKEL), which joins forces with DISY to campaign for its acceptance. While unlikely, this scenario provides a response to those who wonder what would have happened if AKEL had decided to campaign in favour of the Plan. Indeed, we can predict that the 'yes' vote would have been much higher – but still far from reaching majority approval of the Plan. More precisely, the model predicts a 38 per cent 'yes' vote. Though AKEL and DISY theoretically cover over 60 per cent of the electorate, other factors, mainly regarding the Plan's provisions (especially security) but also the concerns of specific groups (refugees, women), would push the 'yes' vote down. This begs the question: what if, in a future round of negotiations, significant improvements were achieved in the security aspect of the Plan, and AKEL's support was procured alongside that of DISY? Would that be sufficient for a 'yes'?

Table 2.3 Predictors of a 'yes' vote in a possible future referendum: Greek Cypriots

	Regression coefficients	Actual scores (%)	Scenario A	Scenario B	Scenario C	Scenario D	Scenario E
Political party support for the revised Plan	1.96	29	63	63	63	63	82
Revised Plan security provisions	1.30	33	33	55	55	55	55
Revised Plan property rights	0.64	32	32	32	55	55	55
Revised Plan settler provisions	0.60	14	14	14	55	55	55
Revised Plan legal status	0.52	47	47	47	60	60	60
'I would not mind having Turkish-Cypriot neighbours'	0.77	57	57	57	57	30	57
'Our side is also to blame for the Cyprus problem'	0.75	79	79	79	79	79	79
'The two communities should go their separate ways from now on'	–0.68	22	22	22	22	60	22
Famagusta district resident	1.58	5	5	5	5	5	5
Refugee status	0.51	31	31	31	31	31	31
Higher education (college+)	–0.60	25	25	25	25	25	25
Low family income (less than CYP750)	–0.66	30	30	30	30	30	30
Female gender	–0.70	50	50	50	50	50	50
Adjusted constant	–3.10						
z-score		–1.15	–0.48	–0.20	0.26	–0.20	0.63
Projected percentage 'yes' vote		24	38	45	57	45	65

Scenario B – Plan extensively revised in its security aspects, and with AKEL support

This scenario hearkens back to the original pre-referenda proposal made by AKEL – that the referenda be postponed until the security aspect of the plan had been clarified. AKEL has now moved beyond this proposal, but, given how important the security aspect appears to be in this model, this scenario seems worth testing. By 'extensively revised' we do not mean adjustments to the Treaty of Guarantee, such as a faster withdrawal of troops, or even an abrogation of the provisions allowing a guarantor state's intervention in its kin-constituent state. Rather, what we mean here is the development of a new security system, mainly in the hands of the Cypriots, with some non-Cypriot involvement to guarantee neutrality, and only a last-resort option for Turkey or Greece to intervene if the primary security system failed to protect the communities. Such a proposal could achieve a small majority of support among Greek Cypriots, while also being acceptable to the Turkish Cypriots (Lordos, 2005). Based on this finding, a target of 55 per cent in favour of the revised Plan's security provisions was set in this scenario. The outcome approaches a 'yes' vote, at 45 per cent. Unfortunately, other concerns, in relation for example to property and settlers, would bring the overall vote down to a point where the final outcome could not be predicted with certainty. Thus, the next scenario to be tested involves a more extensive revision of the Plan, where all the key areas of concern have been reconsidered.

Scenario C – Plan revised in all key areas of concern, and with AKEL support

This is the scenario that we can hope to achieve if the two sides engage in extensive negotiations to define a revised Plan under the auspices of the United Nations (UN). Some such compromise solutions have been tested, and it seems that a 55 per cent target for Greek-Cypriot approval is a realistic aim. Specifically for the property aspect, it is possible to maintain the Annan Plan's principle that refugees currently using another refugee's property would not be disturbed, and significant investments in properties would on the whole be respected, but that the additional one-third quota restriction on property restitution would be abolished, and refugees who would not be entitled to their original homes could be guaranteed an alternative home in the same town or village. For the settlers issue, a criteria-based approach could be used, whereby children of Turkish origin who were born or raised in Cyprus would receive full citizenship, while their parents would receive residence and work permits to stay in Cyprus but without receiving full citizenship. Regarding the legal status of the new state of affairs, the legal continuity of the Republic of Cyprus could be explicitly acknowledged, while the Turkish-Cypriot administration could be retrospectively acknowledged as an interim Turkish-Cypriot authority. In both cases, the 'law of necessity' could be invoked. It could also be highlighted that the Republic of Cyprus has always been constitutionally bicommunal in nature, and that this bicommunality is developed with the Republic's evolution into a bizonal federation. All these possible provisions have been tested. Among Greek Cypriots they score between 52 and 59 per cent approval, while among Turkish Cypriots they are equally acceptable as the equivalent provisions of the original Annan Plan (Lordos, 2005). Thus they could reasonably be considered the target of a new round of negotiations, and in this context they form the basis of the scenario being presented here.

If AKEL support is also posited for this revised Plan – a reasonable assumption since these proposed revisions are within the stated acceptability margins of AKEL – then we could expect a clear, if somewhat narrow, 'yes' vote, at 57 per cent. Yet we have so far not considered the effect of a possible shift in underlying attitudes to reunification, which is what we do in the next scenario.

Scenario D – Plan revised in all key areas of concern, with AKEL support, but with deterioration in Greek-Cypriot attitudes to reunification and coexistence

In spring 2006, opinion poll data were made public which showed Greek Cypriots turning against the idea of coexistence with Turkish Cypriots. While such a shift in attitudes remains to be verified in further polls, it is reasonable to wonder what would happen if, while the leaders strive to agree on a revised Plan, the Greek-Cypriot public loses faith in the idea of reunification and coexistence. The answer is unsettling: the Greek-Cypriot 'yes' vote would deteriorate, perhaps to about 45 per cent of voters, as they would vote against the underlying idea of reunification, rather than against the details of the proposal. Given this result, it seems that from now on it would be wise to consider 'underlying attitudes' as a critical aspect of any serious effort to reunify Cyprus. In this context, further research is urgently required.

Scenario E (target scenario) – Plan revised in all key areas of concern, with AKEL and DIKO support, while attitudes to reunification hold without deteriorating

We conclude this analysis of alternative scenarios with a final 'target scenario': the ideal towards which efforts for reunification could aim. In this final scenario, we can begin to estimate the realistic maximum Greek-Cypriot 'yes' vote in a future referendum. Working to maximise the Greek-Cypriot 'yes' even beyond the strictly required 50 per cent + 1 is worthwhile, since a strong 'yes' would serve as a solid foundation for the new state of affairs, as citizens would strive to make the new constitution work. According to this scenario, achieving a 65 per cent Greek-Cypriot 'yes' is possible, so long as the following conditions are satisfied.

First is the political support of DISY, AKEL and DIKO. The support of these three principal parties is possible, since DIKO, alongside AKEL and DISY, is officially committed to a bizonal, bicommunal federation. It is true that DIKO is more demanding than either of the two larger parties regarding the specific terms of the Plan, but if the revised Plan is deemed functional, and if the improvements in the provisions regarding security, property, settlers and legal status described earlier are viewed as a tolerable compromise, then there is no reason why DIKO, together with AKEL and DISY, should not campaign in favour of a revised Plan. The same cannot be said with any certainty of the smaller parties, which seem more hesitant about the concept of a bizonal and bicommunal federal solution.

Second, the Plan would need to be revised in all key areas of concern. These possible revisions have already been described, although achieving these amendments would prove difficult insofar as they are likely to be resisted by the Turkish-Cypriot leadership and Turkey. It is estimated that the easiest provisions to renegotiate would be those concerning property, followed by those concerning settlers and legal status. The hardest aspect would be the provisions concerning security, for which the consent of the conservative Turkish military establishment would be necessary. Ironically, it is precisely this aspect that most needs revision to alter the Greek-Cypriot vote.

Third, attitudes towards reunification must not deteriorate. If recent opinion polls are to be trusted, we may be heading for a serious deterioration of attitudes. This phenomenon must be carefully measured and analysed, while any worthwhile proposal to re-establish inter-communal trust at grass-roots level must be seriously considered. It seems that the prevailing doctrine that confidence-building measures merely distract from the real issues at stake in the conflict should be rejected and that these measures should instead proceed hand in hand with negotiations on a comprehensive settlement, if we wish to prevent painful surprises in future.

Model findings: Turkish Cypriots

We now turn to an examination of Turkish-Cypriot attitudes, starting with a presentation of the equivalent Turkish-Cypriot regression model, which similarly purports to explain why citizens voted the way they did in the April 2004 referendum (table 2.4).

Table 2.4 Predictors of a 'yes' vote in the April 2004 referendum: Turkish Cypriots

	B	SE	Wald	Sig.	Sample scores
UBP supporter	–2.17	0.29	58.07	0.00	0.22
DP supporter	–1.48	0.31	22.72	0.00	0.12
CTP supporter	1.14	0.29	15.11	0.00	0.48
Annan Plan security provisions	0.96	0.23	17.09	0.00	0.56
Annan Plan power-sharing provisions	0.80	0.25	10.24	0.00	0.70
Motive: to be able to enjoy the benefits of EU membership	0.68	0.27	6.42	0.01	0.69
'We have much in common with the Greek Cypriots'	0.61	0.21	8.27	0.00	0.48
'I would find it natural and acceptable if someone in my family chose to marry a Greek Cypriot'	0.51	0.23	4.88	0.03	0.42
'The two communities should go their separate ways from now on'	–0.42	0.21	3.87	0.05	0.50
'Religion is important in my life'	–0.46	0.22	4.37	0.04	0.53
Iskele district resident	0.84	0.33	6.37	0.01	0.10
Low family income (up to YTL1,500)	0.48	0.23	4.58	0.03	0.67
Old age (55+)	–0.87	0.25	11.70	0.00	0.18

Table 2.5 Predictions of the Turkish-Cypriot vote

	Predicted		% correct
	No	Yes	
Observed			
No	254	65	79.6
Yes	68	582	89.5
			86.3

As shown in table 2.5, this model is also powerful in explaining voting patterns in the April 2004 referendum, correctly allocating 86.3 per cent of the sample into the appropriate category, a slightly better performance compared with the 85.3 per cent figure for the Greek-Cypriot model.

As in the Greek-Cypriot model, variables from all four categories (political allegiance, Plan-specific attitudes, underlying attitudes and demographics) entered the model, which suggests that the Turkish-Cypriot referendum vote was also underpinned by a multifactorial and multifaceted evaluation process. We now examine the parameters of this model in detail.

Party allegiance: UBP supporter (B = −2.17), DP supporter (B = −1.48), CTP supporter (B = 1.14)

Being a supporter of the National Unity Party (UBP) was a very strong negative predictor of a 'yes' referendum vote. The UBP was against the Annan Plan and the party had substantial success in persuading its supporters to accept its official policy. Being a supporter of the Democratic Party (DP) was also a negative predictor, though to a lesser extent than being a UBP supporter. This stands to reason, given that the DP was officially neutral towards the Annan Plan, rather than opposed to it. Yet despite this neutrality, 'DP supporter' was a strong negative predictor, which suggests that the socio-cultural make-up of DP supporters led them to vote against the Plan, despite not being told to do so by their party. The leader of the party, Serdar Denktaş, later admitted that he had also voted 'no' at the referendum. Conversely, being a supporter of the Republican Turkish Party (CTP) was a strong positive predictor of a 'yes' vote, as was the case for smaller parties, such as the Peace and Democracy Movement (BDH).

It seems that party politics was very closely related to the referendum vote among Turkish Cypriots, perhaps more so than among Greek Cypriots. This can be interpreted to mean either that Turkish-Cypriot parties – having taken early positions on the Annan Plan – were more successful in swaying their voters, or that Turkish-Cypriot parties are ideologically and sociologically more cohesive than their Greek-Cypriot counterparts. A bridging hypothesis is that Turkish-Cypriot parties were originally created and then differentiated from each other on the basis of their views on the Cyprus problem and, thus, it was to be expected that referendum voting would more closely follow the contours of party affiliation. By contrast, Greek-Cypriot parties cannot be so easily categorised along pro-unification versus anti-unification lines, since (officially at least) they all have always supported reunification. A corollary of this hypothesis is that Turkish-Cypriot parties are inevitably vulnerable to swings in public opinion regarding the desirability of reunification. A pro-unification mood among the Turkish-Cypriot public will eventually translate into a stronger share for the CTP, while an anti-unification mood will eventually strengthen the UBP. The possible consequences of such a dynamic will be explored later in this chapter.

Annan Plan security provisions, B = 0.96

Following political party allegiance, the strongest predictor of the referendum vote among the Turkish Cypriots was whether a voter approved of or opposed the Annan Plan's security provisions. Turkish-Cypriot voters who could not bring themselves to accept the Plan's security provisions were very likely to vote 'no', all else being equal. This finding closely echoes the Greek-Cypriot model, where security concerns were also found to be the prime determinant of the vote after political party affiliation. Interestingly, only 56 per cent of the Turkish Cypriots found the Annan Plan's security provisions acceptable, a significantly lower score than their overall 65 per cent acceptance of the Plan. Hence, the security aspect of the Plan, though acceptable to the majority, dampened rather than enhanced Turkish-Cypriot enthusiasm for the Plan.

In hindsight, this finding is not surprising. Though the Treaty of Guarantee that was to be reconfirmed in the Plan had the 'positive' aspect of affirming Turkish intervention rights, it also had the 'negative' aspect of affirming Greek intervention rights. In a separate analysis of this survey's data, it was found that the extent to which Turkish-Cypriot citizens trusted Greece was strongly correlated with their referendum vote ($r=0.202$, $p=0.00$). In other words, a Turkish Cypriot who felt that Greece was likely to abuse its right of intervention was likely to vote 'no'. It should be recalled that, from a Turkish-Cypriot perspective, Greece bore a large share of responsibility for Turkish-Cypriot sufferings in the 1960s. Though on balance a majority of Turkish Cypriots found the Annan Plan security provisions acceptable, a large share of this support had to do with the assumption that Turkey was closer than Greece and more willing to intervene in case of trouble.

Annan Plan power-sharing provisions, B = 0.80

Along with security, the only other aspect of the Annan Plan that was a critical factor in determining the referendum result was the power-sharing arrangements. The Turkish Cypriots tended to see the Annan Plan as a power-sharing proposal, which they either approved of and voted 'yes', or disapproved of and voted 'no'. About 70 per cent of the Turkish Cypriots considered the power-sharing arrangements of the Plan acceptable and this added a strong impetus to the Turkish-Cypriot 'yes' campaign. It is interesting to note at this point that the Plan's power-sharing provisions were not an equivalently significant factor determining the Greek-Cypriot vote. This finding disproves those who assert that with their vote, Greek Cypriots said 'no' to power-sharing. Similarly, the other aspects of the Plan which the Greek Cypriots did see as critical to their decision – property, settlers and legal status – were not equivalently significant factors for Turkish-Cypriot voters. Turkish Cypriots may have approved or disapproved of the way the Plan dealt with these questions, but either way this was not among the major factors that determined their vote.

Motive: to be able to enjoy the benefits of EU membership, B = 0.68

For Turkish Cypriots, an indirect aspect of the Annan Plan was that it would immediately render them full members of the European Union (EU). This was a prime determinant of the vote: for Turkish Cypriots, the Annan Plan referendum was partly a referendum on EU accession. Given that 69 per cent of the Turkish-Cypriot respondents felt that EU membership was a worthwhile goal, we can say that this was a primary factor in the 'yes' campaign.

'We have much in common with the Greek Cypriots', B = 0.61

As with Greek Cypriots, underlying attitudes played a role in the Turkish-Cypriot referendum decision. The most important attitudinal predictor was a sense of commonality with Greek Cypriots. Those who saw Greek Cypriots as fundamentally different and members of another nation and culture tended for this reason to vote 'no', all else being equal. Since according to the survey only 48 per cent of Turkish Cypriots felt a sense of commonality with the Greek Cypriots, this factor dampened the Turkish-Cypriot 'yes' vote.

'I would find it natural and acceptable if someone in my family chose to marry a Greek Cypriot', B = 0.51

While for Greek Cypriots the critical attitudinal predictor variable was whether they felt that having Turkish-Cypriot neighbours was acceptable, in the case of Turkish Cypriots the extent to which inter-marriage between the two communities was considered acceptable was a more reliable predictor. There are sound theoretical justifications behind such a finding. While for the more populous and economically developed community the critical issue is whether everyday coexistence with the poorer community can be tolerated – and hence the significance of the 'I would not mind having Turkish-Cypriot neighbours' variable – in the case of the less populous and less economically developed community, everyday coexistence is taken as a given and the issue becomes whether cultural assimilation can be tolerated. Many Turkish Cypriots feared that with reunification their separate culture would be eroded, as their children would inter-marry with the children of the more populous and developed Greek-Cypriot community – and for many, this was enough reason to vote 'no'. Since only about 42 per cent of the Turkish Cypriots felt that inter-marriage was acceptable, this factor served to dampen the Turkish Cypriot 'yes' vote at the referendum.

'The two communities should go their separate ways from now on', B = –0.42

Like the Greek Cypriots, loss of faith in reunification was a negative predictor of a 'yes' vote. What is interesting and surprising is that while among Greek Cypriots, who overall said 'no' to reunification, only 22 per cent agreed that the two communities should go their separate ways, among the Turkish Cypriots – who overall voted 'yes' – a full 50 per cent believed that partition was the way ahead! Of course, this is an issue on which the Turkish-Cypriot community has always been divided. Even today, the actual strength of pro- and anti-unification parties is divided, and it remains highly unlikely that a fully pro-unification coalition government could be formed. If the Turkish Cypriots voted 'yes', this was thus despite their underlying attitudes towards reunification. Their 'yes' vote reflected, primarily, their views on EU accession, political equality and better living standards. Not all those who voted 'yes' voted in favour of coexistence; this is a disturbing reality, but a reality nonetheless.

'Religion is important in my life', B = –0.46

The more religious among the Turkish Cypriots had a greater propensity to reject the Annan Plan. Presumably, this finding is also linked to their greater fear of cultural assimilation. Religion is always a guardian of culture, and religious individuals thus tend to be more attached to their cultural heritage than non-religious individuals. This variable was not significant in the Greek-Cypriot model, presumably for the same reason that the inter-marriage variable failed to show up in the model: the more populous community does not fear cultural assimilation in the same way as the less populous community.

Iskele district resident, B = 0.84

Residents of the Iskele district (i.e. the Karpas peninsula) were more inclined to vote in favour of the Annan Plan, all else being equal. This was not an expected finding, since in this region property restitution would be more extensive than elsewhere. Despite this, residents of this region were more likely to vote 'yes'. A working hypothesis is that the residents of the Iskele district have never ceased to coexist with Greek Cypriots, due to the presence of enclaved Greek Cypriots in this region, and are therefore free of the Greek-Cypriot stereotypes that residents of other districts might have. It should be recalled that the previous Turkish-Cypriot regime made deliberate use of historical narratives to discourage unification, by focusing on how domineering, violent and dangerous the Greek Cypriots could be. Living alongside Greek Cypriots, the residents of Iskele may have been immune to such stereotyping.

Low family income (up to YTL1,500), B = 0.48

In sharp contrast with the Greek Cypriots, low family income was a positive predictor of a 'yes' vote among Turkish Cypriots. While the poorer Greek

Cypriots saw reunification as an economic threat, the poorer Turkish Cypriots saw reunification as an economic opportunity. Neither finding is surprising given the economic disparity between the two communities. Given that 67 per cent of the Turkish Cypriots fall within the low-income category (earning less than YTL1,500 monthly), the expectation and hope of higher living standards contributed significantly to the strongly positive referendum result.

Old age (55+), B = -0.87

The older Turkish Cypriots exhibited a propensity to oppose the Annan Plan. This is the generation that lived through the 1960s and thereafter pursued security in separation from the Greek Cypriots. Thus, it is not surprising that this age group would have greater misgivings about reunification. It is encouraging to see that younger Turkish Cypriots did not generally share these misgivings, but tended to focus on the opportunities for social development and economic growth that reunification would offer.

Overall evaluation

On the whole, the Turkish-Cypriot 'yes' vote in April 2004 was helped by the prospects of EU accession and higher living standards, and by the overall favourable evaluation of the Annan Plan's power-sharing arrangements. At the same time, the 'yes' vote was dampened by lingering doubts regarding the desirability of reunification and coexistence, and these doubts were especially strong among the elderly. Finally, the security arrangements of the Plan, though on the whole tolerable, also served to dampen support by echoing the troubled times of the 1960s, when these very provisions failed to protect the Turkish Cypriots.

From explanatory model to predictive model: Turkish Cypriots

We now turn to the use of the Turkish-Cypriot regression model in a predictive capacity, as was done for the Greek Cypriots above. Using this model, three separate scenarios were tested, as shown in table 2.6.

Scenario A – Nationalist and anti-Greek-Cypriot shift in Turkish-Cypriot attitudes and politics

The first scenario assumes that the overall political balance between the CTP and BDH, on the one hand, and the UBP and DP, on the other, depends on

Table 2.6 Predictors of a 'yes' vote in a possible future referendum: Turkish Cypriots

	Regression coefficients	Actual scores (%)	Scenario A	Scenario B	Scenario C
UBP supporter	–2.17	22	32	35	22
DP supporter	–1.48	12	15	17	12
CTP supporter	1.14	48	35	30	48
Revised Plan security provisions	0.96	56	56	30	65
Revised Plan power-sharing provisions	0.80	70	70	35	75
Motive: to be able to enjoy the benefits of EU membership	0.68	69	69	69	69
'We have much in common with the Greek Cypriots'	0.61	48	25	48	60
'I would find it natural and acceptable if someone in my family chose to marry a Greek Cypriot'	0.51	42	35	42	42
'The two communities should go their separate ways from now on'	–0.42	50	75	50	40
'Religion is important in my life'	–0.46	53	53	53	53
Iskele district resident	0.84	10	10	10	10
Low family income (up to YTL1,500)	0.48	67	67	67	67
Old age (55+)	–0.87	18	18	18	18
Adjusted constant	–1.15				
z-score		0.61	–0.08	–0.48	0.85
Projected percentage 'yes' vote		65	48	38	70

underlying public attitudes along the 'pro-Cypriot, pro-unification' versus 'pro-Turkish, pro-separation' scale. In this scenario, the Plan remains unchanged but underlying attitudes towards Greek Cypriots and reunification deteriorate. In a climate of confrontation with Greek Cypriots and disappointment with the EU and the international community, Turkish Cypriots would turn towards Turkey and nationalism. As a knock-on effect, the CTP would lose ground in favour of the more nationalist UBP and DP. If a new referendum were to take place under such circumstances, the 'yes' vote might not reach the 50 per cent threshold, reaching only 48 per cent.

Scenario B – Unacceptable changes in security and power-sharing, with loss of confidence in the CTP

In this scenario, Turkey agrees to make further concessions, fearing that Cyprus might become an obstacle to Turkey's own EU accession, and pressurises the Turkish-Cypriot leadership to accept revisions to the Annan Plan that are deeply unacceptable to the Turkish-Cypriot public. Specifically, changes are made to the security provisions, such that Turkish protection and intervention rights are removed without a convincing alternative security framework being provided, while changes are also made to the power-sharing arrangements, with a move towards majority rule. While this revised Plan is being negotiated, the public lose faith in the CTP and turn towards the UBP or DP for protection. Under such a scenario, the new referendum would be equally disastrous to the April 2004 one, but this time it would be the Turkish Cypriots who defy Turkey and the international community: their 'yes' vote would reach a mere 38 per cent.

Scenario C (target scenario) – Improvement in security provisions, 'win–win' changes in power-sharing, attitudes to reunification slightly improve, pro-unification parties remain strong

Finally, we conclude this analysis with a target scenario towards which efforts for reunification could aim. This scenario attempts to estimate the maximum realistic Turkish-Cypriot 'yes' vote in a future referendum over a revised Plan. Though in practice it would not matter if the future Turkish-Cypriot 'yes' vote were narrower than that achieved in April 2004, from a psychological viewpoint such an outcome would be experienced by Turkish Cypriots as a defeat. On the contrary, if an increased 'yes' vote were achieved, the psychological message would be that the revised Plan was an improvement for both communities. According to this target scenario, improving on the April 2004 Turkish-Cypriot 'yes' is possible, to the extent that a 70 per cent endorsement is conceivable, but only if all of the following conditions are satisfied.

First, there would need to be an improvement in the Plan's security provisions. As we saw earlier, the Turkish Cypriots had some misgivings over the Annan Plan's security provisions. While the intervening role of Turkey was acknowledged in theory, in practice such intervention could take place only as a last resort and would most likely be coupled with an escalation of Greece's military presence on the island, combined with the presence of unauthorised armed militias, as was the case in the late 1960s and early 1970s. If, in contrast, an integrated security force was instituted as part of a revised Plan, composed of Cypriots themselves but with a sufficient non-Cypriot element to guarantee neutrality, and if this force had a specific mandate to quell any possible incidents of terrorism, civil unrest or ethnic violence, then a greater sense of security could be provided to the Turkish Cypriots. The role of Turkey and Greece could be reconsidered within the context of this new security system. The survey indeed revealed that such a security system would be significantly more acceptable to the Turkish Cypriots than the Annan Plan's provisions (Lordos, 2005).

Second, there would need to be 'win–win' changes in power-sharing. The current Greek-Cypriot leadership expresses strong doubts about the functionality and viability of power-sharing arrangements. This concern with functionality could be met either through 'win–lose' revisions (i.e., a shift towards majority rule), in which case the Turkish-Cypriot 'yes' vote can be expected to deteriorate sharply, or in a 'win–win' manner. One such 'win–win' proposal, advanced by AKEL, is that the governance of various federal institutions need not be undertaken by a Greek-Cypriot representative and a Turkish-Cypriot vice-representative, but instead a quota could be instituted, so that each institution would be led by a stronger chair without being hampered by a second-guessing vice-chair, while an agreed number of chief executive positions would be held by Turkish Cypriots. Another 'win–win' proposal is to reconsider the make-up and workings of the Supreme Court. Instead of three Greek-Cypriot, three Turkish-Cypriot and three non Cypriot judges, the Supreme Court could be made up of five Greek Cypriots and five Turkish Cypriots, without any non-Cypriot judges. Deadlock resolution competences could also be shifted from the judiciary to a specially instituted political council comprised of Cypriots only, which would be appointed through the widest possible bicommunal consensus. Finally, weighted cross-voting could be instituted for the election of the Senate, so that federal politicians would be made accountable to both communities. None of the above suggestions would be consistently viewed as a deterioration of the Plan from a Turkish-Cypriot viewpoint, and some of these proposals, such as cross-voting, have been shown in the survey to be particularly popular among Turkish Cypriots (Lordos, 2005).

Third, attitudes towards reunification would have to improve slightly. As shown above, the Turkish-Cypriot community was, even in 2004, divided regarding the desirability of coexistence. Such a situation is not a good omen for what might happen after reunification, when the two communities would have to cooperate with each other actively, on a personal and a collective level. Thus, improving underlying Turkish-Cypriot attitudes towards coexistence with Greek Cypriots should be a primary goal of any serious reunification effort. At the moment, however, attitudes are moving in the opposite direction, with Greek Cypriots being seen as standing in the way of Turkish-Cypriot development by blocking the lifting of their international isolation. To reverse this trend, the two leaderships need to work together to improve the image of Greek Cypriots among the Turkish-Cypriot community.

Finally, Turkish-Cypriot pro-unification parties would have to remain strong. A strong CTP and strong other pro-unification parties would automatically translate into a strong pro-unification current, whereas a weakened CTP and a weak presence of other pro-unification parties would translate into a dampened desire for reunification. Thus, supporting and strengthening these parties should also be seen as a strategic common interest of the current Greek-Cypriot and Turkish-Cypriot leaderships.

Implications for the Cyprus conflict and conflict resolution

This chapter began by posing a question: should Greek-Cypriot and Turkish-Cypriot voters be seen as 'rational agents' who carefully weighed the pros and cons of the 2004 Plan, or rather 'unthinking followers' who simply obeyed the official positions of their political leaders? After the statistical analysis of the preceding pages, it should by now be evident that such a question is entirely false: the voting behaviour of the Cypriots cannot be reduced to a simple dichotomy. In reality, voters of both communities were rational agents to an extent, but also subtly influenced by the official positions of their political parties. This influence, however, was not so strong as to overcome either deeply held personal views regarding the specifics of the Plan or overall attitudes towards reunification and coexistence.

Greek Cypriots in particular were strongly influenced to vote 'no' by the perceived inadequacy of the Plan's provisions on security, property, settlers and legal status, while the lack of extensive political support for the Plan served to enhance and solidify this already negative tendency. The economic fears of those Greek-Cypriot citizens who were less well off also worked against acceptance of the Plan, while the response of the refugees was less positive than one might have hoped. Underlying attitudes towards reunification were, on the other hand, quite positive among Greek Cypriots, and served to restrain rather than enhance the trend towards a 'no' vote. The Turkish-Cypriot 'yes' vote, in contrast, was driven by the prospect of EU membership and better living standards, and by strong support for the Annan Plan's power-sharing provisions. Other factors, such as the desire for coexistence, served to restrain the Turkish-Cypriot 'yes' vote.

Looking beyond the April 2004 referenda, a future drive for reunification must succeed on multiple levels if the aim is to achieve a strong and simultaneous 'yes'. Political support is essential; but it is also crucial to draft a revised Plan that will satisfy the fundamental concerns of both communities. At the same time, even the best Plan could conceivably fail the referenda test if the underlying attitudes of Greek Cypriots and Turkish Cypriots towards reunification and coexistence were allowed to deteriorate further. In this respect, it is important to engage in confidence-building measures alongside negotiations for a comprehensive settlement.

Beyond Cyprus, this chapter highlights several aspects of wider relevance to studies of conflict resolution. The use of public opinion polling in the context of conflict resolution is a comparatively new approach, which was first used by Professor Colin Irwin in Northern Ireland during the years prior to the Good Friday Agreement (Irwin, 2002). In an age of expanded democratic rights, where conflict resolution is no longer seen as a mere act of high-level diplomatic brokering, the use of public opinion polls can fill an important political gap; this is especially so in cases where referenda over a peace agreement have to be won, as was the case successfully in Northern Ireland, where public opinion polls did take place before the referendum, or unsuccessfully in Cyprus, where unfortunately the idea of conducting opinion polls in order to calibrate the proposed Plan and render it acceptable to the people was turned down. In any event, it is true of all realms of human endeavour that important lessons often need to be learned through painful experience. In the years since the failed referenda in Cyprus, it has become surprisingly commonplace among diplomatic circles to refer to the need for reliable public opinion information as an insurance that efforts made in technical negotiations will not be wasted due to a lack of insight into what people wish to have.

As the top-down, realist model of conflict resolution – in which strong mediators propose a settlement that local leaders sign up to after negotiations – comes under increasing criticism, and as the idea of local ownership gains a foothold in peace efforts worldwide, the use of opinion polls in which the acceptability of alternative proposals is first tested with the public informally before their formal consent is asked for should be seen as a matter of common sense. The science of polling and of statistical analysis, while extensively utilised for decades wherever people need to make a profit or win an election, has so far not been used adequately in the one field that represents the essential foundation for human well-being and progress: the making of peace. It is hoped that the experience of the failed referenda and subsequent polling in Cyprus will add to the strength of the few lone voices advocating greater grass-roots ownership of peace processes, until 'peace polls', to use a term coined by Professor Irwin, become an accepted and central element of efforts at conflict resolution worldwide.

Appendix: model variables

The variables that were tested in the model as potential predictors of the April 2004 referenda votes belong in four general categories, as follows:

a. Underlying attitudes

- We have much in common with the Greek Cypriots/Turkish Cypriots.
- I would not mind having Greek-Cypriot/Turkish-Cypriot neighbours.
- I would find it natural and acceptable if someone in my family chose to marry a Greek-Cypriot/Turkish-Cypriot.
- If my cultural rights and my security can be guaranteed, I can imagine myself living under a local administration that is primarily Greek Cypriot/Turkish Cypriot.
- The Greek Cypriots/Turkish Cypriots cannot be trusted to adhere to an agreement we might make with them.
- The two communities, Greek Cypriot and Turkish Cypriot, should go their separate ways from now on.
- Cyprus should really be considered a Turkish/Hellenic island.
- Religion is important in my life.
- We should all strive, from now on, to be Cypriot first, and Greek or Turkish second.
- To achieve a comprehensive settlement, we have to understand and seek to alleviate the concerns of the Greek Cypriots/Turkish Cypriots, as well as our own concerns.
- The only way to solve the Cyprus problem is through an armed struggle.
- Our side is also to blame for the Cyprus problem.

While the data collected for the above twelve questions was along a five-point Likert scale (strongly disagree, partly disagree, neither agree nor disagree, partly agree, strongly agree), for the purposes of this analysis the variables were recoded into dummies, with 'partly agree' and 'strongly agree' receiving a value of 1, and all other responses, including non-responses, receiving a value of 0. This recoding was done, firstly, to cancel out the inherent subjectivity of Likert scale responses ('partly' and 'strongly' do not necessarily mean the same thing to all people) and, secondly, to ensure that no further cases would be lost from the analysis due to missing values.

b. Political allegiance

Political allegiance was measured, for the purposes of this model, using as a basis the declared vote of respondents in the most recent parliamentary elections of their respective community (May 2001 elections for the Greek Cypriots, January 2005 elections for the Turkish Cypriots). The following dummy variables were constructed to denote a vote in favour of each particular political party (party supporter = 1, other responses = 0):

- AKEL supporter;
- DISY supporter;
- DIKO supporter;
- EDEK supporter;
- CTP supporter;
- UBP supporter;
- DP supporter.

(EDEK is the Greek-Cypriot Movement for Social Democracy.) It was decided not to include data from the most recent presidential elections in the two communities, primarily because it would be very difficult, theoretically, to distinguish cause from effect: was someone who voted for Papadopoulos then led by the President into voting 'no', or did someone who intended to vote 'no' vote for Papadopoulos because he would oppose the Annan Plan? Such questions are intractable on a statistical level, and it was therefore decided to exclude the issue from the analysis. Political party support is, on the other hand, a more enduring personal characteristic, and it thus becomes somewhat easier to discern cause and effect: if, for instance, DISY voters tended to vote in favour of the Annan Plan more than the average, then it is reasonable to assume that DISY voters were at least partly influenced by their party into voting 'yes'.

c. Plan-specific factors

Regarding the specifics of the Annan Plan, five distinct questions regarding different aspects of it were asked in the survey and included in the analysis.

The response scale for each of the questions was explained to the interviewees beforehand, as shown below:

- *Totally unacceptable.* This proposal is completely unacceptable under any circumstances.
- *Tolerable if necessary.* This proposal is not what I would like to see, but I would be willing to put up with it for the sake of reaching an agreed settlement.
- *Acceptable arrangement.* This is a proposal I can accept without difficulty.
- *Very positive arrangement.* This is a proposal which would make the overall plan much more acceptable in my mind, and it would be a strong reason for me to vote 'yes' in a future referendum.
- *I am not sure.* This proposal has both positive and negative aspects for me, and I cannot at this moment decide which aspect outweighs the others; or, I do not fully understand the implications of this proposal.

The respondents were encouraged to ponder each proposal, after hearing it repeated to them twice. The proposals were deliberately complex and multifaceted, in order to simulate the real dilemmas that citizens were faced with in striving to evaluate the equally complex and multifaceted Plan which was presented for their vote at the April 2004 referenda.

- *Annan Plan security provisions.* 'On the issue of security, the UN Plan provided for the continuation of the Treaty of Guarantee between Greece, Turkey and the UK, which means that each one of those three countries will be allowed to intervene militarily anywhere in Cyprus. Furthermore, under the Treaty of Alliance, Greece and Turkey will each maintain troops in Cyprus, 6,000 each until the year 2011, 3,000 each until the year 2018. After that, 950 Greek soldiers and 650 Turkish soldiers will remain on the island indefinitely, but Greece, Turkey and Cyprus will review troop levels every three years with the objective of total withdrawal, if all parties agree.'
- *Annan Plan property rights.* 'On the issue of property rights, the UN Plan provided for the return of some territory to Greek-Cypriot administration – making the Turkish-Cypriot state about 28 per cent of Cyprus – and in that area which will come under Greek-Cypriot administration all property will be returned to original owners, while current occupants will be rehoused elsewhere. As for Greek-Cypriot property that will remain within the Turkish-Cypriot state and Turkish-Cypriot property that will remain within the Greek-Cypriot state, original individual owners will be entitled to one-third of their property, but current occupants will have priority control of a particular property they are using if they are themselves

refugees or if they have made a major investment in the property in question. Agricultural land will not be returned to original owners if this necessitates subdividing the property into plots of less than five donums [one donum is 14,400 square feet], or less than two donums for irrigable land. For any property not returned, the original owner will be compensated.'

- *Annan Plan settler provisions.* 'On the issue of immigrants from Turkey ("settlers"), the UN Plan provided for a list of 45,000 persons who would be given citizenship of Cyprus the day after the settlement and, furthermore, allowed for anyone who has already been a permanent resident in Cyprus for at least five years before the agreement to be able to claim citizenship by naturalisation four years after the settlement. In practice, this would have meant that 60,000 to 75,000 immigrants (settlers) would have been able to remain in Cyprus and become its citizens.'
- *Annan Plan power-sharing arrangements.* 'On the issue of power-sharing in the federal government, the UN Plan provided for a system whereby all decisions would require the positive participation of both communities. For instance in the Senate, for a law to be passed it would be necessary for at least one-quarter of Turkish-Cypriot present senators and one-quarter of Greek-Cypriot present senators to agree with it, as well as the requirement that at least half of the overall number of present senators must be in favour of the proposal. Similarly, in the Presidential Council at least one member from each community must be in favour of an executive decision before it can take effect.'
- *Annan Plan legal status.* On the issue of legal status, the UN Plan approach was that the two sides would not be required to agree about the previous legal status of the two sides' administrations, and instead a 'virgin birth' would take place, leading to a 'new state of affairs'. The two sides would be asked 'to agree about their future without necessarily agreeing on their past'.

For the purposes of this analysis, responses to all five statements were recoded as a trichotomy, where 'tolerable', 'acceptable' and 'very positive' were all coded '1', while 'I am not sure' was coded '0.5' and 'totally unacceptable' was coded '0'. By recoding in this manner, the defining issue becomes whether a person felt they could 'live with' the provisions of the Annan Plan, regardless of whether he or she actually liked them or merely tolerated them for the sake of reaching a solution. This choice was made because very few interviewees from either community could bring themselves to score the various provisions of the Annan Plan as anything better than 'tolerable for the sake of a compromise', and thus it did not make sense from a statistical viewpoint to focus on more subtle gradations between different positive responses.

For the Turkish Cypriots in particular, an additional aspect of the Annan Plan was also tested: the fact that through acceptance of the Annan Plan the Turkish Cypriots would immediately join the EU. More specifically, interviewees were asked to evaluate a range of possible motives for wanting a solution. The variable 'To enjoy the benefits of EU membership' was included in the model, for which responses were coded as a trichotomy where 1 = a primary motive, 0.5 = a secondary consideration, 0 = not at all a motive.

d. Demographics

A number of demographic variables were included, though all of them were recoded in such a way as to yield dummy '0/1' variables. Gender, for instance, was encoded as female = 1, male = 0.

Age was recoded as three dummy variables: 'Young (18–34)', 'Middle age (35–54)' and 'Old age (55+)'. Similarly, education was recoded as three dummy variables: 'Primary education only', 'Up to secondary education', 'Higher education'. Recoding the variables in this manner renders the model more sensitive to differences which apply for only one particular age or education group, without necessarily having a uniformly linear relationship between age/education and referendum vote.

In a similar way, level of family income was recoded, for the Greek Cypriots, as 'Low family income (up to CYP750)' and 'High family income (CYP1,500+)'. It was considered unnecessary to encode the middle-income ranges (between CYP750 and CYP1,500) separately. For Turkish Cypriots, only one income category was encoded 'Low family income (up to YTL1,500)'. The income structure among the Turkish Cypriots is pyramidal, with 67 per cent of the sample falling in this lower-income category; thus it was considered unnecessary to encode another variable for the highest income range – since it would merely be the inverse of the low-income variable.

A regional element was also included in the analysis, firstly in terms of the urban/rural dichotomy, and then additionally in relation to particular districts: for the Greek Cypriots, residents of Famagusta and Paphos districts were encoded as separate dummy variables, while for the Turkish Cypriots Güzelyurt, Lefkoşa and Iskele districts were also encoded as separate variables. The rationale behind including these particular districts was that, in different ways, each would be greatly affected if the Annan Plan had gone ahead. Famagusta district – currently entirely rural – would 're-acquire' its capital city, Paphos district would conceivably suffer as a tourist destination, Güzelyurt (Morphou) would have to be evacuated and essentially rebuilt in a different area, Lefkoşa would merge with Greek-Cypriot Nicosia, a wealthier urban body of over 200,000 population, while Iskele district would witness the return of large numbers of Greek Cypriots who would have had their properties returned to them. Thus, it was hypothesised that residents of any of these regions might have exhibited different voting patterns to the population average at the Annan Plan referendum.

Naturally, refugee status was also included as a variable, both for Greek Cypriots and for Turkish Cypriots. Additionally for Turkish Cypriots, a variable to denote whether someone was currently using a Greek-Cypriot property was encoded, since the Annan Plan included complex provisions for users of such properties, which would have affected them in various different ways.

A variable specific to the Greek-Cypriot sample that was included among the demographics was whether the individual was a state-sector employee. This was done in order to test the hypothesis that doubts and rumours expressed in the days prior to the referendum, along the lines of 'if the Annan Plan goes ahead then civil servants might lose their jobs', affected voting patterns.

A variable specific to the Turkish-Cypriot sample that was included in the analysis was whether the individual was of Turkish rather than of Cypriot origin. This variable was encoded through responses to the question 'Where were your parents born?' The response 'father and mother born in Turkey' was coded 1, while all other responses were coded 0.

Notes

1 All interviews took place within a two-week period, between 10 and 25 May 2005.

2 That is, in each household, the adult who had most recently had a birthday was invited for an interview.

3 More specifically, $z = C + B_1{*}X_1 + B_2{*}X_2 + B_3{*}X_3 + B_4{*}X_4 + B_5{*}X_5 + B_6{*}X_6 + \ldots$ where C is a constant, X_1, X_2, X_3 etc. are the predictor variables and B_1, B_2, B_3 etc. are the coefficients linked to the predictor variables.

3

Economics and the politicisation of civil society: the Turkish-Cypriot case

Canan Balkır and Galip L. Yalman

Introduction

The beginning of the new millennium witnessed a new 'state of affairs' in one of the most protracted conflicts of the twentieth century. The resolution of the Cyprus conflict gained new saliency because of its influence on relations between Turkey and the European Union (EU). Not only has the EU become an integral part of this age-old conflict, but the prospect of becoming incorporated into the EU emerged as a key determinant of the ways in which the Turkish-Cypriot civil society actors in general, and the business community in particular, positioned themselves in their quest for a way out of the stalemate. However, it is also indispensable to take into account the impact of the severe economic and political crises encountered in Turkey as well as in the Turkish-Cypriot part of the island during the period in question, so as to come to terms with the political realignments in the latter. Put differently, the dynamics of change which eventually led to the acceptance of the Annan Plan by the Turkish-Cypriot electorate could be summed up as the transformation of a vibrant civil society into a political society in the context of deteriorating economic conditions.

But there is hardly any analysis of these dynamics on either side of the Green Line which contributed to the perpetuation of the stalemate for many decades. This chapter attempts to fill that void, at least partially, by providing such an analysis for the Turkish-Cypriot side during the rather hectic period of crisis and fluidity that led to the much publicised referenda of 24 April 2004. An analysis of the process by which several social and economic actors increasingly became politically active – forming political platforms and joining forces – in order to end the domestic as well as the international political impasse is pertinent in bringing a new dimension to studies of conflict resolution. The chapter highlights the extent to which the developments that led to the end of an era in Turkish-Cypriot political history have altered the parameters within which the resolution of the conflict could be sought. Such an analysis may also provide a better understanding of the huge disappointment observed since then among both the Turkish-Cypriot people and those observers who seemed to think that the enlargement of the EU would alter the fundamentals so as to put an end to the stalemate, thus bringing a new dimension to this supranational entity, in the form of an agent of conflict resolution.

As it has been cogently put, there was a set of rising expectations at the time, both within the Turkish-Cypriot community and outside it, that 'the simultaneous re-unification of Cyprus and accession to the EU could transform the political structures and interests that have up to now made it impossible to resolve the division of the island' (Emerson and Tocci, 2002: 3). Indeed, the Secretary-General of the United Nations (UN), Kofi Annan, also seemed to believe that:

> a unique set of circumstances was emerging and that the potential existed to make a true impact on the attitudes of the protagonists and bring about the required qualitative changes of position.... [The] European Union factor in particular offered a framework of incentives to reach a settlement as well as deadlines within which to reach it. (UN Secretary-General, 2003: 2)

Thus, he would set himself the task of ending the rather poor record of the UN in paving the ground for a solution of the 'Cyprus problem' by heeding, in his own words, 'Jean Monnet's advice that in order to solve intractable problems it is sometimes necessary to change the context' (*ibid.*). However, the hopes that were pinned on the EU for changing the context within which the protracted conflict had been perpetuated would soon be dissipated, as there was little concern about the factors that motivated the parties to the conflict and made their leaderships, in turn, appear intransigent.

With the benefit of hindsight, writing in the summer of 2007, it becomes clear that the kind of images framed in the form of potential solutions to the stalemate as perceived by different parties in general, and by the Turkish-Cypriot civil society actors in particular, are losing their relevance. The EU, in turn, emerges as a peculiar entity which tends to lose its saliency as 'an idea' motivating the conduct of people who are looking for a way out of their predicament, while being portrayed as an actor increasingly involved in the process. Put differently, the EU seems to be losing its capacity to develop a lived system of meanings for many Turkish Cypriots, as it drifts away from a position constituting a sense of reality for them, confirmed by their real life experiences, unless they opt for the citizenship of the Republic of Cyprus (RoC). Thus, it is not surprising at all to observe the emergence of a variety of ideas not necessarily coherent in their own terms, reflecting a sense of desperation for the realisation of a 'solution' closely identified with the prospect of EU membership under a unified state. However, it does not necessarily imply a reduction in or loss of the EU's so-called transformative capacity; rather, it possibly reinforces the sceptical view of the so-called 'catalytic effect' of EU involvement in removing the obstacles to a lasting solution (cf. Christou, 2006; Diez, 2002b,c).

It therefore becomes imperative to differentiate between the search for a resolution of the conflict setting two communities and/or two geographies against each other and the strong inclination on the part of the Turkish-Cypriot civil society actors to bring an end to their own political regime, which had been portrayed as the major stumbling block preventing the resolution of the conflict. The fact that the two dimensions have been conflated on the part of Turkish-Cypriot civil society actors at a particular historical conjuncture makes it all the more necessary to disentangle them, so as to come to terms with the politicisation of this relatively small but increasingly vocal civil society. In this regard, the ideological significance attributed to prospective EU membership in the Turkish-Cypriot context, albeit as part of a putative reunification process, so as to overcome a particular political and economic crisis that the community had been engulfed in at the turn of the millennium needs to be underlined. Yet it is also necessary to point out that this ideological significance does not necessarily stem from the EU's alleged 'post-modern' qualities in contributing to the rearticulation of identities (cf. Diez, 2002c). Rather, the EU's ideological significance has to be understood in terms of the appropriation of EU membership in the attempt to gain the consent of the Turkish-Cypriot people to the Annan Plan.

History in the making: the evolution of a Turkish-Cypriot political entity

> 'Please tell the world that the TRNC [Turkish Republic of Northern Cyprus] is an open prison,' Ahmet Barçın, president of the zone's secondary-school teachers' union, said. 'It's one big, militarised zone and all the gates are locked. Our only key to freedom is a quick peace settlement [with the Greek-Cypriot south of the island], entry to the EU and reintegration with the rest of the world.' (*Guardian*, 25 September 2001)

Statements such as the above, which proliferated prior to and in the aftermath of the Annan Plan, indicate very clearly the kind of perceptions which prevailed among Turkish-Cypriot opinion-makers as regards the predicament that confronted them as representatives of civil society organisations and/or political parties in opposition. Ironically, their conception of a peaceful resolution would not necessarily be distinct from, or might even be identical to, that of those that they would be portraying as the stumbling block. That is, there were hardly any disagreements between the Denktaş presidency, which was staunchly against the Annan Plan, and the opposition, which seemed to favour it. For both sides would agree on the indispensability of a bizonal federal state based on the political equality of its Turkish-Cypriot and Greek-Cypriot components.[1] They would differ, however, over the means to achieve that ultimate objective, while at the same time accusing each other of deploying tactics that would hinder rather than facilitate its realisation. In fact, one of the first acts of the 'This Country Is Ours' platform (which brought together a panoply of opposition parties and trade unions against the Denktaş presidency at the peak of an economic crisis during the summer of 2000) was to send a message to Kofi Annan underlining its determination to support the creation of 'a bizonal, bicommunal federation with political equality' which would eventually be a member of the EU.[2] This seemed to be in line with the 'primary objective' of the Turkish-Cypriot side as reflected in Kofi Annan's description of the Denktaş presidency's stance during the negotiations leading to the referenda in 2004 (UN Secretary-General, 2004). There is nothing surprising about this seeming concurrence of opinion, as it had also been the basis for negotiations between the Turkish-Cypriot and Greek-Cypriot sides as underlined by the 'Set of Ideas on an Overall Framework Agreement on Cyprus' presented by the then Secretary-General of the UN, Boutros Boutros-Ghali, in 1992 (Hoffmeister, 2002). Yet it also entailed one of the main points of contention within Turkish-Cypriot society in relation to the future form of the Turkish-Cypriot polity and the nature of its relationship with the outside world in general, and with Turkey in particular. This, in turn, requires a brief historical excursion.

The Turkish-Cypriot community lived under various forms of regime since the breakdown of the power-sharing arrangements of the 1960 Cypriot constitution in 1963. The first was the Provisional Turkish-Cypriot Administration in 1967, which reflected an adherence to the 1960 constitution with its depiction of itself as a 'provisional administration'. Yet it also underlined its precarious nature, which would eventually prepare the ground for the Turkish-Cypriot insistence on bizonality as the basis of political equality as well as the security of its people. Concomitantly, the 1977 and 1979 guideline agreements between the Greek-Cypriot and Turkish-Cypriot sides can be considered the reflection of the same line of reasoning attempting to secure bizonality, albeit on the basis of geographical division of the island.[3] Similarly, the acceptance of the Annan Plan by the Turkish-Cypriot electorate in the April 2004 referenda could be seen as indicating their readiness 'to establish a new state of affairs and a new partnership state with the Greek Cypriots on an equal footing in the EU' (Özersay, 2005: 395). However, this does not necessarily justify the interpretation presented by Kofi Annan that, by accepting his Plan, 'the Turkish Cypriots have broken with the decades-old policies of seeking recognition of the "state" they purported to create in 1983' (UN Secretary-General, 2004: 21). For it did not necessarily imply a readiness to give up their statehood, even though the particular form of this could not be pre-figured in advance. As there had been a succession of institutional arrangements since 1974 for the development of statehood for the Turkish-Cypriot community, there was no reason to expect that the present one, the Turkish Republic of Northern Cyprus (TRNC), dating back to 1983, should be the last. Yet it is also necessary to underline that the disappointment in the aftermath of the 2004 referenda seems to be increasingly giving way to a determination to adhere to the TRNC, albeit without seeking recognition.

It is noteworthy that those who were increasingly becoming critical of the Denktaş presidency would equally be adamant in claiming their right to self-rule. This was expressed, however, in two distinct modalities. On the one hand, it reflected an abhorrence of the Greek-Cypriot rejection of political equality, since it was interpreted as nothing short of implying a minority status for the Turkish Cypriots.[4] On the other hand, and as had been reflected in the demands of 'This Country Is Ours' platform, it entailed explicit criticism of the involvement of the Turkish state in the running of the TRNC, through its civil and military representatives in northern Cyprus.[5] Opposition to this kind of involvement gained momentum in parallel to the deterioration of the local economic conditions from the summer of 2000 onwards. No doubt the imposition of a stabilisation package by the Turkish government on its Turkish-Cypriot counterpart in the autumn of 2000, similar to the one imposed on itself by the International Monetary Fund (IMF) a year earlier, did play a critical role in provoking further outcry and galvanising the opposition to the regime.

The banking crisis that broke out during the winter of 1999/2000, nearly a year before the major financial crisis experienced in Turkey, might be considered a watershed, not only in terms of deterioration of the domestic economic conditions but also in instigating a traumatic change in the relationship between the civil society actors and those exercising political power in the north of the island. The deep economic trauma had caused a major dislocation in the economy, resulting in a substantial loss of output and massive unemployment. Yet, at the same time, it created an atmosphere in which the struggle to overcome domestic political opponents prevailed over all other considerations. Thus, it appeared as if, once the opposition forces triumphed over the Denktaş presidency, a solution to the 'Cyprus problem' would soon be forthcoming, notwithstanding the differences between the parties to the conflict about the nature of a contemplated bizonal, bicommunal federation. This also provides a clue to understanding why the prospective EU membership, as envisaged by the Annan Plan, was perceived as changing the context so as to solve an intractable problem of a domestic nature.

The blame of the political regime personified by the presidency of Rauf Denktaş for instigating the crisis was commonplace, as the regime was criticised for its clientelism and nepotism. Yet it is noteworthy that the local banking community had also played a part in instigating the banking crisis, which saw the collapse of a significant number of local banks by the end of 2001, since it had prevented the implementation of a proposed banking law in 1999 which sought to strengthen the banking system.[6] This rather unfortunate episode highlighted the political links of the banking community, which they effectively utilised, at least until the crisis, as they reckoned the introduction of a new law would favour the banks from Turkey at their own expense (Şafaklı, 2003). It also contributed to the loss of legitimacy by the political regime in the eyes of the Turkish-Cypriot community, as depositors of the failing banks became disenchanted with their own state, which seemed unable to provide a solution to their predicament.

As the economic crisis rapidly evolved into a political crisis, with the erosion of the legitimacy of the regime, the political actors who had taken part in different coalition governments under the Denktaş presidency during the 1990s increasingly raised their voices to condemn the nature of the political regime.[7] In the eyes of many, it was a regime which did not even respect the judiciary. However, it is noteworthy that the European Court of Human Rights had rejected such allegations and concluded in May 2001 that 'there has not been an administrative practice of violating the Turkish Cypriots' right of assembly, their freedom of expression, or their rights to liberty and to protection of private life'. 'It had no evidence beyond reasonable doubt that there was a general practice of suppressing all dissent against ruling parties' (Hoffmeister, 2002: 448). Nonetheless, the Turkish-Cypriot political regime would be looked upon as 'the Turkey-dominated political-administrative structure', which, in turn, produced a 'limited democracy [that] disabled the civil society towards being influential in affecting public policies' (CIVICUS, 2005: 158, 218).

Meanwhile, the business community had been undergoing its own, equally salient political overhaul, which had no doubt made an impact in diminishing the perceived 'democratic deficit'. A crack had already started to emerge between the political establishment and the business community, which, in general, had previously toed the line in relation to the negotiating stance *vis-à-vis* the Greek-Cypriot side adopted by the Denktaş presidency, in close collaboration with the Ankara government. This could be observed even on an individual basis as those business people who had been considered to be very close to the Denktaş presidency started to shift ground. Yet, as has been pointed out, this public distancing would not necessarily mean a complete rupture, as regular contacts continued behind the scenes. The message from the members of the business community, however, was that Denktaş's negotiating stance would be weakened if he did not heed their advice.[8] The change in attitudes had also been reflected in a change of leadership of the main business organisation, the Turkish-Cypriot Chamber of Commerce, in the spring of 2001, at the peak of the economic crisis. The new board increasingly adopted a different vocabulary so as to express their views not as an interest group but as the representative of the interests of the Turkish-Cypriot people in general. The outspoken president of the board, Ali Erel, made this shift in positioning apparent:

> The economic crisis and the lack of response from the politicians to our suggestions are creating distress among both the members of our society and our Chamber; and the Chamber Board of Directors is getting many demands to start some kind of action for urgent measures to our problems. In case the message from our economy and public is not heeded, action will be inescapable.[9]

While the weakening of the political regime was a significant outcome of the economic crisis, the latter also paved the ground for the restructuring of the state in accordance with the dictums of neoliberal political economy, so that the state would act as a 'third party', to put an end to 'rent-seeking'. The reforms from October 2000 onwards aimed to strengthen the financial system and establish the 'independence' of the Central Bank of the TRNC as the major mechanism of crisis management and/or prevention. However, they have not alleviated another perceived weakness of the administrative structure of the TRNC, namely its dependency on Turkey. As a matter of fact, the tradition of appointing an employee of the Central Bank of Turkey as the governor of the Central Bank of the TRNC continued, along with the tradition of signing 'protocols' between the two governments to augment the Turkish-Cypriot economy.[10] The continuation of such practices, however, was perceived as curtailing the political autonomy of the state rather than allowing it to act as a 'third party' (CIVICUS, 2005).

This dependency has also been reflected in a strong parallelism in the economic policy of the two countries, which can be observed over a period of three decades. It could be argued that the changes in economic policy orientation that have been experienced in Turkey were mirrored in the Turkish-Cypriot economic policy-making structures. Such parallelism is also indicative of the role assumed by the local civil society actors, trade unions and business associations in the policy-making processes. While they could be effective in striving to defend the interests of their members in terms of negotiating wages or securing entitlements, their capacity to influence policy orientation has been rather limited, if not negligible. More saliently, this relative incapacity was also reflected in the way in which their views were eschewed by the policy-makers in Turkey while taking decisions that would be of direct concern to them. As regretted by the late İsmail Cem, former Minister of Foreign Affairs, one fundamental weakness of Turkey's foreign policy *vis-à-vis* Cyprus was not to have developed any awareness of the need to take into consideration the views of the Turkish-Cypriot civil society actors in determining its means as well as its ends (Cem, 2004: 237).

The parallelism in economic policy as well as the adoption of the Turkish lira as the currency of the Turkish-Cypriot entity had a series of adverse consequences, as officially acknowledged by the Turkish-Cypriot State Planning Organisation:

> Not being able to have a monetary policy of its own, because it is using the same currency as Turkey, the TRNC is highly dependent on changes in the external balances of Turkey, therefore inflation in the TRNC, to a large extent, is a variable imported from Turkey.[11]

However, the total lack of monetary policy autonomy meant the importation not only of inflation, albeit with a short time lag, but also of the stabilisation measures to deal with the consequences. Allegedly, all economic evils were being imported from Turkey, including the crises which had characterised the Turkish economy intermittently. This gave the Turkish-Cypriot politicians a continuous excuse for their apparent mismanagement of the economy. For, in the absence of international recognition, Turkey would also play the role of the IMF for the TRNC economy, by initiating stabilisation programmes through the signing of economic protocols, whenever it deemed it necessary. It is noteworthy in this regard that Turkish-Cypriot governments would send a letter of intent to Turkey outlining the sort of policies they intended to pursue as part of the stabilisation programme. The only constructive exception, from the Turkish-Cypriot point of view, was the financial support provided by Turkey for infrastructure investments and some aid with budgetary deficits. While the financial aid from Turkey to the TRNC was on average $70 million per annum until the mid-1990s, this was more than doubled following the signing of the economic protocol in 1997 between the two countries (Yılmaz, 2002). Paradoxically, the TRNC's annual foreign trade deficit with Turkey tended to exceed the amount of aid received. Due to high costs of production, weak capital structure and low technology, domestic industry was short of satisfying domestic demand, which was met mainly by imports. Dependency of the economy on imports while the export possibilities were limited resulted in a chronic foreign trade deficit, no doubt exacerbated by a decision of the European Court of Justice on 5 July 1994, which declared direct imports from the TRNC to the EU to be illegal.[12] The aid, which amounted to over $3,071 million for the period 1974–2004, was actually used, in large part, to pay public sector salaries and retirement pensions. It was also instrumental in overcoming the fallout from the banking crisis, as it provided a source of finance for the liquidation of the public sector's debt to the banking system. In other words, its contribution to the accumulation of capital for productive investment was insignificant.

Ironically, while the reforms instituted from the autumn of 2000 onwards would normally have been expected to have gained the support of the business community,[13] which had increasingly been voicing its demands for transparency, accountability and good governance in the conduct of the economy, it seems that they rather caused more consternation. As Ali Erel put it:

> The reform packages have not been able to improve the economy; they have managed only to apply taxes and raise prices, while being unable to carry out any structural reform to improve the condition of the economy. The level of public welfare has deteriorated.[14]

While the restructuring of the banking sector has diminished its fragility under the guidance of an 'independent Central Bank',[15] the stabilisation programme put in place by two economic protocols during 2001 created the usual deflationary pressures that further eroded living standards. No less saliently, it prompted ill feeling not only towards the government which put the programme into effect, but also towards Turkey, in much the same way that the IMF would be held responsible by those who carried the brunt of the contractions caused by the implementation of such programmes in different parts of the world.[16] Demands for urgent steps to correct the situation in the economic domain were complemented by demands for a new strategy to resolve the 'Cyprus problem'. More fundamentally, disenchantment with the economic conditions accelerated the process of the emergence of the business community as a political actor in its own right. In Gramscian terms, the latter would increasingly attempt to provide moral and intellectual leadership, and thus play a key role in the process of collective will formation. Not surprisingly, the business community would be engaged in coalition-building with other forces of opposition already under the umbrella of the 'This Country Is Ours' platform, thereby paving the way for the emergence of a new platform, the 'Common Vision of Turkish-Cypriot Civil Society' in August 2002, a mere three months before the announcement of the Annan Plan.

The Annan Plan: end of an era or demise of false expectations?

> 'The [Annan] plan is the only way to prevent our obliteration as a community,' said İzzet İzcan, the leader of the United Cyprus opposition party. (*Guardian*, 29 December 2002)

> 'The Greek Cypriots now see EU membership as an alternative to a settlement and as a means by which to negate the Turkish military guarantee and exert pressure upon Turkey to deliver the Turkish Cypriots into their hands.' (Stephen, 2001: 67)

There are indications that the members of the business community were given clues about the ways in which the Annan Plan was going to present a blueprint for the resolution of the 'Cyprus problem'. In particular, they were encouraged to hear that it would entail a framework parallel to that of the 'Common Vision of Turkish-Cypriot Civil Society'.[17] The representatives of the business community, through their various associations, were making clear their determination for the 'problem' to be resolved through acceptance by both sides of a bizonal, bicommunal federation with political equality. They were not prepared to accept minority status for Turkish Cypriots under any circumstances. Certainly, they were not lured by the so-called carrot/catalyst argument that 'there would be legal benefits providing societal security for Turkish Cypriots because of minority rights and democracy being part of the *acquis*' (Diez, 2002b: 144). They were also keen on the continuation of the guarantee power of Turkey and the protection of the strategic interests of Turkey in the eastern Mediterranean. Realising that Turkey's EU membership application would be a long process, a few began to voice their aspiration to see the Cyprus conflict solved and the new Cyprus become part of Europe regardless of Turkish accession. Of course, they wanted to see the accession talks begin between the EU and Turkey, in a parallel process, but they would not accept being kept hostage until Turkey became a member. In that respect, it is plausible to suggest that a convergence of opinion was emerging, since this was a view long held by the left-wing opposition to the Denktaş presidency.[18]

As stated by the declaration of the 'Common Vision of Turkish-Cypriot Civil Society' in August 2002, the opposition formations were of the opinion that 'the chance for Turkish Cypriots to reach an agreement based on equality and to obtain the right to equal representation in the European Union will be lost' if a solution could not be found before the end of that year. The business community in particular was aware that if the period after the publication of the Annan Plan was wasted, without negotiations, the Greek-Cypriot side would unilaterally become a member of the EU. A deal had to be struck before the Greek part of the island joined the EU, given that the bargaining position would be weaker after accession. In an effort to enhance the possibility of what could be described as a win–win result from the referenda to be held for the Annan Plan, the Turkish-Cypriot Chamber of Commerce succeeded in getting the RoC Chamber of Commerce and Industry on board to make a joint declaration on 15 March 2004. Having expressed their optimism for a solution before 1 May, they reiterated their vision for a reunited Cyprus joining the EU:

> the solution should provide for a fully functioning market economy while any transitional measures and periods should not exceed what is absolutely necessary. The aim must be that the economy becomes fully integrated as soon as possible and that the economic inequalities between the two communities disappear rapidly. We underline the importance of the EU funds to alleviate the economic disparities. (Turkish-Cypriot Chamber of Commerce, 2004)

The business community recognised that its members as well as the public should be informed of the merits of joining the EU, and so promoted understanding of the opportunities that would be gained through EU membership. The Turkish-Cypriot opposition in general seemed to be convinced that a genuine deal could be reached in accordance with the deadlines set by the UN Secretary-General, provided that the intransigence of the Denktaş presidency was overcome. Yet there seemed to be a naïve expectation that the Greek-Cypriot side was prepared to give up their long cherished objective of a unitary state by accepting the Annan Plan. Outside observers, too, were no doubt playing a part in the entrenchment of that misconception. For example, a Brookings Institution policy brief from 2002 noted:

> Greek Cypriot leaders genuinely seem to want to see a reunified island before EU accession and may be prepared to make some concessions on autonomy and territorial adjustments to reach one. (Barkey and Gordon, 2002)

This view was apparently shared by representatives of the EU as well. As reflected in a rather unusual outburst by the then EU Commissioner for Enlargement, Günter Verheugen, during his speech to the European Parliament after the Greek-Cypriot government called for a rejection of the Annan Plan:

> Let me be quite undiplomatic. Ladies and gentlemen, I feel personally cheated by the Government of the Republic of Cyprus. For months on end I have done my utmost, like everyone else, in good faith and trusting in the promises made by the Greek-Cypriot Government, to establish parameters, which would enable the Greek Cypriots to endorse this plan. Sadly, this has not been achieved.[19]

Similarly, according to the British press, Chris Patten, the then EU External Affairs Commissioner, 'accused the Greek Cypriots of betrayal':

> There has always been an implicit understanding that we would make Cypriot accession to the union easier and in return the Greek Cypriot community and leadership would argue the case for a decent settlement ... so I think we feel that we have, as it were, handed over the chocolate and they have refused to hand back the crisps. (*Guardian*, 26 April 2004)

Yet any cursory reading of Greek-Cypriot aspirations would reveal the fallacy of such expectations, as disclosed, for instance, in the following, from Lobby for Cyprus, a London-based voluntary organisation with the aim of reuniting the island:

> The solution is the entry of the whole of Cyprus into the European Union under a politically united government, the government of all Cypriot men and women working under the rule of law and under the guidance of the European Union itself.[20]

Cogently put, the 'Greek Cypriots' predicament lies in how to return to an approximation of the situation that existed in 1974' (Dodd, 2000: 153). It is important to point out that the Annan Plan would not have met the sensitivities of the Greek Cypriots, in that it was perceived as failing to reverse wholly the outcome of the military intervention by Turkey in 1974. Thus, in the Greek-Cypriot view, 'the Plan not only failed to answer their concerns but also seemed to be contrary to both UN and EU norms and values' (Avineri, 2004).

Notwithstanding the huge disappointment which followed its rejection by an overwhelming majority of the Greek-Cypriot electorate, the Annan Plan, no doubt, provided a field day for the Turkish-Cypriot civil society actors to establish their credentials as a social movement with political effectiveness. But it also revealed the inability of such activity to accomplish the ultimate objective. The emergence of civil society as a social movement reflects the degree of separation of the people from constituted authority; thus, it also mirrors the latter's lack of legitimacy. However, this, in turn, should not imply the separation of civil society from political society, as if the boundaries between them are given in the nature of reality. In fact, the opposite is true, as has been illustrated by the Turkish-Cypriot experience. Several social and economic actors have become increasingly politically active, forming political platforms and political parties, joining forces in order to end the domestic as well as the international political impasse.[21] It looked as if the Turkish-Cypriot opposition movement was about to attain the status of what Gramsci had called the political moment, albeit temporarily. As he put it:

> It is the phase in which previously germinated ideologies become 'party', come into confrontation and conflict, until only one of them, or at least a single combination of them, tends to prevail, to gain the upper hand, to propagate itself throughout the society.... In other words, the development and expansion of the

> particular group are conceived of and presented as being the motor force of a universal expansion, of a development of all the 'national' energies ... [thus,] the life of the State is conceived of as a continuous process of formation. (Gramsci, 1971: 181–2)

This is exactly how the constituent members of the Common Vision platform, and the leading representatives of the Turkish-Cypriot business community in particular, apparently felt in the wake of the public announcement of the Annan Plan, as they perceived the Denktaş presidency as having no choice but to bow to the final eventuality. Having no doubt been encouraged by the perception of a change of attitudes on the part of the new government in Ankara following the general elections in November 2002, the contending forces of the Turkish-Cypriot opposition movement were obviously feeling that they had at last gained the upper hand in leading the way forward for the resolution of the stalemate between the two communities. Put differently, the possibility of a resolution of the conflict on the basis of the Annan Plan, albeit in a substantially revised form, seemed to bring about what Gramsci described as 'not only a unison of economic and political aims, but also intellectual and moral unity' (*ibid.*) for the rather diverse set of interests comprising the Common Vision platform.

However, as Gramsci further argued: 'It is also necessary to take into account the fact that international relations intertwine with these internal relations of nation-states, creating new, unique and historically concrete combinations' (*ibid.*). In other words, it is essential to grasp the complexity of the nexus of international and domestic relations for the development of a successful strategy to fulfil the expectations of a mass movement in overcoming this decades-old stalemate. Not only was there a failure to develop a realistic assessment of the interplay of forces in the particular historical conjuncture on the part of the Turkish-Cypriot actors; it seems that the EU on its part had overestimated its capacity to act as an agent of conflict resolution, thereby betraying the hopes raised on both sides of the Green Line in Cyprus.

It was not only the representatives of the EU who would rue the fallout from this failure in conflict resolution: the Turkish-Cypriot social movements would equally be rueful. Relations between civil society organisations and political parties took a twirl in the aftermath of the Annan Plan referenda. This was reflected in the subsequent fortunes of the two movements, which had played leading roles in the politicisation of civil society. In fact, one of the main differences between 'This Country Is Ours' and the 'Common Vision of Turkish-Cypriot Civil Society' was that the political parties had been involved in the former from the beginning, but not in the latter, at least not formally. Common Vision served basically as a platform to bring together representatives of different social strata for the realisation of a common objective in a historically determined conjuncture; but it turned out to be a more temporary phenomenon, and seemed to wither away with the rejection of the Annan Plan. On the other hand, while 'This Country Is Ours' has survived in the post-referenda debacle, the relationship between civil society organisations, trade unions in particular, and the leading beneficiary of the whole process, the Republican Turkish Party (CTP), steadily deteriorated:

> The party used to expand its influence through its party members or associates who were the active members of the civil society organisations. This enabled CTP to convince civil society actors to follow its own political priorities ... [and thus] to develop a degree of leverage over civil society activities. (CIVICUS, 2005: 149)

The CTP, having first achieved political power in parliamentary elections in December 2003 and then got its leader elected as President of the TRNC in April 2005, attempted to tame the activism of civil society. As its leadership allegedly contended:

> there should be a silent period or an interval in the activities of civil society because almost all [its] targets ... were achieved and more activism would be harmful to the community. (CIVICUS, 2005: 149)

However, it would be wrong to conclude, as (CIVICUS, 2005: 149) did, that the civil society organisations in question lost their autonomy or that they 'work in tandem, if not at the behest, of the political leadership'. For what followed was a period of rising tensions between the trade unions, which had spearheaded the social movement from its beginning, and the CTP-led governments of the post-2004 era, as the relationship turned into a more conventional one, focusing on economic demands. Meanwhile, the leading force in the emergence of the Common Vision, the Turkish-Cypriot Chamber of Commerce, witnessed a change of leadership once again, to complete the reconfiguration of the balance of forces within the domestic context. The outgoing and outspoken chairman of the Chamber, incidentally, echoed the assertions mentioned above, as he, too, claimed that the underlying motive which instigated the change of leadership was 'to render the Chamber of Commerce subservient to "government" policy' (CIVICUS, 2005: 144).

Ironically, the period from November 2002 to April 2004, which had seen a scurry of political activity and significant changes in the domestic balance of political forces, also witnessed an economic recovery for the TRNC, coinciding with the recovery of the Turkish economy. While the crisis management strategies in both cases had striking parallels, it is not plausible to suggest that the latter necessarily had an effect on the former. The rate of growth in gross national product (GNP) had been rather unprecedented for the Turkish Cypriot economy, as it increased to 11.4 per cent in 2003 and 15.4 per cent in 2004, while on average it had been 3.8 per cent over 1977–2000, wildly fluctuating between –7.5 per cent and 10.2 per cent (Yılmaz, 2002). There was, though, a parallel increase in the foreign trade deficit as imports soared while exports continued to stagnate, largely because of the TRNC's continued economic isolation. What is conventionally considered to be one of the main risk indicators for an economy, the ratio of current account deficit to GNP, rocketed to 35 per cent in 2003 and nearly to 63 per cent in 2004.[22] As had also been the case for the Turkish economy in the aftermath of the 2001 financial crisis, the post-2002 recovery of the Turkish-Cypriot economy was thus largely dependent on the inflow of money from foreign accounts.[23] This took a variety of forms, including property sales to foreigners, an increase in tourism revenues and the wages earned by the thousands of workers who commuted daily to the south after the opening of the borders in April 2003, while the loans from Turkey either remained stable or showed a slight decline.

More saliently, the practice of signing economic protocols continued, as the rejection of the Annan Plan by the Greek Cypriots maintained the status quo ante. Indeed, the 2004 protocol with Turkey could be identified as an important cause of the deterioration in the relations between the public sector unions and the newly elected CTP administration, since it entailed the objectives of capping public employment and basically prohibiting real increases in public sector wages (World Bank, 2006: vol. II, 1.19).

The opening of the border mentioned above led to the emergence of a conflict of interest between the domestic commercial and industrial bourgeoisies. While the former were trying to push the doors more open, the latter had more protectionist instincts.[24] Yet they did not refrain from presenting a united stance by continuing to call for a political solution even in the aftermath of the 24 April 2004 referenda. Interestingly enough, it was possible to notice a change in the rhetoric, as they identified their newly reformulated economic objective as the integration of the northern Cypriot economy with others in the region, which included Turkey and southern Cyprus, as well as the EU.[25] This was meant to be a means of integrating with the global economy, thus ending the traumatic experience of economic isolation, rather than an end in itself. It is true that the EU felt obliged to find a way to end the economic isolation of the Turkish Cypriots, as EU Commissioner Verheugen indicated immediately after the referenda (*Guardian*, 26 April 2004). But the ultimate aim was still 'to facilitate the reunification of Cyprus by encouraging the economic development of the Turkish Cypriot community', as categorically stated by the European Council.[26] At a time when the post-referenda actions of the EU in this regard have clearly left a lot to be desired,[27] it is noteworthy that the Turkish-Cypriot business community will be seeking a new set of mechanisms to realise its elusive objective. Significantly, the leading bodies which comprised the Turkish-Cypriot business community established yet another 'platform of economic organisations' in October 2006.[28] Its very title, however, can be seen as an indication of their new stance: as an economic interest group within the existing state rather than aiming to initiate substantive changes in the nature of the political regime.

The politicisation of civil society will no doubt continue to unravel, as the Turkish-Cypriot community will intensify its efforts to seek a 'comprehensive solution' to 'the Cyprus problem', which remains unresolved despite the transformation of the political structures and interests that were perceived to be an obstacle, at least on their side of the divide. As acknowledged rather belatedly:

> Superficial agreement on key terms like 'bizonal' or 'federal', however, disguise deep differences about what they mean. The gap between the goals of a unitary state (Greek Cypriot) and a two-state federation (Turkish Cypriot) has swallowed many past initiatives. (International Crisis Group, 2008)

Being swallowed within the same gap, it seems, would also be the fate of the Annan Plan, in the light of initial declarations made by the newly elected Greek-Cypriot presidency in March 2008, which seemed to be adopting a somewhat more conciliatory attitude towards the resumption of negotiations, but while ruling out the ill-fated Annan Plan as a basis for them.

Notes

1 See also Diez (2002c) for noting such commonalities between these seemingly adversarial positions within the Turkish-Cypriot polity.

2 Letter to Kofi Annan, 26 September 2000, sent along with a petition carrying 17,980 signatures.

3 See Gürel and Özersay (2006) for an illustration of the rather contrasting meanings attributed to the notion of 'bizonality' by the Turkish-Cypriot and Greek-Cypriot sides.

4 See Kızılyürek (2006) on the deep historical roots of the Greek Cypriots' determination to keep the Turkish-Cypriot community as a minority and their repugnance of the 1959 Zurich–London Agreements conferring a kind of 'political equality' on both communities.

5 The CIVICUS (2005) Civil Society Index Report for Cyprus noted that 'civil society organizations organized demonstrations against the "government" arguing that "decisions relating to economic and budgeting issues are taken by the Turkish Embassy in Nicosia" and that "Turkish Cypriot community lacks necessary instruments to rule the country"'. Yet it is noteworthy that the same report would consider the Turkish embassy in Nicosia (as distinct from the Ankara government) as 'embedded in the northern Cyprus community affairs'.

6 It is interesting to note that December 1999 witnessed not only the Helsinki Summit of the European Council and the start of a new three-year stand-by agreement between the IMF and Turkey, but also the taking over of a small bank by the Savings Deposit Insurance Fund in Turkey, which, in turn, triggered a banking crisis in the TRNC. See Şafaklı (2003) for a detailed account of this episode.

7 Both opposition parties in the National Assembly, the Republican Turkish Party (CTP) and the Communal Liberation Party (TKP), were expressing their concern about the authoritarian tendencies of the regime, the use of violence in silencing the voices of opposition in the press and the curtailing of democratic rights and liberties in an unconstitutional manner; see for instance speeches by M. Ali Talat and Hüseyin Angulemli in *KKTC Cumhuriyet Meclisi, Tutanak Dergisi*, session 20, 11 December 2001.

8 Interview with a prominent member of the Turkish-Cypriot business community, 30 November 2002.

9 Turkish-Cypriot Chamber of Commerce, Economic-Political Opinion, Lefkoşa, November 2001. See www.ktto.net. (Authors' own translations here and below.)

10 See Yılmaz (2002) for documentation of these protocols; see also Balkır (2005).

11 'Macroeconomic Developments, Main Objectives and Macroeconomic Targets of the 2007 Program', www.devplan.org/Macro-eco-eng/MACROECONOMIC%20DEVELOPMENTS.pdf.

12 One of the consequences of this decision was a shift in the orientation of the TRNC's trade relations: the EU's share of its foreign trade declined steadily from a peak of 40 per cent prior to 1994, and Turkey became the dominant trading partner. See Balkır (2005) for a detailed analysis of this shift, which had a devastating effect on the local economy in general, and export-oriented food and textile industries in particular.

13 A group of business people at İŞAD (the Businessmen Association) had thought that Turkey ought to act as the IMF for the TRNC. There should be, as they put it, performance criteria (i.e. policy conditionalities). Interview by the authors, 4 March 2000.

14 Turkish-Cypriot Chamber of Commerce, Economic-Political Opinion, Lefkoşa, November 2001. See www.ktto.net.

15 Press announcement by the TRNC Central Bank, 29 July 2004, No. 2004/5. See www.kktcmb.trnc.net.

16 As one businessman-cum-politician put it during an interview with the authors, 29 November 2002, because of the deterioration in living standards resulting from the implementation of the stabilisation programme, people became scared that Turkey might be determined to take the TRNC economy down the drain.

17 Interview with the chairman of Turkish-Cypriot Chamber of Commerce, 29 November 2002.

18 According to the late Mr Özker Özgür, former chairman of the CTP, however, Turkey would not be prepared to accept such an eventuality, on the grounds that it would undermine the balance between Turkey and Greece in the eastern Mediterranean. Hence, he was not sharing the euphoria prevailing among opposition circles at the time. Interview with the authors, 30 November 2002.

19 See European Parliament, Debates, Strasbourg, 21 April 2004, at www.europarl.europa.eu/sides/getDoc.do?pubRef=-//EP//TEXT+CRE+20040421+ITEM-001+DOC+XML+V0//EN&language=EN.

20 See www.lobbyforcyprus.org/newsletters/newsletter12/Cyprus_news_12.htm, issue 12, spring 2000.
21 See Balkır (2005) for a review of the political developments and the mushrooming activities on the part of non-governmental organisations during that period.
22 *Monthly Bulletin of Turkish Cypriot Chamber of Industry*, No. 58, February/March 2007.
23 'Macroeconomic Developments, Main Objectives and Macroeconomic Targets of the 2007 Program', at www.devplan.org.
24 The President of the Chamber of Industry, Salih Tunar, voiced this concern on 10 October 2004, in his opening speech of the nineteenth general assembly of the Chamber.
25 Joint Declaration by the Turkish-Cypriot Chamber of Industry, Turkish-Cypriot Chamber of Commerce, TRNC Businessmen Association, TRNC Young Businessmen Association, Northern Cyprus Hoteliers' Association, Lefkoşa, 27 December 2004.
26 Council Regulation (EC) 389/2006, 27 February 2006, available at http://eur-lex.europa.eu.
27 According to some commentators, the credibility of the EU is undermined by its inability to overcome Greek-Cypriot objections to an ending of the economic isolation of the Turkish Cypriots (Sommer, 2005).
28 See www.ktto.net/turkce/sto20060710.html.

4

Cypriot media and the production of conflict: newsworthiness versus the possibility of peace communication

Mashoed Bailie and Bekir Azgin

Introduction

The media provide ways of thinking about what counts as important as they partially shape the boundaries within which we make sense of our social worlds. Thus, when we engage media knowledge, we are exposed to information that has been purposefully constructed from particular points of view and with specific interests in mind. Our limited access to direct experience of heightened politicised events often inhibits our capacity for genuine reflection, analysis and critique of media representations (Morely and Robbins, 1995). Ultimately, this process impresses upon readers, viewers and listeners a certain 'truth value', inasmuch as the event itself has been deemed 'worthy' of its status in the hierarchy of the news agenda. As Wolfsfeld (2004: 12) argues, 'it is the news media that determine who gets to speak and what is considered an appropriate form of argument'.

Naveh (2002: 10) focuses on the role of the media in the formation of foreign policy and also claims it is significant not only in influencing the general public but also in swaying decision-makers. The media play an active role in providing a context for how both the general public and decision-makers think about the political climate surrounding conflict and initiatives intended to move communities towards peace (First and Avraham, 2003: 2).

The key point here is that the media do not merely report on a world that exists independently of media constructions but rather they partly shape the way we come to think about that world; moreover, as political decision-making becomes more distant from the citizenry, the influence of the media increases. This highlights the necessarily *constructed* nature of media knowledge and raises questions concerning the rationale behind the choices that media workers make in their deliberate construction of stories about events, people, policies and places. Do media workers challenge the dominant political and social storytellers of their time, or do they reproduce the underlying ideological premise upon which their own stories are constructed?

Especially with regard to news reports of social conflict, it is difficult not to take media agendas as foundations for thinking through solutions to historically protracted problems, or as starting points from which to consider actions that might lead to peace or, at the least, to the resolution of conflict without violence. This is a central concern for our present analysis of the media in Cyprus, as we first highlight the role that Cypriot journalists in both north and south Cyprus have played in the historical bicommunal drama and then suggest the most fruitful strategies for challenging the dominant storytelling approaches that have been embraced by both the Greek-Cypriot and the Turkish-Cypriot media, with the goal of promoting more peace-oriented journalistic forms. What is required in order to move journalism from didacticism to dialogue, from confrontational language to increased cooperation, from listening to hearing and understanding, from enmity to empathy and cooperation?

What role do the media play in historical, social, political and cultural conflict? Our focus is on the press in Cyprus and the role journalists play in constructing stories about each other's community. While we argue that this study reflects the tendencies of Cyprus media news reporting of the 'other' in general, we engage the specific case of journalistic constructs of the recent negotiations over the opening of the Ledra/Lokmacı: a barrier at the heart of the capital, Nicosia, that became the symbol of a divided city (1964–74) and then a symbol of the division of the whole island. This barrier, separating Greek and Turkish Cypriot since 1964, now symbolises a division of the communities that has persisted for over forty years, even after the opening of various other crossings between the two communities since 2003. We then consider the possibility of opening spaces for alternative journalistic discourses that might encourage the gradual abandonment of conflict-based journalism and, ultimately, the construction of a journalism founded on the possibility of peace. It is worth repeating at this point that we perceive news stories about events as *constructions* of reality. Thus, when journalists draw upon one particular discourse or word choice rather than another, or when they highlight particular components of an event at the expense of others, we understand this active use of human agency to be a contributing factor to the overall perception of social reality and not merely a 'reflection' of a reality that existed independently of the journalist's contribution.

Drawing out frameworks informed by scholars and researchers concerned with the cultural production of news and with the role of the media during times of war, conflict and peace negotiations (Galtung, 1993, 2006; Galtung and Ruge, 1965; Hackett, 2006; Kempf, 2003; Lynch, 2006; McGoldrick, 2006; Roach, 1993; Shinar, 2003; Wolfsfeld, 2004), we evaluate the production and circulation of information in the Cypriot mainstream media and highlight the often unquestioned role that journalists play in *helping to shape* knowledge environments in which publics and policy-makers (often the publics and policy-makers in the 'other' community) take their cues and consider their options for intervention and action in the seemingly intractable Cyprus conflict.

In order better to understand the media's general propensity for peace-oriented or conflict-oriented reporting, we first draw out the implications from the work of two contemporary peace studies scholars: Gadi Wolfsfeld and Johan Galtung. Their work provides frameworks that we will subsequently use for categorising the potential of media content for promoting dialogical spaces or their tendency to close off such avenues prematurely and shut down debate. Wolfsfeld (2004: 16) suggests the four central categories of immediacy, drama, simplicity and ethnocentrism for core editorial values in the production of news stories; of these, immediacy plays the key role. We have adapted Galtung's (2002: 261) analytical model in order to consider those aspects of Cypriot media reporting (journalism in particular) that accentuate either peace/conflict resolution or war/violence.

The frameworks provided by these two scholars offer complementary entry points into the problematic role that the media play in the reporting of conflict. Where Wolfsfeld commends greater understanding of the contemporary institutionalised values that are driving news production in order that we become 'media savvy' enough to navigate through news stories, Galtung identifies these same professional news values as culprits in the perpetuation of war and violence, seeing these values as underpinning a form of journalism that encourages and perpetuates a zero-sum game among a general population and one that ultimately legitimises policies of violence and war. Recognising that neither struggling for peace nor reproducing the discourses of war are 'objective' or 'value neutral' practices, Galtung calls for an approach that highlights the journalist's human agency: the active role that journalists unavoidably play (consciously or not) in constructing the media environments (taken up by citizenries as part of their social environments) that develop around peace processes.

Where Galtung can be read as emphasising the potential for the social transformation of the media, Wolfsfeld emphasises the role media actually play, while highlighting ways in which policy-makers can 'use' that understanding in order to 'manage' the ways in which the media respond to conflict resolution and peace negotiation. Wolfsfeld's (2004: 15) starting point is a media driven both by the madness of violence and war and by a set of institutionalised professional news values that normalise the practice of gathering information from elites, while habituating journalists to a narrow and limiting set of routines. Furthermore, Wolfsfeld's primary audience is not the media and not the journalists who construct stories about events but rather governments and policy-makers, who have to become more creative in their approach to an otherwise antagonistic media (Wolfsfeld, 2004: 228–9). Thus, for Wolfsfeld, the media are relatively monolithic and fixed in their approach to global events; to survive, social and political agencies with specific agendas must learn to play the media game in order to circumvent (unchanging) journalistic barriers to producing and distributing particular kinds of stories.

While Wolfsfeld's model provides one entry point into an analysis of the Cypriot media's propensity for either peace- or war-oriented reporting – locating those tendencies in the production of media knowledge that correspond to generally accepted notions of 'newsworthiness' – its focus on how social and political agents might circumvent media barriers falls short of providing a convincing avenue for exploring how journalists themselves might transcend the social and institutional constraints that impede them.

Galtung's model, on the other hand, suggests a primary focus on media workers and is of potential benefit to those keen to engage journalists and other media workers in transforming contemporary media practices. The focus is on demystification and it is here, at the level of intervention and the potential transformation of journalistic practices, that Galtung's focus on the journalists themselves may prove fruitful, by 'changing the discourse within which something is thought, spoken of and acted upon' (Galtung, 2002: 262). Kempf (2003: 8) clarifies this crucial component of journalistic transformation and argues that precisely because journalists are members of their societies and not apart from them, they must develop both the capacity for critical reflection on the basic convictions of those societies and an increasingly questioning attitude towards their own society's dominant interpretations of reality.

Journalists, as with the publics exposed to the stories that journalists tell, are enmeshed in histories that partially shape the way they think about contemporary events. This is a crucial point when it comes to considering the language Cypriot journalists use to shape their descriptions of events, from the mundane to the extraordinary, as we will see below. We will argue that problematising received histories and challenging journalists to rethink the grounds upon which their storytelling is ultimately shaped must be central components of any intervention, as this will provide the necessary stimulus for the development of new ways of thinking and thus forms of storytelling.

For Wolfsfeld, journalists are both limited and motivated by institutional values that are internalised and reinforced by routine, news values, editors and owners. The operationalisation of these institutional values leads journalists habitually to embrace conflict-centred approaches to storytelling, valued for their immediacy, dramatic energy and simplicity. Stories are events that are happening now; they are highly charged but nevertheless can be easily grasped as journalists reduce the complex structural and institutional problems to the superficial and highly misleading level of personality and opinion while accentuating the rightness of 'our side'. For Galtung, this is journalism in the service of war.

Drawing from both Galtung and Wolfsfeld, it is possible to construct an analytical framework for evaluating the Cypriot press: firstly in terms of how closely they parallel Wolfsfeld's criteria for newsworthiness; and secondly in terms of how they satisfy Galtung's criteria of peace/conflict-oriented reporting. Galtung's 'peace/conflict journalism' category corresponds to Wolfsfeld's 'not newsworthy' category, while Wolfsfeld's 'newsworthy' category corresponds with Galtung's war/violence category (table 4.1). Thus we have our two focal points for an analysis of news reporting on conflict that has as its goal an emancipatory potential: identifying those criteria provided by Wolfsfeld that focus on the primary values of immediacy, drama, simplicity and ethnocentrism while considering those dynamic institutional relations and practices that resist a move towards Galtung's model of peace/conflict-oriented journalism.

Table 4.1 Analytical framework for evaluating the Cypriot press: Wolfsfeld's and Galtung's criteria

Wolfsfeld's 'newsworthy' category (Galtung's war journalism)	Galtung's peace journalism (Wolfsfeld's 'not newsworthy' category)
Immediacy. Focus on events	*Solution oriented*. Focus on complex processes.
Drama. Focus on conflict and violence	*People oriented*. Focus on human suffering
Simplicity. Opinion, personality, images	*Peace oriented*. Complexity of institutional processes
Ethnocentrism. Our myths, beliefs, suffering	*Truth oriented*. Expose all points of view and perspectives

Our analysis started in 'real time' with a decision in early November 2005 to begin collecting news stories from both Greek-Cypriot and Turkish-Cypriot journalists as they were printed, precisely in order to consider how those news stories drew upon previous discourses as they constructed the meaning of one particular event that they were purportedly merely 'reporting'. It became increasingly clear as our collection of stories increased that journalists were constructing stories by drawing on discourses about 'us' and 'them' that were part both of the dominant contemporary political discourse and of their own previous socialisation within their respective communities. Below, we analyse a selection of those stories as reported in both the Greek-Cypriot and Turkish-Cypriot press between November 2005 and February 2006, using the criteria established by Wolfsfeld and Galtung above. The media event concerned the opening of a passage between the two communities in the capital city of Nicosia, at what the Greek Cypriots call Ledra Street and the Turkish Cypriots refer to as the Lokmacı barricade.

From November 2005, when the story surfaced in the Turkish-Cypriot and Greek-Cypriot press, through to February 2006, we collected seventy-six newspaper articles (thirty-eight from Turkish-language Cypriot newspapers and thirty-eight from Greek-language Cypriot newspapers) specifically focused on the Ledra/Lokmacı story. Methodologically, we chose the largest circulating dailies from both communities during this period, including the Greek-Cypriot newspapers *Phileleftheros*, *Politis*, *Simerini*, *Haravgi* and *Alithia*, and the Turkish-Cypriot newspapers *Kıbrıs*, *Yenidüzen* and *Afrika*. Given that the event was 'happening' as we collected the journalistic constructions of it, we were in a position to extract the stories from each of the newspapers as they appeared that day and consider the ways in which each re-presentation of the past day's events were interpreted by the various communal newspapers. As the project continued, it was clear how readily each of the stories fitted Wolfsfeld's criteria for newsworthiness and, simultaneously, reproduced the standard discourses prevalent in each community.

As a supplement to an analysis of the newspaper articles, we conducted personal interviews with editors and other decision-makers in the Greek-Cypriot and Turkish-Cypriot press and analysed their answers according to those same criteria, in order to highlight the underlying assumptions driving journalistic practices in the Cypriot media.

Central to our concern was whether the newspaper articles: explored processes; considered long-term policy issues; promoted or reported on calm; highlighted moments when crisis was subdued; accentuated periods of co-operation and moods of moderation; gave more weight to opportunities rather than drawbacks; highlighted internal consensus; or underlined the possibility of incremental progress. We further wanted to know: whether they explored underlying ideological similarities or differences; whether appearances of conflict were presented as multi-sided; and whether the beliefs and pain of the 'other' were ever considered. Did the Cypriot media news stories on the Lokmacı/Ledra 'event' suggest the possibility of empathy, cooperation or hope? Ultimately, we came to understand that the more important question was this:

did journalists challenge their own received knowledge in the process of constructing stories about those 'others', or did that received knowledge form the foundation upon which they evaluated and reconstructed the unfolding story?

Ultimately, what we find appears as reactionary journalism rooted in unproblematised assumptions concerning the journalist's prior knowledge. While this in itself is an assumption taken from a reading of the newspaper articles, the stories themselves do consistently, in both their language and their interpretations, undermine the very possibility of hope and bicommunal dialogue – falling squarely into Wolfsfeld's 'newsworthy' category and Galtung's 'war and violence journalism'.

Major editorial news values

At the centre of Wolfsfeld's criteria for newsworthiness is the value placed on sensationalism, which takes the sub-forms of immediacy, simplicity, drama and ethnocentrism (Wolfsfeld, 2004: 17). This category is especially important with regard to the Lokmacı/Ledra story because not only was the story itself 'immediate' when reported, but each twist and turn in the development of the story was also an event or an action in its own right. That is, the story was never told as a process; even internally, the developing story was never referred back on itself to explore or explain its development – how it came to be where it currently was. Journalists and editors are often driven 'by' events, because of the news value of immediacy, even while they (perhaps unwittingly at times) play a crucial role in creating the negative media environment within which audiences are encouraged to think or feel about important social processes. Indeed, immediacy as an initial category focuses attention on the propensity in the Cypriot press to be drawn to actions and events rather than to the processes that lie behind them. One danger here is that while the media produce many stories around an issue, the overall result is that the citizenry is left without a clear understanding of the deeper, historical and contextual details necessary for making sense out of them. As Wolfsfeld (2004: 17) argues, it leaves citizens and policy-makers with 'an extremely narrow and simplistic view of what is happening' in the world around them. This, while not determining, has a direct impact on the social dialogue and the ways in which publics respond to the world around them.

Where immediacy drives the initial process of 'getting the story first', drama highlights crisis, internal conflict and discord, potential violence and danger. The sensational environment within which media performances are enacted in Cyprus encourage a habitual production of such dramatic cues in news storytelling.

The story of Lokmacı/Ledra could have been constructed within a 'win–win' frame, accentuating, for example, the benefits to be gained by both communities (not least the Greek-Cypriot and Turkish-Cypriot shopkeepers) as the opening of the Lokmacı/Ledra would certainly have encouraged the revitalisation of the Old City, which both communities are already spending large sums on in attempts at reconstruction on both sides of the divide. Moreover, historically this area was the centre of the city's culture: the marketplace of the capital. Thus, news frames could have accentuated the 'economic sense' of opening the barrier for both communities – and especially for those whose livelihoods depend in large part on the shops that they own in that vicinity. Newspaper articles, however, lacked any explanatory value, economic or otherwise, and thus failed to account for the complexities emerging between the two communities and the multiple points of view that were at work behind the scenes. Newspapers simply presented ongoing events; more explanatory value would have been yielded by a contextualisation of these events in terms of either previous or possible future events. The conflict orientation increased the tendency in the media to accentuate dangers associated with what might happen to 'us', while ignoring completely how 'they' perceive dangers associated with what might happen to 'them'.

In the examples provided in tables 4.2 and 4.3 and discussed in the next section, the newsworthiness of conflict as a category for reporting had implications not only for Greek-Cypriot and Turkish-Cypriot newspapers but also for the media that work in cultures in conflict generally. Greek-Cypriot newspapers increasingly interpreted the possible opening of a pathway between the two communities as a matter of 'them' encroaching on 'our' territory and the potential threat that this would bring to 'us', while the Turkish-Cypriot media presented the Greek-Cypriot attitude to the opening of the pathway as a dangerous precedent for 'our side'. What could have been portrayed as a cooperative enterprise between two yielding Cypriot communities in early November underwent a metamorphosis. For the Greek Cypriots, the media represented the impending threat of a Turkish invasion; while the Turkish-Cypriot media were flooded with representations of Greek Cypriots as power hungry, uncompromising and driven by a desire to dissolve Turkish Cypriots into a Greek-Cypriot-dominated Cyprus.

Furthermore, in December 2005, the Turkish-Cypriot administration removed the Lokmacı barricade in what it declared to be a grand gesture aimed at opening the centre of Nicosia to pedestrian traffic between both communities. This space between the Greek-Cypriot and Turkish-Cypriot parts of Nicosia has been historically referred to as the 'dead zone'. However, although the barricade was indeed removed, a bridge was built in its place – something that the Greek-Cypriot administration reacted strongly to. A year later, under

Table 4.2 Selection of articles from the Greek-Cypriot press

Paper, date	Headline	Summary of content
Simerini, 2 December 2005	They opened roads for Attila	The Turkish-Cypriot plans to open the barricade are wicked and masterminded by Ankara. Mehmet Ali Talat is the occupation leader ... in collaboration with Ankara.
Simerini, 5 December 2005	The division of the dead zone	We believe that we are right. We need to stand firm.
Simerini, 7 December 2005	Even if a Turk becomes a bridge	A Cypriot wise proverb says 'even if a Turk becomes a bridge, do not pass over it'. The hypocrisy, the mockery, the arrogance and the irony/sarcasm of the occupational regime has reached the zenith.
Simerini, 10 December 2005	The Ledra Street	We must find the way to show/prove who really does not want understanding, who is trying to gain points against the solution of the Cyprus problem.
Simerini, 10 December 2005	War of nerves	The occupation forces and Talat turned the opening of the Ledra gate into a war of nerves. The pseudo Prime Minister Soyer announced that the construction at Ledra will not stop. Our government declared that we are prepared to open the gate in 48 hours if the bridge, which was built by the occupation regime, is abolished.
Politis, 13 December 2005		The aim of the Turkish plan is to annex half of the dead zone.
Haravgi, 15 December 2005	Editorial. They should not ruin the common vision	Only yesterday [so-called Prime Minister Ferdi Sabit Soyer] showed that he is the mouthpiece of Ankara and the military and the defender of invasion ... he is continuing to make provocations by talking of the occupied areas as if they are his kingdom or empire as he talks about 'the boundaries'.
Alithia, 18 December 2005	Kiprianou: The responsibility is not ours	The [Greek-Cypriot] government is definitely not responsible for the Ledra Gate ... the responsibility rests with the [Turkish] occupying army and the Turkish-Cypriot leadership. If they try to send abroad false information, we must do our best to counter such a stance.

Table continues opposite

Phileleftheros, 18 December 2005	Ledra Street as a symbol of Turkish arbitrariness	The problem is the Turkish soldier, forced by occupation and invasion. Every effort on the Turkish-Cypriot side is based on lowering the status of our government in parallel with small steps to increase that of Talat and his unlawful regime.
Phileleftheros, 21 December 2005	Opinion of *Phileleftheros*. Free commuting through Ledra	Their actions do anything but help improve the climate between the two communities.
Phileleftheros, 21 December 2005	UN precautions	The UN [United Nations] has informed us that they are ready for any Turkish provocations. The UN police yesterday visited the Ledra gate area and took precautions to avoid the passing of T/Cs [Turkish Cypriots] across the Green Line, thus preventing them from executing their scenarios.
Phileleftheros, 29 December 2005	They received orders	Once again the subjection of the regime by Turkey was proved. The turn of 180 degrees concerning the plans can only be explained by the orders received from the Turkish military, under pressure from the Americans.
Phileleftheros, 31 December 2005		If the Bridge is not demolished, let's one-sidedly close all the gates.

pressure from both communities, the Turkish-Cypriot administration finally demolished the bridge, as it had done the barricade before it, and in December 2006 the Greek-Cypriot administration pulled down the wall on the Greek-Cypriot side of Nicosia. At the time of writing, there had been no further developments in opening a passage between the two communities across the 'dead zone' in the heart of the capital.

The editorial value of 'simplicity', focusing on the paired oppositions of opinion/ideology, image/text, major personalities/institutions, and two-sided conflict/multi-sided conflict, proves instructive. As we explore the choices consistently made by media workers and media institutions across the island, we notice that these choices also make the possibility of a journalism that can promote peaceful coexistence between the Greek and Turkish Cypriots extremely unlikely at this time. Wolfsfeld (2004: 21) underlines the general tendency of journalists and editors to underplay ideology while accentuating 'professional routines', where one merely reports what leaders and citizens say. Ottosen (2004: 13) argues similarly that 'The media consistently fail

Table 4.3 Selection of articles from the Turkish-Cypriot press

Paper, date	Headline	Summary of content
Kıbrıs, 8 December 2005	It seems that nobody will pass the Lokmacı exam	The truth of the matter is that the Greek-Cypriot side doesn't want to open a new gate and improve crossings before an overall solution to the Cyprus problem.
Yenidüzen, 14 December 2005	We cannot be held accountable	They expect us to say 'yes sir, your orders, whatever you order we accept it and put it into practice' but we do not have to get permission from anybody for something we do on our side. We are not forced to abide by the rules of others.
Yenidüzen, 16 December 2005	The bridge at Lokmacı will not be pulled down	The bridge at Lokmacı will not be pulled down. The real problem is that they do not want to open the gate.
Kıbrıs, 19 December 2005	First demolish your wall of shame	The Greek-Cypriot side's stance prevents the opening of a crossing point at Lokmacı.
Yenidüzen, 29 December 2005	Who could not pass from Lokmacı?	The Greek-Cypriot governing elite is not for the solution of the Cyprus problem and as a result [Greek-Cypriot President] Papadopoulos is refraining from the slightest movement towards a solution.
Afrika, 1 January 2006	Lokmacı bridge and other instillations must be pulled down	According to *Haravgi* newspaper, Papadopoulos said that pulling down the bridge is not enough. Anything that is built around the bridge which resembles a military position must also be pulled down.
Afrika, 5 February 2006	Lokmacı on the agenda again.	Nicosia Turkish-Cypriot mayor Kutlay Erk announced to the Greek-Cypriot newspaper *Politis* that the opening of Ledra Street was in stalemate for the last month due to the attitude and the tactics of the Greek-Cypriot leader Tassos Papadopoulos.
Kıbrıs, 8 February 2006	We are waiting for the Greek Cypriots to demolish the wall too	We did all the necessary preparations on our part. Time has proved that we were right in doing that. At this stage the ball is in Greek-Cypriot quarters.

Table continues opposite

Kıbrıs, 13 February 2006	Pedestrians can use the road and the bridge can stay as a monument	We were the ones who opened the Lokmacı barricade and it was the unpredictable Greek-Cypriot administration that did not demolish the wall on their side.
Afrika, 19 February 2006	No hope for Lokmacı	Any move made by the Greek-Cypriot side before their local elections will be nothing more than image-building. The Greek-Cypriot side is hiding behind the excuse of demolishing the bridge.
Afrika, 19 February 2006	No hope for Lokmacı	President Mehmet Ali Talat has accused the leader of the Greek-Cypriot administration Tassos Papadopoulos of carrying out a state campaign to maintain the division of the island.

to explore the deeper ideological underpinnings of conflict or the "hidden agendas"' that may promote a clearer appreciation of the processes at work in an ongoing conflict.

With a compulsion towards presenting opinion, images and personalities, and towards representing the conflict as a two-sided coin (heads wins, tails lose), the Cypriot press, as shown in tables 4.2 and 4.3, heightened conflict, encouraged tension and potentially sowed discord among readers. Furthermore, the examples presented suggest that the primary tactic of both Turkish-Cypriot and Greek-Cypriot journalists is to heighten each community's awareness of the differences between them in what amounts to a zero-sum game, where winning for one necessarily means losing for the other. The tables highlight a small but representative selection of the articles that were published between November 2005 and February 2006. It is worth repeating that these excerpts should be read as purposeful constructs that were intended to influence audience interpretations and not as mere reflections of events 'out there'.

Lokmacı/Ledra in newspaper articles

Tables 4.2 and 4.3 present a selection of the thirty-eight articles from the Greek-language Cypriot newspapers and the thirty-eight from the Turkish-language Cypriot newspapers, respectively. Not only do journalists in both communities reduce possible meanings of events to 'them versus us', but journalists across the political spectrum resort to the same techniques regardless of their political affiliations. This reductionism leaves a citizenry at once with 'information overload' in the sheer number of stories written about an event and 'information poverty', in that journalists leave the underlying interpretive frameworks of nationalism and xenophobia unarticulated – they refuse to challenge them or to offer *alternative ways of thinking* through inter-communal problems. While brief, the selection of drama/crisis-oriented reporting on Lokmacı/Ledra in tables 4.2 and 4.3 highlights the propensity of both Turkish-Cypriot and Greek-Cypriot journalists to construct news stories that accentuate conflict while clearly refusing to make any attempt to encourage empathy or understanding of the other community. It is precisely this seemingly mundane, historically entrenched, 'common-sense', conflict-driven language that journalists have unproblematically taken up in the construction of their stories that has to be made increasingly visible – not primarily so that it can be 'avoided' by the construction of a set of arbitrary rules, but rather in order that journalists may examine their own prior knowledge that naturalises and normalises such practices. The emphasis must be on the journalist's prior knowledge and assumptions and not on any cosmetic attempt to avoid words without also changing consciousness. As we argued above with reference to both Galtung (2002: 262) and Kempf (2003: 8), any transformation of media practices in Cyprus will of necessity require that journalists critically examine and subsequently challenge and transcend the existing discourses within which problems are thought about, spoken of and acted upon.

Newspaper editors' comments

As the story fell from the media's agenda in the second half of January and especially during the visit of the then UK foreign minister Jack Straw to the Turkish Republic of Northern Cyprus on 26 January, we asked editors and columnists of both Greek-Cypriot and Turkish-Cypriot newspapers why the story had been dropped so suddenly and without resolution. Table 4.4 presents highlights from the responses to our questions.

In each of the replies 'immediacy' stands in stark contrast to the drawn-out and complex dynamic processes underlying the issue. Editors and journalists alike express surprise and even confusion concerning how and why the story no longer seems to matter or when it might become important again. While some of the respondents found it difficult to explain why they had dropped the story, they did acknowledge that something else (something new and immediate) had replaced it. Furthermore, they conceded that should a new 'event' take place again around the issue they would probably pick it up again. It is also possible to discern a contradiction on the part of editors concerning whether they wait for a story to 'become news' or whether it becomes news when they

Table 4.4 Highlights of interviews with editors and columnists

Interviewee, date	Comments
1. Chief editor of Turkish-Cypriot *Afrika*, personal interview, 14 January 2006	I am sick and tired writing about the bridge … presumably we'll return to the subject if something new happens
2. Commentator for the Greek-Cypriot *Politis*, personal interview, 17 January 2006	I haven't noticed. It seems that it doesn't sell anymore. We have the 'Straw' problem at the moment and that keeps us busy
3. Loucas Haralambous, *Politis*, 30 March 2006	I was at a loss for words when … a close friend of mine recently asked: 'Have you noticed that suddenly everyone's forgotten about the opening of Ledra Street? Why do you think that is?' I must confess I had a hard time coming up with a satisfactory answer
4. Adviser to the publisher of *Politis*, personal interview, 18 January 2007	We published lots of stories in December and January last year and then the matter died away. As you know, the new mayor was a 'yes' supporter for the Annan Plan. So we hoped that she may help open the Ledra gate. Thus Ledra came on to agenda once again and we started publishing stories about the Ledra last month. Of course, it is the duty of journalists to follow up the stories. But you follow up if and when there is a story out there. What can you do if the story is not there?
5. Chief editor of *Kıbrıs*, telephone interview, 18 January 2006	It is typical journalistic forgetfulness. When other, more urgent themes became popular, the bridge was forgotten. To be honest, as a person in this business, I was not even aware that we had forgotten until you asked me
6. Chief editor of *Yenidüzen*, telephone interview, 18 January 2006	Three reasons come to mind: more than enough was written about the bridge during a certain period. Both the journalists and the readers got bored with it, the long holiday period may have interfered with it, or the bridge itself was out of bounds to the public and journalists were not able to visit it. You don't see anything on the subject in any of the newspapers. That is most interesting. I wonder why? I shall ask one of our journalists to write a story about the bridge. It is a very expensive bridge so we must not forget it
7. Chief editor for *Halkın Sesi*, personal interview, 18 January 2006	It became obvious that the parties cannot and will not agree on the matter and people have lost hope of opening the gate. The visit of Straw became the subject matter and the Lokmacı gate was dropped. It is the result of hopelessness

construct the story – this is clearest in responses 1, 4 and 7 in table 4.4, where the respondents indicate their control over whether an event continues to make 'news' or whether it is dropped from the newspaper.

The value of immediacy and the emphasis on sensationalism may also play a part in the lack of reflexivity apparent in the construction of news stories around the Ledra/Lokmacı event. Hackett (2006: 5) highlights this problem when arguing that 'journalists are citizens of particular states and members of national cultures, and they are not immune to the biases of nationalism in covering ... conflict'. The key issue here concerns unchallenged assumptions that both journalists and editors may carry with regard to the nature of news-making.

Intervention and transformation

While Wolfsfeld provides a framework for recognising the dynamics behind news production, there is little concerning how these values are taken up by journalists or how such institutional practices might be challenged and transformed. Seeing journalists as active agents in the construction of their own identity, and media institutions and practices as both contestable and located upon contestable terrain, opens an avenue whereby we can situate both journalism and journalists as capable of transformation and change. Hackett (2006: 2), for example, argues that an understanding of the logic underlying news production is essential in order to 'identify blockages and opportunities' for the development of alternative media performances, while Panayiotou (2006: 32), speaking specifically of the Cypriot media, asks: 'What kinds of journalism/public discourse can enhance the emergence of local forces that will help in bringing and keeping the island communities together?' The key issue here concerns unchallenged assumptions that both journalists and editors may carry with regard to the nature of news-making.

Reflections on Cypriot journalism

We have drawn out a general framework within which to reflect upon media stories concerning the Lokmacı/Ledra event and have shown that the stories have consistently fallen into Wolfsfeld's category of 'newsworthy' reporting. With this in mind, it is important to consider the possibility for what Galtung perceives as a more peace-oriented journalism in the context of the pervasive editorial values of the news media examined above.

Primarily, this will require journalists to explore conflict from multiple perspectives, make conflicts transparent, give voice to all concerned parties, see 'conflict' as a creative problem requiring creative methods for transformation, humanise all sides and promote ways of thinking among general publics that will encourage both the prevention of violence and an increase in dialogue. Furthermore, the approach anticipates that journalism will expose 'untruths' from all sides, focus on the suffering of marginalised groups, give access to the voiceless in society, and accentuate the role of ordinary people in the peace-making process rather than the 'elites' who tend to be highlighted in contemporary media stories. Finally, peace-oriented journalism would lend weight to peace initiatives by focusing on the possibilities of a peaceful society and by following through peace initiatives with a focus on resolution, reconstruction and reconciliation. It happens that all of these expectations are firmly rooted in Wolfsfeld's 'not newsworthy' category (table 4.1). A few examples will illustrate this point.

First, where our analysis reveals the fixation of the Cypriot media on two parties struggling in a zero-sum game as representative of Wolfsfeld's 'simplicity' category for what constitutes 'newsworthiness', Galtung sees this as 'war/violence journalism' and juxtaposes it with the 'peace/conflict journalism', where all players would benefit from transcending the initial perception of conflict. Second, as we uncovered the tendency of the Cypriot media to ethnocentrism, with an emphasis on 'their' brutality and 'our' suffering, in Wolfsfeld's 'newsworthy' category, Galtung emphasises this as a symptom of 'war/violence journalism' and calls for an alternative orientation, one that accentuates the suffering perpetrated upon and the crime originating from all parties to a conflict. Finally, as revealed in our interviews with editors and others from Cypriot newspapers, there is a tendency on the part of news industries to drop a story when it is overly complex and time consuming and then return to it when another dramatic event ensues. Most often this is because, in the interim, another issue has captured the imagination of the news editors. One example of this is the immediate deflection of the Ledra/Lokmacı story from both Greek-Cypriot and Turkish-Cypriot newspapers with the drama created with the visit of Jack Straw to Mehmet Ali Talat. The Greek-Cypriot government vehemently opposed Straw's visit, and Papadopoulos cancelled his appointment with Straw in protest.

While 'drama' does feature within Wolfsfeld's category of 'newsworthy' (table 4.1), it also finds its place within the 'victory-oriented' subcategory of 'war/violence journalism' in Galtung's model. Galtung stresses the need to move from this victory-oriented approach to what he calls 'solution-oriented' (Galtung, 2002: 260), where journalists follow through with a story in order to promote the possibility of resolution and reconciliation. Thus, Galtung's approach essentially challenges the dominant editorial values that constitute the contemporary Cypriot newspaper industries.

Routine interventions in journalistic practices are insufficient to the goals of peace studies as defined by both peace scholars and critical communication scholars. While Galtung's perceptions have been appropriated in the service of a 'skills oriented' approach to journalistic practices (Galtung, 2006; Lynch, 2006; McGoldrick, 2006), they actually imply a fundamental shift in media structures and a revolution in journalistic performances. Indeed, Galtung has argued elsewhere that without fundamental cultural transformation, superficial changes through lists of 'dos' and 'don'ts' will be of little use (Galtung, 1993: xiii–xiv).

Intervention in the practices of Cypriot journalists and editors must, first, recognise immediate barriers limiting their capacity as information workers and, second, encourage a critical engagement with the usually unarticulated, unquestioned and thus unchallenged assumptions they carry about the issues routinely covered. Further, it is crucial that journalists explore questions concerning the role of communication in democratic life, the social construction of meaning and reality, and, importantly, the hierarchical structural and institutional organisation of the media industries that employ them. Kempf (2003) has similarly highlighted the need for such shifts in media institutions before journalistic performances can change, and further argues that, for journalists to take on the role of promoting the resolution of conflict and the recognition of alternatives to war, they will first have to be emancipated from institutionalised constraints stemming, in part, from contemporary political economic media structures.

Preparing a clear agenda for the promotion of more engaged and socially conscious knowledge workers is crucial for any participatory democracy, given the principal role the media play in the production and dissemination of information in advanced technological societies (Wolfsfeld, 2004: 12). What such an agenda might look like and how it might engage future and current knowledge workers is a decisive question. Mosco (1993: 69) calls for nothing less than a society-wide dialogue to highlight the dangers of centralised media power and the importance of planning the use of information technologies in a participatory dialogue with the widest possible representation of the citizenry; Bruck and Roach (1993: 76) argue that while personal profit is the driving force of the media industries, values such as peace and the resolution of conflict will be relegated to the margins of media production.

Our analysis suggests not only that the Cypriot media are more likely to mystify than to clarify complex issues around peace initiatives, but also that journalists and editors are themselves mystified by the forces that move them, as they are unwittingly drawn, under an illusion of objectivity, to the values of 'immediacy' as the defining characteristic of what constitutes the importance of storytelling. Furthermore, and we believe crucial to further analysis of journalists' practices in conflict situations, a thorough understanding and problematisation of journalists' previous knowledge is called for. As becomes clear in both the news stories and editors' comments, central components of interpretation rely upon previous knowledge in making sense out of current events. These versions of events are interpreted and formed into stories that are then circulated as news and taken up by interpretive communities as 'truths', which are then acted upon. For example, pivotal concepts in the Cyprus media – including 'reunification', 'peace', 'bizonal, bicommunal federation', 'motherland', 'Cypriotness' and 'oppressor' – are both self-explanatory (within the context of the journalist's own community) and oppositional (in terms of the journalist's 'other').

Our concern has been to explore the public media debate on the Ledra/Lokmacı event, taking into account contemporary news values as articulated by Wolfsfeld while using Galtung's model as a gauge with which to evaluate the news media's potential for opening up critical debates that might encourage empathetic understanding between communities. This is all the more necessary because citizens invariably turn to this readily accessible stream of media representations and extract from these reports parameters within which to think about (and offer possible solutions to) their communal and bicommunal problems.

Clarifying the role that the Cypriot media play in the construction of stories that help to shape a general understanding of the current situation in Cyprus accentuates the fact that news stories 'about' events are in fact highly structured media representations that have been shaped for public consumption. The reader is not witness to the 'Cyprus conflict' itself. Instead, readers are situated as witnesses to carefully (or not so carefully) orchestrated 'media events', where journalists and editors highlight and re-present social, cultural, political and economic processes in selective and ideological forms.

5

Intra-communal dynamics: European Union discourses among Turkish-Cypriot political actors before and after the failed referenda

Erol Kaymak and Yücel Vural

Introduction

The European Union (EU) is believed to promise a qualitatively new model for conflict resolution, through conflict transformation (Coppieters et al., 2004). The concept of 'normative power Europe' (NPE) (Manners, 2002) (i.e. the normative power of the EU), initially conceived in economic terms, may also be applied to other areas, including border conflicts. It can be argued that NPE indeed played a constructive role in Northern Ireland and in diffusing border tensions in eastern Europe. However, NPE remains elusive in Cyprus, where the failure of the EU to serve as a 'catalyst' to resolve the Cyprus problem before accession raises questions about the 'construction' of NPE (Pace, 2006a). In the case of Cyprus, now an EU member state despite its *de facto* division, the EU has failed rather spectacularly to resolve the conflict. Unfortunately, by the time a blueprint for a settlement was put to separate, simultaneous referenda on both sides of the divided island, accession had become all but a formality; thus there was relatively little incentive for the Greek-Cypriot community to accept the admittedly difficult compromise put before them. More than 75 per cent of the Greek-Cypriot community rejected the Annan Plan, making the way forward problematic. By contrast, 65 per cent of Turkish Cypriots approved the Plan. Ultimately, the 'transformation' of the Turkish-Cypriot side, which elected a new government committed to reunification prior to accession, came too late (Lacher and Kaymak, 2005). The Republic of Cyprus formally acceded to the EU on 1 May 2004.

The failure of the referenda notwithstanding, the EU still holds the promise of playing a dynamic role in solving the Cyprus problem. Diez (2002c: 8–15), for instance, writing prior to accession, remained sanguine regarding the potential impact the EU could have in the longer term in its role as a 'framework'. Diez considered the EU to be a 'post-modern polity' (Ruggie, 1993) juxtaposed against the 'modern' view of sovereignty. It is this 'post-modern' quality of the EU framework that creates the potential to transform Cyprus. Accordingly, the subversive character of integration could, in time, fundamentally transform the Cyprus conflict. Although Diez's approach neatly differentiated the role of the EU as actor from that of framework, the challenges facing Cyprus today suggest that such a delineation is not fruitful in the analysis of conflict dynamics. Of course, it must be pointed out that Diez's framework potential is based on the assumption of accession including the Turkish-Cypriot community, as he acknowledged the challenges of a scenario whereby northern Cyprus would become a *de jure* but not a *de facto* member of the EU.

This chapter examines the ways in which the role of the EU has been conceptualised by the Turkish-Cypriot community, both before the fateful referenda of 2004 and since. The goal is to point to the ways in which political elites, as well as some of the more prominent civil society actors, have framed the issues related to EU accession and the Cyprus problem. If the EU is to play a role in socialising elites and the public at large, it must be able to articulate a vision of a settlement congruent with the expectations of the Turkish Cypriots and the Greek Cypriots alike: a tall order considering the vastly different interpretations of the origins of the Cyprus problem, both in official historiographies and sentimentally. In this chapter we highlight some of the limitations of the process thus far, and the limited role the EU actually played discursively as well as in terms of mediation prior to accession. In short, it was not only the EU's conditionality policy that failed, but it may also be argued that the EU framework was not utilised in a manner that might have affected discourses in Cyprus, on either side of the Green Line. With the act of accession, the potential of the Greek-Cypriot-led Republic of Cyprus to affect the framework itself also requires consideration (noting the rhetoric among Greek-Cypriot leaders pursuing a 'European solution' as opposed to the demonised Annan Plan). This has meant that, in the case of the Turkish Cypriots, who have little direct contact with EU institutions, the EU and its role have been interpreted in various ways. Today, there is consequently the danger that the EU will come to be conflated with Greek-Cypriot nationalist perspectives. The potential for the resurfacing and reification of 'modernist' discourses, in both communities, is not only very real but already evident.

In the pages that follow we first trace the failure of the Annan Plan to a lack of appreciation on the part of the EU of the dominance of ethnopolitical discourses, which dovetailed with modernist conceptualisations of sovereignty. Whereas the United Nations (UN) blueprint popularly known as the Annan

Plan may have been endorsed by the EU, very little was done to emphasise its 'European' aspects, including its federal arrangements, some of which borrowed from the Belgian model. Post-Annan, EU efforts have been complicated by the accession of the Republic of Cyprus, which insists on unanimity among EU member states in the lifting of the suspension of any aspect of the *acquis* in the Turkish-Cypriot-controlled north. Meanwhile, the Greek-Cypriot side has been pursuing a 'European solution' as a precondition to implementing the suspended *acquis*, which suggests to Turkish Cypriots that Greek Cypriots wish to renege on their commitment to a bizonal, bicommunal settlement, the basis of the UN framework for a negotiated settlement since 1977.

The role of the EU as both actor and framework has been made more problematic by the failure of the referenda, and in particular by the accession of the Republic of Cyprus to the Union. This, in turn, means a potential transformation of the framework itself. The framework should allow for borders to be reconceptualised so as to effect a 'post-modernisation' of the territorial issues of ethnonational secessionist conflicts. Yet in Cyprus the net effect may be the reverse, with the EU's Green Line Regulation and related regulations on aid and trade actually serving to antagonise the sides, thus portending a 're-modernisation' of the Cyprus conflict. Whereas Turkish-Cypriot nationalists, aligned with Rauf Denktaş and anti-EU interests in Turkey, were politically displaced in recent elections held in the Turkish Republic of Northern Cyprus (TRNC), the role of the Republic of Cyprus in frustrating efforts to 'lift the isolation' of the Turkish-Cypriot community has eroded the pro-EU sentiment among Turkish Cypriots. As a result, much of the potential of the framework, in conjunction with the role of the EU as actor, has become problematic.

The effects of the EU as a framework on domestic politics in Cyprus are apparent. The Greek-Cypriot-led Republic perceived the EU framework as a guarantee for extending its sovereignty beyond the Green Line. Brussels also sent a clear message that it recognised the potential sovereignty of the Greek-Cypriot-led Republic in the north. The EU both as a framework and as an actor also affirmed international commitments to basic human rights and generated expectations, directly or indirectly, that territorial unification and demilitarisation of the island would be possible with the implementation of EU laws. The Republic of Cyprus based its expectations on the EU's strong inclination to incorporate Cyprus into an enlarged Europe. This inclination led to the appreciation among Turkish Cypriots that it would be inconceivable to maintain *de facto* gains and that the EU was an appropriate framework for economic development and political stability. The failure of the EU in the process of settlement and encouraging inter-communal cooperation between the pro-EU forces in Cyprus derives from its impotence in acting as an influential political actor and activating its framework. The EU relegated its role as a framework and actor by emphasising the role of the UN. Moreover, the lack of a genuine and shared vision of a settlement on the island culminated in a process in which EU-inspired socialisation encouraged exclusionary discourses based on the reconstruction of otherness in inter-communal relations.

The 'catalytic' effect of the EU cannot be dismissed out of hand, of course. In the case of the Turkish-Cypriot community in particular, the eventual rise of pro-EU forces played a pivotal role in building a consensus in favour of both the Annan Plan and EU accession. The response from the Turkish-Cypriot electorate was belated, coming several years after the 1999 Helsinki European Council, which lifted conditionality on the Greek-Cypriot side, stating that a settlement was not a precondition for Cyprus's membership. However, Cyprus's candidacy did not lead to a settlement prior to accession, as was envisaged. Part of the problem, as noted by Diez (2002b), was that the EU failed to acknowledge ethnopolitics in Cyprus and thus did not take prevailing identity discourses seriously. Moreover, it did not comprehend that the EU was not seen as neutral by the Turkish-Cypriot leadership (under Denktaş), which led to an overemphasis of the economic incentives to persuade the secessionist entity to consider accession and a settlement (Tocci, 2004b). In retrospect, it must be added that the EU underestimated the potential Greek-Cypriot resistance to a brokered settlement. In the run-up to and following the referenda, the Greek-Cypriot leadership was in fact accused of not living up to its end of the bargain concerning the EU accession of a reunified island.[1]

The most crucial element affecting the role of the EU in the process of a political settlement is its capacity to grapple with the issues of ethnopolitics in Cyprus. The EU's role in contributing to peace in Cyprus since the Republic of Cyprus's application in 1990 has generally favoured the Greek-Cypriot side, although there was initially a degree of ambiguity as to whether the EU would admit a *de facto* divided country. In referring to the '*de facto* separation of the two communities' and the 'legitimacy of the Greek-Cypriot-led government of the Republic of Cyprus', as well as to 'the non-recognition of the "Turkish Republic of Northern Cyprus"', the EU helped reframe the solution to the Cyprus problem in terms of the legality of the Republic of Cyprus (Commission of the European Communities, 1993). Despite 'the existence of the *de facto* authorities in the northern part of the island', the EU decided that the application for full membership of the Greek-Cypriot Republic was admissible, as it anticipated that the fundamental economic, political and cultural 'freedoms and rights would have to be guaranteed as part of a comprehensive settlement restoring constitutional arrangements covering the whole of the Republic of Cyprus' (*ibid.*). Although the EU initially stressed the need for a settlement before Cyprus's accession (Nugent, 2000: 137–9), a radical shift came about at the 1999 Helsinki European Council, when the EU enunciated a prospect of accession even prior to a settlement (European Council, 1999). The Helsinki European Council proved to be a turning point in specifying the role of the EU as an actor in the Cyprus dispute. Having dropped conditionality, a crucial responsibility the EU would have had to undertake was to socialise the Cypriot political elite to realise the post-national character of the Union (Wallace, 2002: 10).

For the best part of the decade of Cyprus's accession process, the TRNC leadership perceived EU membership as a threat to the existence of a separate 'Turkish state' in the north. Yet this very process became a central issue realigning ethno-political forces in the island, including intra-communal divisions in the Turkish-Cypriot community, which culminated in a clash between pro-EU and anti-EU groups in the north. The swift rise to power of the Republican Turkish Party (CTP) in late 2003 and its insistent support for a solution based on the Annan Plan constituted an alternative to a separate Turkish state in the north. In doing so, the Turkish-Cypriot conciliatory political forces successfully challenged the legitimacy of separatism by harmonising the idea of a united federal state with the existence of a *de facto* state in the north. Yet after the Annan Plan referenda, inter-communal relations were re-transformed into a political confrontation as a result of the attempt by the Greek-Cypriot leadership to incorporate the north into its domain of political control, without showing any readiness to cooperate and compromise. The reaction of the CTP-led Turkish-Cypriot leadership to this hegemonic policy of the Greek-Cypriot side was to stress the Turkish-Cypriot separate political existence in the north. Therefore, once again, the domestic and international efforts for a peaceful settlement in the island have ended in deadlock, a deadlock which can be broken either by an Annan Plan-like comprehensive initiative or by a constitutional transformation of the existing unitary structure of the Republic of Cyprus into a bizonal, bicommunal federal system.

The early reactions of the Turkish Cypriots to Cyprus's application to the EU

When the Greek Cypriots applied for EU membership, the Turkish-Cypriot leadership at the time considered the application invalid. A number of objections were raised, including the view that the application had been made by a government that suffered from a legitimacy problem insofar as the 'Greek-Cypriot administration' could not represent the whole island, either from a territorial standpoint or from a constitutional standpoint. The Turkish-Cypriot leadership also maintained that full membership of the EU entailed practical impediments, given the division of the island. Moreover, the application was deemed inconsistent with the Treaty of Guarantee and the constitution of the Republic of Cyprus. EU membership would be acceptable only on the condition that the two sides reached an agreement to resolve the Cyprus dispute. Rauf Denktaş, the veteran Turkish-Cypriot leader and President of the TRNC, having the backing of Ankara, was able to resist the EU and its conditionalities on the Turkish Cypriots. The Turkish-Cypriot side refused to take part in accession negotiations, something it regarded as accepting the legitimacy of the Greek-Cypriot-led Republic of Cyprus.

In response to the Republic's accession negotiations, the Turkish-Cypriot nationalist leadership considered a series of reprisals, including withdrawal from inter-communal talks aimed at resolving the Cyprus dispute, as well as raising the spectre of further integration with Turkey, if not outright Turkish annexation of northern Cyprus. The objective of the Turkish-Cypriot leadership at the time was to deter the EU from committing itself to completing negotiations over the accession of the divided island. In parallel with the Greek-Cypriot accession bid, the Turkish-Cypriot leadership suggested alternative bilateral relations between the EU and Cyprus.[2] Over time, as the Turkish-Cypriot initiatives failed to deter the EU, ambiguity gave way to more explicit hostility towards the prospects of eventual EU accession.[3] Thus the EU was treated as part of an Anglo-American conspiracy to hand Cyprus over to the Greek Cypriots. Prior to the formal accession of the Republic of Cyprus to the EU, this nationalist-reactionary perspective was used to generate and spread anti-EU sentiments in the public domain, aiming to prevent the EU from becoming popular among Turkish Cypriots. Additionally, given the pro-EU sentiment among the Greek Cypriots, the Turkish-Cypriot leadership hoped to deepen the ideological division between the two communities. The EU was subsequently portrayed as a pro-Greek entity.[4] Thus, it was argued, if the Turkish Cypriots joined the accession process, they would lose their communal rights, as accession would merely result in Cyprus becoming a 'Hellenic Republic'.[5] In this way, EU accession represented the repudiation of 'motherland' Turkey, and as such it was considered treacherous.[6] The Turkish-Cypriot leadership maintained that Turkish-Cypriot participation in accession negotiations was out of the question, since accession would constitute 'indirect *enosis*' and prove to be an existential threat to Turkish-Cypriot identity.[7] As EU policies regarding Cyprus were against the vital interests of the Turkish Cypriots, the EU should categorically reject the Greek-Cypriot accession bid or, at the very least, postpone the unilateral accession of the Greek Cypriots.[8] The Turkish-Cypriot leadership argued that official pronouncements by the Greek-Cypriot side in support of inter-communal negotiations was a tactical stance aimed at easing membership talks with the EU.[9] As the TRNC was viewed as the only legitimate authority in northern Cyprus, Cyprus's accession to the EU would be problematic as far as the extension of EU laws and norms to the north was concerned. To the extent that such norms entailed the resettlement of Greek Cypriots to the north, this was deemed entirely unacceptable.[10]

The Turkish-Cypriot leadership, together with Turkey, hoped to link eventual Cypriot membership with progress on Turkey's own bid to the join the Union. A more maximalist demand was for diplomatic recognition from the EU.[11] Eventually the Turkish-Cypriot leadership, together with Ankara, went so far as to threaten the annexation of northern Cyprus as an act of reprisal for the accession of the Greek-Cypriot-led Republic of Cyprus to the EU:

> If Europe fails to notice the fact that it is the Greek-Cypriot administration that acts on behalf of 'Cyprus' and if they believe that they can manage to incorporate the whole of Cyprus into the EU, they will fail. The Turks in the north are being compelled to integrate into their motherland. Turkey will do everything and will take all necessary steps towards this direction.[12]

In the face of EU insistence that the Turkish Cypriots participate in accession talks, nationalist elites began to propagate anti-EU sentiments to convince the Turkish Cypriots that the EU was being coercive by 'pressuring and threatening' the TRNC.[13] The nationalist political elite argued that Cyprus's accession independent of Turkey was 'illegal', basing their arguments on an interpretation of the Zurich–London Agreements, and that the EU was thus 'aiding and abetting the Greek Cypriot's illegal application'.[14] The nationalists argued that there were two equally 'sovereign peoples' on the island and that without the consent of the Turkish-Cypriot people, the unilateral accession of the Greek-Cypriot administration would be null and void.[15]

The nationalists did not have sole say in the matter, however. In fact, Turkish-Cypriot discourse was polarised during the period prior to accession. The opposition parties of the left, generally marginalised by the nationalist parties through the 'securitisation' of the Cyprus problem, recognised the EU as an opportunity. Thus, opposition leaders, such as Mehmet Ali Talat, leader of the CTP, called on the government and Denktaş to take part in accession negotiations. The EU, from this perspective, far from a threat, was a reassuring factor that made a settlement realisable. Noteworthy was the emphasis on the promise of political equality within a bizonal federation, something the opposition considered feasible only through negotiations and EU accession. In contrast to the Turkish-Cypriot leadership, which emphasised the negative role of the EU in Cyprus, the leftist opposition formed and aired positive arguments to dignify the EU and justify Turkish-Cypriot participation in the accession negotiations:

> Everything should be done to encourage participation in the process [accession negotiations]. Day by day the Turkish-Cypriot community loses its opportunity

> to claim an appropriate status in this process.... The EU is not a menace, but rather a guarantee for Turkish Cypriots. The settlement of the Cyprus dispute on the basis of political equality, bizonality and bicommunality – with the guarantee of Turkey – is an ideal solution for the EU, too. The interests of the Turkish Cypriots necessitate such participation; otherwise it will be too late.[16]

The opposition made clear that it felt the Cyprus problem had been transformed into a 'European problem', which ascribed a positive or constructive role to the EU.[17] Accordingly, the mission of the EU was associated with its ostensibly post-national character, accentuating its cosmopolitan or multicultural structure, harbouring various national, ethnic and cultural entities and identities. Within the European cosmopolitan framework, the historical conflict between the Turkish Cypriots and Greek Cypriots would become insignificant, as would the rivalry between the 'motherlands' in broader Greek–Turkish relations. Significantly, Turkey's own EU membership bid loomed large, so, unsurprisingly, right-wing nationalists and left-wing opposition in northern Cyprus disagreed over the prospects of this contingency. The right argued that Turkey would never become an EU member, whereas the left played up the chances of this happening. A solution in Cyprus, in turn, served as a catalyst for furthering Turkey's half-century ambition of joining the Union. As a result, the left found itself agreeing with the Greek Cypriots who argued for the need to solve the Cyprus problem and the positive role envisioned for the EU in this process. Moreover, the leftist political parties of the respective communities on the island (i.e. the CTP and the Greek-Cypriot Progressive Workers' Party, AKEL), which have historically represented the pro-solution opposition in Cyprus, seemed to agree on the basic principles of a peaceful settlement, based on the political and economic equality of the two communities, human rights and the equality of all citizens. The two leftist parties employed a common language for constituting a common EU vision by emphasising the importance of European principles and criteria as the basis of a solution.[18]

Political-ideological polarisation among Turkish Cypriots before accession

Despite criticisms by the left-wing opposition regarding its negative stance on the EU, the Turkish-Cypriot leadership persisted in its policies. However, following the publication of the Annan Plan in November 2002, providing for a solution to the Cyprus problem within the EU, political winds of change started to blow in the Turkish-Cypriot community. Accordingly, the parties of the left as well as civil society organisations were granted a rhetorical advantage over the political leadership that had discounted the prospects of

EU membership. The opposition lent wholehearted support to the Annan Plan and used the prospect of membership as a tool to legitimise its stance. More importantly, attitudes towards the EU became the focal point of conflict between the opposition and the regime. Debates on the Annan Plan led to confrontation between right-wing nationalist circles, who considered themselves vanguards of Turkey's strategic interests, and the political parties and civil society organisations that had found common cause in the 'This Country Is Ours' platform, who argued that the presence of the Turkish Cypriots within the EU constituted a strategic goal.

By associating its call for the resolution of the Cyprus problem with the goal of EU membership, the 'This Country Is Ours' platform – which included the left-oriented CTP – proved to be a potent political force, portending political change in northern Cyprus. As a result, the year 2003 saw mass mobilisation, in the form of rallies whereby participation by civil servants and labour unions was maximised. Even private sector workers, housewives, students and some of the less politically active elements of the middle classes took part in a series of unprecedented mass demonstrations. The right-wing nationalist forces that had defended the status quo in the form of the TRNC as a sovereign entity found themselves fractured and disoriented. Whereas the opposition's main political stance was for a reunified Cyprus joining the EU on the basis of the Annan Plan, the right-wing nationalist camp emphasised Turkey's strategic interests and insisted on a settlement that entailed the recognition of the TRNC as a separate state, while the fervour of their anti-EU rhetoric reached a crescendo (Lacher and Kaymak, 2005: 158). The 'This Country Is Ours' platform held symbolic referenda in towns and villages that aimed to demonstrate popular support for the Annan Plan and a widespread desire to join the EU. The right-wing forces that were in power instead attempted to stifle the opposition through harsh measures. The upshot was that the pro-EU, pro-settlement opposition carried the CTP to power after parliamentary elections in December 2003. This was a watershed event insofar it was the first time a party of the left had emerged as the biggest party in parliament and in a position to affect the course of Turkish-Cypriot politics. In short, the period prior to the referenda witnessed the contest of those favouring EU accession and the Annan Plan versus those who opposed EU membership and a federal settlement.[19]

EU perspectives on Cyprus after the referenda

After the referenda, there were compelling reasons inducing the EU to enhance its involvement in the Cyprus dispute: the Turkish-Cypriot willingness to reactivate citizenship bonds with 'member state' Cyprus; the will of the new Turkish-Cypriot leadership to involve the EU in the north; the EU's approach that Cyprus's accession included the whole island; the applications of displaced persons to the European Court of Human Rights; the deceleration of UN conflict settlement initiatives; the inclination of the Greek-Cypriot government to utilise its membership to mobilise EU involvement in Cyprus; and the American disposition to satisfy the minimal expectations of the pro-solution Turkish-Cypriot political elite.

Yet since the failed referenda, the role of the EU in the Cyprus problem has been complicated by the fact that the Republic of Cyprus is now a member of the Union. As a result, the EU cannot apply conditionality *vis-à-vis* the Greek-Cypriot side. Thus, despite the role of the Greek-Cypriot leadership in campaigning against the Annan Plan, the EU is constrained in its ability to pressurise at least one side to the dispute. The EU maintains its existing goal of developing relations with the Turkish-Cypriot community and has emphasised the utility of economic exchange and development as a means of bridging the gap between the Greek-Cypriot and Turkish-Cypriot economies as a prelude to eventual reunification. Through financial instruments, the EU has aimed to demonstrate its commitment to a settlement. In February 2006, a financial aid regulation was approved. EU Enlargement Commissioner Olli Rehn argued that this development will contribute to the end of the isolation of the Turkish Cypriots and raise living standards in the north, thus facilitating the reunification of the island.[20] Despite Greek-Cypriot objections, the EU has continued, through the diplomatic efforts of various presidencies since 2004, to hammer out a deal on an appropriate framework that would allow for the adoption of a direct trade regulation with the Turkish Cypriots as well.

Whereas the EU may be coy about the name of any specific blueprint, the Union maintains its commitment to help resolve the Cyprus dispute on the basis of a federal settlement. By establishing a special committee for the Turkish Cypriots, the Commission has shown its desire to encourage pro-solution dynamics in the north. At the same time, in insisting on the normalisation of relations between Turkey and the Republic of Cyprus, the EU has been exercising moderate pressure on Turkey to hasten this process.[21]

Turkish-Cypriot perspectives on the EU after the Annan Plan referenda

Since the failed referenda and the accession of the Republic of Cyprus as a divided state, the discourse among Turkish Cypriots has become more differentiated. The EU is no longer so unambiguously conceived of as an agent of good or evil as it was in the run-up to the referenda. Here we consider three prominent discourses prevalent since 2004 among Turkish-Cypriot political and civil society elites: the neo-official, the liberal-leftist and the nationalist-reactionary discourse. Although this threefold classification broadly reflects the main perspectives of the Turkish-Cypriot elites, it also demonstrates the perceptions of the people, since the former frames and influences the latter through the activities of political organisations and the media. The neo-official and reactionary-nationalist stances are those which are able to employ most effectively public organisational structures to affect public opinion, while the leftist-liberal opposition garners support mainly from civil society organisations and intellectuals, and is less influential overall.

The neo-official stance

The first discourse is that of the government. It will be recalled that, as a result of the popularity of the Annan Plan, the former opposition party, the CTP, under the leadership of Mehmet Ali Talat, emerged as the principal political beneficiary in the north, partially displacing the nationalists in parliament and forging a coalition government between December 2003 and August 2006 with Serdar Denktaş's Democratic Party (DP), whose politics during the Annan Plan period proved relatively moderate compared with the rhetoric of his father Rauf and the National Unity Party (UBP). Mehmet Ali Talat eventually secured the presidency of the TRNC in 2005, with veteran leader Rauf Denktaş stepping down and choosing to retire from active political life. The CTP–DP coalition government dissolved in August 2006 and a new coalition was formed, between the CTP and the Freedom and Reform Party (ORP), a party consisting of MPs who had splintered from the DP and UBP. The emergence of the ORP proved controversial, as it was alleged that the splinter party was engineered by the ruling Justice and Development Party (AKP) in Ankara. As a result, a small group of MPs forged the ORP to provide an alternative coalition partner for the CTP.

The current coalition government, as well as the former CTP–DP government and President Talat, can be seen as one pole in the new configuration of political forces in northern Cyprus. The discourse emanating from or associated with this pole is dubbed here the 'neo-official stance'. The CTP-led governments have been fragile coalitions that have expected 'rewards' from the EU. The CTP in particular finds itself in a difficult predicament, and has expressed disappointment with the EU since the failed referenda, but thus far has avoided a more confrontational rhetoric on the EU. Short of secession, the discourse on lifting the isolation of the Turkish Cypriots points to the support for the 'Taiwanisation' of northern Cyprus as an interim goal that would, it is hoped, convince the Greek-Cypriot side that containment of the north through EU accession has proved futile. Government and CTP-led discourses thus emphasise the benefits of the current strategy of lifting the isolation, despite their overall frustration in achieving the goals of a settlement and with EU accession.

Behind this perspective lie both long-term ideological positions and shorter-term practical considerations. Beginning with the ideological, the CTP has put forth a neo-official discourse following strained relations with its erstwhile ally, the Greek-Cypriot AKEL, in view of the latter's rejection of the Annan Plan and coalition with the hard-line President of the Republic of Cyprus, Tassos Papadopolous. Beyond ideology, this stance is also based on practical considerations. Because of its political isolation and dependency on Turkey, the CTP has internalised the fact that when determining its strategies it must consider Ankara's preferences and expectations. As a result, the neo-official discourse entails elements that are distinct from the discourses of the CTP before it came to power.

More specifically regarding the EU, the neo-official discourse expresses opposition to and suspicion of an EU that accepted a divided Cyprus into its fold, and that considers the Republic of Cyprus as the sole legal authority on the island. This suspicion has occasionally reached the level of mistrust, with the EU being portrayed as a threat to the Turkish Cypriots. In view of the difficult times in EU–Turkey relations since 2005 and the problems faced by the AKP in Turkey, the neo-official perspective has become increasingly negative towards the EU and its initiatives. Significant in this shift has been the changing balance of power in Turkey's domestic politics. The wave of nationalism and anti-EU sentiment that has gripped Turkey since 2005 has affected not only the AKP but also the CTP, which is dependent on it. Accusations that the Turkish government has made too many concessions on Cyprus – Turkey's national cause – has created a schism between the government and the influential military in Turkey. In turn, both the AKP and the CTP have felt the need publicly to express suspicion of the EU, so as to prevent opposition parties or the military from exploiting foreign policy to their advantage. The conventional wisdom that the EU has not kept its promises to the Turkish Cypriots has induced the CTP to emphasise the complicit role played by the Greek Cypriots within the EU to hinder progress in its relations with both Turkey and the Turkish Cypriots, which in turn leads to a more confrontational stance towards the EU as a whole.

The neo-official circles have also displayed contradictory positions on the EU and reunification. They have rejected the EU as a mediator and framework for resolving the Cyprus problem. This is because of the fundamental questioning of the neutrality of the EU in Cyprus.[22] Therefore, the leadership has decided that it is legitimate to criticise and rebuff EU decisions and actions relating to

Cyprus.[23] In addition, the CTP, which once supported the unhindered pursuit of EU–Turkey relations, has now found itself in the unusual position of rejecting the notion that Turkey should normalise its diplomatic relations with the Republic of Cyprus, as called for by Turkey's accession process.[24]

One nuance in the neo-official discourse can be gleaned from the differences between the former coalition partners, the CTP and the DP. The leader of the DP, Serdar Denktaş, represents a more hawkish version of the neo-official perspective. He maintained that the Turkish Cypriots should not wait for a change of heart from the Greek Cypriots. Nonetheless, these positions remain distinct from the secessionist approach of the previous leadership. The neo-official stance recurrently insists on the establishment of direct ties with the EU and would welcome warmly an EU role in Cyprus to exert pressure on the Greek-Cypriot leadership.[25] Despite its misgivings about the Greek Cypriots and the EU, the neo-official stance also remains committed to reunification[26] and EU accession. In particular, the CTP-led government has stopped short of suggesting reprisals or discontinuing bilateral relations with the Greek Cypriots or the EU. Even those who consider inter-communal cooperation useless and express mistrust of the EU abhor a rift between the Turkish Cypriots and the EU, as ultimately the neo-official stance views the Turkish-Cypriot future as being firmly embedded in the Union.[27]

The perspective of the liberal-leftist opposition

The second discourse is that of the liberal-leftist opposition; this is not an official coalition of forces, but rather different groups that share a similar orientation. Critically, what united this group is the rhetoric of seeking (or demanding) the political rights of Turkish Cypriots within the Republic of Cyprus, thus accepting the legitimacy and legality of the 1960 constitutional framework. This group generally considers the CTP's policies as counterproductive and subservient to the interests of Ankara.

The liberal-leftist discourse emerged in opposition to the neo-official stance of the CTP. Whereas the cause of inter-communal peace and reunification was traditionally represented by the CTP, it now falls more in the ideological domain of the left and liberal intelligentsia. These groups exhibit greater openness towards the Republic of Cyprus and the EU than the CTP does, and still consider the EU as offering an opportunity for a settlement of the Cyprus problem. Beyond ideology, the position of these groups is dictated by political pragmatism. Insofar as the CTP has marginalised the liberal-left opposition, these groups have tried to differentiate themselves from the CTP. Within these groups, formerly middle-of-the-road politicians, such as Mustafa Akıncı, have now shifted to the political margins, by advocating the pursuit of Turkish-Cypriot rights within the existing Republic of Cyprus. In this way, the liberal-left opposition has created a practical alternative to the CTP's strategy.

The leftist and liberal opposition includes the Communal Democracy Party (TDP) and its antecedents the Peace and Democracy Movement (BDH) and Communal Liberation Party (TKP), as well as the United Cyprus Party (BKP), the New Cyprus Party (YKP, formerly the Patriotic Unity Movement, YBH) and other organisations, including the Turkish-Cypriot Chamber of Commerce (until its executive board was out-voted by a CTP-oriented group in 2005), the Cyprus EU Association (KAB), the Cyprus Turkish Primary School Teachers Union (KTOS), the Businessmen Association and several intellectuals. This disparate group opposes the neo-official perspective and to some extent the arguments it presents overlap with those of the EU. It is inclined to legitimise the 1960 constitutional order by reviving the legal rights of the Turkish Cypriots within the Republic of Cyprus. In particular, one group filed an application to the Ministry of the Interior of the Republic of Cyprus demanding the restoration of Turkish-Cypriot political rights (especially the right to vote in separate communal ballots).[28]

The leftist-liberal opposition acknowledges the Cyprus–EU connection as a political reality, and also as an opportunity to demand communal political rights from the Republic of Cyprus; it points out that the whole territory of Cyprus is a part of the EU and that many Turkish Cypriots have reactivated their citizenship bonds with the Republic of Cyprus. The leftist-liberal opposition enthusiastically expresses the 'European identity of Turkish-Cypriots'.[29] Turkey is accused of hindering the implementation of the *acquis* in the north and compelling the Turkish Cypriots to sacrifice their rights for the interests of Turkey.[30] Another crucial initiative undertaken by the leftist-liberal opposition was to support the EU policy of delinking the regulations for direct trade and financial aid and replacing the demand for direct trade with free trade.[31] This perspective, especially as voiced by the then leadership of the board of the Chamber of Commerce in 2005, revealed a schism between the pro-Ankara neo-official perspective of the government and the elements of civil society that considered the emphasis on direct trade with the EU as unnecessary, if not counterproductive.

Most acutely, the leftist-liberal opposition challenges the role of Turkey by demanding the 'immediate transfer of political control in the north from Turkey to Turkish Cypriots'.[32] This demand is reminiscent of the struggle of 'This Country Is Ours' against the nationalist leadership at the time. The leftist-liberal opposition has also introduced novel ideas for dealing with the Cyprus dispute, such as suggesting the reinstatement of property to Greek-Cypriot owners in the fenced town of Varosha and the buffer zone around the Green Line, as well as initiating similar policies which are likely to be supported by the EU and UN.

The nationalist-reactionary perspective

Finally, we focus on the discourse of the 'nationalist-reactionary' forces. This discourse is the most consistent of the three. Following the accession of Cyprus to the EU, nationalists have presented the EU as part of the problem rather than the solution, serving the (widely assumed) Greek-Cypriot policy of 'osmosis' (i.e. rendering Turkish Cypriots a minority within the political institutions of the Republic of Cyprus). These forces owe their existence mainly to ideological factors. They remain firmly opposed to reunification and EU membership. For ideological reasons, they do not consider the lifting of isolation as sufficient and, despite the problematic period they experienced prior to the referenda, they have regrouped, and now champion a political programme grounded on the recognition of the TRNC.[33] In addition, the nationalist-reactionary forces have exploited Talat's limited successes in yielding international links and recognition to their own political advantage.

Not long after the political transformation that saw the rise of Talat, the nationalists regrouped under veteran leader Rauf Denktaş and other nationalist right-wing leaders and parties, including the UBP. Their positions have expressed the conventional nationalist-secessionist discourse in northern Cyprus, having acquired a reactionary character after the electoral victory of the CTP. These conservative elements constitute the main anti-EU movement in northern Cyprus. Referring to the Treaty of Guarantee, the nationalist-reactionary perspectives represent a conservative opinion that argues that Cyprus's accession would be political suicide for the Turkish Cypriots if Turkey were left out of the Union. The rationale for this belief is associated with the idea that Turkey is the 'motherland' and that the destiny of the Turkish Cypriots depends on that of Turkey. Thus, 'without Turkey, we would not go to heaven if they took us, let alone the EU'.[34] This perspective is not anti-EU *per se*, but relates to the belief that the Turkish Cypriots, as a small and peripheral people, can assure their security and identity only through Turkey. The nationalist-reactionary perspective sees itself as having a mission to reiterate the dangers of normalisation between Turkey and the Republic of Cyprus. It is the EU, the partner of the Greeks, which compels Turkey to recognise the Greek-Cypriot-led government at the expense of Turkish-Cypriot existence on the island.[35] Hence, the Turkish-Cypriot leadership should vigilantly defend Turkish identity and interests in the island by refusing the financial aid offered by the EU.[36] The EU is accused of expecting the Turkish Cypriots to succumb to colonisation by the Greek-Cypriot majority.[37]

Ideally, the EU should recognise the legitimacy of the TRNC, meaning diplomatic recognition.[38] The nationalist-reactionary perspective also holds that a two-state model, referring to the case of Czechoslovakia,[39] would be most suitable to Cyprus and only under those conditions would EU membership be acceptable.[40] This perspective has been gaining ground and has become increasingly mainstream as the UN-brokered 'Gambari' process flounders.

Conclusions

The EU's policies since the failed referenda have induced not only intra-communal cleavages but also conflicts within neo-official circles in the north. The neo-official perspective on the EU oscillates between two poles. The first pole is represented by CTP, which decided to split with the DP over – among other points – the question of reunification. The second pole is the ascendancy of the nationalist-reactionist discourse over the pro-EU forces in terms of rhetoric, and possibly portending a reversal of fortunes for the pro-EU parties and organisations that took advantage of the popularity of the Annan Plan in 2002–04. If *de facto* relations between the EU and the Turkish Cypriots persist without incorporating the Turkish-Cypriot community into EU political structures, *de facto* division will continue and this will agitate ethnonationalism in both communities, which will eventually intensify the conflict in the island.

A more active role of the EU in Cyprus today, while receiving the passionate support of the leftist-liberal opposition in northern Cyprus, would divide the neo-official circles and re-empower the nationalist-reactionary discourse. The EU framework as a means of socialising Cypriot local political actors and transforming the relationships between the two communities may, however, produce fruitful results if its vision of settlement guarantees the territorial integrity of the island and the autonomy of both communities. To this end, the EU could express its overt preference for a settlement that would see the Turkish Cypriots and Greek Cypriots transforming the 1960 constitutional order into a bizonal, bicommunal federation and reconfirming their commitments to the 1977 and 1979 High Level Agreements.

More specifically, if the Turkish-Cypriot authorities could accept the notion of 'community authority' within the limits of the 1960 constitution and the principles of federalism, the EU could establish bilateral relations with them. This could be facilitated through the Republic of Cyprus's authority to delegate competences to 'community authorities' akin to the communal chambers established under the 1960 constitution, while the Turkish-Cypriot authorities would be represented at the central level through the principles of political equality, bizonality and bicommunality. The EU could thus contribute to the federalisation of the constitutional system in Cyprus within the legality of the *acquis* precisely by establishing relations with the two communal entities.

Of course, all this is contingent on how EU–Turkey relations evolve. The rise of the CTP coincided with Turkey's own ambitions to join the Union. Today, given the uncertainties of Turkey's accession negotiations, the CTP and Talat cannot rely on allies in Turkey who would actively promote a federal settlement in Cyprus. Moreover, a positive EU contribution to peace in Cyprus is contingent on the willingness of the Greek-Cypriot authorities to pursue a federal settlement, whatever their misgivings regarding the Annan Plan may be. Should Turkish accession talks stall or Greek Cypriots prove incapable of reconciling themselves to power-sharing governance, it is likely that Turkish-Cypriot politics will revert to secessionism, despite the incentives of EU accession.

Notes

1 See the statement by the then EU Enlargement Commissioner, Günter Verheugen, upon Republic of Cyprus President Tassos Papadopoulos's call for a 'no' vote in the Greek-Cypriot referendum, where he draws the 'conclusion from his [Papadopoulos's] words that the government of Cyprus opposes the international settlement'. Verheugen, moreover, continued: 'I will be very undiplomatic now in saying that I personally feel that I have been cheated by the Government of the Republic of Cyprus'. Chris Patten, then EU Commissioner for External Relations, referred to an overall feeling within the EU Commission of 'being badly let down', and repeated Verheugen's comment about deception. For both, see www.hri.org/news/greek/ana/2004/04-04-22.ana.html#29 (accessed 20 February 2005).
2 Official Document submitted by President Denktaş to G. Feissel, assistant of the Special Representative of the Secretary-General. See *Yenidüzen*, 21 January 1995.
3 Statement made by R. Denktas at the meeting organised by Mujaheddins Association. See *Kibris*, 14 June 1995.
4 Statement made by R. Denktas. See *Birlik*, 13 May 1997.
5 Statement made by R. Denktas. See *Birlik*, 6 April 2001.
6 Statement made by R. Denktas. See *Volkan*, 4 October 2003.
7 Editorial: 'Türkiye AB ilişkileri, Kibris – AB İlişkileri ve KKTC Gerçeği I–II', *Birlik*, 3–4 May 1995.
8 Statement made by R. Denktas. See *Birlik*, 29 November 1997.
9 Statement made by Dervis Eroğlu, the leader of National Unity Party. See *Birlik*, 28 June 1997.
10 Statement made by R. Denktas. See *Birlik*, 13 March 2001.
11 Speech made by TRNC President R. Denktas (broadcasted by SKY TV). See *Kibris*, 17 July 2003.
12 Statement made by TRNC President R. Denktas. See *Yenidüzen*, 13 March 1995.
13 Ö. Hatay, 'Kibris için devreye girenler', *Halkın Sesi*, 20 February 1998.
14 Ö. Hatay, 'AB Kibris konusunu kilitlerken,' *Halkın Sesi*, 15 April 1998.
15 Sabahattin İsmail, 'Verhaugen'e yanıt: Asıl işgalci AB'dir', *Volkan*, 4 October 2003.

16 Statement made by CTP leader M. A. Talat. See *Halkın Sesi*, 10 February 2001.
17 Statement made by CTP leader M. A. Talat. See *Yenidüzen*, 8 January 2000.
18 Joint declaration of AKEL and the CTP. See *Yenidüzen*, 25 May 2000.
19 For a detailed analysis of views relating to the future political system in Cyprus, see Vural and Peristianis (2008).
20 Statement made by Olli Rehn. See *Yenidüzen*, 28 February 2006.
21 Statement made by Austrian Minister for Foreign Affairs (and then EU President). See *Yenidüzen*, 11 March 2006.
22 Statement made by M. A. Talat. See *Halkın Sesi*, 1 November 2005.
23 Statement made by F. S. Soyer. See *Volkan*, 10 November 2005.
24 Motion submitted to the TRNC parliament. See *Yenidüzen*, 30 September 2005.
25 Statement made by TRNC President M. A. Talat. See *Volkan*, 10 December 2005.
26 Statement made by TRNC Prime Minister Soyer. See *Yenidüzen*, 2 March 2006.
27 Statement made by TRNC President M. A. Talat. See *Halkın Sesi*, 14 December 2005.
28 The list of applicants included the leader of the Peace and Democracy Movement (BDH), M. Akıncı, civil society activist and columnist F. Azgın, the then chair of the Turkish-Cypriot Chamber of Commerce (KTTO), A. Erel, journalist H. Kahvecioğlu, retired colonel H. Sadrazam, the chief editor of *Afrika* newspaper, Ş. Levent, and economist Ü. Akifler. See *Yenidüzen*, 1 March 2005.
29 Statement made by Ali Erel: 'Vizyonumuz, Kibrislıların AB içerisinde birleşik bir Kibris'ta ortak bir geleceğe sahip olmasıdır'. See *Yenidüzen*, 23 September 2005.
30 Interview with Ö. Nailer, the chairperson of the Businessmen Association in Northern Cyprus (İŞAD). See *Afrika*, 24 November 2005. The leftist-liberal opposition criticised the Turkish military leadership in northern Cyprus for interfering in the internal affairs of the Turkish Cypriots and for showing no respect for the will of the Turkish-Cypriot community. These ideas were expressed in an official letter from the 'This Country Is Ours' platform to the TRNC Prime Minister F. S. Soyer. See *Yenidüzen*, 16 June 2007.
31 Statement made by the KTTO. See *Yenidüzen*, 15 July 2005.
32 Statement made by İŞAD. See *Halkın Sesi*, 5 January 2005.
33 The UBP sees a confederation between the two independent states as the only realistic solution to the Cyprus dispute. See XVI Congress (2006), Decisions of the UBP. Available at www.ulusalbirlikpartisi.com/kibris/16.htm (accessed 20 March 2008).
34 Statement made by TRNC President R. Denktaş. See *Volkan*, 29 October 2003.
35 Speech made by R. R. Denktaş in Aydın, Turkey. See *Volkan*, 28 November 2005.
36 Speech made by DP leader and Deputy Prime Minister S. Denktaş at the General Assembly of the TRNC parliament. See Volkan, 10 March 2006.
37 R. R. Denktaş, 'Ne bekliyoruz?', *Halkın Sesi*, 30 January 2006.
38 İsmet Kotak, 'KKTC meşru bir devletse kurallarına uyunuz', *Halkın Sesi*, 23 January 2006.
39 R. R. Denktaş, 'Görmeyenlerle görenler III', *Cumhuriyet*, 24 February 2006.
40 R. R. Denktaş, 'Daha ne desinler?', *Halkın Sesi*, 20 January 2006.

Part II

The external factors in conflict and resolution

6

Re-imagining Cyprus: the rise of regionalism in Turkey's security lexicon

Alper Kaliber

Introduction

The rise of regional-level politics has been envisioned as one of the main constituents of the post-Cold War security order in international politics. The collapse of the Cold War security architecture rendered the region the main locus of 'cooperation and conflict for states' and as the most appropriate level of analysis for scholars 'seeking to explore contemporary security affairs' (Lake and Morgan, 1997: 6). In this analysis, states, freed from the exigencies of global bipolar rivalry, have found new incentives and instruments to focus on regional conflicts and cooperation (Buzan and Wæver, 2003: 3; Lake and Morgan, 1997: 6). The relative unwillingness of the great powers to intervene in local patterns of conflict and cooperation (Lake and Morgan, 1997: 5), the rise of such soft security threats as migration, human and drug trafficking and environmental degradation, the increasing intermingling of economic and security calculations (e.g. the rise of energy and pipeline politics) can all be identified as factors triggering the regionalisation of security dynamics. Therefore, regions have turned out to be the level at which patterns of amity and enmity among nations concentrate and national and global security dynamics interplay (Lake and Morgan, 1997: 9).[1]

Buzan and Wæver (2003: 27) emphasise the importance of making clear distinctions between what constitutes the regional level and what constitutes the unit and global levels, which they believe is the analytical strength of their theory. To them, 'region' represents a distinct middle level between the other two, 'with an analytical and ontological standing' (Buzan and Wæver, 2003: 27), yet devoid of any actor quality. For the regionalist approaches, the global- and national-level security dynamics have decreased in salience *vis-à-vis* the regional one, since regional security dynamics have become increasingly autonomous (Lake and Morgan, 1997: 6–7; Buzan and Wæver, 2003: ch. 3). In such a regionalising world, national security conceptions of states are necessarily and 'inherently relational' (Buzan and Wæver, 2003: 43), so much so that it is theoretically and empirically meaningless to isolate one such conception from another. The emphasis on the regionality of security dynamics and regional aspects of national security is increasingly echoed in the discourse of policy-makers as well.

This chapter makes the case that Turkey's security language on Cyprus, which has been subject to gradual change in the last decade, does not constitute an exception to this. It argues that, from the second half of the 1990s onwards, Turkey's security language on the issue has gained a more regionalist tone than was the case in previous decades. Throughout its long history, the Cyprus question has had Janus-faced implications in Turkey's strategic calculations and threat perceptions. The geographical proximity of the island to Anatolia has facilitated the articulation of the issue either as a source of an imminent, persistent threat to the Turkish nation and state, or as an integral part of Turkey's national defence and security (Kaliber, 2005). In either case, the island of Cyprus has been imagined as an invaluable geostrategic asset, bound to be used by a hostile power to strike the Anatolian heartland, or one that can be used by Turkey against that aggressive state. It has simultaneously been the cornerstone in the encirclement of Turkey by Greece in particular and its only access to the eastern Mediterranean from the south. This security language has often confined the Cyprus dispute to the realm of bilateral Greek–Turkish relations and has implied that the real threat has been not the Greek Cypriots but Greece itself.

However, within the last decade, thanks to a constellation of internal and external factors, addressed below, this official state line has been subject to change in Turkey. Even if Greece does not completely disappear as a source of insecurity, a new rhetoric has gained prominence, placing Turkey's threat perceptions and strategic calculations on Cyprus in a more complex and regionalist context. The Turkish foreign and security policy (FSP) establishment, other political elites, academics and mushrooming think-tanks in recent years have all begun to talk of the eastern Mediterranean more frequently than ever before. The eastern Mediterranean has been re-invented as a regional – or in some cases sub-regional – context where Turkey's security calculations and interests on Cyprus should be situated. In the new rhetoric, the eastern Mediterranean has signified not only the diversification and multiplication of threats, but also emerging opportunities for economic development and the prospect of becoming an activist, regional power for Turkey.

This chapter mainly aims to trace the regionalist shift in Turkey's security outlook on Cyprus through the analysis of discourses within the Turkish FSP elite. It does not address whether the post-bipolar international order has induced the rise of new regional security complexes or whether the eastern Mediterranean is located at the centre of a new security complex. Rather, it reveals how and through which themes Turkey's security concerns and interests on Cyprus have been reformulated and articulated by the FSP elite within the last decade. The chapter is inspired by the notion that regions are not only geographical but also political, economic and even 'intellectual' constructions (Hemmer and Katzenstein, 2002: 575). Various scholars have aptly drawn our attention to the power politics (Katzenstein, 2005) as well as the economic, cultural and interpretative/cognitive processes (Väyrynen, 2003: 37) behind region formation. Yet the chapter restricts its analysis on the new regionalist turn in international relations (IR) with the regional security complex theory (RSCT) introduced and developed by Buzan and Wæver (2003; see also Buzan et al., 1998). A comprehensive treatment of regionalist approaches to international security is beyond the scope and aim of this study.

In line with its objectives, this chapter first discusses the explanatory power of Buzan and Wæver's RSCT in tandem with their securitisation approach in understanding Turkey's security discourse on Cyprus and the eastern Mediterranean. In this sense, the chapter suggests that the securitisation theory introduced by the Copenhagen School provides an extensively useful research agenda to explore the themes of Turkey's security lexicon on Cyprus and its construction 'as an unfinished security project of the Turkish state' (Kaliber, 2003: 179–216). The securitisation approach also reveals the implications of excessive securitisation and bureaucratisation of Cyprus policy in the internal power struggles between the reformist wing of the political elite and the statist bureaucratic apparatus in Turkey (Kaliber, 2005). However, Buzan and Wæver's later work on RSCT falls short of explaining the ascent of regionality in Turkey's approach to Cyprus accentuating the eastern Mediterranean as the source of new insecurities and geo-economic calculations. RSCT, based largely on the conception of geographically fixed regions, does not question how regions are defined, by whom and for which purposes. Therefore, it is analytically ill equipped to understand the power politics behind the regionalist/securitising discourses of the domestic political elite. Furthermore, Buzan and Wæver's claim that Turkey is an 'insulator state' (2003: 392), also shared by Kazan (2002, 2005), provides too parsimonious an account of Turkey's regionalising security perceptions and interests.

The subsequent section delineates the basic tenets framing Turkey's strategic outlook on Cyprus from the middle of the 1950s up to the present time. The chapter then moves on to address the domestic and international context emerging in the 1990s, which accelerated the regionalist tendencies in Turkey's FSP. In this section, the emphasis is on how the post-bipolar international order is understood by the FSP elite in Turkey. It analyses how Turkey's changing conception of the eastern Mediterranean and surrounding regions has had an impact upon its threat perceptions and geostrategic calculations.

The region as an object of security

Even though the literature on regional security is relatively new for the discipline of IR, the attempts to explain world politics from a regionalist perspective can be traced back to the late 1960s.[2] The first wave of regionalism in IR was triggered by the processes of decolonisation, accelerating integration with the European Community (EC) and the relatively liberal atmosphere of détente in bipolar global rivalry. Yet instead of developing innovative analytical tools, the first wave of regionalist literature contented itself with downscaling 'extant IR theory to regions' (Kelly, 2007: 202).[3] This analysis also holds true for the second wave of regionalist IR scholarship and in particular for its positivist wing inspired by neo-liberal and neo-realist accounts of international politics.[4] The second wave proved more successful in developing a regionalist approach to international security, as it was able to integrate the issues of identity (the sense of belonging to a region), power politics (regions as political creations), multidimensionality and functionality (economic interests and interactions) and transnational activism into the debates on regionalism and the regionalisation of security.[5]

In this section, my aim is not to cover the whole scholarship on regional security and regionalism in IR.[6] The task is rather to critically discuss the analytical power of Buzan and Wæver's RSCT and the securitisation approach to explore Turkey's regionalising security discourse on Cyprus and its domestic implications. As a constructivist analytical tool, securitisation was incorporated into the definition of the regional security complex (RSC) by Buzan and Wæver in their 2003 book entitled *Regions and Powers: The Structure of International Security*. An updated definition of RSC was provided by Buzan and Wæver (2003: 44) as 'a set of units whose major processes of securitisation, de-securitisation or both are so interlinked that their security problems cannot reasonably be analysed or resolved apart from one another'.

Regional security complex theory departs from the assumption that within a process beginning with decolonisation, and accelerating with the demise of the Cold War, security relations among units (states) are increasingly patterned into 'regionally-based clusters' (Buzan and Wæver, 2003: 4). The principle of territoriality, assuming a direct correlation between geographical proximity and intensity of security interdependence, still operates in shaping security dynamics in the post-bipolar international order (Buzan and Wæver, 2003: 4, 29–30, 45–6). It follows that the whole world is divided into 'mutually exclusive' regional security complexes, insulator states and global powers (Buzan and Wæver, 2003: 48). The peculiar structure of each RSC is configured by: the interplay of anarchic international order and its regional balance of power; peculiarities of local geopolitics; durable patterns of amity and enmity among the units constituting the RSC; and the distribution of material power among the members of the RSC (polarity) (Buzan and Wæver, 2003: 45, 53; see also Morgan, 1997: 26). RSCs as the sub-structures of international order have internal structures of their own and external boundaries that allow analysts to distinguish them from other regions, insulator states and global powers.

Even though Buzan and Wæver accept that regions are 'socially constructed' and contingent upon the 'security practices of the actors', they take actors as pre-given and do not problematise their actorness. Not only are regions 'socially constructed' as they suggest, but also regionalism reproduces the actorness of the actors and contributes to the reproduction of their social capital in domestic society. Buzan and Wæver claim that they combine the constructivist and materialist elements of IR theory; however, their constructivism is restricted to analyses of the securitising practices of the given actors with already defined interests in a given region. In contrast, I argue that regions are not pre-established, fixed and objective geographical spaces structuring (constraining and enabling) the actions of the regional political actors. As Hemmer and Katzenstein (2002: 575) suggest, 'regions are political creations and not fixed by geography'.

The process of region-building is a perpetual one and inherent in domestic power relations.

> By understanding discursive practices on regions we can then understand how such practices construct specific subject identities and thereby construct a particular 'reality' in which policy becomes possible as well as through which future policies would be justified in advance. (Pace, 2006b: 37)

As in the case of Turkey's changing language on Cyprus (see below), discourses on region-building/regionalism (re-invention of the eastern Mediterranean) can be part of the elite's securitising discourses through which the geopolitics of the country is remoulded, with new security connotations. Thereby, the discursive practices of region-building by the ruling elite can be viewed 'as part of a wider process of political control – a sort of political engineering by means of which a politically, economically or socially desirable area is constituted' (Pace, 2006b: 37–8). Buzan and Wæver downplay the significance of the domestic elite's regionalist discourses in the social reproduction of regions, for these discourses are regarded merely as part of the intra-elite political struggle. By saying that 'we study security discourses and security practices of actors, not primarily their regionalist discourses and practices' (Buzan and Wæver, 2003: 48), they imply that there may be a clear distinction between the two. However, the ways in which regions are defined, categorised and labelled by the ruling elite are constitutive of political imagination, where the security practices of the state are legitimate, meaningful and necessary. Thus, the limited constructivism and partial objectivism of RSCT do not help us to understand the power politics behind the social reproduction of regions by the activities of actors. To understand the power politics behind the invention of regions by the security and state elite, we should ask such questions as the following. Who defines regions and for what purposes? In what ways is the definition of regions instrumentalised in the securitising practices of the states/political elites? What is the role of the emphasis on regionality in state discourses in the demarcation of state/political identities? Does the invention of new regions as a source of insecurities serve to establish new self/other constructions?

Another shortcoming of RSCT is that it departs from the notion of regions as territorially fixed, exclusive, non-overlapping entities. Regions are assumed to be partly homogenous structures constituted by coherent patterns of security unique to them. In Buzan and Wæver's objectivist approach, RSCs are already established entities that can objectively be observed by analysts under a certain set of criteria. Although they accept that regions may change, depending on patterns of amity/enmity, in their theory the possibility of change is small. Unlike Lake and Morgan, they do not accept that there can be overlapping memberships and that a country outside an RSC can also be a member of it. Even if Buzan and Wæver concede that outside states, especially the global powers, can affect regions, in the end, regional security dynamics are constituted by the members of the RSC themselves. 'However, regional systems are inherently open. The global system, other regional systems, and even "outside" states can have a major impact on a region' (Lake and Morgan, 1997: 9–10). In the case of Cyprus, for instance, through different historical phases of the dispute, Britain, the United States and the European Union (EU) have been the outside powers deeply penetrating and in some cases reshaping regional security dynamics among the disputants. Furthermore, the right of the three guarantor powers of the Republic of Cyprus (Turkey, Greece and Britain) to take action jointly or unilaterally (under article 3 of the Treaty of Guarantee) always makes it possible that there is a dominating 'overlay' of the security balances between these powers in the eastern Mediterranean.

Last but not least, RSCT's claim that Turkey is an 'insulator state' should be approached cautiously. RSCT suggests that in between the RSCs, where (in)security relations intensify, lie either 'zones of weak interaction' or an insulator, such as Turkey, Burma or Afghanistan (Buzan and Wæver, 2003: 41). Insulator states are exposed to security dynamics imposed by those RSCs they are surrounded by (Buzan and Wæver, 2003: 41; see also Kazan, 2005: 589–90). They have (in)security relations with all neighbouring RSCs, yet not as intense as would be the case were they to be a member of any of them. Neither are insulators strong enough to merge these RSCs into one. Buzan and Wæver admit that Turkey has the potential to challenge the passive role – 'absorbing energies from the separate complexes' (Buzan and Wæver, 2003: 394) – assigned to the insulator in their theory. Yet even if Turkey pursues a more proactive policy 'than that traditionally adopted by insulators', to them it will not cease to be an insulator in the foreseeable future (Buzan and Wæver, 2003: 395; see also Kazan, 2005: 589–90). They also imply that any change in Turkey's insulator position does not primarily depend on its activism or its foreign policy dynamics, but on the strategic acts of surrounding RSC members.

I suggest, however, that, as an analytical tool, the term 'insulator' is not well equipped to examine Turkey's intense security interactions with its regional neighbours.[7] It is liable to simplistic and ahistoric generalisations, since it implies rigidity and stasis rather than dynamism and perpetual change. To illustrate, Greece, accepted as a member of the European RSC, and Turkey still enjoy much more complex security interactions than Buzan and Wæver's theory would imply for an insulator and an RSC member state. It can even be suggested that, in the post-1999 era, starting with the recognition of Turkey's EU candidacy, Turkish–Greek relations have been vested with a new and complex set of security connotations. In 1999, Greece drastically changed its policy of blocking Turkey's way to Europe and became a vigorous protagonist of its membership of the EU. This was a natural consequence of the new Greek policy of projecting its vital foreign policy concerns (Turkey and Cyprus) onto the 'European foreign policy-making agenda' (Economides, 2005: 488). The rationale was that the more Turkey approached the EU, the more receptive it would become to Greek security concerns, which are now formulated as European demands. Strengthening of Turkey's EU membership prospects would also produce a *rapprochement* in Turkish–Greek relations, which had been monopolised by a 'cycle of conflict–negotiation–conflict' (Tsakonas and Dokos, 2003: 99). However, the initial impetus in bilateral relations triggered by the 'earthquake diplomacy'[8] and Greece's support for Turkey's EU membership in 1999 gradually dissolved and did not bear any fruit, in particular in security- and sovereignty-related issues, such as the Aegean and Cyprus disputes. Rather, the impact of Europeanisation remained limited to the softening of security tones in their discourses *vis-à-vis* each other, careful management of tensions and sophistication of monolithic perceptions (Keridis, 2001: 14). As Ifantis and Aydın (2004: 1) suggest, what still exists 'is a very disturbing potential for escalation which can lead to a more serious crisis with alarming destabilising effects at a regional level'. The linking of Turkish–Greek (in)security relations to Turkey's EU membership complicated the patterns of interactions between the FSPs of these two countries. Taking into account all these, the term 'insulator' state is by no means helpful to understand Turkey's dynamically changing and intensifying security interactions with its regional neighbours.

In their book *Security: A New Framework for Analysis*, Buzan, Wæver and de Wilde (1998) presented an innovative and comprehensive research agenda to reveal the nature of securitisation as an inter-subjective and political act.[9] Among the central questions of this new research agenda are 'when, why and how elites label issues and developments as "security" problems; when, why and how they succeed and fail in such endeavors; what attempts are made by other groups to put securitisation on the agenda?' (Buzan et al., 1998: 36). As these questions illustrate, securitisation theory takes for granted the fact that there cannot exist objective threats but 'only attempts to saddle issues with security implications' (Eriksson, 1999: 315). Through the articulation of danger and existential threat to sovereignty, the securitiser demands justification from the audience (for which read 'society') for its initiatives beyond the normal bounds of political procedure. Thereby, every attempt to securitise an issue is an explicit, political intervention with seminal consequences 'for which actors can be held responsible' (Buzan et al., 1998: 12).

However, the success of any securitising move is contingent upon the existence of an audience that accepts and tolerates the act by the securitising agent, which is all too often the government and/or bureaucratic establishment (Wæver, 2000: 251). Approval of the securitising act is not necessarily gained through negotiation and free discussion between the securitiser and the audience/society. To obtain the approval of society, the elite may apply imposition, political manipulation through the media and even legal sanctions and restrictions. As in the case of Cyprus, issues may successfully be securitised through various legal and political mechanisms, ensuring the silence of the obedient. To Wæver (1995: 57), 'security is articulated only from a specific place, in an institutional voice, by elites'. Further, the securitiser should have a 'social capital' and 'has to be in a position of authority' (Wæver, 2000: 252–3). What should be added to this analysis is the fact that security may be utilised as a reproducer of this social capital as well. To illustrate, the military wing of the Turkish state elite has customarily utilised its credibility in the eyes of domestic society in declaring what the internal and external threats to the nation and state are. Cyprus has always figured among the issues of top priority for the Turkish state elite, involving vital security interests of the country.

Bearing in mind the assumptions and the research agenda of securitisation theory, one may conclude that the Copenhagen School provides useful analytical tools to explore the power politics of Cyprus, in other words, its implications in the production of power/domination relations in Turkey. As I have argued elsewhere (Kaliber, 2005), from the end of 2002 onwards, the Cyprus issue has turned out to be one of the central 'discursive battlefields' of the polarisation among the conservative/statist and reformist ruling elites. The main reason for the centrality of the Cyprus issue within domestic power relations in Turkey stems from its heavy securitisation by the FSP establishment. Here, the term 'securitisation' refers not primarily to militarisation but rather to de-politicisation, namely insulation from public debate, within a technocratic and authoritarian discursive economy (see Buzan et al., 1998; Wæver, 1995, 1998). The 'lack of a meaningful and critical public debate that goes beyond scientific sounding technicalities' (Yeldan and Cizre, 2002: 15) has hindered the outbreak of genuine alternative arguments and has ultimately eased the bureaucratisation of the Cyprus issue. Hence, the conventional state rhetoric on the Cyprus question substantially contributed to the institutionalisation of a regime fetishising such concepts as security, stability and 'national sensitivities' in Turkey.

Against this backdrop, some crucial implications of Turkey's security language on Cyprus may be outlined as follows. First, the casting of the Cyprus issue as one of national security has severely constrained the power and capacity of the political elite to intervene in the substance of existing policies. It has forced the government, as the political authority, to pursue policies already formulated by the bureaucratic elite, especially if they were labelled 'state policies' and/or 'national causes' (Kaliber, 2003: 217–75). Second, the consistent efforts of the bureaucratic elite to hold the Cyprus question within the sphere of 'the existential' and 'the imminent' thwarted the occurrence of widespread social debate within an autonomous public sphere, and thus led to the de-politicisation of the issue and its fixation as an area of bureaucratic specialty and competence. Labelling the Cyprus issue as a national cause gave the state elite the grounds to delegitimise opposition, since criticising these fixed policies amounted to criticising the regime and the state itself. Third, the effective insulation of 'foreign' policy issues in general, and the Cyprus case in particular, from public debate and the political domain has reinforced the power and hegemonic status of the bureaucratic apparatus, the members of which 'consider themselves as the ideological guardian of the "state"' (Yeldan and Cizre, 2002: 17).

Revisiting Turkey's security lexicon on Cyprus

The discourse and fear of encirclement have always been important components of Turkey's security approach to Cyprus. The notion of encirclement has been instrumental in depicting the extent to which the Cyprus dispute constitutes an urgent threat to the survival of the Turkish nation and state. 'Stuck in its southern underbelly, Cyprus is a major source of concern for Turkey', and 'it is the final, southern element in the containment of Turkey' (Olgun, 1999: 232). The island, which has a 'strategic position to control the important Turkish harbours of Iskenderun and Mersin', could be utilised by a hostile power as a 'springboard for the conquest of Anatolia from the South' (see Kazan, 2002: 58); 'an unfriendly power lodged in Cyprus could easily strike the nation's Anatolian heartland' (İsmail, 1989: 137). From the military and strategic perspective, any state dominant on the island would have a say in 'the fate of Turkey', since 'if this dominant power is also the same dominant power on the islands to the west [of Turkey], Turkey would be *de facto* encircled' (former Turkish Prime Minister F. Rüstü Zorlu, quoted in Kazan, 2002: 58). Encapsulated in all these excerpts is the idea that the real threat is Greece. This is the reason why the discourse and fear of encirclement locate the Cyprus issue directly within the field of 'vitality' and 'emergency' for Turkey. Reinforcing this line of reasoning, Turkey's Aegean coast has already been blockaded by the Dodecanese islands, which belong to Greece. 'Possession of Cyprus by Greece through *Enosis*, would have meant the encirclement of the southern shores of Turkey as well' (İsmail, 1989: 171).

The second component of this 'security speak' hinges upon the notion that Cyprus is an integral part of Turkey's national defence and security. The following statement by Turan Güneş, Turkey's Foreign Minister in Ecevit's cabinet during Turkey's military intervention of July–August 1974 in Cyprus, reveals how the Turkish state elite understands and expresses the nature of the Cyprus question:

> Cyprus is as precious as the right arm of a country which cares for her defence or her expansionistic aims if she harbours any. If we don't keep this strategic importance of Cyprus we cannot understand the peace operation of 20 July [1974] or rather it is impossible to understand the entire Cyprus crisis.... Many states, to a certain extent because it suits their interest, want to see the Cyprus problem merely as our desire to protect the Turkish community on the island. Whereas, the actual problem is the security of 45 million Turks in the motherland together with the Turks in the island and the maintenance of the balance of the Middle East. (*Hürriyet*, 20 July 1980)

The notion that Cyprus is geographically part and a natural extension of an Anatolian heartland, and thus an integral part of its defence, has been articulated by many prominent Turkish bureaucratic and political figures throughout the long history of the dispute. In the words of former Turkish Prime Minister Adnan Menderes, 'Cyprus is but the continuation of Anatolia and constitutes one of the pivotal elements as regards its security' (quoted in Armaoğlu, 1963: 133).

In the 1990s, the notion of continuation was replaced by a new one equating the survival of the Turkish Republic of Northern Cyprus (TRNC) with that of Turkey. Turkish policy-makers began to put much more emphasis on the significance of Cyprus for Turkey's own national defence and security. To illustrate, a joint declaration between Turkey and the TRNC stated that 'both sides have emphasised the increasing importance of the TRNC for the security of Turkey, while Turkey continues to provide effective guarantee for the TRNC' (Turkish Ministry of Foreign Affairs, 1997). The widely used metaphor of 'motherland–babyland' in Turkey's official and popular discourse also implies the inseparability and intertwinedness of the security of the two. This metaphor serves to emphasise both indissoluble and sacred linkages between 'motherland' Turkey and 'babyland' Cyprus and the unity of their fate and destiny.

As is evident in the quotations above, in Turkey's security language, the Cyprus issue signifies two seemingly paradoxical connotations. On the one hand, it implies the existence of a vital and imminent threat to Turkey's national security. On the other, it is an integral part of its defence, the absence of which would create a substantial hole in the protection of Turkey's territorial integrity. Even though these modes of representation seem paradoxical at first glance, they are complementary in the sense that the island of Cyprus is simultaneously the cornerstone in the encirclement of Turkey and its only access to the eastern Mediterranean from the south. The following section explores the regionalisation of Turkey's strategic outlook on Cyprus within the last decade through the re-invention of the eastern Mediterranean as a region of insecurities and opportunities.

Regionalisation of security perceptions and the re-invention of the eastern Mediterranean

The regionalisation of Turkey's discourse on Cyprus can be fully captured only when it is contextualised within the series of internal and external political developments shaping the Turkish state elite's sense of (in)security. A common assumption among the Turkish elite has been that the end of the Cold War dramatically changed the regional security environment in which Turkey is embedded (Adamson, 2002: 173; Sayarı, 2000: 169). For the Turkish FSP elite, the demise of global bipolar rivalry, in which Turkey's position was solidly defined within the Western bloc, precipitated two seemingly contrasting outcomes for the country. On the one hand, it impelled Turkey to become a more assertive regional power, standing at the 'nexus of conflict-prone regions'

(Davutoğlu, 2004) characterised by instability and unresolved intra- and inter-state disputes. According to a widespread analysis among Turkish policy-makers and analysts, Turkey 'stood encircled by 13 of the 16 threat generating regions, identified by NATO at the end of the Cold War' (Aydın, 2004: 85; see also Sezer, 2007). The new security architecture and geopolitical landscape emerging in the post-Cold War era situated Turkey 'in the virtual epicenter of a "Bermuda Triangle"' comprising 'the Balkans, the Caucasus, and the Middle East' (Türk, 1999), each of which is characterised by ethno-nationalist and religious conflict. The dismantling of the former Yugoslav Federation and the Soviet Union, the two Balkan wars of the 1990s, the strengthening of Kurdish autonomy in northern Iraq after the *de facto* partition of the country, and the deteriorating Palestinian–Israeli conflict have all strengthened the conviction of the Turkish FSP elite that Turkey has become much more exposed to insecurities in its vicinity. Hence, its 'tough neighbourhood' (Olgun, 1999) urges Turkey to pursue a more active, multi-track, multi-layered foreign policy in relation to its surrounding regions (Davutoğlu, 2004).

On the other hand, the radical transformation of the geopolitical and strategic landscape in the Balkans and the Caucasus following the break-up of Yugoslavia and the Soviet Union opened up new regions to Turkish influence. Turkey, as an 'anchor of stability' with a unique geopolitical position at the intersection of Europe and Asia, could play a larger and constructive role in the areas 'that were previously closed to Turkish policy' (Larrabee and Lesser, 2002: x). An assumption widely accepted by the current Justice and Development Party (AKP) government is that if Turkey is able to reconcile its eastern and western identities, it can assume 'a conciliatory role' in the polarisations 'between Asia–Europe, Islam–West and North–South' and can promote global and regional peace and constitute 'a centre of gravity' (Davutoğlu, 2004). Thereby, in the new era, Turkey, rather than being depicted as a mere bridge between the east and the west, 'should be defined as a pivotal state' (Davutoğlu, 2004).[10] This line of reasoning is widely echoed by the secular security establishment as well. For instance, to former Turkish President Ahmet Necdet Sezer (2007), Turkey's unique geographical position and its distinctive 'historical and cultural values' facilitate and necessitate Turkey pursuing 'an active and multi-dimensional foreign policy'.

The regionalisation of Turkey's security outlook has paralleled the consolidation of the status of the Turkish military 'as the key interlocutor' (Lesser, 2000: 28) in the formulation of the FSP, 'often in a manner that undermined the authority of the civilian institutions' (Özcan, 2002: 13). In the second half of the 1990s, the military emerged 'more publicly than at any time … as the most important institution, at least in charting the strategic dimension of "foreign" policy' (Robins, 2003: 92). It started to play an active role not only in

Turkey's strained relations with Greece, Syria and Iran, which it blamed for supporting terrorist activities (Uzgel, 2003), but also in initiating the policy of *rapprochement* with Israel, despite the opposition of the then coalition government.[11] Particularly on the military side of the security establishment, a prevalent approach was to associate Kurdish separatism and Islamic fundamentalism with Turkey's immediate neighbours in the Middle East and in the eastern Mediterranean more widely (Özcan, 2004; Uzgel, 2003). Turkey's new regional activism in its immediate surroundings (the Middle East, the Balkans and the Caucasus) and insecurities originating from these regions have also been instrumental in justifying the military's costly and extensive defence modernisation programme.

Furthermore, that a new generation of threats and non-conventional security issues surfaced throughout the 1990s encouraged the Turkish FSP elite to develop a more regionalist outlook to internal and external security. Energy and water security issues, 'uncontrolled migration, ethnic conflicts, religious fundamentalism' (Kışlalı, 2003; see also Larrabee and Lesser, 2002: 4) as well as proliferation of weapons of mass destruction and long-range missiles (Kazan, 2005) have been incorporated into Turkey's security agenda as new challenges requiring a broader regionalist approach to foreign policy. These issues are of course beyond the remit of this chapter, which next examines the basic tenets of Turkey's regionalising security conception with respect to Cyprus.

The rise of regionalism in the Turkish strategic outlook on Cyprus

The two classical themes of Turkey's 'security speak' portraying Cyprus as the source of insecurity and as the indispensable element of national defence have proved their durability and dominance. However, from the second half of the 1990s onwards, this dual mode of representation has increasingly been laden with a regionalist outlook. In fact, Turkey's rhetoric on Cyprus was not totally devoid of regionalist concerns and calculations during the Cold War years. This rather vague regionalism was based on the notion that prevention of *enosis* (union with Greece) and maintenance of Turkey's involvement with the island were vitally important for the sustenance of NATO's stronghold in the eastern Mediterranean (both Greece and Turkey had long been NATO members). That is, the unification of the island with Greece would unavoidably create deficits and cause destabilisation in NATO's southern flank, because of the presence of communist and pro-communist forces among the Greek Cypriots. Greece and the Greek Cypriots would be unreliable in protecting Western interests in the region against the Soviets, who were presumed to be 'aiming at having access to the Mediterranean and the Middle East' (Armaoğlu, 1974: 178). Turkey was the only power, the argument went, able to defend the interests of the 'free world' and to prevent Cyprus from being the 'Cuba of the Mediterranean' (Tevetoğlu, 1966).[12]

However, in the 1990s, regionalism, rather than being a sub-argument in Turkey's Cyprus discourse, steadily gained prominence in mapping out Turkey's new security landscape. As stated before, Turkish policy-makers began to make more frequent references to the term 'eastern Mediterranean', which gained a constellation of new strategic and security connotations. As in the case of Greece (Stivachtis, 2002), the eastern Mediterranean, rather than being a mere geographical expression, accounted for a distinctive region embracing simultaneously new insecurities and opportunities. In what follows, I present the main discursive elements of Turkey's security lexicon on Cyprus characterised by regionalism.

The discourse of encirclement in the 1990s

The fear of encirclement has been continually articulated by the political elite in Turkey throughout different phases of the Cyprus dispute. In the 1990s, however, the emphasis was shifted from Greece only, to Greece plus hostile states in the eastern Mediterranean region which were signing military cooperation agreements against Turkey. For instance, Cyprus was depicted all too often as 'the cornerstone of Greece's policy of enveloping Turkey with a strategic belt of hostile states' (Olgun, 1999: 231–2). The Joint Cypriot Greek Defence Doctrine concluded in 1993 was perceived as 'a direct military threat' (Elekdağ, 1996) and 'an attempt at the encirclement of Turkey and the Turkish Republic of Northern Cyprus (TRNC) by the hostile forces' (Ministry of Foreign Affairs and Defence of the TRNC, 2002). In the same vein, the signing of military and technical cooperation agreements between Armenia and the Republic of Cyprus has been interpreted as a new stride towards this aspiration.

Cyprus, as a 'naval fortress' or 'a natural aircraft carrier in the Eastern Mediterranean' (Balancar, 2003), is deemed indispensable if Turkey is to surmount this encirclement. The island's geostrategic location allows Turkey to control air and maritime routes (Kazan, 2002: 58) and to access sea lanes in the Mediterranean (Larrabee and Lesser, 2002: 153) for defence and trade purposes. In this perspective, dominant among the FSP elite, Cyprus enjoys a unique location, in the sense that 'it is Turkey's only gateway to the Mediterranean and international seas, has the capacity to control Turkey's Mediterranean coastline from the sea and the air, and serves as a base for electronic intelligence to monitor the Eastern Mediterranean and North African regions' (Kandemir, 2004). That the island is closely located to the Anatolian heartland and Turkey's 'soft underbelly' is a thick signifier of the degree of insecurity with which Turkey is faced in the eastern Mediterranean. 'In case a hostile power is lodged on the island and especially if it makes use of its air force, it will have access to Turkey's otherwise inaccessible eastern region from the air.... In geographical terms, any force deployed in Cyprus will pose a grave threat to Turkey' (Kışlalı, 2003).

The Russian factor and the rise of energy security

In early 1997, the security and military dimension of the Cyprus dispute utterly overshadowed all other aspects of the issue with the announcement of the government of the Republic of Cyprus that it was to purchase S-300 surface-to-air missiles from Russia. This deeply concerned the military and the government in Turkey. It was defended by the Republic of Cyprus as a requirement for its defence *vis-à-vis* the strategic supremacy of the Turkish side (Veremis, 2001: 49). For the Turkish state elite, this event symbolised the return of Russia into the Cyprus equation and eastern Mediterranean power politics. The decision of Russia to allow these missiles to be deployed on Cyprus was interpreted as part of its broader 'strategy of influence and presence in the Eastern Mediterranean with the basic motivation of pressuring Turkey' (Lesser, 2000: 34). According to this analysis, what mostly motivated Russia was to weaken Turkey's hand in the rivalry over the transportation of the Caspian oil to western markets. The presence of S-300s on the island would destabilise and disturb the strategic balances in the Mediterranean region at the expense of Turkey (Davutoğlu, 2001: 177–8).

The growth of new energy routes around the Mediterranean basin has irreversibly incorporated the issue of energy security into Turkey's new regionalist agenda on Cyprus. The proximity of the island to the oil-rich Middle East and its critical location along the new routes of oil transportation stretching from the Caucasus to Europe added considerably to Cyprus's geopolitical value in the eyes of the Turkish FSP elite. After the emergence of the Caspian basin as a rich resource for energy, the issue of how the Caspian oil and natural gas are to be transported and through which routes has become a determining factor configuring the strategic calculations of the regional powers. For Turkey and Russia, which favour different routes for oil transportation, pipeline politics has become heavily loaded with geostrategic implications, in that they could use pipeline politics to play a larger strategic role in the eastern Mediterranean, Central Asia and the Caucasus (Larrabee and Lesser, 2002: 110). According to a widespread analysis among the Turkish elite, Cyprus will become even more important when the Baku–Ceyhan pipeline has been built, bringing Caspian oil across Turkey to the Mediterranean (Kandemir, 2004; Olgun, 1999: 243). This argument, shared by some analysts, assumes that the construction of the Baku–Ceyhan and other pipelines transporting oil and gas 'will deepen Turkey's role as an energy entrepôt and will reinforce the position of the Eastern Mediterranean in world oil trade' (Lesser, 2004: 214). Thus, if Turkey wishes to have a strong say in both the sharing of this huge and seductive oil 'cake' and the political future of the region *vis-à-vis* its 'immediate neighbours' (namely Russia and Greece), it has to cling to its involvement with the island.

Energy politics came to re-occupy a central place in Turkey's security agenda when the Republic of Cyprus signed agreements on the delimitation of exclusive economic zones with Egypt and Lebanon in early 2007 (*Turkish Daily News*, 31 January 2007). On 15 February, the Cypriot government also initiated a bidding process to issue licences for oil and gas exploration in accordance with these delimitation agreements (Skordas, 2007). In a statement on 30 January, Turkey argued that the Greek Cypriots did not represent the island as a whole and reasserted its determination to protect its legitimate rights and interests in the eastern Mediterranean and to avert 'any attempt to undermine them' (Turkish Ministry of Foreign Affairs, 2007). In the aftermath of its meeting on 20 June 2007, the National Security Council of Turkey declared that 'the Greek Cypriot Authority due to its initiatives in the eastern Mediterranean continues to be an element of instability in the region' and reiterated that Turkey would 'maintain efforts to protect its rights and interests' in the region (National Security Council, 2007). The then Turkish President, Sezer, also voiced on numerous occasions his conviction that the Greek-Cypriot leadership, 'in an irresponsible and provocative manner, has striven since 2003 to delimit naval sovereign rights in the eastern Mediterranean with the regional countries' (Sezer, 2007). These delimitation agreements pose a direct a threat to both 'Turkey's and the TRNC's legal rights and interests' in the eastern Mediterranean (Sezer, 2007).

Redefining the geopolitics of Cyprus and the eastern Mediterranean

> Cyprus is neither solely an ordinary ethnic conflict between Turkish and Greek Cypriots nor a protracted dispute between Turkey and Greece.... Cyprus turns into a dispute involving Eurasian, the Middle Eastern and the Balkan, that is West Asian and East European regions. Turkey's Cyprus policy should be remoulded to meet the requirements of this new strategic framework. (Davutoğlu, 2001: 175–6)[13]

As is evident in the quotation above, the Turkish political elite is convinced that the emerging geopolitical configurations in the post-Cold War era impel Turkey to develop a broader strategic outlook on Cyprus. This new outlook rests on the relocation of the eastern Mediterranean and Cyprus within the global and regional security dynamics and geostrategic build-up. As argued above, throughout the Cold War years, the FSP elite in Turkey lacked a conception of the eastern Mediterranean as a distinctive regional setting with its own security dynamics and interactions. The Cyprus dispute was more of a Turkish–Greek ethnic conflict and the island's geostrategic salience was always discussed within the confines of military balances with Greece. Within the last decade, however, parallel to the post-Cold War and post-'9/11' security agenda of the West, the geopolitics and geo-economics of the eastern Mediterranean has been redefined by FSP establishment in Turkey. In this reconceptualisation, the eastern Mediterranean, which 'lies at the intersection of Europe, Asia and Africa' (Kandemir, 2004), is a central concern for Turkey, in both strategic and economic terms (Taşhan, 2003). 'The eastern Mediterranean looms over the maritime trade running across Gibraltar, Suez and the Black Sea and the energy hubs in the Middle East and the Caspian Basin' (Kandemir, 2004). Turkish policy-makers also converge on the idea that, in post-bipolar international politics, the fates of the Balkan and Middle Eastern regions are ever bound to each other. 'Therefore, there may not exist, for Turkey, a policy of the Balkans and of the Middle East segregated from each other. It needs a new policy for the regions, at the centre of which the inner balances of the Eastern Mediterranean have been struck' (Davutoğlu, 2001: 177).

It has been a prevalent assumption among the practitioners and analysts of Turkish foreign policy that Cyprus constitutes the cornerstone of the eastern Mediterranean security architecture in the making since the 1990s. It has a dominant position to have a say in the fate of the region 'in political, economic and security terms' (Kandemir, 2004). Any regional or global power nurturing strategic calculations and interests in 'the Middle East, the eastern Mediterranean, the Aegean, the Suez Canal, the Red Sea and in the Gulf' cannot fail to pay heed to the island of Cyprus, as it enjoys the capacity to directly influence all those regions (Davutoğlu, 2001: 180). Turkey should therefore consider it the key element of a general naval strategy (*ibid.*).

Conclusions

The post-Cold War regionalisation of security dynamics has been manifest in Turkey's strategic outlook on Cyprus. Since the 1950s, the Cyprus dispute has been categorised by the Turkish ruling elite primarily as an issue of national security within a discourse imbued with excessive geopoliticism. The geopolitically 'vital' position of the island of Cyprus and its proximity to the Turkish mainland have facilitated the articulation of the issue either as a source of imminent threat to the Turkish nation and state or as an integral part of

Turkey's national defence and security. The fear of encirclement – a prevalent element in Turkish rhetoric – triggered by geopolitical and power political matrices between Turkey and Greece has also implied that the real threat has been Greece itself. However, as revealed in this chapter, within the last decade the security lexicon confining the Cyprus issue to the realm of bilateral Turkish–Greek relations has been subject to change. Thanks to a constellation of domestic and external factors, a new strategic approach has gained prominence, placing Turkey's threat perceptions and strategic calculations on Cyprus in a more complex and regionalist context. This regionalisation has mostly found its expression in the increased use of the term 'eastern Mediterranean' by policy-makers and analysts to resituate Turkey's new security concerns and expectations, both geographically and economically. In the new rhetoric, the eastern Mediterranean has signified not only the diversification and multiplication of threats but also emerging opportunities for economic development and the prospect of Turkey becoming an activist regional power.

The comprehensive research agenda of the securitisation approach poses relevant questions for an exploration of the power politics behind an excessively securitised and bureaucratised Cyprus policy in Turkey. However, the Copenhagen School's later work on RSCs falls short of explaining the ascent of regionality in Turkey's approach to Cyprus and the new domestic and regional security dynamics behind it. RSCT is largely based on the conception of geographically fixed regions, whose internal security dynamics are configured by given regional actors with already defined interests. It does not question how regions are defined, by whom and for what purposes. Thus, the limited constructivism and partial objectivism of RSCT does not help us to understand the power politics behind the social reproduction of regions as objects of security. The chapter has also proposed that RSCT's claim that Turkey is an insulator on the boundaries between different RSCs is not persuasive. The term 'insulator', implying stasis, is liable to simplistic and ahistoric explanations of Turkish FSP dynamics; it is by no means helpful in exploring Turkey's dynamically changing and intensifying security interactions with its regional neighbours. The deepening of Turkish–Greek security interactions in the post-Cold War era, which are complicated by the effect of EU-isation/Europeanisation, is a pertinent example of this.

Notes

1 This chapter is based on research conducted in the framework of the European Common Foreign and Security Policy Studies Programme funded by Compagnia di San Paolo, Riksbankens Jubileumsfond and Volkswagen Stiftung.

2 For a literature review on regional security, see Buzan and Wæver (2003: 77–82) and Kelly (2007). For a concise review of the first wave of regionalism in IR, see Kelly (2007: 202–4).
3 For a few key texts of first-wave regionalism, see, among others, Russett (1967), Nye (1968), Miller (1973a,b) and Cantori and Spiegel (1973).
4 Here I follow the distinction drawn by Kelly (2007: 206) between 'the more positivist formal and the critical normative' approaches to regional security within the second wave of IR regionalism. Though Buzan and Wæver's work is included in the positivist category by Kelly, as will become clear below, their theory has some constructivist elements in it.
5 For the second wave of regionalist theory, see, among others, Hettne et al. (1999, 2000), Farrell et al. (2005) and Hentz and Bøås (2003).
6 For an overall review of regionalism in IR, see Pace (2006b: 22–57).
7 For a counter-argument, see Kazan (2005).
8 This term refers to the revival of government-level negotiations as well as the boost to civil society cooperation between Turkey and Greece following the devastating earthquakes in Izmit and Athens in August and September 1999.
9 They define securitisation as a self-referential practice where issues are 'presented as an existential threat, requiring emergency measures and justifying actions outside the normal bounds of political procedure' (Buzan et al., 1998: 23–4).
10 The term 'pivotal state' was coined by Chace et al. (1996) to refer to such countries as Turkey, Mexico, Brazil, Algeria, Egypt, India and Indonesia. Pivotal states have the potential to influence regional and international stability owing to their population, location, and economic and military potential. See also Larrabee and Lesser (2002: 2).
11 In November 1997, with the military's initiative, there occurred a major change in the national security policy document, which describes the threats to national security and provides policy for state institutions, including the government. In the document, after political Islam and Kurdish separatism, possible cooperation between Greece and Syria and Turkey's need to strengthen its ties with Central Asian republics were stated among Turkey's security priorities (Uzgel, 2003: 194).
12 For the details of the anti-communist rhetoric through the Cyprus issue, see Kaliber (2003: 197–200 and 268ff.).
13 This section draws mostly on the analyses by Ahmet Davutoğlu of Turkish foreign policy and the Cyprus question. He was not only the chief political adviser to the current Turkish Prime Minister, R. Tayyip Erdoğan, from 2003 up to July 2007, but also a very influential figure in the reformulation of Turkish foreign policy during his term in office.

7

From consensus to conflict: changing perceptions of the Cyprus issue in the European Parliament, 1995–2006

Susannah Verney

Introduction

The theme of this chapter is the perceptions of the Cyprus conflict in one international forum, the European Parliament (EP), before and after the 'defining moment' of the April 2004 referenda on the Annan Plan produced by the United Nations (UN) for the reunion of Cyprus. European integration became a key factor in the Cyprus equation following the submission of the accession application by the Republic of Cyprus (RoC) in 1990. The aim of the chapter is to illuminate the stance of the European Union (EU) on Cyprus by highlighting the way in which the conflict was debated and conceptualised within a major EU institution. Adopting a discursive approach, the chapter offers a case study of the policy impact of ideas and of the institutional frameworks within which they are expressed.[1]

It is precisely because the focus of this chapter is less on policy outcomes than on the ideas which shaped them that the plenary sessions of the EP have been chosen as the field for analysis. In the case of the other EU institutions which made policy on the Cyprus question – the European Council, the General Affairs Council and the European Commission – decision-making takes place behind closed doors. The material available in the public domain essentially consists of the policy declarations, which are the outcome of deliberation within these institutions. These formal statements do not provide insights into the perceptions underlying the policies or the variety of views that may have been expressed. In contrast, the EP, like all parliaments, functions as a forum for debate, and it is possible to follow the unfolding of a process of argument and counter-argument. The EP holds its plenary sessions in public and publishes full transcripts.

A further advantage of the EP is its pluralism. In the Council and the Commission, each member state has one representative. Because the Council consists of members of the national governments and the Commissioners are nominated by the government of each member state, they usually belong to the governing party. In contrast, the EP includes multiple representatives of each member state, representing a number of political parties and not just an 'official' national position. Indeed, it has been a characteristic of the EP that it often includes small opposition parties which are not even represented in the national parliaments. Hence, EP debates reflect a multiplicity of national political viewpoints, including positions held by a small minority. Another advantage of the plenaries is that they feature dialogue among representatives of different EU institutions. In the context of parliamentary control, the plenaries serve as a meeting point between the European parliamentarians on the one hand and the Council and the Commission on the other. The EP plenaries can thus be expected to provide a reasonably representative picture of the range of perceptions expressed in the intra-EU debate – and certainly more than the official documentation of the other institutions.

The time frame of the investigation covers eleven parliamentary years, from March 1995 to March 2006, presenting a picture of the evolution of ideas about the Cyprus conflict during the pre- and post-accession periods. In March 1995, the General Affairs Council made a public commitment to begin accession negotiations with Cyprus six months after the end of the Intergovernmental Conference which was due to open the following year. It was thus at this point, following the publication of the Commission's *Opinion* in 1993 and the 1994 Corfu summit statement that Cyprus would be included in the next round of enlargement, that the RoC's accession process became a concrete prospect. The chapter concludes by tracing the change in perceptions following the Annan Plan referenda over the two years following the RoC's EU entry.

The research involved the collection and processing of all references to the Cyprus conflict in the EP plenary debates during the years covered. In the presentation of the findings, greater space is devoted to the pre-accession phase, partly because this was considerably longer and therefore the material is more plentiful. The main reason, however, is to allow the establishment of a picture of the Cyprus conflict in EP discourse before the referenda, in order better to understand the latter's impact. The empirical material is preceded by three explanatory sections that both provide the context of the debate and introduce the institutional context of the EP, in order to suggest how this may have influenced perceptions of the conflict. The chapter ends with a brief discussion of the broader implications of the case study.

The context of the EP debate

At the time the story starts, more than thirty years had passed since the breakdown of relations between the two communities on the island in 1963, over twenty since the *de facto* partition following the Athens-backed Greek-Cypriot coup and subsequent Turkish military intervention, and more than a decade since the Turkish Cypriots' unilateral declaration of independence in 1983. The completely separate trajectories followed by the Greek-Cypriot south and Turkish-Cypriot north following the establishment of the Green Line in 1974 was symbolised by the absence even of direct telephone links between the two parts of the island (*Financial Times*, 19 January 2002). Instead, northern Cyprus was integrated into the Turkish telecommunications and postal networks, used the Turkish currency and was heavily dependent on Turkey for both trade and aid.

The UN-sponsored talks, which began in 1977 with the aim of promoting a single-state solution based on a bicommunal and bizonal federation, had broken down once again in November 1992. A significant recent development had been the July 1994 ruling by the European Court of Justice that agricultural products from northern Cyprus could not be accepted in the EU without official RoC export certificates. The Court's decision had underlined yet again that, for the international community, the Greek-Cypriot RoC was the only legitimate authority on the island.

Before the period examined in this chapter, the European Community (EC), which had signed an Association Agreement with Cyprus in 1972, had not been a significant actor in the conflict. The EC had briefly attempted to play a crisis-management role during the summer of 1974, when the Cyprus problem had erupted as one of the first major challenges faced by the newly launched process of European Political Cooperation (Tsardanidis, 1984). However, the Community's prospects of playing a mediating role in a conflict involving three associates (Cyprus, Turkey and Greece) had essentially dissipated following the Greek membership application of 1975. With one of the states most closely involved becoming a full EC member in 1981, it was no longer possible for the Community to appear in the role of independent arbiter. The EC stance from 1977 onwards has been described as one of 'detached concern', limited to supporting the efforts of the UN Secretary-General in the inter-communal talks (Stephanou and Tsardanidis, 1991). But although it did not undertake an independent mediating role, the EC by no means ignored the Cyprus question.

The EP in particular had a considerable history of engagement with the issue. Over the years, the EP had passed a number of resolutions concerning both EC relations with a divided Cyprus and the Cyprus problem itself. These included issues such as the fate of the missing persons and the destruction of cultural heritage. From the mid-1970s onwards, the EP had systematically put the Cyprus issue on the agenda of Turkey–EC relations.[2] The EP's stand was clear. In November 1983, it had unequivocally condemned the declaration of an independent Turkish-Cypriot state and subsequently pronounced the presidential and parliamentary elections in northern Cyprus to be illegal.[3] Thus, well before the RoC's accession application in July 1990, the EP had a well established policy on the Cyprus conflict, which reflected that of the broader international community.

Nevertheless, the launching of the RoC's accession process created a new situation. If the Cyprus conflict could not be resolved before EU entry, then it would become an internal EU problem. The EU thus faced the prospect of admitting a divided island, part of which was governed by an illegal regime which was not recognised internationally. This raised the thorny question of the status of northern Cyprus and its inhabitants in relation to the EU. A key problem was the long-term presence of Turkish troops, in contravention of repeated UN resolutions, on what would now become EU territory. Turkey was the only state to recognise the Turkish Republic of Northern Cyprus, while it did not recognise the RoC. The latter's bid for EU entry thus appeared likely to further complicate relations with Turkey, an important strategic partner and EC associate for the past thirty years, whose own accession application had received cool treatment in the European Commission's 1989 *Opinion.*

For the EC to import this conflict into its midst was therefore a daunting prospect. A further consideration was the potential impact on the Cyprus problem itself if the island's southern part entered the Union, while the Turkish-Cypriot north and Turkey itself both remained outside. In indication of the difficulties it was facing, the EU adopted an apparently contradictory stance, not committing itself to admitting Cyprus before a solution, even when it officially opened accession negotiations with the RoC in 1998. It was not in fact until the Helsinki summit in December 1999 that the European Council formally declared that the absence of a solution to the Cyprus problem would not be a 'precondition' for the RoC's EU entry. And it was only with the formal closure of negotiations with all the countries of the fifth enlargement, at the Copenhagen Council in 2002, that the decision to admit the RoC even without a solution became definitive.

Thus, the resolution of the conflict became a direct EU interest – and, it would appear, a fairly vital one – from the moment the Union decided to proceed with the RoC's membership application. It might have been expected that such a difficult issue would become a focus of dissent in the EP. Besides the contentious question of whether accession could precede a solution, there were the different interests of the member states to consider, notably those of the two which had been guarantor powers of the 1960 settlement establishing the independent RoC. The former colonial power, the UK, was historically the island's main trading partner and had a particular interest in maintaining its sovereign bases on the island. Meanwhile, Greece was concerned to protect the interests of the RoC, regarded as its 'kin state'.

Nevertheless, Cyprus did not become a source of discord in the EP at this time. This partly reflected the fact that, despite its potential significance for the Union, Cyprus was actually quite low on the EU policy agenda. As Nathalie Tocci has noted, the issue received only 'sporadic attention' from the member states (Tocci, 2007: 52). As in the past, during these years the EU was not playing any kind of direct mediating role in the conflict, but was operating as a supportive bystander to the UN negotiations. The EU gained an enhanced role only during the last phases of the Annan Plan talks, when direct European Commission input aimed to ensure that the solutions proposed could be accommodated within the framework of EU membership. It was only at this point, in March and April 2004, that Cyprus briefly moved to the centre of the EU stage.

Otherwise, throughout the decade preceding the 'big bang' expansion of 2004, the question of Cyprus was overshadowed by the apparently even greater challenges of enlargement to eastern Europe and Turkey – not to mention an institutional reform marathon entailing three Intergovernmental Conferences and a constitutional convention.[4] This lack of focus on the Cyprus question was reflected in the EP's coverage of the topic. Perhaps one of the most striking findings is that throughout the crucial pre-accession period from March 1995 to March 2004, the EP never held a scheduled debate focusing on the Cyprus problem as such. Meanwhile, EP discussions did not frame Cyprus primarily as a strategic issue. Instead, the Cyprus debate in the EP had a quite different emphasis.

The European peace and democracy project

The views of the Cyprus conflict and its implications for the EU put forward in EP plenaries cannot easily be understood in isolation from the institutional context within which they were expressed. The latter has two basic aspects: the first concerns the culture of the EP and the second the technicalities of EP procedures. Both had a significant impact on the way in which the Cyprus issue was framed in the Parliament.

Before the EU's fifth enlargement, on 1 May 2004, the Members of the European Parliament (MEPs) came from fifteen different national contexts and a broad range of ideological backgrounds. Nevertheless, the analysis of the

Cyprus debate suggests that they were united to a quite striking degree by a widely shared set of ideas and beliefs, through which the Cyprus issue was refracted and interpreted. The pro-integrationist MEPs especially, who formed the overwhelming majority in the EP, seem to have been strongly influenced by a particular conception of EU identity. At the heart of this lay the conviction that European integration is a project with a moral purpose.

This idea can be traced back to the launching of the European Coal and Steel Community (ECSC) in 1951. In the founding Treaty of Paris, the ECSC was primarily packaged as a peace project. The plan for international economic cooperation in two specific sectors was presented as a way to 'create ... the basis for a broader and deeper community among peoples long divided by bloody conflicts'.[5] The subsequent development of European integration saw the invention of a parallel and related 'tradition' (cf. Hobsbawm and Ranger, 1983), in which the EC and later the EU were seen as the embodiment and personification of democratic values, deemed characteristically 'European' (see Verney, 2002). With the Copenhagen criteria in 1993, specific principles – the stability of democratic institutions, the rule of law, and respect for human and minority rights – were established as formal requirements for EU entry. The criteria thus formalised the perception of democratic values as the boundary separating 'Europe' from 'non-Europe'. Six years later, at the European Council in Helsinki, the Council added 'good neighbourliness' to the official entry criteria, stressing that 'the values and objectives of the European Union' included the peaceful settlement of disputes (European Council, 1999: para. 4).

The image of European integration as a mission for peace and democracy can be found in the documents of all the major EU institutions, and especially in those of the supranational European Commission and Parliament. In the case of the EP, it seems fair to say that it represented the dominant discourse. This can partly be explained by the EP's relationship to the EU political system. In a national parliament, the majority of members is always linked to the government of the day and hence under greater pressure to toe a party line, often defined primarily by realpolitik. In contrast, operating in the absence of a European government, MEPs are generally under laxer national party control and hence enjoy greater freedom to pursue democratic idealism.

Also significant were the EP's own traditions. Historically, the EP has played a vanguard role in shaping the 'imagined community' (cf. Anderson, 1983) of European integration on the basis of democratic and pacific values. It was the EP, for example, which in its 1962 Birkelbach report first suggested a democratic criterion for would-be entrants. It was also the EP which in the cases of Greece in 1967 and Turkey in 1982 pressed for sanctions against associates which had fallen under dictatorship.[6] Thus, in the early decades of integration, when the EP's powers were essentially only consultative, this role of 'democratic conscience' of the EC had offered major opportunities for the EP to develop an independent voice. As a result, acting as a key defender of the EU's role as a community of values has become inherent to the EP's own institutional identity.

This context, of a dominant discourse promoting the EU's identity as a democratisation and peace-promotion project, illuminates the nature of the parliamentary debate on Cyprus. It helps to explain why the discussion of the Cyprus conflict was not articulated primarily as a question of strategic or other interests but rather, above all, as a matter of consistency with 'European' values, especially those embedded in the political criteria for EU entry.

This also offers some perspective on the question of the Greek influence over the debate. In the case of the EP, at least, it does not seem to have been the case that the Greek presence within an EU institution predisposed the Union to adopt a particular national stance on the Cyprus question. Of course, the Greeks represented rather a small minority in the EP: just twenty-five out of a total of 626 parliamentary seats before the 2004 enlargement. Greek MEPs certainly played an activist role in promoting a view of the conflict favourable to the positions of the RoC. They often intervened in debates and used parliamentary questions to remind Parliament about the Cyprus question. However, the Greeks were by no means the decisive factor. Instead, examining the public debate in the plenaries throughout the pre-accession period, what is striking is the apparent broad consensus among MEPs, more or less regardless of nationality or political group, concerning the Cyprus conflict.

The consequences of procedure

While shared ideas played a key role, the EP debate on the Cyprus conflict was also shaped to a considerable extent by the way in which the Parliament works. At the risk of stating the obvious, the EP is not an academic debating society. Like all parliaments, its discussions focus on matters of pressing political importance. Issues in the EP are also framed essentially in terms of the way in which they impinge on the EU. As a result, during the decade under study, the plenary debates in the EP addressed the Cyprus conflict almost exclusively in the context of the primary issue then facing the EU, that of enlargement. Because of this, the discussion tended to revolve around the implications for EU expansion, rather than to focus on the problem itself and the prospects for a solution.

Moreover, the Cyprus conflict became a significant issue for two cases of enlargement: besides the case of the RoC itself, it was also systematically referenced as a major problem in EU–Turkey relations and a fundamental obstacle on Turkey's road to the EU. A good example of the way in which the Cyprus question was consistently addressed from one or both of these perspectives, and not as an autonomous issue, concerned the case of the dramatic deaths of two Greek Cypriots on the Green Line in August 1996. At its first plenary session following these incidents, the EP decided to discuss them in the context of a debate on Turkey–EU relations rather than as a separate issue.[7] Meanwhile, parliamentary questions raising recent incidents or developments in the Cyprus problem almost invariably referenced either the accession application by the RoC or the implications for Turkey–EU relations. This was to have important consequences for the way in which the Cyprus conflict was presented and conceptualised, for the two accession applications did not necessarily receive the same amount of attention.

In the post-Cold War enlargement debate, the question of relations with Turkey was – and remains – arguably the most vital issue facing the EU. This is not only because the country's sheer size, coupled with its lower economic development level, will necessitate a serious rethinking of the Union's institutional balances, major policies and general capacity for deeper integration if Turkey joins the EU. It is also because the Turkish case confronts the EU with basic questions about its own identity, what it stands for and what it should become.

After several decades of limited advances and even retrogression in Turkish relations with the EU, including the unilateral freezing of the Association Agreement by the Turkish government in the late 1970s and the European Commission's polite relegation of the Turkish accession application to the Community backburner in 1989, spectacular developments took place precisely during the period under examination. The ratification of the customs union in 1995, the recognition of Turkey as 'eligible for membership' in 1997, its endorsement as an official candidate in 1999, and the 2002 decision that Turkey was not ready to open accession negotiations were all preceded by heated debates and considerable soul-searching within the EP. The travails of Turkish domestic politics during this period, including such events as the 'post-modern coup' of 1997, when the army brought down the government, also ensured that EU–Turkey relations remained a constant item on the EP agenda, whether in the form of parliamentary questions or of comments on recent developments made during debates on other subjects. As a result, one of the primary contexts in which the Cyprus problem was raised in the EP was actually that of Turkish–EU relations.

Parliament's mode of operation not only defined the thematic framework within which the Cyprus question was presented. The way in which the topic was framed was also clearly influenced by the EP's rules of procedure. The usual limitation of MEPs to one- or two-minute interventions[8] or to the presentation and discussion of brief oral or written questions to the Council or Commission inevitably resulted in a focus on matters of immediate concern. It clearly militated against analytical discursions into the background to the problem. As a result, especially given that there was never a debate dedicated to the Cyprus problem itself, the EP never explicitly addressed itself to analysing the conflict and its origins, or to assessing specific proposals for a solution. Excursions into the nature of the conflict tended to be telegraphic, presumably based on an assumption that everybody knew what it was about and how it had arisen.

This does not, of course, mean that individual speakers lacked a more sophisticated understanding of the problem. The point is that, within the constraints imposed by parliamentary procedure, arguments had to be kept brief and simple and focused on the here and now. However, this produced a particular outcome: analysis of the debates reveals a picture of Cyprus as a conflict with a present but without a past – or, at least, without a past prior to 1974. This had clear consequences for the way in which the issue was presented and, in particular, for the identification of the key actors or, to put it another way, of who was to blame.

Identifying the actors

The first consequence of this essentially ahistorical approach, which overlooked the origins of the conflict, was the absence of references to the part played by external actors (excluding Turkey). Thus, the role of pre-1974 Greek governments in promoting the goal of *enosis* or union with Greece even after the 1960 independence settlement, or the backing of the military dictatorship in Athens for the Sampson coup in the RoC in 1974, were nonexistent elements of the debate. At the same time, the conflict was presented in complete isolation from its international context. For those familiar with the way in which the Cyprus problem is usually framed in discussions among Greeks and Greek Cypriots, with a central emphasis on the role of Britain and particularly the question of the sovereign British bases on the island, the absence of the latter from the EP plenary discussions is striking. Equally absent is any mention of the former superpower rivalries in the region, considered fundamental in the classic analysis of Attalides (1979), or of the specific role of the United States, which has been the theme of studies like that by O'Malley and Craig (1999).

Moreover, the perception that emerges is that of a local conflict involving a triangle of actors: the Greek Cypriots, the Turkish Cypriots and the Turkish government. The limitation of significant actors to three is particularly notable, given that most analyses refer to a quartet,[9] albeit with the Greek government by the 1990s taking part in a more minor capacity than the other three. This does not mean that the Greek angle is completely missing. There were passing references to Cyprus in the context of Greek–Turkish relations, as one of the problems affecting bilateral relations between the two countries. Expectations were also expressed that the improved bilateral climate following the diplomacy prompted by the powerful earthquake that hit western Turkey in the summer of 1999 and the *rapprochement* between the two countries' foreign ministers, Papandreou and Cem, would facilitate a solution of the Cyprus problem.[10] However, the role of the Greek government as an actor really does not feature in the discussion.

It is possible that the status of Greece and the UK as member states of the EU may have discouraged reference to the involvement of these two guarantor powers of the 1960 settlement, in the sense that MEPs working in the context of transnational parliamentary groups had no reason to alienate colleagues from these countries, with whom they were collaborating on a daily basis. Alternatively, the role of either of these countries may not have been seen as sufficiently central to contemporary developments for them to be worth mentioning in brief EP interventions. But the upshot was that, apart from Turkey, no external player appeared as part of the problem. Instead, the picture of the Cyprus conflict which emerges from debates in the EP is that of an issue with two main components. It was presented as involving, on the one hand, the role and military presence of the Turkish state and, on the other, the nature of relations between the two communities on the island. In both cases, the absence of reference to the pre-1974 past once again coloured the way in which the respective roles of the various parties were depicted.

A Turkish problem

The EP certainly did not endorse the Turkish interpretation of the military intervention of 1974 as a 'peace operation'. Its members were unequivocal in their characterisation of the Turkish 'invasion' and 'occupation'. This terminology seems to have been universal. No speaker in the EP – whether from the Commission or the Council, or MEPs from any national delegation or parliamentary group – appears to have referred to it in any other way. Meanwhile, the EP's emphasis on the here and now meant there was no reference to the events which had led to the arrival of Turkish troops.

In addition, the continued Turkish military presence on the island was deemed the major obstacle to a solution. In the words of Pauline Green, who, as the leader of the Socialist Group during the 1994–99 term, was one of the most influential MEPs:[11]

> For 20 years the Turkish state has occupied one third of the sovereign territory of the island of Cyprus with 35,000 Turkish troops. They and they alone sustained the illegal, unrecognised regime in the north of Cyprus. They and they alone have the ability to do what Mr. Rabin and Mr. Arafat or Mr. De Klerk and Mr. Mandela did and walk the mile for peace. At a stroke they could demonstrate their courage, their vision, their leadership, and break through 20 years of tired old propaganda and the ritual routine of name-calling and apportioning blame. They and they alone can make a real difference on Cyprus. (Pauline Green [PSE, UK], 13 December 1995)[12]

Green's speech has been quoted at length because it reflected in a particularly eloquent manner the EP consensus that the Turkish role lay at the heart of the problem and a change in Turkish policy at the heart of the solution. Not a single speaker throughout this period appears to have dissented from this view.

The Turkish presence in Cyprus came in for tough criticism. The militarisation of the island was an especial concern, with the high ratio of soldiers to civilians in northern Cyprus deemed 'unique in Europe and even in the world' (Poos [PSE, FR], 3 October 2000; see also Hadzidakis [PPE-DE, EL], 19 June 1996). In various debates, MEPs explicitly cited the violation of international law entailed not only in the 1974 landings (e.g. Rothe [PSE, DE], 11 July 1995; Marinos [PPE-DE, EL], 16 May 2001) but also in the illegal settlement of Anatolian colonisers in contravention of the Geneva Convention (e.g. Green [PSE, UK], 19 June 1996) and the denial of access to secondary education and adequate medical care to Greek Cypriots living in enclaves in the north.[13] Turkey was also criticised for its lack of respect for the UN and its resolution in relation to Cyprus (e.g. Sandbaek [EDN, DA], 18 September 1996) and for refusing to accept rulings of the European Court of Justice (Cohn-Bendit [Verts/ALE, FR], 14 November 2000). References were made to Turkey practising both 'cultural genocide' in northern Cyprus (Vanhecke [NI, NL], 18 September 1997) and 'ethnic cleansing' in the enclaves (Papayannakis [GUE\NGL, EL], 10 April 1997).

The resulting picture of Turkey as a systematic and long-term violator of international norms in Cyprus played a central role in the debate on Turkish EU membership. For those opposed to it, Cyprus provided a powerful argument why Turkey should not be allowed to join. Even for those in favour in principle, Cyprus offered strong evidence that Turkey was simply not ready yet. The constant citation of Cyprus in the context of Turkish–EU relations resulted in what at first glance appears a rather curious systematic pairing of the Cyprus and Kurdish questions, which were regularly mentioned by MEPs in the same breath.[14] In fact, this reflected the dominant role of the Copenhagen criteria – as opposed to strategic considerations, for example – as the usual framework for discussion of the Cyprus problem. The repeated linkage of the external question of Cyprus with the domestic issue of the Kurdish minority reflects the prevalent perception in the EP plenary sessions that these two problems were characteristic of Turkey's violation of fundamental rights and general European values. In this sense, to quote a German socialist MEP, the Cyprus question was seen as being 'quite fundamentally about Turkish politics' (Rothe [PSE, DE], 16 February 2000).

In consequence, developments in Cyprus were often interpreted primarily in terms of what they implied for Turkey's aspirations to become an EU member. Not surprisingly, the Turkish threat that the EU accession of the RoC would be followed by the direct incorporation of northern Cyprus into the Turkish state was not well received in the EP. Such threats were totally incompatible with the identity of European integration as a peace project. Turkey's image suffered particular damage from the dramatic deaths of Anastasios Isaak and Solomos Solomou on the Green Line in August 1996. Both these incidents were captured on film and shown on television across the EU, and had a strong emotional impact. In the ensuing EP debate, Ankara was accused of direct involvement, with the accusation being repeated in Parliament that the Turkish Foreign Ministry had financed the trip to Cyprus by the members of the mainland Grey Wolf youth organisation who had killed Isaak (Rothe [PSE, DE], 18 September 1996). Numerous speakers, representing a range of nationalities and political persuasions, expressed a sense of betrayal that their decision nine months earlier to approve the EU–Turkey customs union had not been followed by any improvement in Turkey's record as a respecter of human rights. Some called on the EU to rescind the customs union or cut off funding to Turkey (see the debate of 18 September 1996).

Reading this debate, it is clear how specific episodes, aggravating the disappointment of MEPs with Turkish progress on the Copenhagen criteria, reinforced the emphasis on Turkish responsibility for the Cyprus situation. The warning issued by Enlargement Commissioner, Gunther Verheugen, in 2000 against the simple view that 'one only has to press a button in Ankara to set the wheels in motion in Cyprus' (Verheugen [Commission, DE], 16 February 2000) was a response to a consensus view within the EP, to quote a Greek communist MEP, that 'Turkey holds the key to the Cyprus problem' (Alyssandrakis [GUE\NGL, EL], 3 September 2002).

Inter-communal relations in the Turkish shadow

Compared with the wealth of references to Cyprus as part of the Turkish problem, the question of relations between the Greek Cypriots and Turkish Cypriots received much less attention in the EP. This may have been partly because, before the opening of the Green Line in 2003, contacts between the two communities were extremely limited, with the result that inter-communal relations were not a current news item. Equally important, because the EU did not have official relations with the authorities in northern Cyprus, in the case of the Turkish Cypriots there was nothing like the systematic contact that existed between the EP and the Greek Cypriots. The latter had been developing since the 1970s in the context of the EC–Cyprus Association Agreement. In contrast, Turkish Cypriot concerns were rarely reflected in plenary discussions.

Mirroring the more general emphasis of the EP debates on Cyprus, inter-communal relations were essentially depicted in the shadow of Turkey. Perhaps surprisingly, this picture applied not only to the RoC but also to the Turkish Cypriots. As already mentioned, the conflict on the island was not presented in the historical context of a quadrilateral relationship, in which each community was linked to a 'mother government' across the sea. That only the Ankara and not the Athens connection featured in discussion may appear a logical approach in terms of the EP's focus on immediate problem-solving. By 1995, the Greek government had long since abandoned the pursuit of *enosis*, whereas Ankara retained its umbilical ties to the regime in northern Cyprus. But as a result, there was no reference to the fears and insecurities generated on the Turkish-Cypriot side as a result of past Greek irredentism.

In the period of study, there appears to have been only one reference to the Greek-Cypriot share of responsibility for the breakdown of inter-communal relations in the 1960s. This was in 2001, when a British Liberal MEP protested that:

> In discussing this issue, it is not acceptable simply to say that the problems of Cyprus started with the Turkish invasion in 1974 without mentioning the division of the island from 1963 when Greek Cypriots murdered Turkish Cypriots. If there is to be true reconciliation between these peoples, then complete objectivity is needed. (Davies [ALDE, UK], 4 September 2001)

It is striking that this appears to be the only reference to the inter-communal tensions of the past and to the violence that had occurred on both sides before the Greek Cypriots and Turkish Cypriots went their separate ways. The ahistorical presentation of the Cyprus conflict in the EP plenary debates meant that both the island's communities essentially emerge as apparently blameless for the creation and perpetuation of the conflict.

As mentioned above, one of the themes of the EP discussion was how much the Turkish Cypriots had suffered as a result of the Turkish presence after 1974. The problems of the Turkish Cypriots, living under a military regime, suffering from economic sanctions and with growing numbers emigrating owing to 'the stresses imposed by colonisation', were a favoured theme of Greek MEPs, but were also mentioned by others.[15] As a result, the Turkish Cypriots were presented as victims of the Turkish presence, implying a commonality of interests with the Greek Cypriots. This, however, did not apply to the Denktaš regime.

There was surprisingly little mention of the latter in the plenary debates, perhaps because the lack of official relations meant there were no bilateral issues to discuss. As a result, the few mentions of the government of northern Cyprus were always in the context of the conflict and always with reference to its role as a major obstacle to a solution. For example, it was declared that all the past attempts at UN mediation had failed because of 'the entrenched attitude', 'intransigence' and 'hard line stance' of the Turkish-Cypriot leadership (Rothe [PSE, DE], 11 July 1995 and 16 February 2000; Hadzidakis [PPE-DE, EL], 18 September 1997 and 14 February 2001). When the UN-sponsored talks broke down again in 1997, the Turkish-Cypriot authorities were deemed to have 'made impossible demands', 'sabotaged' the UN peace talks and 'slammed the door' on the UN negotiators (Wolf [Verts/ALE, DE], 18 September 1997; Bertens [ALDE, NL], 18 September 1997). Again, in 2001, following the failure of the proximity talks, MEPs were clear concerning who was to blame, with one speaker noting Denktaš's 'surprising refusal to restart the negotiations' and another declaring that talks were being 'sabotaged by one of the parties' (Lamassoure [PPE-DE, FR], 24 October 2001; Poos [PSE, FR], 4 September 2001), while making it quite obvious whom he had in mind.

Analysis of the debates indicates that speakers made a clear distinction between the Turkish-Cypriot leadership and society. Thus, following the deaths on the Green Line in 1996, Pauline Green maintained that the Grey Wolf activists had been brought over from Turkey because 'not enough anger and hatred exists amongst Turkish Cypriots to do what the Grey Wolf went to Cyprus to do' (Green [PSE, UK], 19 September 1996). As early as 1995, it was claimed by a Greek MEP that 'the real Turkish Cypriots', in contrast to 'the imported colonists', hoped Cyprus would 'cease to be a hostage to invaders' (Lambrias [PPE-DE, EL], 11 November 1995). In June 1996, another Greek MEP, while describing the Turkish-Cypriot side as 'unyielding', noted that there were 'democratic progressive forces' which favoured 'a closer approach' with the Greek Cypriots (Hadzidakis [PPE-DE, EL], 19 June 1996). In November 2000, it was claimed that 'the majority' of Turkish Cypriots desired a solution (Poos [PSE, FR], 14 November 2000). This comment was made shortly after the formation of the 'This Country Is Ours' platform in northern Cyprus but over two years before the mass demonstrations of January 2003 indicated widespread support for the UN's Annan Plan. Even before the major shift in Turkish-Cypriot public opinion was so strikingly manifested, it seems that, in the EP, the Denktaš government was consistently seen as central to the problem, while Turkish-Cypriot society was increasingly viewed as potentially part of the solution.

In retrospect, it seems clear that the plenaries devoted very little attention to the Greek Cypriots. There does not seem to have been any expectation that they might prove an obstacle to peace. It seems rather to have been taken for granted that a solution would be in the Greek Cypriots' interests and they would support it. This was hardly surprising: it reflected a more generally held view within the international community that the Turkish and Turkish-Cypriot governments, with their insistence on the recognition of two separate sovereignties on the island, were the main stumbling block to a solution. In contrast, the government of the RoC had declared its support for the bizonal and bicommunal federation advocated by the UN (e.g. RoC President Clerides quoted in Nugent, 2000: 143). However, in the case of the EP, another factor in its attitude towards the Greek Cypriots may have been a perception of the RoC as a 'European' state.

While Turkey was deemed, even by its supporters, not to meet the Copenhagen criteria, no such issue arose in relation to the RoC. The latter had been given a clean bill of health on this score in the European Commission's first monitoring report, in 1998; that report noted the existence of stable institutions guaranteeing democracy and the rule of law and the absence of major problems regarding the observation of fundamental rights and freedoms (Commission of the European Communities, 1998: 8–9). In fact, Cyprus's European identity was so unquestioned in the EP that it appeared almost unnecessary to talk about it. On the few occasions when it was mentioned, Cyprus was described as 'a firm component of Europe', 'a country that is indisputably European' and even an 'ancient birthplace of Europe' (Melo [ALDE, PT], 11 July 1995; Rothe [PSE, DE], 11 July 1995; Speroni [NI, IT], 9 April 2003). There therefore seems to have been an implicit assumption that, unlike Turkey and the 'Turkish Republic of Northern Cyprus', the RoC was a state which shared European standards and ideals. For the EP, of course, this naturally meant adherence to the aims of European integration as a peace and democratisation project.

Seeking solution

In the context of a Europe reuniting after the end of the Cold War, there was definitely a feeling in the EP that the time had come for the Cyprus problem to be resolved, a sentiment which grew stronger as the fifth enlargement process progressed (e.g. Bertens [ALDE, NL], 11 July 1995; Villiers [PPE-DE, FR], 16 February 2000; Poos [PSE, FR], 3 October 2000). This feeling found its expression in the comparisons of the Green Line in Cyprus to the Berlin Wall (Sacrédeus [PPE-DE, SV], 14 November 2000, 19 November 2002 and 9 March 2003; Morillon [PPE-DE, FR], 5 September 2000), a comparison intended to stress the anachronistic nature of the continued division of Cyprus and the sense that 'this unnatural ... last border of walls and barbed wire, can no longer be sustained' (Swoboda [PSE, DE], 4 June 2003). After years of UN talks, the accession application by the RoC was hailed by MEPs as a 'window of opportunity', which might act as 'a catalyst and driving force' in the search for a solution (Green [PSE, UK], 16 September 1996; Poos [PSE, FR], 3 October 2000). This perception was based on a dual hope. On the one hand, the RoC's impending EU entry could provide a 'stick' with which to press for change in Turkish policy. On the other, the 'carrot' of potential participation in the RoC's accession process might induce the Turkish Cypriots to turn their backs on Ankara and the Denktaš regime.

This reflected a strategy for the solution of the Cyprus conflict centred on what George Christou has called 'the power of attraction', defined as 'a specific logic of "inclusion"' (Christou, 2004: 94). The mechanics of this process and how it would work in the case of the Turkish Cypriots were not very clear. While some reference was made to EU membership as a guarantee for the latter's security and cultural identity (Poos [PSE, FR], 3 October 2000), the main emphasis seemed to be on the importance of the Turkish Cypriots sharing in the economic benefits of accession. This would seem to confirm the observation by Thomas Diez (2002c) concerning the pre-eminence of the 'economic carrot' in EU policy towards the Turkish Cypriots. Economic cooperation was also seen as a way of bringing the two communities closer together, as indicated, for example, by the calls for pre-accession aid to be used to promote reconciliation and the hopes expressed concerning the potential effects of EU-funded programmes (e.g. Villiers [PPE-DE, FR], 16 February 2000; Poos [PSE, FR], 16 February 2000; Rothe [PSE, DE], 16 February 2000). But even more than a matter for reasoned arguments, the expectations concerning the accession catalyst seem to have been based on an implicit underlying faith in the efficacy of the EU as a peace project.

This may explain why the idea that European integration offered a potential route to reconciliation in Cyprus went virtually unchallenged in the EP. An alternative viewpoint, that the accession process would formalise the partition of the island, was expressed by the MEPs of the Greek Communist Party. However, in both the 1994–99 and 1999–2004 parliaments, that party held only three seats. With less than 0.5 per cent of the total, it constituted the tiniest of minorities in the EP. Given that its views do not appear to have elicited audible support from other quarters, the party's protests can be regarded as the exception that proves the rule.

The broadly consensual view within the EP may partly have reflected the lack of discussion of the specific problems dividing the two communities and hence of the obstacles to the island's reunion. For instance, during the period covered, there seems to have been no mention of the missing persons on both sides. This issue was not only guaranteed to inflame emotions, but has also, as Paul Sant Cassia (2004) has shown, helped to perpetuate the conflict by serving as a metaphor of difference between the two communities. Nor was there any extensive reference to other contentious issues, notably the 'three freedoms' of movement, settlement and property ownership that were so fundamental to the UN talks. In addition, there was very little discussion of the early versions of the Annan Plan, with only Greek MEPs raising concerns about the proposal for permanent derogations from the *acquis communautaire* included in the first version, Annan I (Papayannakis, Alavanos [both GUE/NGL, EL], November 2002). The time limitations of parliamentary debates, and the fact the EU was not playing a direct mediating role, inhibited the EP from engaging in any substantive way with the 'nuts and bolts' of a potential settlement. If it had done so, there might have been greater dissent.

The pre-eminent perception of the Cyprus conflict in the EP was not a transitory view, but one which had been consolidated since 1974. Prior to the Annan Plan referenda, the basic conception of the problem remained unchallenged. What did change during the period under examination was the expectation that European integration could play a special role in the resolution of the conflict. Particularly as the EP began to pay more attention to the Turkish Cypriots in the early years of the twenty-first century, there was also some differentiation concerning policy prescriptions. The most notable development occurred from 2002, when some British voices began to be heard in favour of lifting the trade embargo on northern Cyprus, in place since the 1994 decision of the European Court of Justice (Ludford, Duff [both ALDE, UK], 14 May 2002; Van Orden [PPE-DE, UK], 2 and 4 June 2003). This demand was framed in terms of promoting reconciliation between the two communities on the island, with its supporters maintaining that it did not imply recognition of the government in northern Cyprus. While this proposal had no concrete results, in itself it marked a significant departure from accepted EU policy – and an early indication of the kind of issues that were to emerge after April 2004.

Paradigm shift

The period from November 2002 to March 2004 saw a sea change in the parameters of the Cyprus conflict, following the emergence of new leaderships in Turkey, the RoC and northern Cyprus. Thus, in early 2004, it was the

Turkish government which pressed for a resumption of the UN talks.[16] The outcome of the latter, the fifth and final version of the UN Plan, published on 31 March 2004, was accepted by the Turkish government and new Turkish-Cypriot Prime Minister, but rejected by most political forces in the RoC.[17] On 24 April, the failure of the negotiated solution was ratified by the 65 per cent Turkish-Cypriot 'yes' and 76 per cent Greek-Cypriot 'no' votes in the Annan Plan referenda.

This constituted a radical reversal of expectations regarding the roles of the respective actors in the conflict and the search for a solution. The resulting rapid shift in perceptions within the EP had already been apparent in two debates held in April 2004. The first, characteristically concerning Turkey's progress towards accession, took place on 1 April, only hours after the presentation of the final version of the Annan Plan. The second, on 'the prospects for unification of Cyprus before its accession to the EU', was on 21 April, just three days before the referenda. It thus followed RoC President Papadopoulos's dramatic speech of 7 April calling on the Greek Cypriots to vote 'no' and the refusal to allow Enlargement Commissioner Verheugen and other supporters of the Plan, both Cypriot and foreign, access to the Greek-Cypriot media in order to present their case.

In both debates, the Turks and Turkish Cypriots were no longer the centre of attention. The former were praised for their 'constructive and cooperative role' and for having 'worked hard to obtain a just settlement' (Verheugen [Commission, DE]; Van Orden [PPE-DE, UK], 1 April 2004). The latter were deemed to 'have largely thrown off the legacy of Rauf Denktaš' (Rothe [PSE, DE], 21 April 2004), while a 'yes' vote in the referendum would mean 'they will have done everything that we and the UN asked of them' (Davies [ALDE, UK], 21 April 2004). But above all, as Verheugen remarked, 'all the issues ... concerning Turkish responsibility for Cyprus will be resolved as soon as the Annan Plan is accepted' (Verheugen [Commission, DE], 1 April 2004).

Instead, the spotlight had shifted to the Greek Cypriots, who had suddenly emerged as the main obstacle to a solution. During the first debate, the rapporteur on Turkey, amending his own report, claimed that 'Greek Cypriot cooperation in finding a solution to the Cyprus problem is not optimal, to put it mildly' (Oostlander [PPE-DE, NL], 1 April 2004). The second debate was the famous occasion when Verheugen claimed he felt 'cheated' by the RoC government. Other speakers used similarly emotive language, claiming the EU and EP had been 'cheated', 'deceived' and 'betrayed' (Patten [Commission, UK]; Davies [ALDE, UK]; Oostlander [PPE-DE, NL]). The RoC, whose rejection of the Plan was interpreted as a fundamental *volte face* on the long-standing commitment to a bizonal, bicommunal federation, was accused of acting in bad faith. MEPs referred to a 'presumption' that it is 'possible to trick one's way into membership of the EU' and to the need for trust among participants in the EC, meaning that 'pledges must be honoured' (Oostlander [PPE-DE, NL]; Brok [PPE-DE, DE]).

More than this, however, the Greek Cypriots' European credentials were called into question. The lack of press and media freedom during the referendum campaign was denounced as a violation of the Copenhagen criteria, which, if it had occurred in another country, would have led to the breaking off of negotiations.[18] Verheugen excoriated the RoC's stand as, first and foremost, a negation of the principle of European integration as a peace project. He essentially claimed that the Greek Cypriots had misunderstood the real nature of the EU, and noted that, in recent Greek-Cypriot statements,

> the word 'peace', the word 'reconciliation', the word 'mutual understanding' and the word 'different communities and religions living together' are hardly ever mentioned. The focus is almost entirely on trade aspects.

The April 2004 debates not only indicated a striking about-turn in perceptions of the major actors, and particularly in the previous image of the RoC: they also opened a new phase, in which the Cyprus question was to become the object of open dissension within the EP.

A moral battlefield

The criticism of the Greek Cypriots was not unanimous, with some MEPs – and not only Greeks – voicing support for their stand. The Annan Plan itself emerged as a focal point of disagreement. Before the referenda, speakers from the EP's three main political groups tended to stress that it was a compromise which should be supported as offering real prospects for reconciliation (e.g. Brok [PPE-DE, DE]; Rothe [PSE, DE]; Watson [ALDE, UK], 21 April 2004). However, some Greek MEPs, while advocating a positive vote, at the same time voiced strong criticisms, describing Annan V as 'anti-democratic' and claiming that it did 'not put both sides on an equal footing' (Katiforis [PSE, EL], 1 April 2004; Tatsos [PSE, EL], 21 April 2004). Meanwhile, strongly voiced protests – usually from eurosceptic MEPs – roundly condemned the Plan, arguing that it 'tramples over the UN resolutions and international law', 'perpetuates and legalises the Turkish occupation', and failed to apply the principles of 'observance of human rights and respect for democracy' which the EP 'is shouting from the rooftops'.[19]

This was just the beginning of the new divisions around the Cyprus question. The immediate question after the referenda concerned the fate of the Turkish Cypriots, who had voted for reunion in the framework of EU membership but were effectively excluded from the Union by the Greek-Cypriot rejection of the Annan Plan. Disagreement rapidly developed concerning the fundamental responsibility for the Turkish Cypriots' plight. For some, the latter were 'held hostage by the citizens in the south' (Cohn-Bendit [Verts/ALE, DE], 21 April 2004). For others, the basic problem remained the Turkish military presence: 'if the occupying army leaves ... automatically northern Cyprus will enjoy the benefits that southern Cyprus enjoys' (Karatzaferis [IND/DEM, EL], 28 September 2005). The latter view was also supported by Greek-Cypriot MEPs (e.g. Demetriou [PPE-DE, CY], 16 November 2004), whose participation in the EP from May 2004 further contributed to raising the emotional temperature around the Cyprus issue.

These differing assessments led to diverging policy prescriptions. For those who regarded the Turkish Cypriots as wrongfully excluded from the EU by their compatriots, ending the economic isolation of northern Cyprus now became a moral imperative. This had already found expression in the 21 April debate, in renewed calls for the lifting of the trade embargo (Davies [ALDE, UK]; Cohn-Bendit [Verts/ALE, DE]). However, for those who saw the Turkish Cypriots as primarily the victims of the Turkish presence, such concessions would mean rewarding Turkish aggression. In November 2004, the EP became a battlefield over the question of EU funding to northern Cyprus. For some, this was definitely welcome, although criticised as little and very late (Duff [ALDE, UK], 16 November 2004). For others, it meant *de facto* or 'tacit recognition of the occupying authorities and of the illegal Turkish Republic of Northern Cyprus' (Claeys [NI, NL], 16 November 2004; Figureido [GUE/NGL, PT], 17 November 2004).

During 2005, the debate took a new turn, when the Turkish signature of the Additional Protocol, extending the customs union with the EU to the new member states, was accompanied by a unilateral declaration that this did not imply recognition of the RoC or the opening of Turkish ports and airports to the latter's ships and planes. This led to another characteristically heated debate on 28 September 2005, in which two competing moral arguments were once again counter-posed. While one school of thought emphasised the EU's failure to keep its promises to the Turkish Cypriots as a justification of Turkey's stance, the other focused on Turkey's failure to comply with its contractual obligations and the contradiction of seeking membership of a club when it did not recognise of one its members. The prevalence of the latter argument, with the December 2006 decision to suspend the opening of accession talks with Turkey on all chapters related to the customs union, suggested that the centre of gravity of the Cyprus debate was shifting back to familiar ground, prioritising the question of Turkey's accession and the implications of its apparently 'non-European' behaviour.

Conclusions

The preceding analysis suggests that up to March 2004, the Cyprus question was the object of a surprisingly broad consensus in the EP. Obviously, the picture that emerges from examination of the plenaries is of necessity simplistic. It clearly does not represent the whole story with regard to EU parliamentarians' views and activities on the subject. Nevertheless, it seems justified to talk of a basic shared understanding of the nature and causes of the conflict and of the fundamental purpose of EU policy. But then the failure of the Cyprus peace process dealt a major blow to the credibility of the EU as a peace project. The Annan Plan referenda and what preceded them also appeared to overturn all the assumptions on which the EP had judged the various suitors for EU accession. Not surprisingly, this transformed Cyprus into a focus of controversy within the EP. Disagreement concerned both the assessment of responsibility for the perpetuation of the conflict and the course which EU policy should now follow.

A unifying factor between the pre- and post-referenda time periods was the central role of identity in shaping the debate. It was the perception of the EU as a community of shared values and the beliefs concerning the compatibility of the various actors in the conflict with the latter which defined the parameters of the debate. The difference was that in the pre-referenda era, the predominance of one particular interpretation of recent history led to an essentially unitary discourse on the Cyprus conflict. Subsequently, conflicting views of a crucial event – the response to Annan V – brought competing moral imperatives into play, resulting in differing interpretations. In both cases, however, the debate seems to have been rather less about its ostensible subject – the Cyprus conflict – than about confirming the EP's own identity as a guardian of the values on which the EU was based. In this sense, the EP debate on Cyprus can ultimately be regarded as a failure. It concluded by leaving the EP deeply divided concerning the course of action in relation to Cyprus that would be most compatible with its identity as a community of values.

Meanwhile, the EP also proved singularly ineffective in contributing to the resolution of the conflict. As Nathalie Tocci points out, the latter would have required the generation of suitable incentives to persuade all the parties concerned that a settlement would be more advantageous than non-solution. In her view, the EU framework had the potential to offer such incentives (see Tocci, 2004b: ch. 7). But this would have required an assessment of the hopes, fears and particular problems of all the parties and of the special solutions that European integration could provide. However, as we have seen, the EP plenaries did not delve into such specifics. Instead, the parliamentary debate was characterised by a lack of knowledge about the conflict, its origins and dynamics, and hence of what might be required to resolve it. Parliament did not debate a strategy for the settlement of the Cyprus question. Instead, it placed its hopes in the transformation of the conflict through the magic touch of enlargement.

The latter was not conceived as a framework within which specific solutions could be found to the problems dividing the parties. Instead, it was seen as a question of compliance with the accession criteria. The EP policy appears to have been based on the assumption that if all the parties involved could become 'Europeanised', by accepting European values – of which the peaceful resolution of disputes was among the most important – then the problem would be resolved. But this overlooked the need to find incentives to make the parties adhere to the peace project in the first place. And for this, the invocation of European values was simply not enough.

In this respect, the EP debate does not simply illuminate the failure of the EU peace project in the Cyprus case. It also suggests the inherent dangers in the general assumption underlying EU policy more broadly, especially in relation to south-eastern Europe – that drawing states into the enlargement orbit will be sufficient to resolve long-standing conflicts.

Notes

1 The research for this chapter was conducted as part of the Cidel project ('Citizenship and Democracy in the European Union'), financed by the Directorate-General for Research and Technology of the European Commission and led by Arena at the University of Oslo. I would like to thank Sophia Michalaki for research assistance on the European Parliament case study.
2 See for example the EP resolutions of 19 July 1975 and 28 April 1976 on the recommendations of the Joint Parliamentary Committee of the EEC–Turkey Association, reprinted in Republic of Cyprus (1998: 56–60).
3 EP resolutions of 17 November 1983 (reprinted in Hakki, 2007: 616–17) and 13 September 1985 (reprinted in Republic of Cyprus, 1998).
4 The Intergovernmental Conferences took place in 1996–97, 2000 and 2003–04, and the constitutional convention in 2002–03.
5 Treaty establishing the European Coal and Steel Community, Paris 18 April 1951, preamble.
6 For more on this, see Verney (2002).
7 See the statement by Mr Mitchell, President-in-office of the Council, concerning the understanding that the question of Turkey and Cyprus would be taken together, in *EP Debates*, 18 September 1996.
8 With a formal cut-off procedure in the former case for speakers who exceeded the limit.
9 See for example the account by the British special representative for Cyprus in 1996–2003, Sir David Hannay (2005: 10–11).

10 For example a statement by the Portuguese representative of the Council, Mr Gama, in the EP, 11 April 2000 (*EP Debates*: 55).
11 Pauline Green, who had many Greek-Cypriot voters in her north London constituency, took a keen interest in the Cyprus problem. For more on her views, see her memoir (Green, 2003), published following her retirement from the EP.
12 In the remainder of this chapter, references to speeches in the EP (reported in *EP Debates*) are provided as (speaker [party affiliation, member state], date of speech), where the listing of party affiliation and member state follows the EU conventions. The acronyms used for this purpose appear in the list of abbreviations (pp. xv–xvii). For further information, see www.europarl.europa.eu/groups/default_en.htm.
13 See for example the debate of 10 April 1997, including the interventions by Rothe (PSE, DE) and Bertens (ALDE, NL). See also the intervention by Villiers (PPE-DE, FR), 1 September 2003.
14 A random sample: 13 December 1995, numerous speakers; Green (PSE, UK), 19 July 1996; Bertens (ALDE, NL), 16 September 1997; Duff (ALDE, UK), 6 October 1997; Schori (PSE, SV), 1 December 1999. The Cyprus issue was also quite often paired with the issue of the Armenian genocide, for example by Rocard (PSE, FR), 13 December 1995; Faubre-Aubrespy (EDN, FR), 19 June 1996.
15 Examples of Greek speakers included: Daskalaki (UPE, EL), 11 July 1995; Hadzidakis (PPE–DE, EL), 19 June 1996; Tsatsos (PSE, EL), 18 September 1996; Katiforis (PSE, EL), 4 September 2001. Examples of non-Greek speakers included: Green (PSE, UK), 19 June 1996; Bertens (ALDE, NL), 19 June 1996.
16 On the change in Turkish policy towards Cyprus, see Bahcheli (2006).
17 On the line-up of political forces in the Greek-Cypriot and Turkish-Cypriot referenda campaigns, see Christophoros (2004).
18 Verheugen (Commission, DE), Oostlander (PPE-DE, NL). See also the intervention by the President of the EP.
19 Korakas (GUE/NGL, EL), 1 April 2004; Dillen (NI, NL), 21 April 2004; Souchet (NI, FR), 21 April 2004. See also Camre (UEN, FR), 1 April 2004; Alyssandrakis (GUE/NGL, EL), 21 April 2004; Tannock (PPE-DE, UK), 21 April 2004.

8

United Nations peace-making in Cyprus: from mediation to arbitration and beyond

James Ker-Lindsay

Introduction

For the past sixty years, the United Nations (UN) has played a central role in the management and resolution of conflict in international affairs. Under chapter VI of the UN Charter, which refers to the 'Pacific Settlement of Disputes', the organisation is specifically authorised to play a part in the termination and settlement of international disputes. Since then, one of the most protracted UN attempts to manage and resolve conflict has been in Cyprus. For over four decades, starting in 1964, the UN has been at the forefront of efforts to reconcile the Greek Cypriots and Turkish Cypriots and, since 1974, to reunite the island following the Turkish military invasion. Starting first with formal mediation, the UN Secretary-General later offered his 'good offices' to the parties. However, despite considerable efforts, these approaches failed to reconcile the sides.

In early 2004, the UN adopted a different approach. Following an agreement between the parties in February 2004, a new round of peace talks began. This was divided into two phases. The first phase would involve just the two Cypriot communities. The second, shorter phase would also include representatives from Greece and Turkey. If all this failed to produce a settlement, the UN Secretary-General was empowered to produce a final settlement, based on the discussions, which would then be presented to the two sides in twin referenda. This decision effectively marked the introduction of an entirely new type of intervention by the UN, one that did not fit neatly into any category of conflict resolution. It was more than mediation, and went beyond the notion of good offices. Instead, it might be best characterised as 'arbitrated mediation'.

This chapter examines the evolution of peace-making in Cyprus over forty years and shows how the Annan Plan, with its eventual failure, raises questions about the future of peace-making, not just in Cyprus but also elsewhere.

Traditional models of peace-making

A range of conflict-resolution techniques is available to third parties seeking to end protracted civil and inter-state disputes. For example, in the context of the UN, article 33 of the Charter notes that the parties to a dispute may opt for, among other things, 'negotiation, enquiry, mediation, conciliation, arbitration, judicial settlement, resort to regional agencies or arrangements'. However, this wide range of practical options for ending conflicts may in fact be broadly divided into two specific categories of conflict resolution: 'intermediary and conciliatory' and 'arbitral and judicial' approaches (Mitchell, 1981: 255).

At the core of 'intermediary and conciliatory' approaches lie negotiation and mediation. The first of these, negotiation, is traditionally viewed as a process of direct bilateral negotiations between the two sides to a conflict. While external actors may be involved in some way – perhaps to offer advice, assistance or support – the emphasis is on a process that takes place between the parties themselves. In contrast, mediation, by its very definition, involves a third party performing some sort of facilitating role in the peace-making process. This is done by encouraging communication between conflicting parties, either in the context of initiating dialogue or else as an intermediary once a peace process has started. In this latter context, Mitchell has identified six main functions that an intermediary may perform once talks have started between the parties (Mitchell, 1981: 309–10):

1 providing ideas or possible solutions, particularly when the parties are deadlocked;
2 initiating proposals which originate from one or other party, but which could not be advanced for fear of revealing weakness or uncertainty;
3 de-committing parties by providing some formula by which they can gracefully abandon previous positions to which public acts and statements have heavily committed them;
4 acting as a substitute source of ideas or proposals for the two adversaries;
5 excusing the parties for making concessions, both within the discussions and outside to supporters, by providing an alternative to the superior bargaining position or skill of the adversary as a rationale for concession;
6 providing an 'audience' or 'spur' function through the channelling of an expectation from a wider audience that the peace-making function will

continue and some compromise be reached, rather than the whole process collapsing and the conflict being renewed coercively.

At the same time, it is generally accepted that a mediator must exhibit certain traits. First of all, there is an assumption of impartiality. It is expected that the intermediary is neutral and does not represent the interests of one party over another. Secondly, the external peace-maker, the mediator, has no legal sanction against the parties. An intermediary's aim is to coax the parties into reaching a settlement without recourse to violent or judicial means to enforce a peace agreement.

Mediation is also, by its very essence, deemed to be consensual in nature. Of course, this does not mean that the intensity of the involvement of the intermediary is the same in all cases. One can clearly identify a variance in the degree of coercion, short of armed force or legal sanction, which the intermediary attempts to use. In some cases, there is almost no coercion at all. A hands-off approach is taken whereby the third party simply aims to open channels of communication between the parties in the hope and expectation that this will lead to a dialogue that will in turn result in some form of agreement between the sides. At other times, an intermediary may try to adopt a more interventionist approach to conflict resolution by using more direct tactics, such as a threat to move the matter to the Security Council.

In overall terms, therefore, mediation essentially represents 'a non-coercive and voluntary form of conflict management that is particularly suited to the reality of international relations, where states and other actors guard their autonomy and independence quite jealously' (Kleibor, 1996: 362).

Balanced against the consensual approach to conflict resolution encapsulated within the notion of mediation, one can also identify 'arbitral and judicial' roles for third parties. According to traditional definitions, such roles involve the use of legal approaches that are 'highly restricted by known and formal rules' and are backed by sanctions for non-conformity (Mitchell, 1981: 255). Under this form of peace-making, the parties agree to have an outside actor of one sort or another resolve the dispute for them. In some cases, the dispute can be resolved through an established legal institution in a manner analogous to domestic judicial remedies. For instance, the UN Charter vests the International Court of Justice (ICJ) with responsibility for adjudicating inter-state disputes.

However, there is no reason why parties may not opt for other bodies or organisations to play an arbitrating role. This raises the key question of the degree to which arbitration and judicial intervention are binding on the parties. This is where the link between domestic and international legal approaches breaks down. In reality, the parties accept the outcome of a ruling not because the ruling body has any direct coercive power; rather, the ruling is accepted because a decision to ignore the outcome would result either in considerable opprobrium or in actions being taken elsewhere, such as in the Security Council. Nevertheless, even without the use of force, arbitration and judicial techniques of conflict resolution are far more interventionist than mediation.

Constitutional crises and peace-making in Cyprus, 1960–74

On 16 August 1960, British rule over Cyprus ended and the island became an independent sovereign state. The constitutional system that was put in place attempted to create a balance between the island's two main communities: the majority Greek Cypriots, representing 78 per cent of the population, and the minority Turkish Cypriots, who made up 18 per cent. (The remaining 4 per cent was divided between the three religious communities: the Maronites, the Latins and the Armenians.) In most areas of government – such as the Council of Ministers, the civil service and the fifty-seat parliament – power was split 70:30 in favour of the majority Greek-Cypriot community. However, in the security forces, the balance was 60:40. As for the political structure of the new state, a presidential system, akin to the US model, was chosen instead of a parliamentary form of governance. Under this model, the President would always be a Greek Cypriot, whereas the Vice-President would be Turkish Cypriot. Both had a right of veto over vital legislation. At the same time, Britain, Greece and Turkey were given constitutional responsibility for ensuring that the sovereignty and independence of the island remained intact. In order to further this, Greece was allowed to station 950 troops on the island. Turkey was allowed 650. Meanwhile, Britain was permanently granted approximately 99 square miles of (sovereign) territory for use as military bases (see Macris, 2003).

All things considered, for most of the parties the agreement was acceptable. Britain kept a military presence in the region, Greece and Turkey avoided confrontation and the Turkish Cypriots avoided coming under direct Greek rule and were given a strong say in the government. For the Greek Cypriots, on the other hand, independence was a severe disappointment. The constitution banned any future efforts to unite with Greece (Markides, 1977: 88) and many felt that the powers given to the Turkish Cypriots were excessive. At the same time, while many Turkish Cypriots found the settlement to be broadly acceptable, rather than desirable (Dodd, 1993: 6), certain extremist elements within the Turkish-Cypriot community still wanted to partition the island.

Soon after independence, problems emerged between the two communities over a number of issues, such as taxation and the administration of city councils. As a result, in November 1963, the Greek-Cypriot President,

Archbishop Makarios, proposed a number of constitutional amendments that, he argued, would ease the running of the state. In reality, the proposals would have reduced the Turkish Cypriots to minority status, and were immediately rejected by Turkey. As a result, tensions grew on the island and in late December 1963 fighting broke out between the two communities in several of the island's towns. This in turn led to the end of Turkish-Cypriot participation in the government. In response, a peace-keeping force was established by Britain, with the support of Greece and Turkey, which managed to keep serious conflict on hold until a formal UN peace-keeping force – the United Nations Peacekeeping Force in Cyprus (UNFICYP) – was established in March 1964 (see Ker-Lindsay, 2004). At the same time, the Security Council authorised the Secretary-General, U Thant, to try to resolve the political differences between the two communities. He appointed as mediator Sakari Tuomioja, a Finnish diplomat, who quickly made it clear that he viewed the problem as essentially international in nature. While he saw union with Greece (*enosis*) as the most logical course for a settlement, he rejected union on the grounds that it would be inappropriate for a UN official to propose a solution that would lead to the dissolution of a UN member state (Nicolet, 2001: 247).

Despite the appointment of a UN mediator, the first major effort to break the deadlock was initiated by the United States. In early June 1964, following a Turkish threat to intervene militarily in Cyprus, Washington launched an independent initiative under Dean Acheson, a former Secretary of State under Truman. In July he presented a plan to unite Cyprus with Greece. In return for accepting this, Turkey would receive a sovereign military base – most probably on the northern Karpas peninsula – and the Turkish Cypriots would also be given minority rights, which would be overseen by a resident international commissioner. Makarios rejected the proposal. He argued that a sovereign Turkish base on the island was a limitation to full *enosis* and would give Ankara too strong a say in the island's affairs. Soon afterwards, a second version of the plan was presented. This offered Turkey a fifty-year lease on a base, rather than full sovereignty. This time, both the Greek Cypriots and Turkey rejected the offer. After several further attempts to reach an agreement, the United States was eventually forced to give up its effort.

In August 1964, just months after being appointed mediator, Tuomioja died suddenly. In his place, U Thant appointed Galo Plaza Lasso. Rather than approach Cyprus as an international problem, Plaza instead saw it in communal terms. In March 1965 he presented a sixty-six-page report that criticised both sides for not having shown enough commitment to reaching a settlement.[1] While he understood the Greek-Cypriot aspiration of *enosis*, he believed that any attempt at union should be held in voluntary abeyance. He also argued that the Turkish Cypriots should refrain from demanding a federal solution to the problem. Controversially, he also agreed that the abrogation of the core constitutional treaties by the Greek Cypriots should be recognised. Although the Greek Cypriots eventually accepted the report, in spite of its opposition to immediate *enosis*, Turkey and the Turkish Cypriots rejected the plan and called on Plaza to resign on the grounds that he had exceeded his mandate by submitting formal proposals rather than just trying to broker an agreement. But the Greek Cypriots made it clear that if Plaza resigned they would refuse to accept a replacement. U Thant was left with no choice but to abandon the mediation effort.

In March 1966, U Thant initiated a more modest attempt at peace-making. Instead of trying to develop formal proposals for the parties to bargain over, he aimed to encourage the two sides to agree to settlement through direct dialogue. As a result of political upheaval in Greece, which eventually led to the formation of a military government in April 1967, this process failed to make any headway for the next eighteen months. In September 1967, the Greek and Turkish foreign ministers met for two meetings on either side of their border in Thrace. Turkey categorically rejected a Greek proposal for *enosis* (Nicolet, 2001: 370). Greece was now forced to abandon the idea of union for the foreseeable future (Woodhouse, 1991: 293). Just two months later there was another severe bout of inter-communal fighting in Cyprus. Turkey again threatened to invade and Greece was forced to reduce its forces on the island to the limit of 950 set under the 1960 constitution. Capitalising on the situation, the Turkish Cypriots proclaimed their own provisional administration. Although Makarios condemned the move, he nevertheless realised that the Turkish Cypriots would have to have some degree of political autonomy and that *enosis* was not feasible under the prevailing local and regional conditions (Richmond, 1998: 109).

This recognition of the need to accept greater Turkish Cypriot self-rule paved the way for inter-communal talks between the two sides, under the auspices of the 'good offices' of the UN Secretary-General. During the first round, which lasted from May until August 1968, the Turkish Cypriots were prepared to make concessions on the constitutional questions in return for significant autonomy. Makarios refused to accept this. The second round of talks, which focused on local government, was equally unsuccessful, even though the Greek military junta lobbied hard for a settlement. In December 1969, a third round of discussion started focusing on constitutional issues. Yet again there was little progress. When they ended in September 1970, the Secretary-General blamed both sides for the lack of movement.[2] A fourth and final round of inter-communal talks, which also focused on constitutional issues, again failed to make tangible headway before they were forced to a halt by events in July 1974.

Efforts to reunite the island, 1974–2002

Meanwhile, tensions had been growing within the Greek-Cypriot community as well as between the Greek-Cypriot leadership and Greece, which was under military rule. Although Makarios had effectively abandoned the pursuit of *enosis* in favour of an acceptance of independence, many others continued to believe that the only legitimate political aspirations for Greek Cypriots was union with Greece (Panteli, 1990: 224). In the early 1970s, an armed movement – the National Organisation of Cypriot Fighters (EOKA-B) – emerged that sought to unite Cyprus and Greece. Fearing that the new, more hard-line, military rulers in Athens were supporting this organisation, Makarios requested that all Greek troops leave the island. In response, the Greek government ordered the overthrow of Makarios. In his place they appointed Nicos Sampson, a former EOKA gunman who supported *enosis*. Believing that this would lead to the union of the island with Greece, Turkey invaded Cyprus on 20 July 1974. Within days the Greek military government collapsed and democracy was restored. This led to peace talks in Switzerland. However, these fell apart following a demand by Turkey that the Greek Cypriots immediately accept an ultimatum for a federal settlement (see Birand, 1985). Ankara therefore resumed its military campaign, and by the middle of August the Turkish army had occupied 37 per cent of the island. This meant that 160,000 Greek Cypriots, a quarter of the Greek-Cypriot population, had become refugees. Similarly, over 40,000 Turkish Cypriots left their homes in the southern part of the island, either seeking sanctuary in the British bases or making their way north. The island was now completely divided, both geographically and politically.

In April 1975, Kurt Waldheim, the UN Secretary-General, launched a new mission of good offices. Over the course of the following ten months, discussions were held over a range of humanitarian issues. However, no progress was made on the substantive political issues, such as territory and the nature of the central government, and the talks fell apart in February 1976. In January 1977, the UN managed to organise a meeting in Nicosia between the two sides and, on 12 February, the two leaders, Makarios (returned after the short-lived Sampson presidency) and Rauf Denktaş, signed a four-point agreement confirming that a future Cyprus settlement would be based on a federation made up of two states (bizonal) and two communities (bicommunal). The size of the states would be determined by economic viability and land ownership. The central government would be given powers to ensure the unity of the state. Various other issues, such as freedom of movement and freedom of settlement, would be settled through discussion.

The agreement marked a monumental change of direction for the Greek Cypriots. They had been forced to accept that Cyprus would be reunited as a federation, with the Turkish Cypriots controlling their own zone, and that *enosis* was officially dead. Meanwhile, the Turkish Cypriots affirmed their commitment to a united island and put aside hopes of partition. However, despite the apparent agreement between the two sides on the general nature of a settlement, new talks quickly showed that they were an ocean apart on the specifics. The Greek Cypriots presented proposals on territorial issues that took little notice of the principle of bizonality. Meanwhile, the Turkish Cypriots presented ideas on the role and functions of the central government that were more towards the confederal end of the federalist spectrum in nature. The discussions soon came to an end.

The UN remained undeterred. In May 1979, Waldheim visited Cyprus and secured a further ten-point set of proposals from the two sides. These not only reaffirmed the 1977 agreement, but also included a number of new provisions, such as demilitarisation and a commitment to refrain from destabilising activities and actions. It was also agreed that the question of Varosha (the abandoned former tourist district of the city of Famagusta, under Turkish military control) would also be addressed as a matter of priority and that the two sides would deal with all territorial and constitutional aspects of the problem. Shortly afterwards, a new round of discussions began in Nicosia. Again, they were short lived. For a start, the Turkish Cypriots did not want to discuss Varosha, which was a key issue for the Greek Cypriots. Secondly, the two sides failed to agree on the concept of 'bicommunality'. Rather than call a complete halt to the talks, the UN decided to put the negotiations on hold (Richmond, 1998: 154).

The following summer, 1980, Waldheim tried to resurrect the process by putting forward a proposal for an interim agreement. This included measures to promote a more positive atmosphere on the island, such as the return of Varosha to civilian control and the lifting of the economic embargoes placed on the Turkish Cypriots. It also called for the opening of Nicosia International Airport, which had in fact been agreed by the two sides during the first round of the Vienna talks. On 9 August, new negotiations opened under Hugo Gobbi, the Secretary-General's special representative. They focused on four areas: improving levels of goodwill between the two sides; the return and resettlement of Greek-Cypriot refugees in Varosha; constitutional matters; and territorial issues. But this time the talks ran into difficulties over 'bizonality'. The Turkish Cypriots interpreted this in terms of a confederation, and argued that the two states should have their own sovereignty. The Greek Cypriots insisted that sovereignty rest with the central state, in line with more generally accepted notions of a federal political system.

Even though they had accepted the principle of a federation, in November 1983 the Turkish Cypriots unilaterally declared independence and formed the

Turkish Republic of Northern Cyprus (TRNC). The move was almost immediately condemned by the UN Security Council, which called on states not to recognise the new entity and declared that the move represented a setback to efforts to reach a settlement.[3] As a result, the only country to recognise the Turkish-Cypriot state was Turkey.

Despite this, the UN continued its efforts to find a solution to the island's division. In early 1984, steps were taken to resume the peace process. In March, Javier Pérez de Cuéllar, who had replaced Waldheim as UN Secretary-General at the start of 1982, presented the two sides with a five-point suggestion for confidence-building measures. New talks began in September. After three rounds of discussions a blueprint was achieved. Cyprus would become a bizonal, bicommunal, non-aligned federation. The Turkish Cypriots would retain 29 per cent of the island as their federal state and all foreign troops would leave Cyprus. In January 1985, the two leaders of the respective communities, Spyros Kyprianou and Denktaş, met for the first face-to-face talks since the 1979 agreement. While the general belief was that the meeting was being held to agree to a final settlement, Kyprianou insisted that it was a chance for further negotiations. The talks collapsed (Newman, 2001: 139). In the aftermath, the Greek-Cypriot leaders came in for heavy criticism, both at home and abroad. Denktaş walked away with a public relations victory and a reprieve. More importantly, he made it clear that he was unlikely to make so many concessions again (Denktaş, 1988: 142).

Despite the setback, de Cuéllar continued his attempts to broker an agreement. In March 1986, he presented the two sides with a 'Draft Framework Agreement'. Again, the plan envisaged the creation of an independent, non-aligned, bicommunal, bizonal state in Cyprus. However, the Greek Cypriots were unhappy with the proposals. They argued that the question of removing Turkish forces from Cyprus was not addressed, nor was the repatriation of the increasing number of Turkish settlers on the island. Moreover, there were no guarantees that the three freedoms – the freedom of movement, the freedom of settlement and the right to own property – would be respected. Finally, they saw the proposed state structure as being confederal in nature.[4] Further efforts to produce an agreement failed, as the two sides remained steadfastly attached to their positions. Meanwhile, increased Greek–Turkish tension in the Aegean reduced hopes for a solution.

However, a thaw in relations between Greece and Turkey in early 1988, coupled with the victory of a moderate political novice, George Vassiliou, in Cypriot presidential elections, opened the way for de Cuéllar to initiate a new effort in August that year. At a series of meetings in Geneva the two leaders agreed to abandon the March 1986 Draft Framework Agreement and return to the 1977 and 1979 High Level Agreements (Richmond, 1998: 193). Less than a year later, in June 1989, the UN presented a new document to the two communities – the 'Set of Ideas'. It was quickly rejected by Denktaş, who not only disagreed with the substance of the proposals but also argued that the Secretary-General had no right to present formal plans to the two sides, a complaint reminiscent of that made of the Plaza report in 1965.

Following a failed Turkish-Cypriot attempt to open direct talks with the Greek Cypriots, free from UN involvement, the two sides met again in New York in February 1990, under the auspices of the UN. Again, the talks proved fruitless, as Denktaş demanded that the Greek Cypriots recognise the existence of two people in Cyprus and their basic right to self-determination. Matters were further complicated in July 1990 when Cyprus formally applied to join the European Community (EC). Furious at the move, Denktaş called off all talks with UN officials. Undeterred, de Cuéllar tried unsuccessfully to restart the process. In his last report to the Security Council he noted that progress on his proposals could go no further, largely because of Denktaş's demand that the two communities have equal sovereignty and a right to secession.[5]

In January 1992, Boutros Boutros-Ghali took over as UN Secretary-General. He continued to work on the Set of Ideas and, in April 1992, he presented the Security Council with an outline plan for the creation of a bizonal, bi-communal federation that would prohibit any form of partition, secession or union with another state,[6] which the Council endorsed.[7] While the Greek Cypriots accepted this as a basis for negotiation, Denktaş refused to engage in substantive discussions on the plan and again criticised the Secretary-General for exceeding his authority. The Turkish-Cypriot leader again called for direct talks with the Greek Cypriots, free from UN involvement. The offer was rejected. When he did eventually return to the table, Denktaş complained that the proposals failed to recognise his community. In November, Boutros-Ghali called a halt to the process. Although the Turkish-Cypriot side had accepted 91 of the 100 proposals, Denktaş's unwillingness to engage in substantive talks on the remaining nine areas of difference meant that further progress was unachievable.[8] After this, the plan fell by the wayside as the new Greek-Cypriot government, formed under Glafcos Clerides in 1993, also sought to move away from the Set of Ideas.

Despite this wish to abandon the Set of Ideas, the Greek Cypriots remained outwardly committed to the creation of a bizonal, bicommunal federation. The same could not be said for Denktaş, who became more and more hard line in the years that followed. By the middle of the 1990s, he had decided that he would no longer accept a federation as the model for a settlement. Instead, he now insisted that any settlement must be based on a loose confederation in which both states would be fully sovereign. However, the parameters of the Cyprus issue now started to change. In 1998, formal accession negotiations started between the European Union (EU) and Cyprus. At first, the Turkish government believed that there was no chance that the EU would risk provoking a crisis with Turkey, a major state of 60 million people, in favour of Cyprus, with just 700,000 inhabitants. Just to be sure, Turkey threatened to annexe northern Cyprus if the Republic of Cyprus was admitted as an EU member.

UN peace-making 2002–04 and the Annan Plan

However, by 2001 it was clear that the EU was serious about accepting Cyprus as a member. In December 2001, the Turkish-Cypriot leader therefore surprised observers by proposing new talks (Hannay, 2005: 155). These started in January 2002. Although the initiative was warmly welcomed, many suspected that it was little more than a ploy to try to delay Cypriot EU accession. This impression was quickly confirmed. The Turkish-Cypriot leader quickly showed that he had little interest in negotiating in good faith. Despite several attempts by Kofi Annan, the UN Secretary-General, to intervene personally, the talks made little progress. Matters were not helped by the fact that Denktaş was receiving support from the nationalist administration in Turkey.

The situation changed in November 2002, when in Turkey the Justice and Development Party (AKP) won a landslide victory under the leadership of Recep Tayyip Erdoğan and made it clear that its primary policy goal was to secure Turkey's eventual EU accession and that this would include solving the Cyprus issue. It was this commitment to a settlement that paved the way for the UN to present the two Cypriot sides with a blueprint for a settlement. A little less than a month later this document, which quickly came to be known as the Annan Plan, underwent its first revision. This was aimed at improving a number of key provisions in advance of the important European Council in Copenhagen in December 2002, where it was hoped that a final settlement could be reached, alongside the confirmation that Cyprus would formally join the EU, along with Malta and eight states from central Europe, on 1 May 2004.

Because the Turkish Cypriots refused to negotiate, it was not possible to reach a solution in Denmark (Ker-Lindsay, 2005: 45). However, discussions between the two sides nevertheless continued throughout January and February 2003 in an attempt to meet the 28 February deadline for an agreement, which had originally been set down in the Annan Plan. Despite facing growing pressure from his own community, which had taken to the streets in a series of mass demonstrations, Denktaş remained as intransigent as ever. At the same time, the Greek Cypriots elected Tassos Papadopoulos, a known hard-liner, as their President. In view of this, few believed that an agreement could be reached between the two sides and a three-day visit to the island by Kofi Annan in the days before the expiry of the deadline failed to bridge the differences that existed. In a last-ditch effort to reach a settlement, Annan called upon the two leaders to put the plan directly to the people in simultaneous referenda. While Papadopoulos grudgingly accepted the idea at a meeting with Annan in The Hague on 10–11 March, Denktaş refused to accept it. As a result, the UN brought its peace-making efforts to a close.

In the weeks that followed, the Turkish-Cypriot leader was heavily criticised for killing off yet another peace process. At the same time, Turkey also received a clear warning that, as a result of the Turkish-Cypriot leader's behaviour, it own efforts to join the EU would be obstructed. In an attempt to deflect some of this criticism, the Turkish-Cypriot authorities decided, on 23 April 2003, to end the thirty-year restrictions imposed on crossing the Green Line and allow Greek Cypriots the first chance to cross over at will. While the move was widely welcomed, it soon became clear that there was little chance of a resumption of talks. This appeared to be confirmed when Lord Hannay announced that he had stood down as the British special representative, a post he had held for seven years, and Alvaro de Soto, the UN Secretary-General's special adviser on Cyprus, was reassigned to the Western Sahara.

By the autumn, the prospects for new talks appeared to be improving, however. The Turkish government appeared to be increasingly exasperated with Denktaş's consistent intransigence. At the same time, the military also appeared to be increasingly ready to accept the need for a settlement. Attention now focused on the Turkish-Cypriot parliamentary elections, which were held on 14 December 2003. However, the main pro-solution opposition parties failed to win an outright victory and the Republican Turkish Party (CTP), led by Mehmet Ali Talat, was eventually forced into a coalition with the Democratic Party (DP) of Rauf Denktaş's son Serdar. While this ensured that Rauf Denktaş would remain in place as the lead Turkish-Cypriot negotiator, his moral and political position was weakened. This became clear soon afterwards, when, against the Turkish-Cypriot leader's wishes, a high-level meeting of senior Turkish foreign and security policy figures decided to pursue new Cyprus talks. A few weeks later, the National Security Council confirmed this decision. On 24 January 2004, Erdoğan met with Annan on the margins of the World Economic Forum and requested that discussions resume at the first opportunity. Following consultations, Annan summoned Papadopoulos and Denktaş to New York. On 13 February, following lengthy discussions, the two sides agreed to accept a timetable for a new round of discussions.

After a break of almost a year, a new round of talks got underway on 19 February 2004. However, little was achieved. Although the various technical committees were able to make significant progress, the main constitutional differences remained unbridgeable. The situation was also hindered by the bad atmosphere generated by Rauf Denktaş, who appeared determined to scupper the process, and deliberately weakened the negotiations by holding frequent press conferences at which he revealed as much as he could to the media about the talks. On the other hand, while the Greek Cypriots started the discussions in a more constructive manner, by the end they too appeared determined to weaken the process. They did so by overloading the UN with paperwork in an attempt to prevent movement towards a settlement (Ker-Lindsay, 2005: 92). As agreed, this 'Nicosia' round of talks was brought to a close on 22 March. Almost no political progress had been made.

There then followed a further week of discussions in Bürgenstock, Switzerland, where representatives from Greece and Turkey joined the representatives of the two Cypriot communities. Fortunately, Rauf Denktaş boycotted this part of the process. As a result, the main impediment to a solution was seemingly removed from the equation. However, rather than open the way for a settlement, the absence of Denktaş instead created the conditions whereby the extent of Papadopoulos's opposition to the UN proposals was revealed. Despite the best efforts of the UN, he effectively barred any attempt to convene face-to-face discussions. He also ensured that attempts to open up talks by other means failed as well. As numerous officials involved with the process have stressed, President Papadopoulos did not negotiate in Switzerland. However, it goes further than this. Even when concessions that would have made the Annan Plan more palatable were put on the table for him to accept, he rejected them. Although Papadopoulos has rejected these charges, and many others made by the UN, the overwhelming evidence is that he did not have any intention of using Bürgenstock to try to improve the Annan Plan. Instead, the conclusion one is forced to reach is that he went there determined to create the conditions for its eventual rejection in the referendum. As a result, the UN Secretary-General was eventually left with no choice but to fill in the parts of the Plan where no consensus had been reached between the two sides. This fifth and final version of the proposals was presented to the two communities on 31 March for a vote in simultaneous referenda on 24 April.

Despite opposition from Rauf Denktaş, Turkey and the main Turkish-Cypriot opposition parties endorsed the Annan Plan. There was therefore never any real doubt that it would pass in northern Cyprus. In contrast, most Greek Cypriots had been opposed to the agreement ever since it had first been unveiled, back in November 2002. Nevertheless, there were hopes that, with the support of the two main parties, the Progressive Workers' Party (AKEL) and Democratic Rally (DISY), a turn-around in attitudes could still take place. These hopes were dashed when President Papadopoulos called on the Greek Cypriots to resoundingly reject the plan (Papadopoulos, 2004).

Soon afterwards, AKEL backed away from its earlier support for the proposals. Although DISY came out in favour of the agreement, as did a number of leading political figures, including two former Presidents, it was too late to reverse the negative climate. At the same time as 65 per cent of Turkish Cypriots voted in favour of the proposals, 76 per cent of Greek Cypriots opposed the agreement. As a result, the UN's attempt to reunite the island came to an end and just one week later, on 1 May 2004, Cyprus joined the EU as a divided island.

Cyprus and the evolution of arbitrated mediation

In reviewing the activities of the UN from 1964 until early 2004, one can clearly argue that UN peace-making efforts in Cyprus – either in the form of a formal 'mediation' effort or as the mission of good offices, the two of which were 'almost indistinguishable' (Richmond, 1998: 26) – have fallen squarely within the realms of traditional mediation. For a start, it has generally been perceived as neutral. Secondly, it has not had any coercive power over the two sides. While the Secretary-General could, and did, criticise one side for not showing goodwill, or even obstructing talks, there was nothing that could be done to force the two sides to reach an agreement. Extending this analysis to the range of techniques employed by the UN, and applying the six functions of the intermediary described by Mitchell, it is clear that, at some point or other, the UN peace-making activities in Cyprus have corresponded to the standard norms of mediation. For example, the UN has provided ideas or possible solutions. An obvious example of this was the Set of Ideas. It has also acted as a conduit between the two sides for proposals that the sides themselves could not advance. It has provided an opportunity for the two sides to de-commit themselves from previous positions. The most obvious case was the High Level Agreement in 1977, which officially marked the end of *enosis* as a policy objective. Likewise, the UN has provided a vital audience for the two sides that has helped to keep talks going; one example of this was during the inter-communal talks in the 1960s.

However, balanced against this traditional UN approach, the process used at the end of deliberations over the Annan Plan appeared to mark a significant shift in approach. While it appears to have been based on mediation, in fact it is possible to argue that it went well beyond the characteristics most usually associated with traditional conciliatory types of intermediary activity. In fact, one could almost argue that the process bore many of the hallmarks of arbitration, both in terms of process and in terms of the functions performed by the intermediary. Indeed, many Greek Cypriots, including Papadopoulos (*Cyprus*

Mail, 12 September 2007), now openly refer to the process that took place in 2004 as an act of arbitration (Theophanous, 2004: 64–6).

Such a view is justified. In terms of the process, the parties were presented with a very clearly defined timetable and framework for discussion. The open-ended approach was abandoned. Far more importantly, the parties also mandated the UN to decide the final terms of the Plan. In effect, the UN became the arbiter of any areas where a dispute still existed between the two sides at the end of the allocated period of negotiations. Significantly, this was matched by a decision by the political leaders to waive their rights to reject the outcome in any direct manner. The Plan presented would not be a 'proposal' for the parties to discuss further. It was a full-blown 'agreement'. Of course, it would be disingenuous to suggest, as many opponents of the Plan have, that this was an imposed solution that came from nowhere. Instead, it was the distilled product of many decades of negotiation. Nevertheless, by presenting such a comprehensive document, the UN went a lot further than it had ever done before.

Likewise, by accepting this, the parties handed an unparalleled degree of power and authority to the UN over the peace-making process. The parties in Cyprus had never before been subjected to such a robust form of peace-making as they were at that point. While many accept that this was a necessary approach, given the long history of failed efforts to resolve the issue, the process was fatally flawed, insofar as it could be presented to the two sides as fundamentally unrepresentative, given that key elements of the Plan had not in fact been agreed to by the sides themselves, but had been inserted by outsiders. And this is exactly what happened. Papadopoulos used this argument to encourage the people to reject the plan. However, crucially, it could not be described as having fallen unambiguously within the bounds of arbitration, because there was no formal sanction attached.

The future of arbitrated mediation

The obvious question is whether this form on 'arbitrated mediation' will be applied again. Significantly, it appears as though the idea of 'arbitrated mediation' has not in fact fallen by the wayside with the failure of the Annan Plan. More recently, the presentation of the Ahtisaari proposals for the status of Kosovo, presented in March 2007, have borne many of the hallmarks of the approach the UN took in Cyprus three years earlier, in March 2004. In that case, the UN, led by its envoy Martti Ahtisaari, attempted to broker an agreement between the Serbian government and the leaders of the Kosovo Albanians on the future of the province. However, after eight rounds of discussion the two sides remained deadlocked. While Belgrade was willing to consider all options short of statehood, the Albanians would accept nothing but independence. Under these circumstances, Ahtisaari put forward a settlement proposal in which he proposed 'supervised independence'. The difference in this case was that it would not be decided by the parties in separate and simultaneous referenda. Instead, the Security Council would take the final decision. Indeed, it was notable that when the Russian Foreign Minister, Sergey Lavrov, proclaimed that the Ahtisaari proposals had failed, in April 2007, he deliberately created a link with Cyprus by directly comparing the peace-making approach used in both cases. As he explained following discussion with the Serbian Prime Minister, Vojislav Koštunica:

> Certain efforts by the international community to resolve conflicts, such as a plan on the Cyprus settlement or Ahtisaari's plan have failed.... In both cases, the failure was caused by attempts to adopt unilateral decisions and to ignore the interests of all concerned sides. (*RIA-Novosti*, 19 April 2007)

Thus it appears as though the attempt to eschew democratic processes on the ground will now be stymied by the representative voice of international opinion, the UN Security Council.

For all these reasons, it may well be the case that the experiment in 'arbitrated mediation' is likely to be short lived. While it may appear to be a logical way to break the deadlock in long-standing conflicts, it ultimately lacks legitimacy. In fact, one could even argue that 'arbitrated mediation' is designed more to manage the frustrations of external actors – by imposing peace agreements on the sides and thus 'ending' conflict – than to find a more efficient way to broker peace agreements between conflicting parties. For better or worse, in the case of Cyprus, it therefore appears almost certain that the future will see a return to the traditional forms of mediation.

Notes

1 UN Security Council, S/6253, 26 March 1965.
2 UN Security Council, S/10199, 20 May 1971.
3 UN Resolution 541, 18 November 1983.
4 UN Security Council, S/18102/Add.1, 11 June 1986.
5 UN Security Council, S/23121, 8 October 1991.
6 UN Security Council, S/23780, 2 April 1992: paras 17–25 and 27.
7 UN Resolution 750, 12 April 1992.
8 UN Security Council, S/24472, 24 August 1992.

Part III

Cyprus in comparative perspective

9

Compromising with facts, clashing with norms? Revisiting territoriality and sovereignty in Cyprus, Moldova and Bosnia

Eiki Berg

Introduction

> How and when will Kosovo become Europe's newest state? These are questions that European and American diplomats are grappling with at the United Nations. What they are not doing is wasting time debating whether Kosovo should be independent – for it is too late to stop it. (*The Economist*, 22 March 2007)

During Kosovo's final status talks in 2006–07, it became clear that Kosovars would accept nothing less than independence, which the Serbian government was highly reluctant to offer. Despite these contrasting positions, the international community has largely come to accept the Kosovar view that there could be no return to Kosovo's status quo ante, but at the same time it rejected the notion of Kosovo's partition or its union with any other country. Will the Kosovo campaign for independence set a precedent for other breakaway regions? Will it change the notions of self determination and sovereignty in other secessionist conflicts? Will a redefinition of self-determination and sovereignty influence externally imposed or induced power-sharing arrangements? And above all, will it alter the normative international framework which prioritises the preservation of existing state borders?

The answers to all these questions are interlinked and will emerge in the years to come. They all relate to the tensions between facts and norms. In particular, they touch upon sensitive territoriality issues, which seem to have retained their salience despite the much-acclaimed shift away from modernity in international relations in the late twentieth and early twenty-first centuries. Indeed, claims to statehood persist unabated in all corners of the globe. In June 2006, the state of Montenegro was established and recognised after its successful referendum on independence in May that year. This encouraged other non-recognised entities to pursue their claims to recognition through plebiscites. Transnistrians voted on independence and free association with Russia in September 2006. South Ossetia held a referendum on independence in November 2006. And Nagorno-Karabakh adopted a new constitution affirming independence in December 2006. Unlike the case of Montenegro, however, the results of these plebiscites were considered null and void by the international community. Kosovo and Montenegro continue to represent the exception rather than the rule in the international community's stance and thinking about sovereignty and territory.

Although the original Wilsonian solution to the problem of self-determination was precisely that of referendum (Mayall, 1999), Allen Buchanan explains how and why the international community shifted away from this position. He argues that 'the chief justifications for democratic governance within given political boundaries do not support the thesis that boundaries may be redrawn by majority vote' (Buchanan, 2004: 378). Rather than majority approval by one community, broad-brush consensus is normally viewed as being necessary to legitimise and recognise secession. While reasonable at face value, this position has also led to paradoxical situations whereby formerly seceding parties opt for reintegration and reunification, yet their wish may remain a dead letter if the proposal is rejected by the majority community in the metropolitan state. The case of Cyprus in 2004, when 65 per cent of the Turkish Cypriots voted in favour of reunification while 76 per cent of the Greek Cypriots rejected it, forcefully illustrates this point.

Granting international recognition to a breakaway state can no doubt trigger a domino effect in other conflict areas. These fundamental preoccupations of political order and stability underpin the international community's resistance to secession. Yet the shortcomings of existing post-conflict power-sharing arrangements have also been a disincentive for secessionist entities to renounce their claims to *de jure* recognition. This leads to a dilemma. On the one hand, the international community has no interest in modifying existing norms in favour of territorial integrity. On the other hand, neither secessionist entities nor metropolitan states are seriously interested in operationalising complex power-sharing arrangements within existing state borders. Hence, quasi-states (Kolstoe, 2006), *de facto* states (Pegg, 1998) or states within states (Kingston and Spears, 2004) persist, and increasingly widen the gap between facts and norms in the international system.

Sovereignty is a limited property with a strong normative dimension which cannot automatically follow on from empirical facts on the ground. Yet this chapter argues that when post-modern power-sharing solutions to secessionist conflicts are developed and proposed within a modern framework prioritising the territorial integrity of existing states, the gap between facts and norms often remains unbridged. In other words, proposed power-sharing models often legitimise modern solutions rather than transcend them. As such, they do little to erase the zero-sum logic bedevilling ethnic conflicts. The results are often far from satisfactory. Either a *de facto* frozen status quo persists outside the confines of international legality, as illustrated by the cases of Cyprus and Moldova, or a power-sharing agreement within existing state boundaries is imposed by the international community, but one which fails to satisfy the demands of the conflict parties, as demonstrated by the case of Bosnia, in which the *de facto* states in the loose federation persist in seeking greater internal and external recognition while the central authority refuses to renounce its claims over its lost territories and competences.

A normative interpretation of sovereignty

Robert Jackson (1999: 10) defined sovereignty as 'a constitutional arrangement of political life', which should not be viewed as natural, inevitable or even immutable. More substantively, to be sovereign means to have absolute authority over a specified territory without interference by outsiders. In other words, territory is a vital prerequisite of statehood and control over territory represents 'the spatial expression of power' (Storey, 2001: 14). Precisely because of the importance of territory, some actors engage in ethnic engineering and national construction efforts aiming to control portions of space, while being resisted, often violently, by others who attribute equal importance to the same piece of land. Most actors accept there can be only a single governmental jurisdiction over a particular territory, and view sceptically joint government with others, hence the prevailing scepticism among parties to various conflicts regarding the power-sharing arrangements enthusiastically embraced by external mediators.

Territory and territoriality continue to play a key role in international relations and international law. The principle of territoriality upholds the territorial integrity of sovereign states by demanding respect for their existing borders (Jackson, 1999: 25). Although many have argued that information and communications technology has reduced the importance of territoriality, rendering sovereignty more complex and multifaceted, Spears (2004: 19) correctly notes that 'there is a certain irony that at the moment technology has reduced the importance of territory, international law continues to uphold the boundaries of existing states'. Indeed, even as sovereignty becomes increasingly fictive and states devolve competences to supra-state and sub-state levels, territory continues to play an important role, partly because it continues to provide a spatial locus for the exercise of political authority.

Yet territoriality remains an insufficient condition of sovereign statehood. Territorial control alone helps little in providing statehood with the legal attributes of sovereignty so long as international recognition remains elusive. In other words, international law entrenches a black-and-white notion of sovereignty: an actor either is or is not sovereign in international law, and no shades of grey are possible (James, 1999: 41). This is because sovereignty is determined not only by effective control over a given territory, but also and most crucially by the recognition and legitimisation of the international community of states. In the past, the recognition of state sovereignty depended almost entirely upon a state's control over territory, as stated in article 1 of the 1933 Montevideo Convention on the Rights and Duties of States (Kurtulus, 2005: 88). Accordingly, entities were recognised as sovereign states as and when other states accepted their fulfilment of the territoriality criteria and treated them as sovereign. Since the second half of the twentieth century, however, normative standards have changed (Jackson, 1999), and less attention is paid now than in the inter-war period to the factual attributes of sovereignty. It is not only facts that determine the formal recognition of statehood, but rather it is a set of *a priori* norms that create and determine ensuing facts on the ground (Aalberts, 2004). In this way, sovereignty becomes a limited property, with rights and powers emerging from recognised sovereign status rather than the possession of *de facto* sovereignty entrenching those rights and powers (Grant, 1999; Kurtulus, 2005). This shift from empirical statehood to juridical statehood follows from the reality that recognition represents a political decision, and is not the automatic product of facts on the ground. In other words, as Kurtulus (2005: 2) argues, a state's status as 'a subject under international law' has 'clear political implications', implying also that international law does not, by definition, universally and impartially attribute sovereignty to all actors equally and on the same merits.

According to international law, the right of self-determination today applies only to colonies that are separated from their metropoles by sea (Bartmann, 2004: 20). This normative approach in international law discourages small polities from seeking statehood as a means to guarantee stability (Buchanan, 1991). According to Buchanan (2004: 331), 'international law should recognise only a remedial right to secede (when it is the last resort against serious injustices) but not a general right of self-determination that includes the right to secede for all peoples or nations'. In other words, legal arrangements as well as normative arguments are not always 'based on fairness but instead on convenience and prudence'. This entails that many communities are arbitrarily denied recognition as sovereign states (Jackson, 1999: 32). In short, current legal and normative doctrine forbids *de jure* recognition to those territorial units whose political leadership has been successfully resisted by metropolitan central authorities.

Yet as a matter of political fact, the world is rife with legally recognised states that lack effective control over territory and *de facto* territorial entities that are denied the legal attributes of sovereignty. This 'new sovereignty game' encompasses many political entities. Some do not meet the traditional tests of empirical statehood and probably would not exist as sovereign states were it not for their legal recognition by others (Jackson, 1990). This 'juridical approach to statehood simply allows one to overlook empirical aspects of statehood that are clearly deficient in much of the developing world' (Spears, 2004: 17). At the same time, some entities that have empirical existence on the ground are denied external recognition, due to a preoccupation in international law to fix borders and forbid territorial change.

As noted above, the international community values stability and order, and because of this there is little reason to expect a sudden demise of this normative framework. This notwithstanding, sovereignty remains a constructed political arrangement, which by definition can be rethought and redefined. Indeed, a rethinking of sovereignty is in order precisely because of the growing reality of weak yet internationally recognised states experiencing secessionist conflicts that have, in turn, generated empirically viable yet illegal states. So far this rethink has focused on ideas about federalism and power-sharing, induced or coerced by internationally mediated negotiations. It has led either to 'an uneasy coexistence and symbiosis between the state and substate' (Kingston and Spears, 2004: 7) or to extremely loose forms of federalism in which the vestiges of statehood are retained yet internal self-rule is predominant (Dent, 2004: 3). However, it may be argued that these activities have unwittingly contributed to state- and nation-building practices in *de facto* states (Kolstoe, 2006). Furthermore, these arrangements are often viewed as highly unsatisfactory by all conflict parties, rendering them inherently unstable. These shortcomings exist because power-sharing arrangements within the confines of territorial integrity fit into and do not attempt to alter the current sovereignty regime in international relations. In the sections that follow, this argument is developed empirically by considering the cases of Bosnia, Moldova and Cyprus.

A *de jure* quasi-federation: compromising between Bosnian facts and international norms

Because of the enduring compromises between facts and norms, we are faced with 'an absurd combination of states and would-be states in a legal fog' (Bartmann, 2004: 12). Is there a way out that seeks alternatives to the traditional political order by adhering to modern conceptions of borders and statehood while promoting post-modern solutions to modern conflicts (Diez, 2002d)? This route has certainly been explored, and for good reason. First, *de facto* states cannot be easily erased and are often relatively effective in providing stability and communal security internally, making the retention of their effective powers both likely and to some extent desirable. Second, retaining internal sovereignty within a larger independent country (Dent, 2004) could represent an acceptable substitute to the independence of secessionist entities, given that international norms deny legal secession. Yet the case of Bosnia illustrates that the result of these compromises is often a *de jure* quasi-federation (Berg, 2007), in which a federal-like structure is externally imposed yet remains largely dysfunctional in view of its internal make-up and incentive structure.

After its declaration of independence in 1991, Bosnia and Herzegovina (BiH) was unable to secure the empirical properties of statehood insofar as it lacked an effective government and a clearly defined territory. The final settlement of the conflict (1992–95) entailed a *de facto* partition of the territory. The Dayton agreement maintained the 51:49 per cent division between the Federation of Bosnia and Herzegovina and the Republika Srpska (RS). At the same time, the RS became the symbol of 'aborted statehood' (Zahar, 2004: 32). Its constitution in fact reads in many respects as that of a recognised state, declaring that the RS would be 'the State of Serb people and of all its citizens, and that the territory of the Republic shall be unique, indivisible and unalienable'. Insofar as the Dayton agreement virtually created the RS as a state within a state – a status the majority of Bosnian Serbs are determined to preserve – the hope was that formal partition would not be necessary or desirable for the Bosnian Serb people.

The Dayton agreement which ended the war, thus established an independent Bosnian state. Yet they also stipulated that the central state would have only the theoretical power to govern, insofar as it would function under the control and supervision of the Office of the High Representative (representing the members of the Peace Implementation Council), and most public competences would be delegated to the regional entities comprising the central state; moreover, the regional level would enjoy extensive veto rights over the centre (Bieber, 2006b: 47). More specifically, the regional entities would possess all residual powers and functions, and would be empowered to establish and develop special relationships with neighbouring states (Bose, 2002: 44). This decentralised (con)federal government with two semi-independent regional entities would thus represent 'a conception of diffuse and layered sovereignty' (Bose, 2002: 62) and allow multiple forms and levels of citizenship. Yet by doing so, the Dayton agreement achieved two contrasting effects. On the one hand, post-Dayton Bosnia has acted as an undivided territory and state as far as international law is concerned. On the other hand, however, the disaggregation of power in favour of the regions has encouraged the RS to strive for independent statehood and to prepare the local population for self-determination. The architects of Dayton thus succeeded in securing a settlement, but largely failed in creating a single multi-ethnic country with functioning state structures sovereignly governing the country.

The current weakness of federal institutions in BiH, as well as the diverging interests of the main actors in the country, cast doubt on the solidity of this arrangement. Concrete developments and progress have usually come about through external pressure rather than domestic will and consensus. The vast majority of the country's citizens, belonging to two of the three constituent communities, still contest BiH as a united state (Bieber, 2006b: 45–9). The majority of the Serb population feels reluctant to engage in Bosnian state-building, and continues to prefer either independence for the RS or uniting with Serbia. Likewise, parts of the Croat population either support irredentism towards Croatia or the establishment of another political entity in Bosnia – a state within state for the local Croats. Most Bosniaks refuse to acknowledge an equal treatment of aggressors and victims, and thus demand a new and more centralised constitution to replace the Dayton agreement. They support civic state- and nation-building, which would abolish the RS, considered as a bitter remembrance of the war.

The present Dayton constitution is a combination of state- and peace-building efforts articulated through imported power-sharing arrangements (Bieber, 2002). The belief that change in the current status quo is necessary is now largely shared by all internal and external actors. The unresolved questions are how, and in what direction? Today, among the three constituent peoples in BiH, the Bosniaks are in the strongest position to abandon the Dayton constitution and propose a more centralised and cohesive set-up. A draft constitution on the website of the Party for Bosnia and Herzegovina (SBiH), and presented by Ćazim Sadiković, Omer Ibrahimagić and Zlatko Hadzidedic at the tenth anniversary of the Dayton agreement, suggests the establishment of a sovereign and indivisible state with regions that 'may not violate the sovereignty of the State by assuming any of its sovereign prerogatives', and where 'ethnic identity, or any other collective identity, may not serve as a basis for any territorial, legal, political, social or economic privilege or for any form of discrimination, on individual or on collective level'.[1] The argument is that, as it stands, the present constitution will set barriers along Bosnia's path to accession to the European Union (EU) insofar as it is doubtful whether the weak and decentralised state can implement the broad range of rules and measures the EU requires for membership (Hays and Crosby, 2006). Hence the party's leaders have agreed to engage in negotiations about the reform of state institutions, implying an amendment rather than replacement of the Dayton constitution (Hitchner, 2006b). In arguing their case, the Bosniaks make reference to the EU's requirements. In the EU accession framework, Brussels has made conclusion of BiH's Stabilisation and Association Agreement conditional upon internal police reform and the adoption of constitutional amendments (the so-called 'April Package'). Sharing the positions of many Bosniaks, Brussels would prefer to see central structures strengthened at the expense of the sub-state entities, which currently operate virtually as separate countries.

European and international pressure seems to be having some effect. Under international community pressure, Bosnian politicians signed a declaration of intent to implement the constitutional reforms, and vowed to complete the process by the end of March 2006. The parties agreed to establish two new state-level ministries, to delegate more decision-making powers to the central Council of Ministers and to improve the scrutiny of human rights by the federal level.

This notwithstanding, the bulk of the constitutional reform remains paralysed. The reform of the two chambers of parliament, to reduce the powers of the tripartite presidency and eliminate the system of rotation, has remained unresolved (Dayton Project, 2006). Previously agreed amendments by Bosnian political parties and the three principal communities, with the support of the EU and the United States, have remained a dead letter as they failed to garner the necessary support of two-thirds of the House of Representatives of BiH's parliament. Today, the debate over the 'April Package' is practically frozen.

The international community (in particular, US Ambassador Douglas McElhaney and other US diplomats) still pushes the parliament to adopt the once-rejected April Package. Yet virtually all actors in BiH reject the amendments, for radically different reasons. In Bosnia, the SBiH won the last national elections because of its rejection of the April Package, claiming that its amendments legitimised the current constitution by maintaining the voting rights of the separate ethnic entities and favouring the dissolution of the country. The parties in the RS, meanwhile, have coordinated their views around a joint platform: 'yes' to constitutional change but 'no' to any reduction in the entities' powers (Council of Europe, 2006). Their proposal is that, in return for the long-term recognition of the RS's status, Bosnian Serbs would work towards reforming and upgrading the structures at the centre. Hence as and when Bosniaks call for abolishment of the RS they are punctually met by Serbian replies threatening a referendum on secession. The Serbs in Bosnia remain fearful of being politically outnumbered and marginalised in a unitary state based on purely civic values. They seek acceptance of the loose federal structure (and in particular of the RS's status) as a guarantee for their political survival (Hitchner, 2006a). In September 2006, Bosnian Serbs signed a 'special ties agreement' with Belgrade, aimed at promoting economic and institutional cooperation between Serbia and the RS (Council of Europe, 2006). In this light, statements such as 'the Serb people do not see their future in Bosnia' (Dervisbegovic, 2006) or 'Serbia may be plotting to annex large tracts of Bosnia if Belgrade loses the southern province of Kosovo' (Traynor, 2006) clearly express persistent secessionist and irredentist sentiments.

Bosnian society is thus divided over the most basic issues: state legitimacy, the nature of common institutions and the definition of borders (Bieber, 2006c). The eventual settlement of the Bosnia dispute between Serbs, Croats and Bosniaks came about through international coercion, and the post-war state was created as 'a legal fiction' (Bose, 2002: 25): it exists only because both its Croat and its Serb citizens are forbidden from joining their mother countries. As highlighted above, in most policy areas power-sharing has failed to operate effectively, as the 'institutional set-up highlights the problematic link between veto rights and decentralisation of power' (Bieber, 2006a: 20). These power-sharing mechanisms are expected to work through consensual decision-making among 13 prime ministers, almost 100 ministers and about 800 representatives in the parliaments on state, entity and cantonal levels. Far from engendering effective governance, these mechanisms have reinforced ethnic divides and prevented the creation of multiple identities and hence loyalty to the state (Marko, 2006). Without either a sense of civic identity or multiple identities, it seems highly unlikely that the constituent peoples of Bosnia will find a common *raison d'être*.

Post-modern solutions for modern conflicts in Cyprus and Moldova

Since the recognition of their independence, both Cyprus and Moldova have been divided for far longer than they have been united. After the establishment of the Republic of Cyprus in 1960, violence erupted in 1963, leading to the ensuing physical separation of the two communities. The Turkish Cypriots were driven into enclaves, where they continued to live intermittently until 1974, when the Turkish military intervened and took control of the northern part of the island (Kyle, 1997). The Turkish Republic of Northern Cyprus (TRNC) was proclaimed in 1983 with the aim of providing security for the Turkish Cypriots.

In Moldova, the process of emancipation from the Soviet centre brought with it violent clashes, during which pro-independence Moldovans came into conflict with the so-called *soyuzniki*, representing different ethnic communities (Russians, Ukrainians and Russified Moldovans), who resided on the left bank of river Dniester. The first armed clashes between Transnistrian separatists and Moldovan police units occurred in November 1990, a few months after the proclamation of the Transnistrian Moldovan Republic (TMR). Fighting intensified in 1992, when a large-scale military operation involving the Russian 14th batallion took control of the city of Tighina/Bendery; this ultimately led to the *de facto* partition of the country (CSCE Mission to Moldova, 1994).

Since 1975, when inter-communal talks began in Cyprus, both conflict parties have continuously declared their support for an independent, non-aligned and bicommunal federal republic, with independence and territorial integrity adequately guaranteed against Cyprus's partition, or union in whole or in part with any other country (Groom, 1993). These views were reflected in the High Level Agreements of 1977 and 1979 as well as in the 'Set of Ideas', proposed by the Secretary-General of the United Nations (UN), Boutros Boutros-Ghali, in 1989 (see chapter 8). But when it came to moving beyond general principles and signing a detailed peace deal, problems abounded. The difficulty lay in the sensitivity of the Greek Cypriots to anything which might appear to constitute a recognition of the state in northern Cyprus, and the sensitivity of the Turkish Cypriots to anything which might seem to be recognising the Greek-Cypriot authorities as the government of Cyprus (Kyle, 1997). Beyond both parties' rhetorical support for a loose federation, the Greek Cypriots in practice favoured a centralised federation or unitary state, whereas the Turkish Cypriots favoured a confederation (Bindebir et al., 2003). This is principally because of the Turkish Cypriots' fear that they might become an impoverished minority within a Greek-dominated state, and the Greek Cypriots' fear that the TRNC might become a sovereign state inextricably linked to Turkey.

Also in Moldova, a peace agreement has proved elusive. Although the details of the different peace proposals, memoranda and draft agreements have changed over time, the nature of the debate, and in particular the dilemma of whether a solution should be federal or confederal, has remained unchanged (Roper, 2004a). Initially, Moldovan leaders insisted on the principle of territorial integrity, while the breakaway TMR demanded a federation consisting of two sub-state entities with equal rights (Neukirch, 2003). However, when Moldova proposed a special legal statute of autonomy, with considerable rights for self-government for Transnistria, in 1995, the TMR leadership rejected this, and attempted instead to consolidate its statehood and sought external recognition. According to Steven Roper (2004b), the Transnistrian interpretation of power-sharing is characterised by the equality of the constituent parts, agreed and ratified through a state-to-state treaty, both features which are vehemently resisted in Chişinău, the Moldovan capital. One could in fact argue that many Moldovans even oppose a genuine federalisation of the country, while Transnistria holds that any solution should involve the creation of a confederal state (Protsyk, 2005).

Several scholars argue that 'post-modernisation would allow for a sustainable solution to the territorial conflicts over sovereignty and identity' (Diez, 2002a: 8). When minorities are protected and regions recognised as political subjects, territory should in principle lose significance and borders become less important in view of increasing cross-border flows. Rory Keane (2002) presents an equally challenging approach to modern conflict resolution in arguing that the nation state is an anachronism. He sees the solution to these conflicts in the 'disaggregation of power from the centre and in simultaneous emancipation of peoples' (Keane, 2002: 3). His theoretical escape route challenges modern definitions of sovereignty, territoriality and exclusive identities.

In our case studies, both the UN-sponsored Annan Plan (named after former UN Secretary-General Kofi Annan) for Cyprus and the Kozak Memorandum (named after the Deputy Head of the Russian Presidential Administration Dmitry Kozak) for Moldova included post-modernisation approaches, in that they attempted to disperse sovereignty and replace the power configurations created under the Westphalian model (Berg, 2006). On the one hand, both plans provided for a single international personality, sovereignty and citizenship, thus safeguarding the independence and territorial integrity of the metropolitan states. On the other hand, both plans included strong power-sharing elements, intended to establish politically equal constituent states in a loose (con)federal structure. According to the Annan Plan, sovereignty would be shared and would not lie exclusively in one level of government.[2] Instead, both levels would 'sovereignly' exercise the powers granted to them by the constitution, in a non-hierarchical fashion (Tocci and Kovziridze, 2004). Similarly, according to the Kozak Memorandum, the new federation in Moldova would be considered a subject of international law, but its federated entities could become members of international organisations, maintain international relations and conclude international treaties on their own.[3] The Memorandum was strongly criticised by many observers, who pointed out that the proposed federal structures would lack any control mechanism over the federated entities insofar as law-enforcement powers rested in the latter rather than the former (ADEPT, 2003).

In the Annan Plan and the Kozak Memorandum, the proposed status of the TRNC and the TMR was upgraded compared with earlier proposals. Both were supposed to become state entities within the new federation (similarly to the RS in BiH), which would establish their own state structures with their own constitutions, state properties, independent budget and tax systems, and also with their own state symbols and other attributes of statehood. As opposed to BiH, however, these proposed post-modern escape routes in Cyprus and Moldova did not provide an exit from the vicious circle of conflict. This was primarily because both parties continued to view sovereignty and territoriality essentially as indivisible, despite the proposed power-sharing mechanisms. In both conflicts, each constituent state/federal subject was supposed to have a fixed territory and clearly defined boundaries. Each was granted treaty-making powers as a further form of recognition of their national self-determination rights. In terms of individual rights and communal security, however, a modernist discourse of absolute sovereignty and statehood prevailed in the plans proposed for both Cyprus and Moldova. The provisions concerning Turkish immigrants and the freedoms of movement, settlement and property all had strong implications regarding the indivisibility of territory and sovereignty in Cyprus. As put by Stavrinides (2006): 'for Greek Cypriots to be asked to share control of the Republic with Turkish Cypriots might have been a painful necessity in the best of times; but to accept a power-sharing arrangement at the time when there were Turkish troops and settlers in Cyprus was too high a price for Greek Cypriots to pay'. Likewise in Moldova, the public perceived that the acceptance of power-sharing represented a defeatist position and threatened the sovereignty and unity of the country, particularly in view of the presence of Russian troops in the TMR (Protsyk, 2005: 76).

The Annan Plan was put to referenda in the two parts of partitioned Cyprus on 24 April 2004. The proposed deal sought an uneasy compromise, in which power-sharing would be established within a loose (con)federation that would create favourable conditions for sovereignty and territoriality to lose significance. But the proposed gamble did not convince the Greek Cypriots, who overwhelmingly rejected the Annan Plan. The Kozak Memorandum was initially accepted by the Moldovans, but soon thereafter, when large protest meetings were organised to reject the Kremlin's unilateral peace deal, the Moldovan President, Vladimir Voronin, declined to sign. In both cases, the *de facto* states found themselves in a position whereby the proposed conditions of a final settlement were largely satisfactory, but were ultimately rejected by the metropolitan states in view of their power-sharing elements. These power-sharing and decentralisation elements were not dissimilar to those instituted in post-war BiH. The Dayton agreement provided a model for international mediators. Yet that example also encourages *de facto* states to legitimise their existence and reaffirm their claims to sovereignty. Aware of this, they are lukewarm in their acceptance of these deals, and the partitioned metropolitan states are disinclined to pursue these solutions without further guarantees to their sovereignty and territorial integrity.

This seemed to be the case in Cyprus, where, since 2004, the Greek-populated south enjoys EU membership and veto rights over all matters that may come close to implying the recognition of the TRNC. Hence lifting the EU trade embargo on the north or opening Ercan airport for international aviation are matters requiring the sovereign consent of the Greek-Cypriot member state, consent which is regularly denied by Cyprus within the EU. The Greek-Cypriot post-Annan Plan 'osmosis strategy', intending to re-integrate Turkish-Cypriot citizens within the Greek-Cypriot state and society, exemplifies the Greek-Cypriot rejection of power-sharing and denotes the Greek-Cypriot sense of power over the Turkish Cypriots, given their enjoyment of sovereign rights within the EU (Ercakica, 2006). Power-sharing is off the agenda for the Greek Cypriots, who, as the Turkish Cypriots regularly complain, have effectively abandoned serious contact and dialogue since Cyprus's accession to the EU.

In Moldova, there are strong fears of falling deep into Russia's security, economic and linguistic sphere of influence. Under the banner of the 'common state', another proposed reunification plan foresees the preservation of Moldovan territorial integrity in exchange for the legalisation of the TMR regime (Nantoi, 2005). Moreover, in April 2007, there were some rumours that Russia may be pushing Moldova to sign a joint political document with the TMR. The plan set out in that document would see: a dissolution of the Moldovan parliament and the Transnistrian Supreme Soviet, the election of a new Moldovan parliament with a guaranteed quota for deputies from Transnistria, Transnistrian representatives being given a quota within the Moldovan government, guarantees of a neutral status for Moldova, and the continued presence of Russian troops in Moldova for at least another two or three years.[4] Were this document to come into force, a post-modern power-sharing solution would be unilaterally imposed by Russia against the will of majority Moldovans, who consider federalisation as the legitimisation of the TMR's statehood. Having observed the Cyprus precedent, Moldovans are now inclined to settle their conflict at a later date, when the power configuration in the conflict may have shifted in Moldova's favour (Popescu, 2004).

Territoriality and sovereignty unbundled?

The international community in general does not support secessionist entities in their search for recognition. Instead, many attempts have been made to find workable compromises between facts and norms by establishing sovereign lands within larger independent countries. These power-sharing arrangements set within (con)federal structures maintain the territorial integrity and single international personality of the metropolitan states while following a 'confederal' logic in terms of internal decision-making procedures and competence allocation. One may argue that this is a compromise between those who aspire to self-determination without achieving international recognition and those who enjoy *de jure* recognition without in practice exercising sovereignty over lost territories. These compromises usually represent post-conflict settlements imposed or strongly induced by outside powers, while not satisfying conflict parties equally. If and when these settlements are reached, their power-sharing arrangements turn out to be dysfunctional because of an encoded fatal error encapsulated by the lack of political will of the conflict parties themselves. The absence of political will translates into dysfunctionality in state and society, through power-sharing mechanisms that grant veto rights to all parties at federal level, through the definition of separate territories within the state, and through citizens whose primary allegiance remains to their own community. All conflict parties in the post-settlement stage remain committed to a belief in 'one state, one sovereignty and one citizenship', despite the assiduously promoted concepts of 'constituent peoples, constituent states and treaty-based unions' by international mediators.

Although these post-modern settlements are based on the merits of diffused power and fuzzy identities, they do not offer a recipe to end zero-sum logics or to provide communal security. They cannot provide a new normative legal framework either, given their internal inconsistency. On the one hand, these solutions rely on the notion of territorial integrity and fixed borders at federal level, while, on the other hand, they promote the erosion of internal divisions and group boundaries. As illustrated by the Dayton agreement, while squaring the vicious circle underpinning modern conflicts is theoretically possible, post-modern solutions in practice have not made territoriality irrelevant, and nor have they given rise to shared sovereignty and the erosion of group boundaries. Power-sharing is premised on the will of the parties to compromise and work together, but the federal representatives of the three Bosnian ethnic groups have not demonstrated such will. Relying on a strategy of control and influence, ethnic claims to territory have created new conditions for conflict in BiH and imposed new internal boundaries, despite the hope of an escape route from the Westphalian sovereignty regime.

Cyprus and Moldova, *de facto* partitioned states with two functioning administrative apparatuses and economies, have not been able to reach a compromise between facts and norms, because each side securitises territoriality and sovereignty and perceives the future in zero-sum terms. With the implementation of federal solutions, the central governments of Cyprus and Moldova would have to grant legal status to and reduce their control over the federal entities of the TRNC and the TMR. This is what they have learned from the dysfunctional state apparatus of BiH, which has reduced their willingness to renounce their recognised sovereign status, imparted by favourable and biased international legal conditions.

Unlike the cases of Cyprus and Moldova and more similar to the case of Bosnia, the international community has sought a quick compromise in Kosovo, this time, however, bending its normative interpretation of sovereignty and territoriality. The recognition of Kosovo's independence, in contravention of existing UN resolutions, would split the international community, though.

At the same time, shelving Kosovo's independence for the time being also risks causing a major backlash among Kosovo's Albanians, whose expectations of independence are sky-high (*The Economist*, 1 June 2007). It is these considerations, rather than Belgrade's modernist views of sovereignty and territorial integrity, that will determine the international community's response and adaptation of its own normative benchmarks.

Notes

1 The constitution of Bosnia and Herzegovina, draft (2006), available at www.zabih.ba/downloads/19_2.pdf.
2 See the Comprehensive Settlement of the Cyprus Problem, 31 March 2004, at www.cyprus.gov.cy/moi/PIO/PIO.nsf/0/BF93317E0BF0EEF3C2256E6F0030BD70/$file/The%20Annan%20plan%20%205%20-%2031%20march%202004.pdf.
3 See the Russian Draft Memorandum on the Basic Principles of the State Structure of a United State in Moldova, 2003 (Kozak Memorandum), at http://eurojournal.org/more.php?id=107_0_1_6_M5.
4 See 'Russia's New Proposals on Transnistrian Conflict Settlement', 11 April 2007, at www.transnistria.md/en/news/o/246/20.

10

The European Union's competency in conflict resolution: the cases of Bosnia, Macedonia and Cyprus

Emel Akçali[1]

Introduction

Unlike compromises achieved through brokered or imposed bargains, successful conflict resolution through third-party intervention should try to reach agreements which are likely to generate the parties' long-term commitment to a negotiated solution and transform the relationship between them.[2] Through such agreements and the new relationships they engender, conflict resolution aims to be 'conducive to stable peace, mutually enhancing cooperation and ultimate reconciliation' (Kelman, 2004: 112). Conflict resolution is thus not a strategy to use the power of authority to dictate outcomes in a conflict. This would be rather conflict regulation, settlement or management, but not resolution proper (Avruch, 1998: 82). Realists and structuralists in fact argue that there is no room for resolution in conflicts between irreconcilable interests, for which instead power and coercion are the name of the game (Miall et al., 2005: 6–7). Attempted conflict resolution may thus only prolong the fighting and prevent durable peace following a clear-cut military victory by one side (Miall et al., 2005: 6).

The use of force by military intervention has proved helpful in stopping bloodshed in violent conflicts and freezing the situation, thus preventing violence from spreading. However, liberals and critical theorists reply that such interventions have not been successful *per se* in bringing about a viable peace: 'Coercive action treats the symptoms, at worst, by merely suppressing them but rarely treats the underlying pathologies' (Avruch, 1998: 83). They have thus suggested that conflict resolution should deal with the socio-psychological process of conflict, by delving into its root causes, particularly in the form of unmet or threatened needs regarding identity, security, recognition, autonomy and justice; in this way, conflict resolution offers a critical approach to peace-building and peace-making (Burton, 1990; Kelman, 2004). New approaches in conflict resolution have also argued that to achieve lasting peace, the incompatibilities at the heart of a conflict need to be transformed, and this requires broader societal changes in terms of the definition of identities and interests (Diez and Pace, 2007: 3). Conflict resolution efforts by a third party should thus aim at the transformation of conflict to enable actors to change the way they see themselves and relate to each other, thereby eliminating the prospects for the use of violence (see Diez et al., 2006: 565–6).

Conflict resolution in western Europe in the aftermath of the Second World War was, in fact, one of the core ambitions underpinning the creation of the European Community (EC). Its accomplishment through democratic, economic and political means has given rise to the much-quoted process of 'Europeanisation' within, between and beyond member states of the European Union (EU). Despite this, the EU has acted as a third party in conflict resolution only recently. Given that most of the intractable conflicts in Asia, Africa or the Middle East are arguably the results of the policies of European colonial powers – reflecting their bias and preferences – there have always been strong internal and international pressures to bestow upon the Union its responsibilities towards conflict resolution beyond its frontiers. However, it is only during the post-Cold War era that global interdependencies have enhanced the role of non-military powers such as the EU or international financial institutions in world affairs. Moreover, the post-Cold War era has witnessed the eruption of numerous inter-communal conflicts. In contrast to theories based on religion or 'civilisations' (Huntington, 2002), the root causes of these conflicts reflect more traditional lines of divide: competing claims to sovereignty, self-determination and territory, state formation, power-sharing, control over scarce resources and socio-economic exclusion (Lederach, 2004). Most of these post-Cold War conflicts are intra-state ones and as such are marked by the immediacy of having the enemy next door. However, these conflicts still pose a challenge to the search for global security and the defence of universal human values (Crocker et al., 2003).

The decisive events that have prompted the EU to invest in conflict resolution beyond its borders have been two violent inter-communal and intra-state conflicts: Bosnia in the Balkans and Rwanda in sub-Saharan Africa, as well as the political unrest in the Maghreb throughout the 1990s. In addition to the brutality of these conflicts, the flows of refugees and illegal migrants and the surge of organised crime and terrorism they created spilled over into the EU and jeopardised European foreign investments and trade, setting off alarm bells across the Union. The EU chose to develop its conflict resolution capacities by investing in conflict prevention. As early as 1992, at the Lisbon European Council, conflict prevention was stated as an objective of EU Common Foreign and Security Policy (CFSP), insofar as prevention was qualified as the most feasible way for the EU to ensure security both outside and inside its territory. Dealing with violent conflicts was not viewed as a practical option for the EU, both because of institutional shortcomings and because of a lack of political will (Smith, 2004: 145). CFSP-making takes place through the inclusion of a variety of actors, such as the Commission, the Presidency and the High Representative, and its decisions tend to be largely disassociated from the member states. Furthermore, the EU was already well versed in conflict prevention, having acquired fifty years of experience in managing relations between its members. Democratisation, demilitarisation, socio-economic development, regional cooperation and the entrenchment and respect for human rights have in fact become the priorities of European foreign policy in theory, and emphasis has been placed on fostering political engagement and dialogue in practice.

Several EU conflict prevention initiatives have been launched since the 1990s. The 'Barcelona Process', established in 1995 between EU member states and twelve southern Mediterranean countries, aiming to foster economic development, democracy and political stability and to minimise the potential for conflict and illegal immigration, can be said to be one of the first major non-coercive EU efforts at conflict prevention. EU non-coercive conflict prevention initiatives were followed by the Stability Pact for South-Eastern Europe (SPSEE),[3] adopted in June 1999 after the Kosovo war, followed by the Stabilisation and Association Process (SAP), which included Stabilisation and Association Agreements (SAAs) and the Community Assistance and Reconstruction Development and Stabilisation (CARDS) programme. However, in December 2001, the EU added a coercive character to its conflict resolution strategy. At its Laeken meeting in December 2001, the European Council operationalised the European Security and Defence Policy (ESDP) through the Rapid Reaction Mechanism (RRM) and Rapid Reaction Forces (RRF), consisting of national armed forces ready for a rapid deployment in high-risk conflict areas. These ESDP mechanisms were put in practice in Macedonia in early 2003, the Democratic Republic of Congo in mid-2003 and Bosnia in late 2003. The main purpose of these missions has been either to back the EU's civilian conflict resolution instruments, or to intervene if and when conflict prevention proves unsuccessful.

Finally, and perhaps most importantly, the EU has made use of its magnetic power of attraction as a major incentive for both conflict prevention and conflict resolution in its near abroad. In principle, the prospect of integration into EU structures can open the prospects for mutual identification and a reversal of competing nationalist discourses in a conflict. EU integration incentives can further foster the creation of multiple identities, which in turn facilitates conflict transformation. EU financial assistance can support these processes by helping to overcome socio-economic hardships and inequalities. EU legislation can offer a framework to safeguard communities against discrimination and show sensibility towards communal identities, thus reducing fears of collective exclusion. The 1998 Treaty of Amsterdam in fact determined that the EU Council of Ministers, acting by qualified majority, could suspend the voting rights of a member state in the event of serious breaches of rights and constitutional provisions on the part of that member (articles 6.1 and 7.3). Hence, the prospects of joining the EU could generate incentives to tackle the underlying causes of an inter-communal and intra-state conflict. Furthermore, the reforms demanded by the EU accession criteria are also designed to reconcile intra-state conflicts by redefining interests and finding common ground through multi-track third-party involvement (Stern and Druckman, 2000: 5).[4] Indeed, over the course of the eastern enlargement, the candidate countries, supported by the EU, engaged in reforms and created the necessary political space to address sensitive political issues. The accession process also weakened nationalist discourses in most candidate countries and opened the way to institution-building in candidate countries supported by the Enlargement Directorate of the European Commission.

These assets notwithstanding, the EU's methods do not always contribute to sustainable conflict resolution beyond its frontiers. In particular, the aim of democratisation policies pursued through EU accession could induce the peaceful reconciliation of group interests, but could also create political instability by enlarging the political space and legitimising radical political groups (Smith, 2004: 146). Furthermore, EU-inspired economic reforms, aid or trade concessions could create or exacerbate inequalities among different identity groups, thus triggering disintegrative effects. Moreover, nationalist approaches often prevailing in member states' foreign policies create a tendency to use the EU to pursue strictly national economic or geopolitical interests. More poignantly, the stability of certain geographical areas is a more direct concern to some EU countries than others, while some member states are more sensitive to events and issues in some areas than others, reducing the effectiveness of EU conflict resolution policies as a whole (Hill and Wallace, 1996: 8). Besides diverging national interests, conflict prevention is often not the EU's foreign policy priority. Maintaining good relations with Russia, for example, is often prioritised over taking action to end the conflict in Chechnya (Smith, 2004: 169).

Finally, EU conflict resolution strategies still lag behind the times. Conflict resolution has emerged as a critique of the reliance on power politics. Although

EU integration opens ways for interest and identity transformations to take place, the EU still relies on power politics to achieve this end. It does so by offering carrots – be these socio-economic, institutional or, more comprehensively, in the form of EU accession – and using sticks – withdrawing rewards or imposing sanctions. These are the techniques normally employed by third parties with muscle in the framework of conflict management and settlement.

As elaborated by Fetherston (2000) and Stone (2002), Habermas's communicative action theory instead may offer a post-hegemonic window through which to explore active methods of conflict transformation. Communicative action thrives when institutions enable citizens to debate matters of public importance. Ideally, all actors should be endowed with equal capacities of discourse and recognise each other's basic social equality, and their speech should be undistorted by ideology or misrecognition. Communicative action would thus constitute a means of inter-subjective dialogue between communities, enabling them to reconstruct common understandings of their life-world and restore their shared basis for culture, social integration, socialisation and, ultimately, mutual existence (Habermas, 1984a,b). Furthermore, the notion of discourse ethics, derived from the consent-oriented theory of communicative action, provides a means to solve situations of social conflict in a just and impartial manner. It offers a basis for advancing the moral point of view in conflicts, as well as consensus regarding new principles and institutional arrangements, and thus yields solutions which are acceptable to all conflict parties. When it comes to third-party involvement in discourse ethics, the objective is to achieve a non-hierarchical and non-coercive resolution of conflicts by including all affected parties as participants to dialogue, promoting decision-making based on consensus and undistorted communication, and excluding third-party values, visions and interests from the resolution process (Hoffman, 1992: 271–2). The central concern is the nature of the relationship between the conflicting parties and how to change the current meanings, conditions and circumstances (*ibid.*: 271). The dialogue that the third party promotes should open the way to transformation by focusing on the structural, social, attitudinal and interpersonal dimensions of the conflict (*ibid.*).

In order to induce Habermasian conflict transformation, the EU as a third party should be fair and impartial in its understanding of the conflict and it should promote the emancipation of all affected parties, secure their participation in dialogue, reduce injustice and release the conflict from relations of dominance that distort communication. In fact, as a world trade actor, a major donor organisation and a framework organisation enhancing inter- and intra-state interdependencies and multi-tier governance (Tocci, 2004b: 140), the EU has an impressive conflict-transformation potential. Moreover, it aspires to be a global normative power. As Solana (2000) argued in a Council report on the western Balkans: 'The Union is the only institution capable of comprehensive action, ranging from trade, economic reform and infrastructure, humanitarian assistance, human rights and democratisation, justice and police to crises management and military security'. This potential is therefore asserted both in the academic literature and in policy discourse. Taking the cue from this, the following sections analyse the effectiveness in the EU's methods in conflict resolution and suggests where to fill the gap and how. To this end, the chapter delves into three conflict cases, with a particular emphasis on the Cyprus conflict, in which EU played a role as a third party: Bosnia, the Former Yugoslav Republic of Macedonia (FYROM) and Cyprus. All three conflicts are characterised by competing claims to the rights of self-determination, sovereignty, ethnic identity and territorial integrity, as well as by the effort of international mediators to resolve these competing claims. While Bosnia and Macedonia are post-Cold War conflicts, Cyprus is a particularly intractable conflict, whose origins date back to the decolonisation period. The EU became involved in different phases and to different degrees in these three conflicts, and in all three the prospects of EU membership have played a catalytic role, insofar as all the primary parties to these conflicts could and did turn to the EU to satisfy their competing interests.

The case of Cyprus

The EU believed that the accession process for Cyprus could bring about a settlement of the Cyprus problem. This was indeed the main argument advanced by the Greek-Cypriot political leadership and was endorsed in the Commission's *Opinion* on Cyprus in 1993. The Turkish-Cypriot leadership in the Turkish Republic of Northern Cyprus (TRNC), however, questioned the legitimacy of the application at the time, on the grounds that the government of the Republic of Cyprus (RoC) did not represent the whole island. Greece, already an EU member state, however, threatened to use its veto power against the enlargement of the EU, first to the northern member states in the mid-1990s and then to the central and eastern European countries later, if Cyprus's application was rejected and official negotiations with the Turkish Cypriots were opened (Bideleux and Jeffries, 1998: 634; Yiangou, 2002: 5). Hence, not only did the European Council meetings in Corfu in June 1994 and Essen in December that year confirm that the next round of enlargement would include Cyprus, but the EU abandoned its impartial position by deleting all references to the need for a Cyprus settlement before accession. From this point on, the position of the EU shifted from being that of an interested third party to that of an interested secondary one (Eralp and Beriker, 2005: 182).

The Turkish Cypriots did not object to EU integration, but called for a settlement of the conflict before membership and demanded separate negotiations with the EU from those of the Greek Cypriots. The Greek Cypriots instead wanted to proceed with accession negotiations, hoping this would strengthen their bargaining hand in inter-communal negotiations. The EU endorsed the Greek-Cypriot desire to proceed with accession and rejected Turkish-Cypriot demands, not least because of its role as a secondary rather than third party to the conflict. Progressively over the years, major EU decisions on Cyprus were taken in parallel with a deterioration of the conflict. In July 1994, European Court of Justice (ECJ) issued a ruling against the importation of Turkish-Cypriot products without RoC certificates, which seriously damaged the northern Cypriot economy. In 1997, the Luxembourg European Council rejected Turkey, Turkish Cypriots' protector in the international arena, as a candidate for membership. In December 1999, the Helsinki European Council changed the equation, however, by granting candidacy to Turkey. Yet it also emphasised that the RoC's accession would not be linked to a settlement of the conflict.

Since then, EU–Turkey relations have entered a new and virtuous phase and, through its representative on the island, the EU engaged in 'track II' diplomacy with Turkey and the TRNC: pro-European intellectuals, journalists and academics were contacted, networks established and many organisations were funded to challenge the status quo in Cyprus, and pro-solution forces in northern Cyprus were strengthened. The economic and political isolation of the north was being increasingly felt by the Turkish Cypriots in view of Turkey's economic crises in the late 1990s and early 2000s. At the same time, Turkey launched its own reform process and conducted a major review of its constitution, particularly after the political breakthrough that came with the first election of the Justice and Development Party in November 2002. Precisely at this time, the Secretary-General of the United Nations (UN), Kofi Annan, released a comprehensive peace plan for the resolution of the Cyprus issue. Commonly known as the Annan Plan, it proposed the creation of a United Cyprus Republic (excluding the British bases) under a loose federation of two constituent states, one Greek Cypriot and the other Turkish Cypriot. Intensive efforts were made to encourage both sides to sign the document prior to the RoC's membership of the EU. As neither side agreed to sign, in December 2002 the EU invited only the RoC to join the Union. Despite these developments, the UN continued dialogue with the two sides and presented a third version of the Annan Plan, in February 2003, with the goal of reaching a settlement before Cyprus signed the EU Accession Treaty in April 2003. The same month, however, the candidate of the Greek-Cypriot Democratic Party, a hard-liner, Tassos Papadopulos, was elected as the RoC President with over 50 per cent of the votes. His election ended the term of the previous President, Glafcos Clerides, who had engaged in negotiations over the last two years and was favourable to the Annan Plan. The election of Papadopolous was somehow an indicator that the EU had neglected its track II diplomacy among the Greek Cypriots while concentrating all its efforts on Turkey and the TRNC. Meanwhile, the talks on the last phase of the Annan Plan collapsed as the TRNC President, Rauf Denktaş, walked out of negotiations and in April 2003 the RoC signed the Accession Treaty. A week later, the TRNC leadership opened two crossing points on the Green Line, which had been closed since 1974, favouring peaceful contacts between Greek Cypriots and Turkish Cypriots. Moreover, the Turkish Cypriots organised mass demonstrations against Denktaş's intransigence, started to apply for RoC citizenship to acquire EU citizenship rights, and began using RoC state institutions such as the public health service.

In December 2003, a coalition government was formed in the TRNC under the pro-change and pro-solution Republican Turkish Party leader Mehmet Ali Talat as Prime Minister. The Annan Plan was brought back to the negotiating table in February 2004 and Papadopoulos and Denktaş accepted Annan's invitation to resume negotiations. As they met almost daily, numerous technical committees and subcommittees met in parallel in an effort to resolve legal, political and economic issues underpinning reunification. The talks failed to reach a settlement and Denktaş refused to attend the next stage of the talks, scheduled to take place in Switzerland in March 2004. The Turkish-Cypriot coalition partners continued the talks, which nevertheless collapsed, and no agreement was reached. Annan then stepped in as arbitrator and presented a final version of his plan. Denktaş rejected it immediately and started his 'no' campaign for the referendum that was going to be held in April 2004. A week later, in a televised speech, Papadopolous called upon the Greek Cypriots to reject the Plan as well. Together with the Orthodox Church and the left-wing Progressive Workers' Party, Papadopolous started his own version of the 'no' campaign. Talat in the north instead supported the Plan and enjoyed majority support among the Turkish-Cypriot public; together with other pro-solution parties and non-governmental organisations, he launched a 'yes' campaign in the TRNC. The Greek-Cypriot 'no' campaign bothered the EU Commission, which had invested much effort in the Plan. The Enlargement Commissioner, Günter Verheugen, even publicly stated that he had been cheated by the RoC government, and was particularly vexed by the refusal of two Greek-Cypriot television channels to allow him to explain the Annan Plan to the public.[5] Finally, the Annan Plan was put to referenda in the two communities on 24 April 2004 and was rejected by 76 per cent of Greek Cypriots while being accepted by 65 per cent of the Turkish Cypriots. Since the implementation of the Plan was dependent on the approval of the two sides, the plan remained a dead letter.

Since then, Turkey's ongoing accession process has brought further complication to the search for a Cyprus settlement, especially from a Turkish-Cypriot perspective. According to its customs union agreement with the EU, Turkey has to open up its ports and air space to the RoC. However, before a comprehensive peace settlement is reached, Turkey considers that trading and normalising its relations with the RoC would isolate further the Turkish Cypriots and their economy. As a way out, Ankara has called for direct trade between the EU and the TRNC and for the free circulation of goods across the island, incorporated, together with Turkey, in the EU customs union area. This proposal has been rejected by the RoC government, which sees it as a way of upgrading the TRNC's *de facto* status. In late December 2005, half the EU financial aid set aside for Turkish Cypriots was about to be lost, since the TRNC rejected the aid package as it did not have a direct trade component. Both sides met in Brussels, but no agreement was reached and the RoC once again blocked direct trade. Meanwhile, Turkey proposed a revival of Cyprus reunification talks under UN auspices, as a means to escape the Greek-Cypriot threat to block Turkey's EU accession efforts. Turkey proposed an 'action plan', which envisaged the opening of Turkish ports and airports to Greek-Cypriot ships and planes in return for the lifting of trade and other restrictions on northern Cyprus. Following several months of debate, EU foreign ministers approved in February 2006 an aid package of €139 million for the Turkish-Cypriot community (of the originally planned €259 million, €120 million was lost, as the deadline for using the funds from the EU's 2005 budget was missed).[6] Turkey and the TRNC expressed disappointment with the EU, while in the words of the RoC government spokesman, Georgios Lillikas, 'the fairy tale of Turkish Cypriot isolation is now removed with the EU decision'.[7] Meanwhile, EU participation in the conflict is being further problematised as Turkey's possible accession to the EU raises ardent debate between members. France and Austria would like to leave the process open-ended. German Chancellor Angela Merkel has suggested a privileged partnership with Turkey and all-Turco-sceptic member states have used the Cyprus issue as a shield against and source of leverage over Ankara. Although the negotiation process between Turkey and the EU started in October 2005, France and Austria have pledged to hold referenda on Turkey's future accession.

It is highly debatable whether the enlargement process without conditionality attached to the Greek-Cypriot side served conflict resolution in Cyprus. It would be incorrect to deny the catalytic effect the EU had on preparing the ground for negotiations on the island and in reversing the incentive structure in northern Cyprus, where for years the status quo had been regarded as the only possible solution. Furthermore, the opening of the border has given the possibility to the 'post-'74' generation to see the 'other side' for the first time. However, the EU became too dependent on the effect of membership negotiations (Eralp and Beriker, 2005: 187) and missed the opportunity for resolution by promising accession to the Greek-Cypriot community alone, without fostering a common ground for collective social construction (Boedeltje et al., 2005: 36). Besides, by lifting conditionality on the RoC and failing to convey to the Greek Cypriots the potential repercussions of entering the Union as a divided island, EU actors were partially responsible for the latter's rejection of the Annan Plan (Tocci, 2004b: 165). Developments in the post-Annan period have revealed that conflict settlement efforts under the EU framework following the RoC's membership have also been unsuccessful, as the EU has now become a primary party to this protracted and intractable conflict.

The case of Macedonia (FYROM)

The 1974 Yugoslav constitutional preamble described Macedonia as 'the state of the Macedonian people and the Albanian and Turkish minorities'. The new Macedonian constitution in 1989 defined it as a Macedonian nation state. Moreover, previously existing minority rights were abolished or restricted. In 1992, the Albanian minority held a referendum on the territorial autonomy of the Albanians in Macedonia, which was interpreted by the Slavic Macedonian majority as a confirmation of Albanian separatism. As happened in Serbia and Kosovo, a scare campaign was begun that argued that the Slavic majority would be outnumbered in the long run by the Albanian ethnic group in view of their higher birth rates and immigration from Kosovo. A war of numbers on demographics prevailed between the two communities throughout the 1990s.

The Kosovo crisis in 1999 further challenged the imperfect balances in Macedonia. An estimated 360,000 Kosovo Albanians took refuge in the country and, despite their departure after the war, Albanian nationalists, members of the National Liberation Army (NLA, which had emerged as the successor movement of the Kosova Liberation Army, KLA), began to infiltrate into the northern parts of FYROM from Kosovo, clashing with Macedonian security forces. The UN Security Council adopted Resolution 1345, condemning the violence by Albanian nationalists. The EU followed the UN and supported the Macedonian government in its fight against terrorist acts, but urged the former also to open a dialogue with the elected Albanian political parties on future political reform. The major EU concern at the time was to prevent another intractable conflict in the region.

The EU's High Representative, Solana, opened round-table talks in March 2001 between the political parties under the auspices of the Macedonian President. Albanian proposals included the postponement of the national census due to take place in May–October 2001, to allow the return of refugees who had fled the conflict, state funding for the University of Tetovo and the conversion of the state television's third service into an Albanian-language channel. However, the Macedonian government continued to reject these demands and refused to amend the constitution in order to grant equal rights to the Albanian population.

In April 2001, Macedonia signed its Stabilisation and Association Agreement with the EU, which came into effect in April 2004. In the context of adaptation of EU standards of democracy, human rights and the rule of law, the parties had thus to resolve their problems. 'This formula was also used as a face-saving strategy towards Slav Macedonian politicians who did not want to appear as making any concessions to the Albanian extremists' (Schneckener, 2002: 31). At the same time, the EU Commission offered further financial and technical assistance to Macedonia, especially to the Albanian-dominated areas. The violence ceased during this period but erupted again, at the end of April 2001, when Albanian militants killed eight Macedonian soldiers. This led to civilian Slavic Macedonian riots against Albanian property. Government troops launched an offensive against Albanian positions near Kumanova, after two more Macedonian soldiers were killed.

In response to the re-escalation of the conflict, the EU and the North Atlantic Treaty Organisation (NATO) acted together. Solana and NATO General Secretary Lord Robertson met jointly with the Slavic Macedonian and Albanian leaders and persuaded them to establish a coalition government. On 29 June, NATO formally approved an operation to deploy a 3,500-member multinational force in Macedonia to assist the disarmament of the NLA. The EU announced at the same time a substantial aid package, in case of a peaceful solution. It also appointed former French Defence Minister François Léotard as EU Special Representative to Macedonia (Schneckener, 2002: 34). Léotard and US Special Envoy James Pardew acted as a joint EU–US mediation team, which was later complemented by the High Commissioner appointed by the Organization for Security and Co-operation in Europe (OSCE). This time, the tripartite team did not leave the negotiation process to the conflicting parties but imposed their own proposals in the form of a Framework Document, which proposed decentralisation, non-discrimination in public service, special parliamentary regimes and other major laws concerning education and language.

The negotiations began in Ohrid, and step by step disputed issues were discussed and resolved. Finally, on 13 August 2001, the conflicting parties signed the Ohrid Framework Agreement, which provided for the amendment of the constitution to grant greater rights to the Albanian community. EU and OSCE monitors supervised the implementation of the peace agreement, while NATO troops remained in the country to protect them. In January 2002, new Macedonian legislation allowing greater authority to local governments in Albanian regions was approved by the parliament. In March 2003, the remaining NATO contingent was replaced by an EU-led mission, Operation Concordia, which was deployed at the official request of the Macedonian President, Boris Trajkovski, to maintain security during the implementation of the Ohrid Agreement. On 17 December 2005, the EU granted Macedonia candidacy, but with no promise of when accession negotiations would start. France made a budget deal as a condition for granting Macedonia candidate status while Greece agreed not to veto the decision, with an EU understanding that its dispute with that country over the name 'Macedonia' would be resolved. According to the EU, the main obstacles before Macedonia for an eventual membership are good relations with its neighbours and reforms to the judicial and police systems.

The Macedonian case demonstrates that EU actions in a violent conflict were successful only in conjunction with other powerful international actors, including NATO, the OSCE and the United States (Schneckener, 2002: 37). Nonetheless, the EU's integration process with Macedonia presents an example of non-coercive methods of conflict resolution. The EU's use of sticks and carrots proved successful by suppressing the intransigence of all sides. In 2001, 87 per cent of Albanians indeed asserted the importance that the country remains united, not least in view of the ongoing accession process with the EU (Hatay, 2005: 90). The Ohrid Agreement, brokered by the EU High Representative and agreed upon by the parties, included commitments from both sides to the country's territorial integrity and the preservation of its unitary structure. It also ruled out territorial solutions to ethnic disputes. At the same time, the Framework called for reforms to transform the state from an ethnic Slav Macedonian one (which privileged the majority population, including its language, religion and culture), into a multi-ethnic or more precisely a bi-ethnic state (Jakobsson Hatay, 2005: 91). These reforms were initially met with enthusiasm by Albanians. However, Slav Macedonians were far less impressed. In 2003, a survey by the United Nations Development Programme (UNDP), 38.0 per cent of Macedonians and 91.6 per cent of Albanians declared their strong support for the agreement (UNDP, 2003). However, over time, more Slav Macedonians came to appreciate the advantages of the settlement, insofar as they also benefited from the structural changes that came with peace, including better economic performance and EU candidacy.

The EU's policies of conditionality may be viewed as successful in incentivising conflict settlement in the short run and in inducing accommodation in the medium run. But for veritable conflict resolution and transformation to take place, a far deeper process of change, including the transformation of underlying interests and identities, must be ushered in, and can be expected only in the longer run (Coppieters et al., 2004: 4). For this to take place, a large share of responsibility is borne by the local actors themselves. Yet for the EU to play a constructive role in this process of resolution and transformation, it must also operate to improve the conditions in a conflict. In particular, it must promote socio-economic development, a major weakness in Macedonia at present. As a third party in this conflict resolution, the EU should also pay far greater attention to safeguarding the other minorities' rights in Macedonia, hedging against the possible negative consequences engendered by the transformation of a mono-ethnic state into a bi-ethnic one, comprising Slavic Macedonians and Albanians. Finally, the EU should constantly ensure that its third-party role in the conflict remains a neutral one, despite its close involvement in the country through the accession process. Only in this way can the Union facilitate the development of communicative action in the country.

The case of Bosnia

The EU was a confused and controversial third party during the Bosnian war insofar as its members were divided by contrasting policies. Germany was the main political supporter of the Croat and Bosniak governments. France and the UK supported non-intervention and the arms embargo on Bosnia. Volunteers from Greece fought in Srebrenica (Michas, 2002). As Sokolović points out, if the Dutch battalion of the UN Protection Force had actually defended Srebrenica, it could have led to Greek and Dutch soldiers shooting at each other (Sokolović, 2005: 17).

Despite these controversies during the war, the EU reached a consensus to act collectively through international organisations to implement the 1995 Dayton peace agreement. This settlement, while legitimising the partition of Bosnia and the ethnic cleansing that came with it, sought to loosely revive the country's multi-ethnic past. Moreover, developments since then, proceeding in parallel with deepening ties with the EU, have increasingly turned Bosnia away from its war-ridden past. In June 2003, at the Thessaloniki European Council, the EU announced the opening of the enlargement process to south-eastern Europe. In November 2003, under pressure from the Office of the High Representative (OHR) in Bosnia and Herzegovina (BiH), which largely comprised EU member state officials, the investigation into the Srebrenica massacre was broadcast on Bosnian Serbian television. The Republika Srpska authorities conceded for the first time that Bosnian Serb forces had perpetrated the killings.

During a visit to Sarajevo later in the month, Svetozar Marović, the President of Serbia and Montenegro, issued a formal apology for the atrocities committed against the Bosnian civilians during 1992–95 and urged reconciliation. Following a Venice Commission 'Opinion', the OHR proposed transforming itself into an EU-led mission and in August 2005 it announced its further downsizing. In October 2005, the Republika Srpska adopted a police reform plan in accordance with EU principles and that same month the European Commission recommended that member states open Stabilisation and Association negotiations with BiH. In November 2005 the EU Enlargement Commissioner, Olli Rehn, declared the opening of negotiations, making BiH a potential candidate for the EU. In March 2006, BiH's Bosniak, Serbian and Croatian communities agreed on a constitutional reform package that would strengthen the country's central government.

Despite these positive developments, influenced by the EU integration process, several dark shadows hang over Bosnia's reconciliation process. The country's segregated educational system based on three distinct nationalist approaches persists, Bosnian Serb nationalists still tend to view the Republika Srpska as part of Serbia proper, Serbian authorities in Bosnia are considered as complicit in their support for the indicted war criminals Karadžić and Mladić, political balances between the Croats and Bosniaks at the federal level remain highly unstable, and poverty in the country remains widespread. The German High Representative, Christian Schwarz-Schilling (2006), has suggested that the burden of transition naturally falls more on the BiH authorities than on the international community, although the continuation of the EU's impartial and competent third-party role remains essential to progress in Bosnia. In turn, BiH continues to present key challenges to the EU.

The parties to the Bosnian conflict are well aware that the EU is the most promising remedy to their frozen ills. First of all, the EU cannot bear the economic, political and above all the moral cost of another Bosnian war. As such, the Union is ready to allocate financial, political and military assets to secure justice and basic human rights to prevent renewed violence in the country. Second, BiH is geographically at the heart of Europe and it has no geopolitical alternatives to association with and integration into the EU. Moreover, the EU is planning to integrate the entire western Balkan region. Hence, BiH's destiny is tied to the EU, beyond the EU's aspirations to play a constructive third-party role in the conflict. To this end, the EU should help the parties to seek an agreed political framework, address unattained justice and overcome the lack of enduring security. More broadly, it should promote effective reconciliation. As argued at the outset of this chapter, conflict resolution and conflict transformation as methods were borne from the criticism of realist approaches to conflict settlement. These approaches should thus aim to transform conflicts in order to reach genuine reconciliation between conflict parties on all the different issues on the conflict agenda, including security, the political and constitutional framework, justice and basic human rights, and socio-economic development. The challenge facing the EU in Bosnia is to help achieve such reconciliation before the accession of Croatia, so as to avoid repeating the mistakes made in Cyprus and becoming a primary party to the conflict. The EU's biggest weakness in Bosnia, however, seems to be that, despite BiH's strong European orientation, its citizens do not share the same conviction and do not have full confidence in the EU, in view of their memories of the Union's controversial role during the war. Opinion polls in BiH show that Bosnians hold the international community responsible for the war (Jakobsson Hatay, 2005: 83) and European powers have not yet spoken openly about their own share of responsibility in the conflict. As put by Irwin (2004: 83): 'In respective blame games, Bosniaks blame the Serbs and the international community, the Serbs blame the US and the NATO and Croats blame the Serbs and the international community'. Furthermore, according to a Bosnian attorney, NATO membership is what matters most to Bosnians, as their primary concern is to avoid another war. This implies that the EU is still not viewed as the most reliable actor on security matters in the country. This attorney also asserted that EU integration has not yet opened the way to reconciliation, insofar as the country remains internally divided in terms of the division of competences, and the federal state level (the Directorate for EU Integration) carries out vertical and horizontal coordination, without having visible impacts.

Findings and assessment

In all three cases, the EU used its current conflict resolution methods (integration incentives, financial assistance and policies of conditionality). In the cases of Bosnia and Macedonia, the Union has also tested its military capabilities as a means of post-conflict stabilisation and conflict prevention. It has thus far achieved progress, especially in Macedonia. But in all three cases, the EU has not fostered the ground for a genuine and comprehensive reconciliation between the conflict parties.

With the persistence of socio-economic inequalities and exclusion in these conflict areas, the root causes of conflicts are not eliminated. Funds and financial assistance can help but do not provide long-term remedies to revive the economic sectors, benefiting all segments of society and helping thus to create a space where inter-subjectively produced mutual understanding becomes possible. The EU has contributed to reconstruction and development significantly in Bosnia and Macedonia and to a lesser extent in the TRNC.

As put by Kristoff Bender, a senior analyst leading research projects in Serbia, Montenegro and FYROM: 'While most people in BiH and FYROM are worse off than 20 years ago, in the absence of aid, today, they probably would be further worse off'.[8] The EU has also supported small and medium-sized enterprises, vocational, management and human resource training, as well as the efficient management of public finances to combat unemployment, especially in Macedonia. However, it has not made a long-term contribution to socio-economic development in any of these cases. With the exception of the banking sector and investments in Macedonian telecommunications, cement factories and breweries, there have not been significant EU foreign investments in BiH or FYROM, while the TRNC remains isolated from the rest of the EU. The widespread poverty in Bosnia,[9] the high unemployment in Macedonia and the economic isolation of northern Cyprus all represent major obstacles to successful conflict resolution, and are not sufficiently tackled by the EU. Furthermore, the EU's allocation of development assistance and trade concessions in Cyprus has actually exacerbated inequalities between the conflict parties. The EU has also paid little attention to the fact that the comprehensive and rapid privatisation processes in Macedonia and Bosnia may result in greater ownership by one ethnic group, further aggravating segregation and inter-communal inequalities.

When it comes to creating an environment for undistorted communication between the conflict parties, the EU has also not been a very reliable third party. The EU has attempted to promote socialisation, but without fostering communicative action. In this respect, a statement by a Greek-Cypriot politician, Lyssarides, concerning Turkey is revealing: 'We support Turkey's accession to the Union. Not because we love Turkey, but it's better to have her in the family and make her behave according to the family rules than keep her outside'.[10] At times, this patronising 'civilising' approach within the EU can become exclusivist. The Internal Market Commissioner, Frits Bolkestein, stated that if Turkey were admitted to the EU, 'the liberation of Vienna in 1683 would be in vain'.[11] As analysed by Ramonet, the debate about Turkey's impending membership of the EU in particular has been characterised by overblown rhetoric and a lack of finesse: 'Framed in terms of the "clash of civilisations", it testifies to the identity crises of western societies when faced with Islam' (Ramonet, 2004). Moreover, while the EU discourse continues to uphold the principle of flexible, multi-tiered cross-border identities, in practice a 'post-9/11' syndrome has rendered EU borders extremely exclusive, with the exception of selected allies. As put by Hungarian academic Böröcz (2001: 6):

> In the enlargement scheme, identities that posture themselves as less Oriental than a chosen Other have systematically latched onto the synecdoche notion of 'Europe equals EU'and perpetuate that schema as a core element of their identity

> focus. Acceptance vs. postponement for accession to the EU is read, in this frame, as reinforcement or rejection of Europeanness (i.e. non-Orientalness) and hence ultimately of 'whiteness'.... The diversity and multi-culturality stressed by the plurilingual label 'Europa, Europa' is also strictly internal to EU.

This exclusivist approach reduces and at times eliminates the EU's potential to promote conflict transformation and its ultimate goal: reconciliation. With this approach towards the 'other', how can the EU, as a third party, persuade its Orthodox Christian Slavic Macedonian partners to reconcile their differences with their Muslim Albanian compatriots, Christian Serbs and the Croats with their Muslim Bosniak neighbours, or the Orthodox Greek Cypriots with the Muslim Turkish Cypriots? True, EU assistance, investments and conditionalities would continue to affect these conflict zones, but as long as exclusivist discourse bedevilled the EU itself, this approach would contaminate different policy areas and instruments within and beyond the EU's territory, reducing the EU's ability to create spaces for communicative action to transform conflicts and achieve reconciliation.

This chapter argues that the EU has significant potential to act as a catalyst in bringing conflict parties to negotiate their differences and work together, thanks to its developing conflict-prevention mechanisms and the incentives embedded in the integration process. Through its treaties and legislation, the EU also has the potential to create an open and emancipatory ground to resolve conflicts over competing political interests. However, the Union has a structural weakness in the field of conflict transformation because of its own deficiencies in tackling socio-economic inequalities and in fostering undistorted communicative action between conflict parties. An impartial and successful conduct of conflict transformation would instead be the most promising method to induce reconciliation, not only beyond EU frontiers but also within the EU itself.

Notes

1 The author would like to express her gratitude to Antonija Petričusić, Džemal Sokolović, Kristof Bender, J. C. Tordai and Zoran Ilievski for providing suggestions, corrections and information during the preparation of this chapter.

2 The primary parties to a conflict are those who are directly affected by it (Rubin and Rubin, 1989; cited in Eralp and Beriker, 2005). An interested secondary party is one which has an indirect interest in the outcome of a conflict and supports one of the disputants accordingly. An interested third party is one which has an interest in the successful resolution of the conflict and engages in active settlement efforts (Wilmot and Hocker, 2001; cited in Eralp and Beriker, 2005). A disinterested third party is one which does not take an active part in settlement efforts despite its general interest in a solution (Eralp and Beriker, 2005).

3 The SPSEE aims to develop and promote free trade, democracy, human rights in and among Albania, Bosnia and Herzegovina, Bulgaria, Croatia, the Former Yugoslav Republic of Macedonia, Moldova, and Serbia and Montenegro.
4 Multi-track third-party involvement implies that besides the top-level ('track I') leaders, between whom high-level negotiations take place, the third party includes mid-level leaders ('track II') to organise problem-solving workshops, and grass-roots leaders ('track III') to establish local peace commissions. All sectors of society are thus expected to participate in building peace, 'with middle-range rather than top-level leaders having a particularly important role to play' (Lederach, 2004: 39).
5 *Le Monde*, 22 April 2004.
6 Com (2004) 465 final, 27 February 2006.
7 See www.euractiv.com, EU news, policy positions and EU actors on line.
8 Email interview, March–April 2006.
9 According to the World Bank (2003), poverty is so widespread in BiH that there is a constant danger that it may lead to social unrest and upheaval.
10 Interview with Dr Vassos Lyssarides, founder of the movement of Greek-Cypriot Social Democrats, Nicosia.
11 *Financial Times*, 8 September 2004.

11

The Cyprus conflict in a comparative perspective: assessing the impact of European integration

Elise Féron and Fatma Güven Lisaniler

Introduction

The process of Europeanisation raises questions concerning the transformation of collective identities and the organisation of democracy, especially in states where a range of social processes coalesce around generally shared perceptions of community difference. Is such a thing as community coexistence possible, or does peaceful coexistence imply some kind of erosion of community? We cannot assume that integration in Europe will automatically bring a solution to these conflicts. Indeed, European integration may even sharpen them, by making claims for autonomy or even independence more credible. Because the relevance of the territorial integrity of nation states has been lessened by European integration, it seems easier for smaller communities to claim their independence, or at least a greater degree of autonomy.

The fact that the European Union (EU), through its Common Foreign and Security Policy (CFSP), has set itself the task of intervening in the conflicts raging in its vicinity, has led to various interventions with a strong EU dimension. But direct intervention is not the only way in which European integration affects conflicts: European institutions and norms have been exerting their influence on modes of conflict management, and European officials have been offering their good offices and advice.

In order to understand what kind of impact the process of Europeanisation is having on current conflicts taking place on the European continent, we have to put together two sets of questions. The first set of questions deals with the shape and nature of current conflicts. Europeanisation is unlikely to have a similar effect on different types of conflicts. Therefore, we need to disaggregate conflicts in order to better understand them, and more specifically to understand which of their characteristics Europeanisation might influence. A second task is to understand what kind of mechanisms are implied by 'Europeanisation' and how these processes can positively or negatively affect conflicts taking place in Europe and its vicinity.

Starting with an overview of the main dimensions displayed by conflicts, and identified in the literature, this chapter locates the Cyprus conflict among other conflicts taking place in Europe, and assesses its specificities as well as the features it shares with other cases. This chapter subsequently focuses on the impact of European integration on the structures of the conflict itself, going beyond the question of the political implications of membership, and inquiring whether it has led to a shift in its key issues and dimensions.[1]

Key dimensions and features of conflicts in Europe

The causes of conflicts that pitch communities in Europe against each other are not immediately obvious, as cultural, ethnic or religious groups seem to integrate smoothly in some cases but not in others. Many diverging theories on the emergence and persistence of conflicts in Europe can be found in the literature; these emphasise different factors, with various combinations possible. According to some authors, identity and ethnicity are at the root of most conflicts, while some theories stress the importance of competition over territory or natural resources. Others explain conflicts mostly by political factors. This divergence can be explained partly by the fact that conflicts constantly feed themselves: they are self-perpetuating. The initial conditions give rise to new frameworks, in which new grievances can develop. In other words, the causes of a specific conflict – the reasons why it initially developed – may not be reflected in what it is currently about – its core issues. This peculiarity poses a great challenge to analysis, because some processes which are rightly pointed out as the root causes of a conflict, like, say, colonisation in Ireland, may be a lot less relevant than other factors for characterising or even understanding its current shape. For the sake of clarification, this section of the chapter focuses on the main possible issues or 'symptoms' of current conflicts in Europe, as identified in the scientific literature, and classifies them in four main clusters (cultural factors, socio-economic and territorial factors, political factors, and external factors). These issues or dimensions often overlap or even merge, as none of them is able in itself to provide an overall and encompassing explanation for the emergence or endurance of conflicts.

Cultural factors

A first series of theories explain or characterise conflicts by cultural factors, understood in a very broad manner. They often focus on so-called ethnic conflicts, and point alternatively or simultaneously at three main features of a conflict. The first feature is *identity*. Here, the literature describes conflicts as oppositions between communities, which relate to primordial affiliations, in the sense that communities are supposed to exist in advance of any other kind of affiliations. These primordialist theories also focus on the importance of the past, of traditions and of myths, in the making of the community (Duffy Toft, 2002). Conflicts are thought to arise between groups that are long-standing rivals (Geertz, 1973; Isaacs, 1975). In almost all cases, the stress put by a group on its identity allows for its differentiation from the rest of the world. However, the virulence of these identity claims can be more or less important. In the Basque country, for instance, there is a strong insistence on the Basque collective identity, even by moderate nationalists, but this is not necessarily accompanied by a denigration discourse on other groups' identities; this identity discourse nevertheless legitimises a confrontational attitude towards the central Spanish state. Another example is found in Kosovo, where antipathies are not very old, but are depicted as such, and justify aggressive attitudes towards the other community.

The second feature is *religion*. Some authors (for instance Reynal-Querol, 2002) argue that religiously divided societies are more prone to intense conflicts than are societies in which people have conflicting claims to resources, say, or language divisions. However, research has demonstrated that no straightforward conclusion can be drawn concerning the impact of religious differences without a closer look at the real influence of clergy and faith in the conflict, and at the extent to which actors in the conflict frame it in religious terms (Féron, 2008). In the case of Sandžak, of the former Yugoslavia, for instance, it was in fact the pre-existing conflict between ethnic groups that increased the religious consciousness of the population. A growing faith can in turn generate its own dynamic of estrangement and distanciation from other groups. Even in cases where a conflict is framed in religious terms, by both internal and external actors, religion is not necessarily the main issue or cause of the conflict. In Northern Ireland, for instance, conflict is not a function of the ritual and doctrinal content of the religions themselves, but of the cultural significance of religion as a marker of identity (Cronin, 2002).

Linguistic and *cultural* differences make up the last main cultural feature of conflicts, as identified in the contemporary literature. When the survival of a language is at stake, conflicts are said to be more intractable, because cultural identity, of which language is an important part for many peoples, is non-negotiable and not open to compromise. This element of cultural or linguistic opposition is present in many conflicts taking place in Europe, even if it is not always the main current issue or cause of the conflict (Joseph et al., 2006). In some cases, however, as in the case of the Slovene minority in the Carinthia region in Austria, linguistic cleavages are the main explanation for the maintenance of group boundaries, and for suspicious attitudes, fostered more by German nationalists than Slovenes. Likewise, in South Tyrol language corresponds to a deep division in society, which has sometimes had violent implications, but which has nevertheless been overcome through the setting up of consociational premises. In this case, language is used as an ethnic mark, and linguistic divisions have given birth to 'parallel societies', which are largely autonomous.

Socio-economic and territorial factors

Another group of theories concentrates on the socio-economic and territorial issues underlying conflicts. Instead of focusing on group identities, they insist on the environmental settings in which conflicts take place. They point firstly at socio-economic issues, such as differences in the level of economic and social development inside a state's boundaries, and argue that conflict arises when modernisation and development follow uneven patterns (Deutsch, 1966; Horowitz, 1985), or when a specific ethnic, linguistic or cultural group is economically and socially discriminated against (Gurr, 1970). What is striking is that both economic discrimination and privilege can politicise or reinforce the political relevance of cultural and community identities. Indeed, it is often in those territories which are wealthier than the rest of the country that regionalist or autonomist feelings are strongest. This can be explained by the fact that these regions contribute more than they receive from the national state. These kinds of arguments are very clear in Belgium in the discourses of the Vlaams Belang party, for example. But the counter argument, for economically disadvantaged regions or groups, seems valid too. For instance, the feeling, established or not, of being or having been despised or treated unfairly in the past by the central state very often gives a strong basis for opposing the state or the specific cultural group that embodies it.

This group of theories also insists on *demographic* factors. Population shifts and demography indeed play an important role in contemporary conflicts. This is in two main circumstances, which may overlap: first, when large waves of migration modify the demographic balance of a geographical zone; and second, when demography is the basis for the sharing of political power and positions, and an increase in the demographic weight of one of the communities induces changes in the political landscape as a whole. In the first case, migrants or refugees can be seen as invaders, who jeopardise political structures as well as political cultures, especially if they are claiming political rights. In the second case, when two or more communities of comparable size share the same political space and demographics is the basis for the sharing of political power and positions – especially in democratic societies – any demographic change will induce change in the political landscape as a whole (Weiner and Teitelbaum, 2001). These changes are often seen as a threat by some of those communities who wish to retain their positions and privileges.

Territory makes up a third crucial issue linked to socio-economic resources. It can be at the centre of the conflict whether it is its symbolic or material signification that is stressed, or both (Duffy Toft, 2002). In Kosovo, there is a strong link, at the discursive and symbolic levels, between territory and identity, which are considered non-negotiable and absolute values, and which make accommodation and peace settlements difficult. As discussed below, in Cyprus, the control of territory has become a complex geopolitical issue that is accompanied by local and 'smaller' territorial ones.

Political factors

A third set of theories explains conflicts by political factors, which can be disaggregated further in four main dimensions. The first one is the *centre–periphery* cleavage, which explains conflicts as the result of power relations between the central – or 'foreign' – state and a specific region or territory which tries to gain or regain more independence or rights (Rokkan and Urwin, 1983). Some examples like the Corsican one indeed show that regionalist claims can at least partly be understood as reactions against centralist policies (in this case, French centralist policies), and that feelings of specificity as well as desire for a specific status do not always pre-date the centre–periphery cleavage (Crettiez, 1999).

A second political dimension relates to the *security dilemma* (see for instance Fearon, 1994; Posen, 1993). It argues that political uncertainty and lack of information concerning threats lead groups to take measures to reinforce their security and identity, thus further isolating them from the outside world. This paradigm fits more specifically the case of multinational states that, when faced with decline and risks of fragmentation, can no longer protect the interests of cultural groups and minorities, who then feel politically, culturally and even physically at risk. In the Sandžak case, the attitude of the Serbian central state towards the Bosnian minority has clearly led to its radicalisation, to its estrangement as well as to its tendency to look elsewhere – in Bosnia and Herzegovina – for protection. Autonomist and separatist feelings, or conflicting attitudes towards other groups, also develop when a group prefers to secede rather than to participate in the regime and possibly weaken its position (Hechter, 1995).

Elite manipulation makes up a third political dimension. Here, conflicts are understood as a result of identity manipulation efforts by political entrepreneurs whose main goal is to gain or retain power (see, for instance, Gagnon, 1995). In that sense, elites 'construct' the conflict in order to serve their own interest, and they manipulate group identities (Brass, 1997; Haymes, 1997). They thus drive the conflict 'from above'. In Belgium, for instance, political elites are the major defenders of community cultures and identities, and nationalist elites in Corsica have managed to draw the French government into a series of negotiations, despite the fact that only a small minority of the population favours the independence option.

Finally, conflicts can also relate to a problematic access to *citizenship*, especially in countries characterised by the strong nationalism of their majorities. In some cases, there is a tendency to give to minorities only rights that are thought of as non-threatening in the eyes of the majority, and to grant a preferred status to the majority (Smooha, 2002). Such is the case in Estonia, whose population, after its declaration of independence in 1991, comprised a one-third minority of Russian speakers. Restricted access to citizenship is one characteristic of the Roma's situation in central Europe, too, especially in the Czech and Slovak Republics, where difficult access to citizenship has led not to political mobilisation but rather to a specific social behaviour reinforcing the estrangement of the Roma from the society they live in.

External factors

Finally, a last group of theories focus on so-called external factors, such as globalisation and decolonisation. For many authors, communal opposition is often linked to globalisation and the transition to a market economy, for instance in eastern Europe. Economic reforms and institutional transformations bring about new rules and norms as well as power shifts, and break old 'social contracts' on which the distribution of resources was grounded (Crawford, 1998). Decolonisation factors also lead to the disintegration of states or of political structures that used to provide a link between different cultural groups (Ignatieff, 1999). The impact of colonisation in Cyprus was particularly interesting and strong during the first half of the twentieth century, as it generated diverging affiliations and political options on the Greek-Cypriot and Turkish-Cypriot sides.

Many conflicts are also analysed as 'unfinished business' from the First or Second World War (Gellner, 1995). In many European countries, irredentist nationalisms have been kept under control, or made subordinate to the outcome of the Cold War. As a consequence, the collapse of the Soviet empire allowed for the resurfacing of these conflicts.

Closely related to the question of decolonisation, neighbouring countries, bordering communities and diasporas often play an important role in enacting or sustaining conflicts in contemporary Europe where there is an imperial background. Neighbouring countries are sometimes competing for territorial control and are thus favouring the allegiance of one of the communities in opposition; or they can be used by communities in conflict themselves as a way of legitimising their secessionist claims. The case of South Tyrol perfectly illustrates the case of a territory disputed by two bordering countries, and whose fate has long been depending on factors other than the will of its population. The presence of diasporas coming from neighbouring countries can also be an important dimension of conflicts, as these neighbouring countries can feel entitled to intervene and intercede in favour of the members of their diasporas. Even if this involvement is not very important, it can cause a state of tension in the wider population, and can make relations between neighbouring countries more difficult, as in the case of the Hungarian diaspora in the Vojvodina region.

All these conflict dimensions or issues reflect the variety of situations on the ground, but they can also be related to various ways of understanding a conflict or of trying to solve it, as well as to diverging theoretical backgrounds and focuses. In most current conflicts, several of these issues interact, and have very different implications and meanings on the ground, both for the actors and in terms of conflict resolution. This means that there can be no uniform impact of Europeanisation on these conflicts, because they are extremely complex social constructs that react in various ways to the process of Europeanisation, which is nearly as complex and multiform. In other words, it is only by pointing at these different characteristics, and by adopting a case-by-case approach, that we can assess the impact of Europeanisation. We thus turn our attention to the Cyprus case.

Assessing the specificities of the Cyprus conflict

Historical background

The population of Cyprus is a mix of Greek Cypriots, Turkish Cypriots, Armenians, Maronites and Latins. The Mycenaean migration that started in the fourteenth century BC and the mass settlement of Moslem inhabitants just after Ottoman conquest of the island in 1571 led to the creation of the two main communities: a Greek-speaking Orthodox Christian community and a Turkish-speaking Moslem community. During the period of Ottoman rule (1571–1878), Greek Cypriots and Turkish Cypriots lived together, side by side, in peace, mostly in mixed settlements, even though their identities, shaped by religion and religious institutions and a dual education system, were distinct. Despite the existence of distinct and diverse identities on the island, there was no violent ethnic conflict between the Christian and Moslem inhabitants, even in the context of events such as local riots against heavy taxes imposed by Ottoman rulers. The years of British colonial domination were the years of identity transformation. British colonial rule changed traditional institutions, which had once served to maintain cultural identities, into modern political institutions with an ethno-religious basis (from pre-modern/religious/traditional identities to modern/national identities). Through the Westernisation of educational institutions on the basis of nationality, reform of the bureaucracy and so on, British colonial rule pushed the modernisation of daily life to conform to the communal identities. But the patterns of Westernisation/modernisation were different in the two communities, as Turkish Cypriots – owing to Kemalist influences from Turkey at that time – were developing a secular national identity, while Greek Cypriots, as was case with Greece's independence from the Ottoman empire, constructed their national identity around the Orthodox Church, which was playing the leading role in the anti-British/anti-colonial struggle. This not only led to different nationalistic patterns among Greek Cypriots and Turkish Cypriots, but also caused different reactions towards British colonial rule as well. While Greek Cypriots were fighting against British colonialism under the influences of Greek ethno-religious nationalism, Turkish Cypriots did not side with them, because of their double (religious and national) exclusion. Meanwhile, the British colonial administration used the Turkish Cypriots to counter Greek-Cypriot riots. Thus, the communal identities of the two main ethnic groups were reshaped not as 'Cypriots', the only possible ground for developing a common anti-colonial struggle, but as Turkish and Greek, under the influence of their respective 'motherland' nationalisms.

This period was when 'the seeds of the present dispute were effectively sown' (Coppieters et al., 2004: 65). It shaped the main determining feature of the present conflict as an economic, political and cultural power struggle between 'Greeks' and 'Turks' of the island, who saw themselves as extensions of two 'great' nations. What is more, this power struggle has been taking place on an island that has been seen as strategically important by all the international powers that have an interest in the region; discussions on the future of the island have therefore been constantly open to external interference.

To cut a long story short, the recent history of Cyprus can be read as the history of two communities who were not able or not allowed to create a common concern for a peaceful coexistence; instead, they have tried to be part of their respective (mother) homelands. The conflict between the two communities was mainly caused by nationalistic claims, but those were always accompanied by religious (although less so among Turkish Cypriots), economic and cultural claims. This power struggle has been dominated by the discourses of the majority (Greek Cypriots), who see themselves as the indigenous community. The construction of this discourse of the majority was in line with the dominant discourse of that time, nationalism, which was characterised by its exclusiveness. The political vision of the second largest community, the Turkish Cypriots, who had governed the island for 300 years, can be understood as a reaction to the majority's claims; thus, instead of deconstructing the dominant frame of the majority, they simply reproduced it in their own nationalist separatist discourse.

Following the emergence of pan-Hellenic sentiments calling for *enosis* – that is, the incorporation of Cyprus into Greece – the two communities entered a collision path. In the 1950s, the Greek-Cypriot guerrillas of the National Organisation of Cypriot Fighters (EOKA) struggled against British rule and for integration with mainland Greece, but Turkish Cypriots, fearing for their fate under Greek rule, sided with the British authorities or advocated *taksim* – the division of the island in two areas – as an alternative to *enosis*. Neither side received what it sought with the creation of the Republic of Cyprus in 1960, a 'state without a nation' (Kızılyürek, 2005: 16). Its population was divided in two distinct communities, Turkish Cypriots and Greek Cypriots, with different languages, religions, identities, socio-economic statuses and feelings of belonging. The fact that neither of these communities used this state as a space to define its own identity is one of the most important distinguishing features of the Cyprus conflict, which can be found in few other places in Europe apart from Northern Ireland. The constitution of the new Republic enshrined the equality of the two communities and expressly prohibited annexation by other nations. Nonetheless, *enosis* and *taksim* apparently remained alive in the minds of many Cypriot leaders from both communities. By 1963, only three years after the establishment of the Republic, Greek-Cypriot attempts to modify the constitution, and to reduce representation and political power of the Turkish Cypriots in the administration, resulted in the withdrawal of Turkish Cypriots from the central and local administration.

Inter-communal violence in 1963–64 and in 1967 turned thousands of Turkish Cypriots into refugees. Under the Treaty of Guarantee, Greece, Turkey and Britain were to serve as protectors of the new Republic and had the right to intervene on the occasion of severe violations of the constitutional order. However, it was not until 1974, when a newly installed military regime in Athens supported a coup against the government of the Republic of Cyprus, that a guarantor nation intervened. Fearing that the coup would be followed by a declaration of *enosis* and by attacks on Turkish Cypriots, Turkey intervened, capturing about 40 per cent of the territory of the island by the time a ceasefire was arranged. *Enosis* had been thwarted, but in order to guarantee the safety of the Greek Cypriots and Turkish Cypriots caught on the wrong side of the front line, the two sides agreed to population exchanges; this was a *de facto* division of the island, with thousands of additional refugees from both communities (about 60,000 Turkish Cypriots and 150,000 Greek Cypriots had to abandon their homes).

Conflict dimensions

Initially, Greek Cypriots used Greece as a space to define their identity, while Turkish Cypriots used Turkey as a space to define theirs (Güven Lisaniler and Rodriguez, 2002; Kızılyürek, 2005). Subsequent redefinitions of these identities have not diminished the distinctions between those two groups: indeed, after 1974, Greek Cypriots developed a more independent identity, differentiated themselves from mainland Greeks and began to ground their identity primarily on Cyprus. In the northern part of Cyprus, the 'Cypriotness' of Turkish Cypriots began to face the challenge of their new 'internal' others – Turkish settlers, illegal immigrant workers, the Turkish army, and Turkey's political and cultural elites. In other words, many Turkish (Cypriots) discovered their Cypriotness or the Cypriot part of their identity when they had to directly face their 'distant relatives' ('mainland Turks'). Nowadays, Greek Cypriots use the Republic of Cyprus (Cyprus as a whole) as their mainland and as the space to define their identity, whereas Turkish Cypriots use the Turkish Republic of Northern Cyprus (the northern part of the island) as their 'baby land' (still not their mainland) and the place to define their identity.

In Cyprus there is therefore a strong link between processes of identity-building and territory, a link that has been reinforced by the geographical separation of the two communities. They now live in different parts of the island, a feature which distinguishes the situation in Cyprus from most other contemporary conflicts taking place in Europe and which renders it similar to an inter-state conflict. From 1974 until 23 April 2003 (with the re-opening of the checkpoints dividing northern and southern Cyprus), there was no (peaceful or violent, social, cultural or economic) contact between the two communities, except for limited inter-communal relations organised and sponsored by international actors, which took place either in another country or in the buffer zone, and informal relations through the initiatives of organisations such as unions (Broome, 2005). This detached life resulted in the erosion and denial of common pains and joys (traditional Cypriot foods, music, folk dances, folk poems), which in turn have made the two communities even more detached and ignorant of the feelings of 'others'. Visions of the future also follow two distinct paths: while Turkish Cypriots imagine an independent and internationally recognised Turkish-Cypriot state, or a loose federal state with Greek Cypriots, Greek Cypriots imagine a unitary Greek-Cypriot state with minorities – Turkish Cypriots, Maronites, Armenians and Latins.

Partition has also reinforced socio-economic divisions between the two communities, and Turkish Cypriots tend to hold Greek Cypriots responsible for their poor socio-economic situation. According to them, their low socio-economic level results from the 1963–74 period, when Turkish Cypriots were expelled from the public positions of the Republic of Cyprus and were forced to live in enclaves until 1974; since 1974, economic embargoes on the Turkish Cypriots, exercised by Greek-Cypriot authorities, have further impeded the economic development of the northern part of the island. What makes these socio-economic differences all the more relevant for understanding the current stalemate in Cyprus is the fact that many Greek Cypriots consider the economic difficulties faced by the north as a significant obstacle to reunification or even enhanced cooperation.

Concerns over physical security and economic viability are also intimately tied to the questions of property reinstatement and the freedoms of movement and residence in a (confederal) Turkish-Cypriot state. The unrestricted reinstatement of all property to pre-1963 (or pre-1974) owners would severely reduce the meaning of bizonality as well as displace a significant number of Turkish Cypriots and the vast majority of post-1974 Turkish settlers. Turkish Cypriots fear that the widespread haemorrhage of property back to the original Greek-Cypriot owners would place them in a position of economic subordination. The restoration of full freedoms of movement and residence also causes alarm. The fear is that a massive resettlement of Greek Cypriots in Turkish-Cypriot territory could result in threats to the physical security of the Turkish-Cypriot community as well as its economic domination by Greek Cypriots.

Since the partition of the island, the international context has changed a lot, but the Cyprus conflict remains to be shaped and characterised by external factors. In particular, the (conflicting) relations between Greece and Turkey have always been a determining factor of the degree of intensity of the Cyprus conflict. Greek–Turkish rivalry hinders the creation of shared or coexisting identities in Cyprus. A full settlement between Greece and Turkey, and greater cooperation between them, seem necessary for the settlement of the Cyprus conflict.

The geographical location of Cyprus has always been another determining factor of the conflict. The interest of international actors has resulted in a set of attempted solutions (in 1977, 1979, 1983, 1989 and 2004), none of which has led to a sustainable agreement (Tocci and Kovziridze, 2004). The Cold War has ended, and new international political actors have emerged on the Cyprus stage, such as the EU, and transnational agencies, which limit the sovereignty of nation states. Globalisation also creates new threats and opportunities. The flows of refugees, workers and immigrants make nation states more heterogeneous. Cyprus is no longer the country only of Greek Cypriots, Turkish Cypriots, Armenians, Maronites and Latins, but also of Turkish, Sri Lankan, Indian, Pontus Greek, British, German, Bulgarian Turk, Pakistani and Russian settlers, and others (Yaşin, 2000).

What many now see as crucial for the resolution of the conflict is the creation of a new identity, a 'Cypriotness', which would be more inclusive, beyond nation state identity formulation; this would be favoured by the creation or recognition of common interests or common concerns, like the local environment, which is threatened by population increase, technology, mass tourism, population flows and so on. Globalisation, which requires economic cooperation in order to cope with threats such as drug trafficking and money laundering, and the black economy, also seems to invite such an evolution.

If we refer to the conflict dimensions identified above, the salient dimensions of the Cyprus conflict thus seem to point at religious differences, identity claims, culture and language differences, socio-economic disparities, population shifts, territory claims, decolonisation/globalisation processes, and neighbour/borders claims. Among these salient dimensions, culture and language, territory, decolonisation and neighbour interferences seem to be dominant. In this perspective, the situation in Cyprus displays striking similarities with other cases of conflict in Europe. For instance, as far as culture and language differences are concerned, the situation in Cyprus bears many resemblances to Belgium, Estonia and the former Yugoslavia. Cyprus also displays similarities with Belgium or Estonia as far as socio-economic dimensions are concerned, but the socio-economic disparities in the Cyprus case follow the territorial border of the EU itself, a division which significantly hinders the Union's capacity to intervene. In fact, territorial claims can be considered the most salient dimension in Cyprus. Finally, the impacts of colonisation and decolonisation, as well as of globalisation and the transition to a market economy, can also be traced in other cases of conflict, for example in Estonia. And just like in Cyprus, the conflicts in Kosovo and in Northern Ireland have been marked by a constant interference of neighbouring countries, and/or by the existence of powerful diasporas.

What seems specific to the situation in Cyprus, however, is the enduring significance of external factors, such as 'motherland' involvement, and colonisation/decolonisation, which seemingly cannot be found at such a level of salience in any other conflict in Europe. It is also characterised by the low importance of political factors such as centre–periphery cleavage or access to citizenship – even though some political dimensions might have been decisive in the past, such as the security dilemma in the Turkish-Cypriot case. This does not mean that these factors explain by themselves the difficulty in resolving the conflict, but that, together with its other main characteristics such as territorial claims, socio-economic differentials and cultural and linguistic differences, they create a specific conflict scheme that must be taken into account when trying to assess the impact of European integration on the evolution of the conflict.

The impact of European integration on the Cyprus conflict: rule or exception?

It is not our purpose here to enter the ongoing debate about the definition of Europeanisation. In line with the definition proposed by Claudia Major (2005), we do not equate Europeanisation and European integration, insofar as Europeanisation is not limited to changes to state and sovereignty, but also covers domestic institutions and actors. What is more, there are organisations other than the EU within the European arena, such as the Organization for Security and Co-operation in Europe and the Council of Europe, which have an impact on national policies, especially on the management of conflicts. In addition, the study of the impact of Europeanisation should not be limited to EU member states, as institutional and policy changes related to the attraction of the European/EU model are occurring elsewhere, mainly in candidate or neighbouring countries. Finally, Europeanisation should not be confused with globalisation or homogenisation, since our research shows that these processes lead to different adaptations or evolutions at national and local levels. In terms of concrete mechanisms, following Radaelli, Europeanisation is here defined as:

> processes of (a) construction, (b) diffusion and (c) institutionalisation of formal and informal rules, procedures, policy paradigms, styles, 'ways of doing things' and shared beliefs and norms which are first defined and consolidated in the making of EU decisions and then incorporated within the logic of domestic discourse, identities, political structures and public policies. (Radaelli, 2000: 4)

Diez et al. (2006) have identified four main paths through which the EU can affect conflicts, depending on whether they are driven by the concrete interventions of EU actors, or through the discursive, legal and institutional framework of the EU: path 1, 'compulsory impact', refers to a direct approach of 'carrots' and 'sticks' used by the EU in order to solve a conflict; path 2, 'enabling impact', relates to the more indirect influence of the institutional and discursive framework of the EU, through the *acquis communautaire* and the socialisation of policy-makers into a European discourse; path 3, 'connective impact', refers to financial or organisational support for inter-communal activities; and path 4, 'constructive impact', relates to the more long-term change of conflict identities enabled by the introduction, under the impulse of European integration, of new discursive frameworks. This detailed approach of the various levers the EU can use in order to reduce or even resolve conflict is useful for our purposes, even though those levers are mainly 'top-down' instruments (apart from path 4), and 'work' obviously better on territories and populations which are already in the EU, or are likely to be so in the near future – a perspective which is far from given as far as the northern part of Cyprus is concerned. These various paths suggest that European integration should help pacify conflicts characterised first and foremost by political and socio-economic dimensions – as these are the main features of European integration itself – and that it should impact positively in the long term on other dimensions.

As far as direct instruments and concrete schemes are concerned, Coppieters et al. (2004) have developed a theoretical model which distinguishes two types of actions the EU can undertake in order to settle a conflict: first, providing a framework for resolving constitutional issues; and second, acting as a mediator or supporting mediation efforts between conflict parties. They then distinguish between three levels of impact EU institutions and policies can have: first, the level of legal and administrative structures of domestic institutions; second, domestic economic, social or security policies; and third, societal changes in general. In cases of protracted and complex conflicts, such as the Cyprus case, no sustainable peace can be envisaged without changes affecting all three levels.

How do these paths of influence affect the dimensions of conflict we have identified? Because the EU is both a framework and an actor, it can certainly positively influence the cultural dimensions (but only in the long term), especially through paths 4 and 2 as described by Diez et al. (2006), namely by gradually changing discursive frameworks, at both elite and grass-roots levels. Admittedly, in conflicts such as the Northern Irish one (Hayward, 2006), the EU has been pushing towards the creation of a situation in which various identities can be peacefully expressed, rather than radically changed or suppressed. However, the more entrenched conflicting identities are, the longer these transformations are likely to take. And because identities are not frozen, but are, on the contrary, influenced by the evolution of the context, it is unclear whether European integration might not in fact lead to further identity claims. Many advocates of European integration present the nation state as an outdated reference, and invite EU (future) members to overcome their divisions, and collaborate. As such, a large part of the pro-integration discourse stands in contradiction to the classical political identities of many communities in conflict, as in Cyprus, the Basque country or Kosovo, to take only a few examples. Moreover, there is a possibility that disagreement on the EU's role in these conflicts might in effect reinforce divisions and tensions which already exist between communities, because there is a portion of these populations that believes that its identity is threatened by the blurring of sovereignty caused by European integration, and by the setting up of cross-border institutions. More often than not, communities in conflict see EU involvement in radically different ways, a trend that may reinforce other cleavages. What is more, European integration is sometimes perceived as threatening the community's perceived specificities, by including them in a wider political space, where small communities play only a minor role. As a consequence, the impact of European integration on these cultural dimensions can be extremely ambiguous, and in any case very long to come about.

As far as the socio-economic dimensions of conflicts are concerned, the impact of European integration seems much more direct and effective, as Europeanisation can reduce socio-economic differentials and grievances, through the granting of various types of economic aid, as stressed by Coppieters et al. (2004). For instance, the EU actively underpins and monitors the peace process in Northern Ireland; in order to support it, it has raised its subvention through the Structural Funds and, to a lesser extent, through the International Fund for Ireland, and has since 1994 led other initiatives, such as the Special Support Programme for Peace and Reconciliation (Hayward, 2004). However, these efforts have not always been successful; for example, the funds available through the Programme for Peace and Reconciliation have not yet been completely taken up by local organisations. It is also important to recall that the socio-economic impact of European integration can be called 'positive' only if both sides benefit from it. In this perspective, the accession of Cyprus to the EU 'creates' a new difficulty, because it makes the reunification of the island even less desirable for Greek Cypriots. This problem does not appear in other cases of 'border' conflicts, such as Northern Ireland, where both sides of the border are integrated – and were integrated at the same time – into the EU.

This ambiguous impact of European integration is even more obvious when it comes to dealing with territorial issues, which are, as we have seen, central in the Cyprus case. By fostering cooperation and exchanges between states, the EU can provide an incentive for the settlement of territory-related conflicts – as long as communities in conflict give a predominantly material meaning to 'territory', rather than a symbolic and emotional one – and it can help in managing the cultural diversity resulting from demographic shifts.

But peace-building strategies are much less effective when territory is first and foremost given a symbolic rather than a material value, as we can witness in Kosovo. In the Cyprus case, territory bears both a symbolic and a material value, and is closely linked to the development of separate identities. As such, it is disputable whether the EU can provide an effective framework or even an incentive for resolution, since it has allowed the accession, in effect, of the southern part of the island alone. As a consequence, it cannot use any longer the accession prospect as a carrot for convincing the most reluctant parts of the Greek-Cypriot community, and its multi-level system of governance cannot work as a pattern for a solution on the island. In other words, proposing joint sovereignty over the island no longer seems to be an option, and the two communities' mutually exclusive conceptions of statehood have been reinforced rather than undermined.

The same kind of reasoning seems to apply to border issues. It is common to read that Europeanisation is provoking the blurring of territorial boundaries by the increase in cross-border cooperation and migration. For instance, in the Northern Irish case, it is possible to observe an increase in the exchanges between the northern and the southern part of the island (Tonge, 2004). But it is worth keeping in mind that this territorial blurring primarily applies to institutionalised and well established nation states (Féron, 2002). In other words, the European construction may have some influence on the states' boundaries, but it is less likely to do so on local territories. However, on this border question, the Cyprus case differs considerably from the Northern Irish one, because it is characterised by the existence of one major border, and not by the existence of a series of internal borders, as in Northern Ireland, where most Catholics and Protestants inhabit different parts of the same cities. For the time being, the integration of the southern part of the island alone within the EU has created a new obstacle to conflict resolution, but we can suppose that, provided the north and south of Cyprus are one day integrated in the Union, European integration will help to lessen the meaning and importance of the border.

The impact of European integration on the political dimensions of conflicts is seemingly easier to trace, mainly because Europeanisation has a direct effect on access to citizenship, and on the political opportunities and rights offered to minorities. However, as we have seen, these issues are not very salient in the Cyprus case. Admittedly, some political factors play a role in the perpetuation of the conflict, insofar as political elites on both sides of the border do not seem to have reached the famous 'hurting stalemate' that will lead them to compromise (Groom and Webb, 2007). But if European integration does indeed influence the priorities and ideologies of political and cultural elites, as stated by Diez et al. (2006), it is doubtful whether it can similarly affect opposing elites further divided by the accession process. What is more, this political and ideological impact is much less obvious on the greatest part of the population, and it is worth remembering that those who suffer the most from conflicts are often those who have only a very vague experience of what European integration could be. The question therefore remains how much of such change in elite cooperation, if any, will find an echo among the 'masses', and whether European integration will effectively compensate the vested interest that some elites have in the perpetuation of the conflict. However, the European construction has obviously helped to disqualify violence, terrorism and other violent methods traditionally used in community conflicts, and democracy and dialogue have become the only legitimate means to resolve them. The development of the EU has initiated changes not only in the terminology of conflicts, but also in political concepts and substantive priorities. The risk of a violent confrontation in Cyprus has accordingly decreased, and now seems rather unlikely. But at the same time, the division of the island seems thoroughly entrenched.

Finally, other cases of conflict show that the impact of European integration on the external dimensions of conflicts (involvement of neighbouring countries, diasporas, etc.) can sometimes be positive. Even if EU officials tend to favour the freezing of current state borders, and seem rather reluctant to see the creation of new states, they can also be pragmatic when necessity arises, at least regarding territories not yet included in the Union, as shown in the cases of Kosovo and Montenegro. The EU can also provide a framework for managing (de)colonisation and neighbouring factors, through mechanisms such as joint sovereignty, as in the case of Northern Ireland (Hayward, 2006). But here again, the 'joint sovereignty' model can work only if the two sides of the border are either in, or out, of the Union. In the current configuration, a joint sovereignty scheme in Cyprus seems very unlikely.

Similarly, on territories sharing the same status *vis-à-vis* the EU, European integration can help both to reduce the influence of diasporas and to defuse problems created by the existence of border communities, thanks to the opening of borders and the free movement of persons. But this cannot happen if both sides of the border are not part of the EU. In the case of Cyprus, the problem is further complicated by the properties question and 'resettlement'.

Conclusions

From this general overview, it seems that European integration can have a positive impact on conflicts characterised primarily by the salience of socio-economic and geographic dimensions, especially socio-economic differentials (provided that it does not deepen them in the case of an existing border, if both sides are not at the same stage of integration *vis-à-vis* the Union) and territory (especially if it is given a material rather than a symbolic value, and if communities in conflict inhabit different parts of this territory). It can also positively influence some political dimensions, such as access to citizenship and a centre–periphery cleavage, as well as external factors, provided that all sides of the conflict are integrated, so that joint sovereignty schemes and the principle of the free movement of people can apply. In contrast, its impact should be rather blurred or slow to come about for conflicts in which cultural dimensions are salient.

If we accept that these hypotheses are correct, or at least plausible, then European integration would definitely have a very positive impact in the short or medium term on the situation in Cyprus, if both sides were integrated, possibly meaning by this not only the northern part of Cyprus, but also Turkey, which would be part of a joint sovereignty scheme that could be set up. In a scenario where northern Cyprus, but not Turkey, were included, a positive effect would still be possible (especially on the socio-economic and territorial dimensions of the conflict), but it would be limited, as long as the process of identity redefinition had not led both communities to put stress first and foremost on their 'Cypriotness' – which presupposes deep cultural evolution. Our research, however, suggests that the current situation (with the integration of one side but not the other) may lead to a deepening of divisions between the two communities, and to a perpetuation of the conflict. This does not necessarily mean that it is likely that Cyprus will witness further outbursts of violence, but simply that the reunification of the island is less plausible, at least in the medium term.

Comparing Cyprus with other cases of conflict thus sheds light on its very specific current evolution. Not only has it become more entrenched after the integration of the southern part of the island into the EU, but it also increasingly mixes inter-state and intra-state features. The accession of the south has reinforced the cleavage between both sides of the border, and thus renders less and less effective peace-building activities traditionally set up and implemented in communal (intra-state) conflicts. The solidification of the border, its quasi-institutionalisation, cannot be undermined by the opening of a few gates, or by meetings between political elites who sometimes seem to agree only on disagreeing. At least in the short term, the main impact of European integration has been to strengthen the already strong external dimensions of the Cyprus conflict, as well as the disparities between the two parts of the island. This evolution has to be taken urgently into account in conflict resolution activities set up at the EU level, by giving renewed importance to diplomatic activities, and by negotiating with Turkey some sort of transitional status *vis-à-vis* the Union of the northern part of the island, and possibly of Turkey itself.

Note

1 This chapter builds on the results of the PEACE-COM project, a three-year research project (2004–07) funded by the European Commission's Sixth Framework Programme. Further information is available at http://peacecom.spri.ucl.ac.be.

12

The refugee factor in two protracted conflicts: Cyprus and Palestine compared

Peter Loizos and Tobias Kelly

Introduction

In the early years of the twenty-first century, two peace processes at the eastern end of the Mediterranean, both of which had once widely been seen as very promising, came to a halt. In Cyprus, the Annan Plan was rejected by the majority of Greek Cypriots. In Israel/Palestine, the Oslo peace process collapsed into the second *intifada*. Despite their obvious differences, not least in the levels of political violence, the fate of the refugees caused by both conflicts has played a major role not only in determining how the relative paths of the conflicts in Cyprus and Israel/Palestine developed, but also in the eventual collapse of the respective peace processes. This chapter is a comparative exploration of the roles that refugees, as individuals, as groups and as political issues, have played in the failure of both peace processes. Although there have been Turkish-Cypriot refugees from the southern part of the island, and Jewish refugees from the Arab states, this chapter focuses on Greek-Cypriot refugees and Palestinian refugees, as it is the way in which the rights of these two groups have been treated that has been the most controversial issue in both peace processes.

In five comparative sections, this chapter explores the historical conditions, legal statuses, economic conditions, access to political representation and the geopolitical factors that have influenced the ways in which the two conflicts and the refugees have been dealt with. A further section explores the failures of the Annan Plan in Cyprus and the Oslo process in Israel/Palestine, and the role of the refugee issue in these failures. We conclude with some wider suggestions about the implications of the refugee issue for attempts to settle long-term political conflicts.

The development of the refugee problems

The Palestinian refugee crisis was produced by a struggle between an indigenous Arab nationalism shaped by the British colonial project in the Middle East, and a Jewish settler nationalism rooted in European anti-Semitism. Following the creation of the British Mandate for Palestine at the end of the Ottoman empire, the Balfour Declaration of 1917 committed the British to the promotion of a 'Jewish national home' in Palestine. In the mid-1940s, militant Zionists turned their guns on the British with the aim of establishing a Jewish state and, following the holocaust, Jewish immigration to Palestine increased greatly. By 1947, the British Mandate could no longer control either the Jewish or the Arab communities. In response, the United Nations (UN) passed Resolution 181, which supported the partition of Palestine into two states: one Jewish, one Arab. The British left it to the two groups to fight it out. The Zionist forces accepted partition, while the Palestinian leadership, divided or in exile, rejected partition on the basis that Palestine was not a legitimate British possession and so could not be granted by the British to the Zionist movement. Throughout 1947 and 1948, Zionist and Palestinian Arab forces fought across Mandate Palestine. The better trained, organised and equipped Zionist Haganah was largely victorious against the *ad hoc* Palestinian Arab forces. When the leadership of the Jewish community declared Israeli independence in mid-May 1948, the surrounding states of Egypt, Jordan, Syria, Lebanon and Iraq sent in their troops. However, the efforts of the Arab states were limited by their often contradictory agendas. By the end of October, Israeli forces controlled over 78 per cent of Mandate Palestine, a space considerably larger than that which had been allotted to Israel under the UN partition plan.

Following its declaration of independence in 1948, the new state of Israel was quickly recognised by the international community. The Arab state envisaged in the UN partition plan was never established, and the areas of Mandate Palestine not under Israeli control were either annexed to the Hashemite Kingdom of Jordan (i.e., the West Bank and East Jerusalem), or placed under Egyptian military rule (i.e., the Gaza Strip). The majority of Palestinians became stateless persons. By the time the armistice agreements were signed in January 1949, only 150,000 of the original 950,000 Palestinian Arab residents remained in the area now under Israeli control. The refugees had fled, fearing forced removals or worse from the rapidly advancing Zionist forces. By 2003, the UN estimated that these people and their descendants numbered over 4 million, spread across Jordan, Syria, Lebanon, the West Bank and Gaza Strip, and elsewhere.[1]

After the signing of armistice agreements between Israel and its neighbouring Arab states, the border areas remained sites of sporadic conflict. In the summer of 1967, after rising tension, the Israeli military defeated the Egyptian, Jordanian and Syrian armies in a matter of days and occupied the West Bank, Gaza Strip and Sinai peninsula, causing another exodus of refugees. After the 1967 defeat, the Palestinian Liberation Organization (PLO), established in 1964, became an increasingly influential actor and for the first time the Palestinians had a political organisation that spoke directly in their name. However, although the PLO was a diplomatic success, in that at one point it was recognised by more states than Israel was, it was militarily ineffective (Sayigh, 1997). The political power of the Israeli state became unchallengeable, in large measure because of the strategic alliance forged with the United States after 1967.

The Cypriot refugee crisis was formed, as in the Palestine, in the twilight of British imperial power in the eastern Mediterranean. When the British acquired Cyprus in 1878 from the Ottomans, a minority of Greek Cypriots were attracted to *enosis*, a political union with Greece. Those Turkish Cypriots mindful of the bloody expulsion of their co-religionists from the Morea and Crete viewed *enosis* with alarm.[2] It was these conflicting nationalist visions which were to produce the island's refugees between 1955 and 1974. Greek-Cypriot pro-*enosis* agitation was peaceful until the October 1931 disturbances. From then on it dominated relations between the British and the Greek Cypriots. On 1 April 1955, the National Organisation of Cypriot Fighters (EOKA), a Greek Cypriot guerrilla movement for national liberation, exploded its first bombs in an effort to further the *enosis* project. These actions were politically supported by Greece, whose leaders had lost patience with Anthony Eden's refusals to show flexibility over the future of the island. Turkish-Cypriot nationalists soon formed a clandestine armed organisation of their own, known as the Turkish Resistance Organisation (TMT), which promoted the idea of partitioning the island between the Greek and Turkish populations (Bahcheli, 1990; Stephens, 1966).

The Zurich–London Agreements in 1959–60, in which three allied members of the North Atlantic Treaty Organisation (NATO), Britain, Turkey and Greece, had decisive voices, resulted in an independent Cypriot state with a complex power-sharing constitution, which excluded both *enosis* and partition (*taksim*). However, this compromise failed to satisfy the more extreme nationalists in each community, and after three troubled years the fragile state was ridden by fresh inter-communal fighting. In 1964, Turkey threatened to make a full-scale military incursion, and only decisive intervention by the US, the UK and the UN prevented this. A further flare-up in 1967 led to a second invasion threat by Turkey, which again the US spent more political capital on preventing. Subsequently, the Greek Cypriots sought to pursue *enosis* through diplomacy. However, in 1967 an anti-communist military dictatorship had taken power in Greece and in 1972 it started to bankroll a new insurrectionary movement among the Greek Cypriots, aimed at achieving *enosis* by overthrowing the democratically elected Cypriot President, Makarios. This movement carried out a coup on 20 July 1974 and, having crushed the pro-Makarios democrats, found themselves facing invasion by Turkey, which then occupied 38 per cent of the island. The resulting violence meant that, within a few months, there was an almost total separation of the two major ethnic groups, behind two opposed armies, with a UN peace-keeping force in between. Technically, the situation in Cyprus remains a ceasefire. The south of the island, which the Greek Cypriots control, has international recognition as the Republic of Cyprus (RoC). The north of the island, occupied by Turkey, has declared itself the 'Turkish Republic of Northern Cyprus' (TRNC) but is recognised only by Turkey, while Turkey refuses to recognise the RoC.

The Palestinian and Cypriot refugee crises were the result of clashes between an indigenous nationalism and a settler colonial movement on the one hand, and a clash between two indigenous ethno-national movements on the other. Both conflicts developed in the wake of the Ottoman empire and as the British empire weakened and contracted. Although sizeable proportions of both populations were displaced, the ultimate result was a Greek-Cypriot state, but no state for the Palestinians. The comparative statehood and citizenship of the two populations would remain a major difference between the two situations. At the same time, although Cyprus remains tense and deadlocked, there are only rare casualties; in contrast, Palestine/Israel is regularly caught up in cycles of lethal violence.

The comparative legal statuses of the refugees

Since 1948, the Palestinians refugees have existed in a legal limbo. The Israeli state refused to allow the 1948 refugees to return to their homes, arguing that they represented a security threat which would endanger the Jewish majority in Israel, and their property was also confiscated, without compensation. In 1950, the UN established the United Nations Relief and Works Agency for Palestine Refugees in the Near East (UNWRA) in order to deal with the immediate humanitarian aspects of the crisis. Although most of the Palestinians who fled had not crossed an international frontier, the UN decided to designate them as 'refugees' on a needs basis. Refugee status was also passed down to the descendants of those initially displaced, meaning that the number of official refugees has now more than quadrupled. In this context, Palestinian refugees were granted limited legal rights by the various states in which they were hosted. In general, this meant that most Arab states treated the refugees as a temporary presence and gave them some residency rights but no permanent legal footing. The notable exception was Jordan, where, after 1948, all Palestinian residents were claimed as Jordanian citizens. However, although, or even because, over 70 per cent of the population of Jordan was of Palestinian origin, the Jordanian government has attempted to stress their status as Jordanians rather than as Palestinian refugees. The vast majority of the other 1948 refugees have remained stateless persons, and have relied on refugee documents issued by the states in which they are resident. The Casablanca Protocol issued by the League of Arab States in 1965 was supposed to stabilise their rights of movement, residency and work, but it has been honoured more in the breach. In practice, Palestinian refugees have almost only contingent rights to residency, movement and work, making them subject to discrimination in virtually every Middle Eastern state (Shiblak, 1996).

The legal status of the Greek Cypriots displaced in 1974 is more straightforward. In contrast to most Palestinians, who became stateless, the Greek-Cypriot refugees remained citizens of the RoC. In international refugee law, they are 'internally displaced persons' (IDPs) rather than refugees. However, some of those who left the island after 1974 have claimed refugee status in the countries to which they migrated – chiefly the UK, Canada, the US and Australia. Like Palestinian refugees, the Greek-Cypriot refugees also lost access to former properties in the Turkish-controlled part of Cyprus, which were occupied either by Turkish Cypriots or by settlers from Turkey. However, in addition to their retention of citizenship rights in a modern democratic state, Greek-Cypriot refugees received special entitlements granted by that state to ease their transition to a semblance of normal life. In contrast to the Palestinian refugees, displacement for the Greek Cypriots granted them more, not fewer, social and economic rights than those of their neighbours.

The major distinction between Palestinian and Greek Cypriot refugees is that of citizenship and statehood. Greek Cypriots enjoy full citizenship rights. With the notable exception of Jordan, most Palestinians are stateless, and have only temporary residence rights. Although both populations lost property and livelihoods, most Palestinians were also denied residency, social, political and civil rights.

The comparative economic conditions of the refugees

The precarious legal status of most Palestinian refugees has translated into their economic conditions. Whereas middle-class and upper-class refugees were often able to make use of the contacts and relatives they had in Beirut or Damascus, the majority of refugees were small-scale peasant farmers who, when they lost their land, also lost their only means of livelihood. Furthermore, propertyless and largely unskilled, the refugees have faced the same difficult economic conditions as the citizens of the countries in which they reside. Syria, Jordan and Egypt have long-term stagnating economies, whereas Lebanon has faced the instability of years of civil war. Ironically, the refugees in Gaza and the West Bank have, until recently, fared best economically, as, like the other residents of the area, they have often found employment in Israel.

As well as facing the economic conditions of the countries in which they live, many refugees have had additional problems arising from their legal status – such as severe restrictions placed on their employment, particularly in Lebanon. Even where they have not been subject to legal discrimination, they have often faced socio-economic prejudices on the basis of their refugee status. In Jordan, for example, despite making up the majority of the population and formally having full rights of citizenship, Palestinians represent only 10 per cent of all government employees. Many refugees work in the black market or fill the lowest-paid jobs in agriculture, construction and industry. The PLO also became a major employer of camp residents. As a result of this economic marginalisation, Palestinian refugee camps have been centres of deprivation and poverty. In the Gaza Strip in 2002 over 40 per cent of the refugees were unemployed, and in Jordan 31 per cent of all camp households fall below the poverty line (Shiblak, 1996: 43). A survey by the United Nations Children's Fund (UNICEF) in 1993 found that in Lebanese refugee camps only 37 per cent of men aged between fifteen and forty-nine years were employed (Shiblak, 1996: 43). Refugees also receive few, if any, social services from the states in which they reside. Refugees in Lebanon, for example, are entitled to no state services, despite the fact that they pay social insurance contributions on their wages.

In stark contrast, although the Greek Cypriots faced relatively major economic losses in 1974, they have managed to turn a potential economic and political disaster into what has been termed an 'economic miracle'. Mass unemployment lasted less than eighteen months, and major reconstruction projects, both state-led and private, redeployed refugees as a development resource, a labour force keen to work on almost any reasonable terms (Christodoulou, 1992; Strong, 1999; Zetter, 1992). Furthermore, after 1974, trade unions agreed to suspend confrontations with employers, a concordat lasting into the late 1980s. The Greek-Cypriot economy grew rapidly from the late 1970s and throughout the 1980s, due to the purchasing power of the nearby oil-exporting countries, the growth of mass tourism from northern Europe, the backwash effects of the Lebanese civil war, and the development of the Cyprus merchant fleet, one of the world's largest. The consequence for those displaced in 1974 was that there were many opportunities for them to remake their livelihoods, and these were energetically grasped. Few of them were forced to remain in refugee camps for more than the first year of displacement. While rehousing the poorest refugees typically took three to four years, by 1980 virtually everyone displaced in 1974 had a weatherproof home and an economic stake, however small.

Although both the Greek-Cypriot and Palestinian refugees largely originated in rural and relatively poor areas in their home countries, the Greek Cypriots have fared a great deal better economically than their Palestinian counterparts. In large measure this is due to three factors. First, the Greek Cypriots had a recognised state, which allowed them international credit and trade. Secondly, the secure legal status of the Greek-Cypriot refugees meant that they could plan for the future, and also receive considerable economic support from the state. In contrast, Palestinian refugees have always faced an uncertain future, have received little in the way of welfare and social support from their host states, and have often had their economic opportunities restricted. Thirdly, when it mattered most, that is, in 1976–85, Cyprus boomed, unlike war-torn Lebanon, stagnant Jordan and sluggish Egypt.

The comparative political representation of the refugees

Although the 'right of return' has been a central feature of the wider Arab and Palestinian national agendas, refugees themselves have largely remained politically marginal. There was, for example, no refugee representation at the armistice talks between the Arab states and Israel in February 1949. As stateless persons, the refugees have had little influence on the decisions of the states in which they dwell that directly affect them. Although Jordan and Lebanon both set up branches of government with direct responsibility for Palestinian refugees, these mainly took on regulatory rather than representative functions, being closely linked to the security forces. The dispersal of refugees across Lebanon, Syria, Jordan, the West Bank, the Gaza Strip and further afield, all with very different economic, political and legal experiences, has also meant a dilution of influence of the refugees, making a unified 'refugee' position hard to produce.

However, a common experience of discrimination, combined with the 1967 defeat of the Arab states by the Israeli military, prompted a sense that only through an independent Palestinian infrastructure could the refugees improve their individual positions and national aspirations. It was this realisation that led to the support for the PLO. Although, in its early years at least, the expressed goal of the PLO was the return of refugees, and refugees held senior positions in the original leadership, they have played a decreasingly important role in decision-making. The majority of senior PLO positions have gone to people from the West Bank and Gaza Strip (Sayigh, 1997: 671). Furthermore, there has been even less representation of Palestinian refugees as *refugees* within the PLO. Although the PLO has a Department of Refugee Affairs, this has been a largely administrative body, rather than a forum through which refugees can voice their concerns. This situation reflects the wider process of PLO state-building, which has tended to favour the reproduction of top-down resource allocation rather than grass-roots mobilisation (Robinson, 1997). Since the start of the second *intifada* in September 2000, refugee camps have arguably played a central role in popular militancy, but it is difficult to tell to what extent they are doing so as refugees, or merely as part of a wider group of politically and economically marginalised people.

In large part, the relatively marginal role of the refugees as political actors has been due to the very centrality of the refugee issue to the Palestinian national movement. No one political faction could be said to be more refugee-orientated than another. Fatah, Hamas and smaller parties have all placed the refugee issue high on their agendas. Refugee expulsion was not seen as a tragedy for individual refugees only, but as a national catastrophe, that has thwarted attempts at national self-determination (Khalidi, 1992: 30). Until 1968, the 'right of return' was usually subsumed within the wider struggle for the liberation of all of historical Palestine. It was implicitly assumed that once Palestine had been liberated, the refugees would return. However, following the 1967 war, the occupation of the West Bank and Gaza Strip, and the increasing dominance of the two-state solution, the 'liberation of Palestine' and the 'right of return' became distinct issues. This has left a crucial ambiguity over the meanings of 'return'. In particular, there is a dispute over whether 'return' should be seen as an issue of individual rights to return to former homes, or as an issue of national self-determination, and therefore one that could be fulfilled through the creation of a Palestinian state, wherever that maybe (Khalidi, 1992: 19).

In contrast to the Palestinians, displaced Greek Cypriots remained citizens of the RoC and, as a result, their right to political representation was never in doubt. They could vote in elections and make their preferences known. For much of the last thirty years the President of the day has consulted an all-party National Council, and throughout these years national unity has been a dominant theme. As a result, it can be argued that the refugees as an interest group have never felt forgotten or left out. They have their own national association which speaks directly for them collectively, and they also have regional political associations, with more or less symbolic functions most of the time, but which make their voices heard whenever a political solution is under national discussion.

The Greek-Cypriot refugees were sufficiently numerous that, had they acted in a concerted manner, they might have become enough of a radical force to demand a major restructuring of the polity (Loizos, 1981: 135–8). Their discontent was potentially explosive. However, no important radical pro-refugee movement arose, nor did any radical challenge to the pre-1974 modes of politics arise. Although the refugees have been inscribed on the electoral register by reference to their pre-1974 communities of residence, this appears to be more of a symbolic than a substantive matter. The refugees have voted for the four major pre-war political parties, and have distributed their votes across the party spectrum in such a way that their impact as a collective pressure group has tended to be diffused and incremental rather than radical and anti-systemic. In an important sense, the way non-displaced Greek Cypriots responded to those who were displaced meant that a politics of radical challenge was neither necessary nor particularly appropriate. One senior member of the Planning Bureau, which authored the three 'emergency plans' which were to take Cyprus from the threatened economic collapse of 1974 to healthy development, said: 'My mother was from Kythrea. She was a refugee. We did not have to be told to think about the refugees – they were our parents and grandparents!'[3]

In both the Palestinian and the Greek-Cypriot cases, the refugees have been seen as a concern of wider nationalist politics. However, the Greek Cypriots had greater levels of electoral leverage, largely because they were incorporated into an already functioning democracy. The Palestinians, stateless, faced the task of building their own representative structures through the PLO, which developed largely as a top-down organisation. Although refugees were a central part of the nationalist agenda and numerically dominant, they were relatively marginalised and had little access to mechanisms of accountability.

Comparative geopolitical issues

The Israeli–Palestinian conflict and the Palestinian refugee issue are heavily internationalised and subject to wider geopolitical pressures. Not only are refugees subject to the foreign-policy considerations of their host countries, but also US support for Israel has been increasingly influential. At a military level, US support has made the position of Israel unassailable. As a result, in the late 1970s and 1980s, the pragmatic wing of the PLO sought to play down the armed struggle in favour of a diplomatic approach, and in 1988 the PLO implicitly recognised the two-state solution. Such a diplomatic approach, which recognises Israel, has increasingly found favour among the Arab states. Egypt signed a peace agreement with Israel in the late 1970s, and Jordan eventually followed suit in the 1990s. Even Saudi Arabia and Syria have indicated their willingness to accept a two-state solution. However, at the diplomatic level, Israel has also received considerable support from the US, and in particular the US has vetoed critical resolutions on Israel in the UN Security Council. After 11 September 2001, support for Israel seemed to become increasingly entrenched, with the administration of George W. Bush becoming allied with successive right-wing governments in Israel. Within this general approach, the US has largely favoured the integration of Palestinian refugees into their host countries, rather than their return to Israel. In this context, pressure on the Israeli state to accept the return of Palestinian refugees is very unlikely to come from the US. In practical terms, the influence of the European Union (EU) in the area is limited, partly because of Israeli mistrust of Europe's alleged pro-Palestinian sympathies, and partly because of an unwillingness to force the issue with Israel.

The Greek-Cypriot refugee problem has also been internationalised, albeit largely at a regional rather than a global level. As the very essence of the conflict has concerned the relationship between Greece and Turkey, it has never been a simple matter of whether the two local communities 'got on with' each other. The very way each saw the other was, for many years, increasingly affected by how they saw their 'mother countries', and how their left-wing movements saw the UK, the US and the USSR. This situation is best characterised as a 'double-minority problem'. The Greek Cypriots were a majority on the island, but a minority in an Ottoman-dominated province or, later, in an eastern Aegean dominated by Turkey. The Turkish Cypriots were a minority *vis-à-vis* the Greek Cypriots and feared they would be even more powerless if Cyprus were to become a province of Greece (Loizos, 1976).

When in 1952 Greece and Turkey entered the North Atlantic Treaty Organization (NATO), the relations between the Alliance and the island became complicated by the anti-communism of the bloc, as the communist movement in Cyprus was strong among workers in both communities. The US decided in the mid-1950s that the British had mismanaged the EOKA rebellion, and favoured a pro-*enosis* solution for some years (Nicolet, 2001). The 1959 Zurich–London Agreements were an attempt by the British to keep both Greece and Turkey sweet after a period (1955–58) of estrangement, particularly between London and Athens, and Athens and Ankara. President Kennedy, in 1962, was worrying about Cyprus becoming a Mediterranean Cuba, and the Greek-Cypriot communist party's fraternal solidarity with Moscow aggravated those anxieties, as did reports of Greek Cypriots receiving training in the deployment of light missiles from Russian instructors in Egypt (Stephens, 1966). Over 1960–2003, the UK and the US attempted further damage limitation as the conflict in Cyprus threatened to disrupt the eastern flank of NATO, while the

USSR attempted to exploit the situation by overtures to Turkey and arms sales to the Makarios regime. Since 1964, the UN, and more recently the EU, have sought a negotiated settlement to the island's divisions.

Both the Cypriot and Israeli–Palestinian conflicts have been heavily influenced by wider geopolitical concerns. At a regional level, both Greece and Turkey have played major roles in Cyprus, and the neighbouring Arab states are an integral part of the Israeli–Palestinian conflict. It is at the wider international level that the contrast is more marked. Although the US, the UK and NATO have been involved in the Cyprus conflict, it has mainly been in order to maintain stability between NATO allies Greece and Turkey in the eastern Mediterranean. Engagement has therefore been tactical, rather than reflecting a deep-seated ideological commitment to either side. In contrast, US and to some extent European support for Israel has been based on what is seen as a strong moral commitment to the existence of the Israeli state (Allin and Simon, 2003). As a result, neither the US nor the EU has been willing to push solutions to the Palestinian refugee crisis which they felt would be unacceptable to majority opinion in Israel.

The failures of the Oslo process and the Annan Plan

By the late 1980s, the unofficial consensus, albeit a highly contested one, had been reached by many Israelis and Palestinians, as well as the international community, that any eventual solution to the conflict, if there was to be one, would have to be based on a two-state model. Important questions remained, however, about the exact nature of these states and the place of the refugees within them. In the early 1990s, Israel and the PLO, under the supervision of the US, the UN and Russia, signed the Oslo accords. For the PLO, Oslo came at a key juncture in its relationship with the West, as it had been marginalised by its support for Iraq in the first Gulf War. For the Israelis, Oslo instead offered the opportunity to hand over day-to-day responsibility for the occupied Palestinian population, after the violence of the first *intifada* in the late 1980s had demonstrated that it was difficult simultaneously to maintain claims to be a liberal democracy and to repress an occupied population. Crucially, Oslo was not a final peace agreement but a process, to lead to 'final status' negotiations. Central issues, including refugees and borders, were to be left unexamined and delayed until these negotiations took place. In the interim, Israel retained ultimate security control over the West Bank and Gaza Strip, but devolved limited administrative powers to the newly created Palestinian National Authority (PNA). Final status negotiations were scheduled for 1999, but were delayed several times and have never been completed.

There was a general perception among Palestinians that the Oslo process had at best left the refugee issue on the back burner and at worst threatened to shelve the question altogether. In the 1990s, the main focus of the PLO became the West Bank and Gaza, rather than the refugee camps in the diaspora. When PLO leader Yasser Arafat and the PLO sided with Iraq in the first Gulf War, the Arab states cut off funds to the PLO, which therefore could no longer fund the refugee camps. The PNA, restricted to the West Bank and Gaza Strip, became the main centre of focus and source of power for the Palestinian national leadership.[4] The result was a further marginalisation of the refugee populations outside the West Bank and Gaza Strip. There was also a widespread sense that the replacement of the PLO by the PNA as the main centre of gravity in Palestinian politics had created further incentives for the Palestinian leadership to compromise on the refugees in favour of issues such as settlements, which were of significance mainly to the West Bank and Gaza Strip. However, despite the marginalisation of the refugee issue, opposition to Oslo did not primarily come from the refugees *as refugees*, but from nationalist organisations such as Hamas, the Popular Front for the Liberation of Palestine and Islamic Jihad, as well as younger generations within Fatah. Furthermore, in general, refugees did not see Oslo solely through the refugee lens, and assessed its likely impact in terms of other factors, such as the continuing building of Jewish settlements across the West Bank and Gaza. However, there is no doubt that refugees did feel increasingly marginalised by the Oslo process. The constant deferral of final status negotiations in which refugee issues (and the status of Jerusalem) were to be addressed, and the lack of precise communications from the PLO, led to a sense of confusion and dislocation among the refugees.

Grievances around the issue of refugees have to be understood at two interacting levels. The first level relates to the individual political and civil rights of the people displaced, dispossessed and denied return since 1948. It is hard (although not impossible) to see how those displaced in 1948, or their descendants, can ever return to their original homes and property. Many of those homes have been destroyed, or are now occupied by Israeli citizens. Most acutely, Israel, intent on retaining a Jewish demographic majority in the state, abhors the return of Muslim and Christian Palestinian refugees to their homes. The issue of return therefore represents a claim to political and economic resources for a marginalised population, as much as a desire for a physical return. The second level concerns Palestinians as a collective. Here the issue of return has a much broader political significance than individual displacement and dispossession. The events of 1948 were a humiliating disaster for Palestinians at a collective and a national level. The 'return' of refugees would symbolically signal that the Palestinians were wronged in 1948. The legacy of the past sixty years has meant that very few are willing to forgive Israel or forget the 1948 *nakba* (disaster).

When final status negotiations collapsed in the summer and autumn of 2000, the issue of refugees was a decisive, if not the most important, factor in them doing so. Although the course of events is much disputed, according to several commentators considerable agreement was reached on the issues of the borders of the Palestinian state, the nature of its sovereignty and the future of Israeli settlements (Pressman, 2003). However, refugees (and the status of Jerusalem) remained the most sizeable gap between the two negotiating positions. Israeli Prime Minister Ehud Barak claimed that through the implementation of the 'right of return', the PLO was seeking the destruction of the state of Israel as a Jewish state via the back door. Before the final status negotiations, he publicly stated that the resolution of the refugee issue would have to be found in the countries in which they currently resided, and not in Israel (Tamari, 1999: 86). The PLO negotiating position is hotly disputed, but it seems that the PLO was trying to separate the moral, symbolic and legal recognition of the right of return from its practical implementation (Pressman, 2003). While it argued that Israel had to recognise the absolute right of return of all Palestinians refugees, it was willing to negotiate various mechanisms through which this could be realised, thus limiting its practical impact, and argued that the vast majority of refugees would not seek to return to Israel. However, the Israeli negotiators would not accept moral responsibility for the refugee issue, would not trust Palestinian promises that most refugees would not return to Israel and feared that their return was a euphemism for the 'destruction of Israel' as a Jewish state. The talks eventually collapsed, with no agreement on the refugee issue, and have since been sidelined by the reciprocal violence of the second *intifada.*

It is hard to tell whether both sides were right in arguing that they could not have sold the other side's proposals to their own populations. Polls suggest that 76 per cent of Jewish Israelis would refuse any deal that saw anything more than a token number of Palestinian refugees settled in Israel (*Haaretz*, 7 August 2000). It is even more difficult to tell exactly what Palestinian refugees felt about the various options that were put forward. This was partly due to the lack of political mechanisms through which they could express their views. It was also due to the politically sensitive nature of the refugee issue, which went far beyond the concerns of individual refugees. In large measure, refugee opinions were not distinguishable from those of the wider Palestinian public. According to one report, more than 95 per cent of Palestinians saw the 'right of return' as a 'sacred right that can never be given up' (Palestinian Center for Policy and Survey Research, 2003). However, the same poll also showed that only 10 per cent of Palestinian refugees would seek to exercise the right of return if it meant living under Israeli security. Since the collapse of the Oslo process, there have been several 'unofficial' draft peace agreements, most notably the Geneva accords. The most controversial aspects of these agreements, among

Palestinians at least, have concerned the refugee issue. While the Palestinian participants were keen to stress that they had not formally renounced the 'right of return', they were widely criticised for treating the refugee issue merely in terms of immigration and not as a national issue.

More so than in the Middle East, the most likely 'shape' of any agreed constitutional settlement between Greek Cypriots and Turkish Cypriots has been implicitly clear to the political leadership of both sides for decades. Since the Makarios–Denktaş High Level Agreement of 1977, a settlement has implied a state with two ethnically homogenous and largely self-governing components. Greek Cypriots have sought a state with stronger central powers, while Turkish Cypriots have sought equality in all governmental institutions. It has also been supposed that the Turkish-Cypriot-controlled component would amount to at least 25 per cent of the island. However, as in Israel/Palestine, the issues over which there has been speculation have involved the refugees' right of return, their right to property reinstatement and matters of compensation for those who would not or could not return.

Crucially, as with the Palestinians in 1948, 1974 did not affect the Greek-Cypriot refugees alone. All Greek Cypriots were affected in two ways. First, in a practical, materialistic sense, they could not visit the occupied lands, nor invest in them. Thus, although they were themselves not IDPs they were affected by the shrinking of opportunities in their already small state. Secondly, most Greek Cypriots felt spiritually impoverished and politically less secure from the humiliation of 1974. As in Palestine, the creation of the refugee crisis was a major blow to national pride. Prior to 1974, Greek Cypriots had made economic progress, seen their children increasingly educated, fought a successful campaign to remove the vastly more powerful colonial state, and worsted the Turkish Cypriots in several inter-communal conflicts. Just as 1922 was 'the Catastrophe' for mainland Greeks, and 1948 was *al-nakba* to the Palestinians, so 1974 was the catastrophe for the Greek Cypriots. The article of faith they had learned in primary school, a catechism of confident and resurgent Hellenism, was 'Cyprus is a Greek island!' After 1974, that sentence had to continue 'but a portion of it is under occupation'.

However, unlike in Israel/Palestine, the political leadership of both sides in Cyprus came close to agreeing to what the UN and the EU hoped would be a final peace agreement. The 2003 UN-sponsored Annan Plan would have seen the establishment of the United States of Cyprus (Palley, 2005). In essence, this would have been a federal umbrella state, with two 'constituent states', territorial in character, and with implicitly ethnic criteria for residence. To get to the new state, Turkey was required to release some 9 per cent of the island's territory under its occupation, which would have reduced the zone reserved for the Turkish Cypriots (and Turkish settlers) to 25 per cent. Graduated Turkish troop withdrawals were envisaged. The Greek-administered zone would thus have increased to 75 per cent, and the present 'buffer zone', the 2 per cent of territory under UN control, would have been reabsorbed by the two constituent states. The property issue was to be dealt with in rather complex ways. The Greek Cypriots in the 9 per cent of Cyprus to be returned as a Greek-administered zone would get all their property back, but would not be able to return until fresh provision had been made for the current Turkish occupants. For the remainder of formerly Greek-Cypriot land, there was a formula that would allow the current occupant to retain the property if he or she had spent more on it since acquisition than it had originally been worth in 1974. If this was not the case, the Greek-Cypriot owner would have a right to reinstatement or compensation. There were to be restrictions on the number of Greek Cypriots who could return to the Turkish-Cypriot constituent state as residents, and the formula would allow the oldest back first, and accept the next age groups downwards, until that ceiling was reached. For those not able to reside in their properties, there was to be compensation. For Turkish Cypriots, the basic provisions of rights to reinstatement and compensation would have been the same as those for the Greek Cypriots, but the Greek Cypriots did not fear any demographic 'swamping' by returning Turkish Cypriots because the numbers of Turkish Cypriots in the Greek-Cypriot constituent state would have been too small to change the majority–minority relationship. As the settlers from Turkey owned no property in the Greek-Cypriot constituent state, there was no question of their 'returning' to the south.

The Annan Plan was rejected at a referendum. While two-thirds of the Turkish Cypriots voted in favour of it, following a strong rejection speech from Greek-Cypriot President Tassos Papadopoulos, three-quarters of the Greek Cypriots voted against it. For Turkish Cypriots, the Plan had offered an end to their marginal status as persons in a non-state living in limbo under administration from Turkey, and it also offered immediate and much desired entry into the EU. The Greek Cypriots instead had been guaranteed entry into the EU on 1 May 2004 as the RoC, and to them the 'leap in the dark' meant too much economic and political uncertainty, fear of possible instability, a continuing Turkish military presence in the island, but no defence force of their own. This added up to a perception of more risks than guaranteed benefits. The Plan was seen as offering too little, and many voters insisted that a better Plan was possible and would be forthcoming.

How far has the existence of the refugee issue been the main obstacle, or one of the core obstacles, to a settlement in Cyprus? There is no doubt that all Greek-Cypriot negotiators have had a careful eye on the demographics of proposed settlement packages (how many refugees could have returned to their properties, how many would have been permanently excluded?). The

Turkish Cypriots and Turkey's minimum demands – 25–30 per cent of the island under their near exclusive control – would always have made a negotiated settlement 'risky' for any Greek-Cypriot leader who might have been tempted to 'sign away' the towns of Kyrenia and Karpasia in northern Cyprus. Despite the ideological importance of recognising Greek-Cypriot claims to the north of the island, more people would have voted for the Annan Plan had it not been for the uncertainties attendant on major change. The 'return' of the refugees, in and of itself, was not the major reason for rejecting the Plan. A recent analysis (Trimikliniotis, 2006) suggests that 35 per cent of the Greek-Cypriot refugees voted 'yes' to the Annan Plan, as against 25 per cent of the non-refugees. This is a notable difference, but hardly an overwhelming one. If it had been a much greater difference, we might have had measurable indicators of the strength of the refugees' desire to return. However, the fact is that those refugees who cared most – because they put most of their lives into the pre-1974 homes and properties – are now dead or elderly. Many who were young in 1974 are now rooted in the south and see their children and grandchildren's futures as keeping them there.

Conclusions: refugees and peace processes

What lessons do the collapse of the Annan Plan and the Oslo peace process have for the ways in which refugee issues are dealt with in attempts at settling long-term ethno-political conflicts? Talk of 'solutions' to such protracted and complex disputes is, of course, overly simple. There are no magic formulas, but only complicated and painful compromises, that must build up trust and address the grievances of all involved in a meaningful way. However, at least four important points can be taken from a comparison of the different place that refugees have in both conflicts, and the very different ways in which both peace processes collapsed.

The first and perhaps most important point is that refugees became a national issue and not just a sectoral issue for the refugees and their descendants. In this sense, it is difficult to separate refugees from non-refugees in their opinions and demands over refugee issues. This means not only that non-refugees have strong opinions over how refugees should be treated, but also that refugees do not look exclusively through the lens of their 'refugeeness' when they assess the implications of a peace process. As a result, agreements made over the fate of refugees do not have to be sold only to refugees, but also to the wider population.

The second, related point is that refugees represent an issue of morality and memory, as well as of rights, citizenship and property. While the restitution/

recognition of rights is undoubtedly an important issue for both Palestinians and Greek Cypriots, the creation of the refugee problem is above all perceived as a national humiliation. This means that, in addition to dealing with individual claims, any serious attempt to deal with refugees needs to find ways of coming to terms with this sense of damaged national pride. Crucially, this is not possible without some form of restitution, but it also requires those responsible for the creation of the crisis to admit moral agency.

The third point is that access to political and economic resources matters. While Greek Cypriots feel better off than the people who now occupy their former homes, Palestinians not only are worse off than the Israelis who inhabit their former villages, but also are worse off than those Palestinians who remained in what is now Israel. Many Greek-Cypriot refugees would find 'return' to northern Cyprus economically difficult and disruptive, and would need major economic resettlement packages, which are not on offer; meanwhile, they have adjusted politically and economically to life in the south. In sharp contrast, the widespread economic and political marginalisation of the Palestinian refugees means that the political and civil rights that are attached to their claims to 'return' are very much a live issue. While they may not want to return to their former homes (and it is unclear whether they do), a claim to 'return' is a way of making a claim to wider political, economic and civil rights which they presently lack.

The fourth and most tentative point relates to the very different ways in which the Annan Plan and the Oslo peace process collapsed. An unsolved refugee issue is not enough, on its own, to lead to violence. For Greek Cypriots, while the refugee issue can be seen as a perceptual or psychological obstacle, the heat seems to have gone out of it, as the primary refugees have grown old, or died. For Palestinians, although the rights of those displaced in 1948 are as hot a political issue as they were sixty years ago, it would be problematic to reduce explanations for the violence of the second *intifada* to the refugee issue. While the impasse over the refugee issue did play a key part in the collapse of the Oslo process, any comprehensive analysis of why the second *intifada* broke out would have to include the wider economic and political disenfranchisement of Palestinians in the West Bank and Gaza Strip, the resort to disproportionate violence by the Israeli military, and the tactical decisions made by a disjointed Palestinian leadership. However, in seeking to understand why the Annan Plan and the Oslo process collapsed in such different styles, the crucial difference between the two cases is that the Greek Cypriots have a politically and economically stable state, with attendant rights and resources, whereas Palestinians are stateless. Armed struggle has never quite made sense in the same ways for Greek Cypriots as it did for Palestinians, as they had far more palatable economic and political options.

Notes

1 See www.un.org/unrwa/english.html.
2 For the character of Greek–Turkish hostilities during the Greek struggle to break out of the Ottoman empire, see Clogg (1979: 43–104) and Holland and Markides (2006: 81–161).
3 Interview, 2001, Nicosia, with Iakovos Arestides.
4 The PNA is formally a subsidiary of the PLO, but in practice the PLO has been starved of funds and has become largely moribund.

Part IV

Cyprus beyond political science

13

Women of Cyprus at the crossroads between traditionalism, modernity and post-modernity

Maria Hadjipavlou

Alternative ways of knowing

Human experience is gendered and this understanding is central to the radical implications of feminist theory, which emerges from and responds to the lives of women. The recognition of the impact of gender and an insistence on the importance of the female experience has provided the vital common ground for feminist research and thought. Listening to women's voices, studying women's writings and learning from women's experiences have been crucial to the feminist reconstruction of our understanding of the world. Women's personal narratives are, among other things, stories of how women negotiate their 'exceptional' gender status, both in their daily lives and over the course of a lifetime (Personal Narratives Group, 1989: 4–5).

Methodology thus matters within feminism because it is the key to understanding and unpacking the overlap between knowledge and power (Stacey, 1997). Women's stories and personal narratives today constitute a valid scientific field of study, in which new methodologies have given rise to a new history of women; this is the product of interaction between the political perspective of the contemporary women's movement and feminist methodology, and an emphasis on the new social history. For women, according to Sandra Harding, to name and describe their experiences 'in their own terms' is a crucial scientific and epistemological act:

> Members of marginalized groups must *struggle* to name their own experiences *for* themselves in order to claim the subjectivity, the possibility of historical agency, that is given to dominant groups at birth, or at least as psychoanalytic theorists report, in infancy. (Harding, 1986: 103)

This chapter analyses parts from a pioneering study of women's experiences, voices and desires in *all* Cypriot communities – Greek, Turkish, Armenian, Maronite and Latin. It unravels the complexity of Cypriot women's voices and thus challenges the 'bicommunality' discourse. The discussion largely builds on data and prevalent themes from focus group discussions in each community held in 2003. One of the general findings demonstrates that the women from all Cypriot communities find themselves in a transitional context, where modernity and traditionalism are mixed in both the private and the public realms of their lives. This can explain the many contradictions, confusion, dilemmas and ambivalences the women expressed in relation to the different issues about which they were interviewed. We found that the women's education on gender issues and their sensitisation to the prevalence of the male-dominant culture in Cyprus were exceedingly low (Hadjipavlou, 2004, 2006). While some women were critical of their own oppression and were looking for ways out, others 'internalised' the gendered understanding of their socially constructed roles as the 'natural way' due to their biology.

In conflict societies, the 'national problem' historically dominates and downplays social issues, including women's issues, voices and their different experiences (Cockburn, 2004; Hadjipavlou, 2006; Sharoni, 1995). The conflict is viewed as genderless, with the implication that men's and women's experiences of the conflict are the same; or, if they are different this is considered irrelevant. The predominance of the official masculine and militaristic discourses in the Greek-Cypriot and Turkish-Cypriot communities about the duty to protect the homeland and fight the 'enemy' for justice and recognition led many women, as 'sacrificing mothers', to offer their sons to the military institution unquestioningly. Cypriot women internalise their ethnic and national duty roles in safeguarding the nation (Anthias, 1989; Anthias and Yuval-Davis, 1992; Kanaaneh, 2002; Yuval-Davis, 1997). Thus, many women do what the system and the community would expect them to engage in, and they are denied the right to be full participants or active agents in the peace processes. In the last thirty years of official negotiations, no Cypriot woman has ever been appointed a member of the negotiating team. The absence of a feminist movement in Cyprus further helped the internalisation of male political discourses, since all women's organisations are closely associated with political parties and most often are expected to adopt the male party agendas and ideologies.

In a patriarchal society such as the Cypriot one, the two sexes are socialised into different roles, based on biological differences, and are associated with different values and spaces. It is expected of each sex to behave according to these roles and gender stereotypes and to fulfil societal expectations. In addition, the space in which each gender is expected to move and to be self-actualised is socially determined; that is, the private space is associated with the female, and the public with the male (Ascher et al., 1984; Hadjipavlou, 2006; Peterson and Runyan, 1993; Tickner; 2001). When one gender (and it is often women) moves from one space to the other or chooses to be in both, then a social 'disturbance' is created and any resultant social problems are usually blamed on this 'anomaly'. We often hear comments such as: the anti-social behaviour of children is due to the fact that women have left their household duties to work outside the home; or, the increase in divorce and spousal infidelity is due to women's economic independence and their wish to create careers for themselves.

Separating public from private space leads to a separation of mind and body, whereby women are associated with nature, something that is mortal and corrupt, whereas men are associated with civilisation/culture, which is immortal and significant. Instead, we should explore, according to Virginia Woolf in *Three Guineas* (1938), the ways in which mind and body can be made to cooperate and discover what new combinations make good wholes in human beings. In an environment of segregation, both genders lose (Baker-Miller, 1976; Janeway, 1971; Ortner, 1974; Rosaldo, 1980). Each sex is deprived of the full spectrum of choices and a holistic development in a community structured by a variety of connections, rather than by separation and opposition (Eisler, 1987).

In a patriarchal, conflict-ridden society we also experience a hierarchy in the value system, whereby the feminist values of connection, caring and creating a consciousness that is relational, contextual, integrative and life affirming are considered as inferior to or of less importance than those engendered by men's activities such as competition, the exercise of power, rationality, hard-headedness, ambition and efficiency. Thus, as Bell Hooks (2000) would argue, simply changing the structures is not enough. We also have to change the prevalent value system.

Although there is evidence (Cockburn, 2004; Hadjipavlou, 2004; Women's Organization of United Democrats, 2006) that Cypriot women *have* advanced in a number of aspects of their lives in the last twenty years, namely in education, the workplace, travel and personal development, still it is noteworthy that, according to a qualitative study for the Women's Organization of United Democrats in 2001, the criteria and points of reference Greek-Cypriot women use to define themselves as 'successful women' are those that men have developed and have been taken to be the norm, leading to 'women thinking and behaving like men'. This is exactly what had been challenged by the early feminists in the 1960s and 1970s and later in the 1990s, such as Judith Butler, who supported the view that sex is part of a system of meaning, produced by language, and that power is exercised not only through direct coercion but also through the way in which language shapes and restricts our reality. Thus, radical and post-structuralist feminisms and women's movements have struggled to achieve the legitimisation of equal value of women's thinking and experiences, as well as their autonomy as individuals (Donovan, 1994; Faludi, 1991; Firestone, 1970; Gilligan, 1982; Hooks, 1981, 2000; Janeway, 1971; Klein, 1984; Marshment, 1997; Millet, 1970; Stacey, 1997; Threlfall and Rowbotham, 1996).

Using the approach of group in-depth interviews, we wanted to highlight each community's legitimacy and to promote the politics of appreciation of each other's commonalities and differences on specific issues. We believe knowledge is produced not only from rational scientific models but also from inter-subjective experiences and interactions with each other and other 'others' (Collins, 1998). These focus groups were accompanied by a questionnaire survey, which consisted of fifty-nine questions, conducted with 1,697 interviewees from the four Cypriot communities (the Latin community participated only in the qualitative part of the research, owing to demographic difficulties). The focus groups expanded on issues such as self-definition, relations of women with other women and the dominant community (i.e. issues of discrimination and exclusion), the 'crossings' (i.e. the partial opening in 2003 of the Green Line separating the two communities), violence and women's expectations from the European Union (EU).[1] This chapter concentrates on the themes of women and their self-definition, and issues of discrimination and violence. Representative quotes from each ethnic group are given, as these highlight the bigger theme of the chapter, the crossroads between traditionalism and modernity. More than eighty women participated in the implementation of the different phases of the project.

The process we used to carry out the project was as important as its products. In our study, we chose to listen only to women because, as Belenky et al. (1986: 9) tell us in their book *Women's Ways of Knowing*, 'the male experience has been so powerfully articulated that we believed we would hear the patterns in women's voices more clearly if we held at bay the powerful templates men have etched in the literature and in our minds'. The focus group discussions relied on five partner non-governmental organisations (NGOs) representing all the communities: the Peace Center, a bicommunal women's organisation; Hands Across the Divide; the Armenian Relief Society; the Maronite Graduates Association; and the Latin Association for Support of Foreign Workers.

One practical aim of the research project was to develop a safe thinking space for women from all communities in which to articulate their opinions, their concerns, their values and voice, in addition to realising their differences within and between their groups. Another aim was political, that is, to raise awareness and develop a social consciousness of the right of women to participate in a world shaped by both men and women. Women need their own space to listen to each other and to affirm that knowledge is also produced through reflecting on experiences, which become the most important data upon which to construct our realities. The level of commitment among the partners increased as we built trust and confidence and the project moved ahead.

The political situation in Cyprus changed during the implementation phases of our project and this included three historic events: the submission of the Annan Plan for a Comprehensive Settlement of the Cyprus Problem (2002); the signing of the Republic's Accession Treaty with the EU on 16 April 2003; and a week later (23 April) the partial opening of the Green Line, when contacts and communication among the communities on the island developed an amazing dynamic towards peace-building. This new dynamic facilitated the implementation of our project, since Turkish-Cypriot and Greek-Cypriot women could cross to each other's side and hold meetings without the previous militaristic hustle to get permissions. All these historic events, in the context of the deep-rooted Cyprus conflict, have had an impact at both the community level and the personal. Thus we included discussions of such changes in our focus groups.

The analysis

After transcribing the texts from all the focus groups, we tried to elicit broad categories of the themes that emerged in the discussions. Some of these issues were shared, for instance the role of religion and church in the lives of women, social pressures from external authorities and ignorance about the EU. Certain issues of less importance to some women were highly articulated by other women, for instance the economic aspect, which was crucial to Turkish-Cypriot women but not so for the women in the other communities, who lived in the Republic of Cyprus. We observed both complexity and uniqueness within and across communities. In general, we noted a shift in women's lives towards more gender awareness, but not an adequate one. There was still a lot of confusion due to lack of appropriate education and familiarisation with certain world-views and concepts that describe women's condition and issues. The absence of relevant gender courses in education and the absence of a feminist movement in Cyprus did not allow alternative discourses and public debates on women's issues and rights to take place.

Women: the self as embedded in the 'other'

It is often very difficult in Cypriot culture to get women to talk about themselves, tell their own story and reflect on who they are, what they want and their achievements. This is because the collective and communal identity is stressed more than the individual. The individual belongs to the group and the female self is embedded in all the others. This is also attributed to gender socialisation processes, which promote the norm for women to speak very little about themselves and when they do they are judged as inappropriately egoistical or showing off or too talkative. Another explanation related to their socialisation is that women are expected to listen more and speak less, and to focus on caring and serving the needs of the other or others (father, brothers, husband, children, parents, community, the nation, the world, etc.). Their own needs and self-development as autonomous beings become secondary. The equal importance to both the individual and the communal is not stressed. One of our participants from the Latin-Cypriot community, who came from Poland, expressed this as follows:

> To talk about myself is very difficult because it sounds as if you are either very egotistical or very arrogant to do so. In general, in Poland we say that whoever is taking pride in one's self is worthy of disregard. Thus we were socialised to say only a few words rather than more. Because all about yourself sounds insignificant.

Most of the women in the Latin group expressed the same hesitation to talk about themselves but afterwards with encouragement and after the significance of their personal story in the process of learning and producing knowledge was pointed out they became more at ease. It is noteworthy that all tended to use the 'you' pronoun and had difficulty speaking in the first person ('I'), indicating embarrassment or even a sense of 'self-undermining'. This also indicates how deeply sometimes women internalise their subordinate roles and follow traditional norms and prescribed gendered etiquettes, and thus reinforce the patriarchal order.

We met the same hesitation from the Maronite group, but the resistance was easier to handle. The Armenian and Greek-Cypriot groups were more willing to talk about themselves. The Turkish-Cypriot women spoke about the self always in relation to the 'other' and the social system, thus stressing the self in the community context. Here we note that both the individual agency and the social structure need to be reconsidered and challenged.

> When I talk specifically about myself it was firstly me who felt uncomfortable as when I do something for the first time. Afterwards I questioned myself, why did I do that, why did I go there, did I have to do it? ... When the social structure changed after 1974, I thought about my involvement in the trade union. In order to do this, I had to leave my two-month-old baby at home with someone else in order to attend the meetings. I really felt bad about doing this but later I decided it was the right thing to do for me, but it was a struggle. Today I have not regretted it ... I was able to get out of the house. (Turkish-Cypriot participant)

Such insight into their own self-awareness and struggle for self-definition, expressed by some of the women, challenges the prevailing Cypriot culture and gender socialisation. It involves a process, but it also tells us that the patriarchal structures within the institution of the family have not changed, and working mothers are still expected to undertake the main responsibility within the household and for the upbringing of the children.

Most of the Greek-Cypriot women, however, focused their pleasure and satisfaction on their children and the gratification they derived from being 'good mothers'. Often this was not a choice but a compliance with social expectations. This explains why some of these women regretted that they either focused excessively on the needs of others or worked too many hours, and thus neglected themselves, and when asked to talk about themselves they were not sure where to locate themselves. Could motherhood have a higher status than selfhood? How can both coexist? In a patriarchal structure, this seems impossible, as motherhood is closely linked to women only and is often 'romanticised'; moreover, the state and its institutions often exalt mothers, thus giving primacy to the biological reproductive capacity of women, which is another form of patriarchal control. In so doing, the state makes the issue of 'motherhood' the exclusive responsibility of women, instead of looking at it as a social issue:

> When my children were small, I stayed at home until noon and then left for our business to the clothes factory. But I never neglected taking my children to private lessons. Both of them are university graduates. Every day I had to drive them home, go to work, then be with them to do their homework and watched them so that they did not waste time playing. I am proud of them. But my biggest regret is that I was working 18 hours a day and had no time left for myself. My husband never helped. I had no time for my personal life; I always had to steal time as if I were a thief. (Greek-Cypriot participant)

In many of these women's stories the husband/father is absent. The separation between private/household and public/career spaces still prevails.

Another theme that we noted concerned mother–daughter dependency. A Turkish-Cypriot participant described a 'bitter experience'. She had decided that she would begin her university studies abroad, as she wanted to get away from the family to develop her own ideas and self-autonomy. Her relatives and neighbours, though, tried to convince her mother not to send her daughter abroad because the mother would regret it in her old age. (There is still the tradition in Cyprus that the grown-up children are expected to look after the aged parents.)

> A woman neighbour came up to my mum and said, 'you are making a mistake here. You should have kept her with you; you know she is the youngest kid and she has to stay with you to look after you, don't send her away'.... There is a sequence

> in what we should do as women: we go to school, then get married, have kids, get them married, look after our parents, and so on. If you don't behave in the way the community wants you to, then the pressure starts. (Turkish-Cypriot participant)

The self is prescribed to exist within the community parameters as part of the patriarchal agenda. Women as mothers reinforce the notion that women are the vessels through which traditional cultural values and by extension the nation are preserved and reproduced. Even when young women return from abroad after finishing their university studies and decide to have a life of their own, both family pressure and community pressure start demanding compliance with the traditional women's role. Thus, the self-autonomy they tried to develop while away from home collides with the lack of appreciation of other (non-traditional) achievements and abilities of women as individuals. As one of our Turkish-Cypriot participants said:

> When I returned to Cyprus, after I finished my studies abroad, I decided, against my mum's wishes, not to marry. I started work, got my economic independence and decided to stay single. This was something my mum could never understand. Whenever she gets together with her friends, that's all she can talk about. I do have many other positive features; can't they talk about them? Instead of looking at my life and see that I am happy the way I am, she becomes critical of the way I act and have chosen to live. She is disappointed because I ignore the socially expected 'natural' roles for a 'normal' woman.

Not only are young women who struggle for their autonomy as individuals not appreciated, but they are often made to feel guilty for doing so. In general, patriarchal societies are not appreciative of the development of an individual sense of self. Another view expressed was that often women themselves undermine their own strengths and abilities, which can lead to self-oppression. As one of the Greek-Cypriot participants stated:

> We, as women, have a lot of power and talents but we do not really utilise them. This is because we get tired and end up by saying 'let the other do it'. There is, however, a contradiction here because we ourselves become demanding of others and our environment but not so from ourselves. We live a contradiction, as if trapped.

In a deeper sense, what this woman is describing is the development of the self in a social context which, on the one hand, demands that women's strengths be used to serve society but which, on the other hand, marginalises them, making women internalise this contradiction, which leads to disempowerment. Some choose to avoid this contradiction through the adoption of styles of behaviours and traits that would help them survive both as women and as 'successful' professionals in a male-dominated society. They adopt the male ways of doing business as a means of protection, so as to feel that they would not be taken advantage of. For instance, one of the Greek-Cypriot participants, a businesswoman, described herself as follows:

> I have learned to be in control; otherwise I will not be able to survive. I have learned, thus, to dominate others irrespective of whether they are men or women. I was once gentle, romantic; I was very sensitive, but not any more. I have learned to be aggressive and to demand my rights, otherwise I feel used by others. Especially the men.

In other words, some women constructed a self to fit the social, male-dominated context, to the extent of abandoning intentionally parts or traits of their self. This is a pattern we often see in women politicians, too, who, in their effort to be accepted and survive politically, have to adopt male values and styles because in this way they do not constitute a threat to the established system. Moreover, young, married women expressed a sense of guilt if they dared do something for themselves such as going to the hairdresser and leaving their child with their husband. Their psychological discomfort was so great that they preferred to return to the old, traditional family values. Feminisms have challenged this psychological oppression through socialisation and inequality. Such oppression is a form of violence:

> Even when we go to the hairdresser we feel guilt because we leave the children with our husbands, and we worry in case he is not able to take care of them, or if the children give him a hard time. Many of us are tortured by the remorse so we favour a return to the old family values and even wish that our daughters will marry someone who will not allow them to work, so that they can devote their life to the family. (Greek-Cypriot participant)

What we have observed, in general, is that women in Cyprus are still struggling to establish a space for the self and to accept their identity as individuals. The prevailing perception still demands that women comply with their assigned traditional roles, thus making it difficult for them to engage in personal gratification and self-actualisation in ways beyond these assigned roles, beyond guilt, social resistance and pressures from above. When they do choose what is perceived as the modern way of defining themselves, they often experience loneliness and marginalisation, even within their own families, which is still a strong institution in Cyprus.

Discrimination and prejudices

A great deal has been written about issues of discrimination as it manifests in different ways, in the context of minorities, gender, ethnicity, class, sexuality, race and age. The dominant group usually tries to impose its norms and values on the other. Prejudice is one of the most destructive aspects of human behaviours, often producing acts of violence, both overt and covert. The classification of social groups into 'us' and 'them', whereby we attribute negative characteristics, attitudes and behaviours to members of the out-group, creates a culture of polarisation and a tendency to homogenise communities (Hadjipavlou, 2003). In our study, women spoke about gender and community discrimination as well as about prevailing prejudices.

Gender discrimination

In our focus group discussions, the issue of gender discrimination was more evident and intense in the experiences of Greek-Cypriot and Turkish-Cypriot women, whereas other forms of discrimination, such as workplace and community discrimination (discussed below), were more intense in the Maronite and Armenian groups. For instance, Greek-Cypriot women emphasised the undermining of women in the domestic sphere – the sex-role stereotyping and degrading images of women as these are promoted through the media and school textbooks – as well as in the larger social context. All these phenomena constitute different forms of violence, according to these women.

In addition, women who experienced sexual harassment at the workplace said that the support system was weak. Women do not support other women, owing to structural factors and the absence of a feminist solidarity movement. The power asymmetry was usually felt to be a factor. Women are fearful to report such incidents because of either losing their jobs or not being taken seriously. Or, once they do, they are made to feel shame and guilt. One Greek-Cypriot participant had been sexually harassed by her supervisor and because she did not give in, he made her life unbearable. After a while, she was forced to resign because he showed no respect for her work. Similarly, a Turkish-Cypriot woman gave an example of being ignored and her work devalued because of her sex:

> When I go to a customer [as a consultant] they don't respect me because I am a woman. They dismiss me and ask for a male colleague to advise them on their business ventures. Will this change when we enter the European Union and, if so, how long would this take? When I go somewhere, I don't want to be judged according to how I look or the way I dress; I demand equal respect.

Some of our participants experienced discrimination exercised by other women, which is indicative of the lack of women's solidarity and sisterhood. This experience also challenges any essentialisation of 'women', which would imply that women share the same issues by virtue of belonging to the social category 'woman', ignoring other divisions such as class, ethnicity, race, sexuality and age. It becomes a power issue through age and status. For instance, when women school inspectors had to evaluate the work of other women teachers, in their effort to exercise and maintain their power and status they appeared to be very strict, dominating, distant and unfair. Younger, more educated women in lower positions felt that their supervisor, who had less knowledge and fewer qualifications than them, used her power over them, creating an unhealthy relationship, not conducive to learning and professional development. Research has shown that not all women who acquire power are gender conscious. They simply reproduce the male patriarchal definition of 'power' as it is understood as 'power over', that is, to dominate and control others, and not the feminist understanding of 'power to', meaning empowerment and doing things together (Brock-Utne, 1985, 1989). A Greek-Cypriot young teacher thus felt that when women acquire power, they are no different to men and she complained:

> I expected my female supervisor to be different from the male supervisor I had last year. This is not the case. She terrified me with her demeaning comments and did not allow much of a dialogue. How could women become so insensitive once they acquire power, I wondered.

This question was often raised, that is, why do many women in powerful positions or in public life not behave differently from men? First, the expectation itself is a fallacy, because not all women in powerful positions have a gender consciousness. And, thus, they are not all expected to be sensitive to gender issues and women's concerns and needs. Even in the hierarchy of the family structure, as some Turkish-Cypriot interviewees said, woman can experience their mothers' control and domination; some mothers would not allow their daughters to go out and date different men, because society does not approve of such practices, whereas sons are allowed (or even encouraged) to date many girls. On this issue, the Turkish-Cypriot and the Maronite communities seemed to be more 'traditional' than the other communities. For instance, in our quantitative study we noted that a higher proportion of married women in these communities had had arranged marriages (51 per cent of Turkish Cypriots and 41.5 per cent of Maronite women). In response to a survey question asking whether an unmarried woman was considered a 'failure' in their community, three out of ten Greek Cypriots said 'yes' and in the Maronite community four out of ten said 'yes'; the percentages in the other communities were much smaller. The position of women in a society indicates the level of social development of that society. Our data situate Cypriot women at the crossroads between traditionalism, modernity and post-modernity, and surely the national question, that is, the Cyprus conflict, has not provided the space for such kinds of public debate.

Community discrimination

Discrimination and prejudices are equally prevalent at the community level. Such behaviour is often expressed in terms of power relations, leading to feelings of superiority and inferiority. Often the dominant group feels superior and does not really care to get to know and understand the minority cultures. The dominant group assumes that it knows what is fair and best for the less powerful ones, who in turn often internalise their lower status as if it were the natural state of affairs (Baker-Miller, 1976).

Maronite women, coming from a small community and having to struggle for their cultural and social survival, encountered more discriminatory practices in their social interactions with both the dominant group (i.e. the Greek Cypriots) and also the Armenian community. In general, Maronite women perceive, for instance, both the living standards and the level of education of the Armenian Cypriots and Greek Cypriots as being higher than their own. In addition, they perceive the Armenians as having a historical advantage, in that they share a 'common enemy' with the Greek Cypriots (i.e., the Turks), which in their opinion makes the Armenians feel closer to the dominant group. They also think that the others perceive them as 'peasants with little education' and speaking a strange language, which characterises them as 'less civilised'.

On the issue of historical advantage, the Armenians do not see it in the same way. In fact, there emerged a contest as to who suffered more. The Armenian women argued that, because of the genocide against their nation by the Turks, they had suffered much more than the Maronites. They invited the Maronite women to understand their historical pain and trauma. The impact of the Cyprus conflict on women in the different communities varied too. One Armenian participant said:

> Many of us lost our homes and properties in the northern part of Nicosia in the 1963–64 inter-ethnic violence. There was a rich Armenian neighbourhood then, especially in the northern part of the walled city of Nicosia.... Later, with the 1974 partition of the island, it hit us badly again. Such experiences hurt us a great deal, but we try to avoid talking about them.

The Maronite women also stressed the disastrous effects of the 1974 war on the cohesion of their community, and their displacement from the four Maronite villages in the northern part of Cyprus – apart from a few hundred who stayed at Kormakides, a village in the north, as 'enclaved persons'. They repeatedly mentioned their concern about the shrinking of their community and the loss of their sense of cultural identity. In fact, many minority groups feel such concerns when their minority rights of cultural distinctiveness are not observed by the state.

Another traumatic experience of religious prejudice against the Maronites was vividly described by one of the participants in the focus groups, who felt rejected by a member of the dominant community, the moment it became known that she was a Maronite by religion. She described her painful experience as follows:

> When I was 18, I had an operation at the general hospital in Nicosia and in the same ward there was a Greek-Cypriot woman from another village who had had an operation too. One day, my mother came to visit me and told me that she would not come the next day to see me because of Easter preparations. The other patient hearing this she remarked that Easter was in two weeks' time. And then my mother told her that we are Maronites and that we celebrate Easter earlier than the Greek Orthodox. The Greek-Cypriot lady then turned to me in great surprise and said, 'so you are a Maronite?! It is a shame that such a good girl like you is a Maronite!' Although she was very friendly to me, as soon as she heard that I am a Maronite she changed her attitude and I felt rejected and thereafter she avoided talking to me, as if Maronites were atheists or bad people.

Other Maronite women said that they could be working with their colleagues for years with them not knowing they were Maronites. But once the issues of religion and identity came up in conversation, Greek-Orthodox colleagues often showed their disappointment:

> The stereotypical response is 'you don't look it'. The word 'Maronite' sounds as if we come from outer space, something strange ... or as if we carry a kind of a disease.

Many Maronite women tend not to reveal their Maronite identity for as long as possible. The Greek-Cypriot community often shows intolerance and does not know how to deal with difference, as if, at an unconscious level, 'difference' poses a threat to their own identity, which is still a contested issue.

At home, however, young Maronite mothers try to transfer to their children a sense of pride in being Maronites coming from Kormakitis village or from the other inaccessible villages in the northern part of Cyprus, of which, of course, the children have had no lived experience. Their effort to make visible the Maronite part of their identity has been gaining ground recently. They demand recognition of their differences and social acknowledgement; this is something they believe accession to the EU will help to achieve, and they have begun an information campaign in their community on how to reactivate and preserve their cultural distinctiveness.

Some Latin women had also experienced communal discrimination. In particular, one woman described her own experience in the workplace. She was considered a non-Greek-speaker, although she had completed Greek secondary school and came top in her class in both Greek and Latin. Despite her repeated applications for promotion, in the end she resigned rather than receive another letter of 'we regret to say that the promotion committee…'. She believed both her gender and her religious background influenced the decisions reached by that committee. Other Latin women also described their disappointment concerning delays in governmental procedures, such as getting a Cypriot passport, despite the fact that they had been living on the island for many years, or even decades, and had the right to vote.

Some Armenian participants also described discriminatory practices against their community. In particular, emphasis was given to the degree of ignorance the other communities exhibited towards their community. For instance, one participant, gravely disappointed, explained how the majority of Cypriots could not tell the difference between the Armenian and the Turkish languages. This is an indication of the 'arrogance' of the dominant group, who normally would not be interested in learning about the minorities' cultures and histories:

> Something I do mind is when we talk with each other [in Armenian] and they [Greek Cypriots] listen to us and ask whether the language we speak is Turkish. They do not understand, they don't want to understand the difference. We have been here for so many decades, and I believe they ought to have known by now to distinguish who we are and our language.

In other words, discrimination arises out of ignorance, lack of social contacts (Hadjipavlou, 2003) and the invisibility of the Armenians in the mainstream mass media, but also in school textbooks. Both sides have a responsibility for such social phenomena: the Armenians for not making the necessary effort to inform the other Cypriot communities about their history on the island, and the dominant group for not giving enough opportunities to all minorities (or religious communities) to do so and feel included. As a result, both the Maronite-Cypriot and Armenian-Cypriot women expressed their concern about the cultural survival of their communities. Some younger Armenian participants mentioned that their parents encouraged them to get married to an Armenian man; thus loyalty to the community and its reproduction became a personal duty. Such a practice could be read as an expression of a different kind of oppression and control of personal choice from within the community:

> Yes, my parents want me to get married to an Armenian. I have been hearing this since I was a little girl and I know inside me that I will marry an Armenian. I do not blame them because we are a small community and have to stick together.

Furthermore, they stressed the fear that by going either to Greek or English schools (instead of Armenian ones) in order to integrate with the larger society, their minority language might become extinct.

However, despite the discriminatory practices some Armenian-Cypriot women expressed positive feelings as well. One participant said:

> I have not experienced any discrimination at the workplace. I have worked in a lot of enterprises and I have observed that some managers prefer Armenian employees. They say that Armenians are more hard working and more trustworthy than others.

As far as the state contribution was concerned, the participants seemed very satisfied with the governmental financial support of their community. More specifically, they talked about state infrastructure support:

> We are proud that the Cyprus government has donated money for our school to be built. A church was built in 1981 with a significant donation from the government. Our children go to school for free, and our priests receive their pensions.

It should also be noted that other Armenian participants reported experiencing no discrimination when it came to engaging in civil society activities with Greek-Cypriot women.

Some Turkish-Cypriot women expressed a stereotypical view about the Greek Cypriots:

> Very good business people. They are well organised, and work hard, but I think we are happier people. We are more cultured than them, and more creative. They are stuck with materialism and consumerism and are under pressure to make money. Art is a rebellion and they have no such urge inside them. We are richer in that sense.

Certainly, the lack of communication and contacts with the other gives rise to prejudices, misperceptions and stereotypes, and makes such an environment difficult to challenge. There exists now the opportunity (since the opening of checkpoints along the Green Line) to dispel such stereotypes through interpersonal contacts but also the media and NGOs on both sides of the divide have an important role to play in presenting a more complex and diverse view of Cypriot societies.

Violence

Another predominant theme that emerged from the focus group discussions concerned the issue of violence against women. When the radical feminists in the 1970s promoted the position that the 'personal is political', this brought to the public discourse the issues of domestic violence, sexual abuse, women's rights for reproduction and women's ownership of their bodies, among others. The implication is that women's private life is shaped by power asymmetries, domination of the male gender over the female; such issues are not rooted in individual characteristics but rather in social structures and hierarchies of values. So, individual problems often have systemic causes and many so-called personal decisions about issues of sexuality, appearance, consumption and family life have political implications.

In 2004, the Greek-Cypriot parliament passed a law making punishable any act of violence against women, including sexual harassment in the workplace and domestic violence, as well as psychological violence. Women need to be informed about this law and become aware of their rights to resist abuse and mistreatment, which often has disastrous effects on their general health. Studies done in Cyprus since the 1990s have noted a tremendous increase in domestic and other forms of violence, which needs to be addressed urgently.

In our focus group discussions, it was primarily the Greek-Cypriot participants who raised the issue of violence in the family and inter-personal relationships. Women spoke very openly and sincerely about abusive relationships with their husbands, feelings of humiliation, psychological abuse and lack of communication. Such dysfunctional relationships lead either to estrangement in the relationship and complete alienation, or to the woman leaving the house, or applications for divorce. Sometimes, because of social pressure, they are forced to stay in a meaningless, abusive relationship.

The fact that the patriarchal structures within most Cypriot households have not changed, despite the evidence that Cypriot women have more economic independence and more education, means that the mothers are still expected to be in charge of household duties and children's needs. A Greek-Cypriot high school teacher explained that she had problems in her relationship with her husband because she was overworked with her household duties and children's needs. Her husband would not help or even think of sharing responsibilities. This raises the need to train men to take responsibility within the domestic sphere and help remove the dilemma working women often feel, which is to decide to have either a career or a family. Domestic life is the responsibility of both sexes. Some commented that the separation between the domestic and the public leads to psychological abuse and exclusion. They believe the wife still takes care of everything in the house but when serious decisions are made it is the husband's opinion that carries all the weight.

Another serious issue many women faced was their husband's infidelity, a frequent problem in Cyprus, especially since the 1990s. The Greek-Cypriot women said that even when they confronted their husbands with evidence of their infidelity, they not only denied it but they also shouted at them: 'You are a fool; you are crazy, ready to be admitted to the psychiatric hospital. You imagine things and have no evidence.' Such abuse leads women to doubt their own self-worth, and their state of mind. Their husbands even tried to induce

chances of strong and sustained growth (International Monetary Fund, 2005: ch. 3). Openness and undistorted trade can be seen as factors favouring sustainable growth and thus helping to buttress peace.

The relevance of these considerations in the case of Cyprus is clear. Some interest groups on the island (or in Turkey) may flourish on rents derived from distorted trade patterns, and become defenders of the status quo. Others, including consumers, may see major gains if trade is regularised. Property rights in the north are contested, and this adversely affects foreign investment and banking. Some new possessors of housing or commercial real estate, after population movements, may have developed a vested interest in avoiding regularisation, unless new holdings are in some way acknowledged and protected; and parties throughout the island are concerned to achieve compensation for property losses experienced during those periods of population movement.

More broadly, a regularisation of political relations in Cyprus could lead to significant economic disruption as the structure of production (and the role of the state in supporting production) would change in the north – a possibility illustrated in a more systemic fashion during the economic transition in eastern Europe. Such disruption may be a concern for the population as well as the elites; but, nonetheless, they may see it as a price worth paying to secure improved medium-term economic prospects. Changes in trading patterns can also affect neighbours: economic actors in a regularised northern economy might emerge either as strong competitors or as valuable partners in markets (such as tourism and education) that are important to neighbours, including in the south. Economic interests located in these neighbours may thus be drawn into play.

In all these fields, perceptions of economic realities may or may not be well founded, yet either way they play a fundamental role in determining political outcomes. In conflict situations, information flows can be as distorted as trade flows. It is plausible that political opinions may at times be influenced by incorrect perceptions of economic realities, and in such circumstances the role of credible analysts – perhaps from international organisations or from academia – could be valuable in correcting misperceptions. In any event, there can be little doubt that economic factors, and the perception of such factors, are a potentially important influence on conflict resolution.

Economics and the spring 2004 reunification talks

In the Cyprus discussions in 2004, during which the author of this chapter was an economic adviser to the UN team, there was only limited time to analyse in depth the economic challenges of reunification. Partly as a result of this, some key issues were never fully analysed from an economic standpoint, and this added to the inherent difficulty of reaching a political agreement on them. In particular, three important questions were not effectively tackled and resolved during discussions:

- What was the income gap between north and south? A major concern on both sides, cross-cutting many key issues on the conflict resolution agenda, lay in the potential costs and forms of support for income convergence within the island. But both sides overestimated this gap during the discussions, and were probably too pessimistic on convergence prospects (this is discussed below, under 'Synergies in a converging intra-Cyprus economy', p. 264).
- What would reunification cost, and who would pay? Even at a late stage in the talks, some key costs were unquantified, including steps needed to regularise public- and private-sector balance sheets in the north. Moreover, the strategy for resettlement in the north was still at a formative stage, with a range of possible costs and risks.
- How could a credible fiscal federalism be created which would work well in the EU framework? The exchanges did not achieve a shared vision of the challenge, which needed to be addressed in the context of an island with a relatively heavily indebted south, an unquantifiably indebted north, an ex-reunification fiscal deficit peaking at perhaps 10 per cent of gross domestic product (GDP), an exchange rate peg, and plans for early adoption of the euro.

These questions were recognised as important, and were debated, but were not resolved with a deep consensus. A fourth question was no less important, but received even less attention:

- How might the dynamics of the two economies – north and south – evolve in the aftermath of reunification? What would be the convergence mechanisms and requirements? What challenges would have to be faced by the labour market? Would firms in the south face opportunities or threats, and in which sectors? Would labour in the south stand to win or lose in terms of income growth over the medium term, and under what conditions? Could the north be assured that there would be mechanisms – public and private – to finance the infrastructure needed to benefit from intra-Cyprus convergence and access to new markets?

These are not necessarily elements that could be planned in advance, in the old-fashioned sense of state planning. But some shared analytical framework and sense of common policy priorities seemed essential for a successful economic outcome. Addressing such questions upfront would help ensure greater clarity among voters about the future – and this could have complex effects on their assessments and preferences. In April 2004, voters may have been guided by economic perceptions that, in some cases, left important considerations out of account.

More specifically, in the north, there was in April 2004 a convincing intuition that EU membership offered a source of income convergence and new job opportunities. But convergence is highly policy dependent: voters may have underestimated the adjustments needed to achieve sustained convergence. Economic liberalisation and reform of the public sector are agendas that clearly need to be pursued in the north under all circumstances, but they will bring some painful adjustments as they affect different interest groups in the economy. Such adjustments are easier if undertaken at a time of buoyant growth. Thus, in principle, reform and conflict resolution may work in a mutually reinforcing manner. Nonetheless, the share of the capital stock that could prove unviable, the number of jobs that might be lost and the political as well as the economic repercussions of these developments should not be underestimated.

These factors can be important, of course, in any environment where the economy has been distorted, as in the case of the transition economies. The additional consideration in a conflict situation, however, is that they may influence not only the willingness to support reform but also the readiness to support and act in favour of conflict resolution and, where relevant, the legalisation of an entity's status. In north Cyprus, these facts represent a potentially negative factor that inevitably will need to be addressed.

In the case of northern Cyprus, a bridge in this direction (discussed further below) would be the staged shadowing of the *acquis communautaire* (which is formally suspended in the north), thus moving to harmonise laws and economic practices with the EU before a settlement. However, constraints on the trade of the north reduce the scope for it to benefit from a reorientation of the economy. The economic incentives and opportunities to gain from a full shadowing of the *acquis* are not present. Moreover, hard budget constraints have not been fully applied by Turkey, the principal aid donor in north Cyprus, to set the stage for more fundamental public-sector reforms.

By contrast, in the south, as noted in the report of former UN Secretary-General Annan in 2004, voters may have perceived mainly the risks of reunification, including the economic and financial risks: uncertainties or costs that could hamper growth after thirty years of progress (UN Secretary-General, 2004). This may have left important factors out of account: there is substantial scope for synergies in economic development that would benefit the south as well as the north. As acknowledged in the authorities' submissions for the EU's Lisbon dialogue on growth and job-enhancing reforms, the economy in the south needs continuing structural change to enhance its competitiveness. Reunification – on the right terms – could be a source of stimulus, synergy and opportunity to serve this end.

We should note also, from the standpoint of people in the south, that the economics of the property settlement were complex, finalised at a late stage, and perhaps not widely understood by the public: people were not convinced it was in their true interest to vote in favour of reunification. A recent study by Stelios Platis and others sheds some interesting light on the dynamics of the proposed Property Board, which can be interpreted rather favourably (Platis et al., 2005).

These considerations could lead to a schematic representation of the interests of the parties that might win or lose from reunification in Cyprus – though in some cases the scope for gain or loss may be misperceived, and in some cases policy actions or developments on the ground could change the relevant perceptions in the future (for a discussion, see under 'Economic reforms and the convergence challenge', p. 266). Further work to clarify this issue, to find ways of addressing concerns, and to correct mistaken perceptions, would be a valuable preamble to resumed negotiations on the island.

To be clear, during the UN-sponsored negotiations in 2002–04, there was very limited time to explore these issues. But if economics is indeed an important driver in political affairs, then the negotiators were labouring under a significant disadvantage. One conclusion would be that, if we do not learn from this history, we may repeat it – at some point re-entering discussions with a sense of urgency, but on the economic front being still rather ill-prepared. Informal bodies, such as the Wolfson Cyprus Group, have organised bicommunal discussions on key economic issues, but these have taken place against a political backdrop that has been unpromising for a restart of formal technical talks.

The income disparity between north and south

During 2003–05, growth accelerated in both north and south. This narrowed the intra-island income gap and boosted convergence towards average EU income levels. In the south, growth averaged 2 per cent during the run-up to EU membership, but then accelerated to nearly 4 per cent in 2004–05 (table 14.1) and was set to remain at this level over the following two years. In 2004, per capita GDP stood at 84 per cent of the EU average. In the north, growth averaged 6 per cent in 2001–02, in the wake of economic volatility in Turkey and a banking crisis there. It accelerated in 2003, and GDP rose by 42 per cent between 2002 and 2005. With the acceleration of growth in the north, the income gap across the island shrank, although the pace and pattern of growth in the north did not appear to be fully sustainable.

Table 14.1 Real percentage growth rates in gross domestic product in the north and the south of Cyprus, 2001–05

	2001	2002	2003	2004	2005
South	4.1	2.1	1.9	3.8	3.9
North	5.4	6.9	11.4	15.4	10.6

Source: World Bank (2006).

In addition, the World Bank (2006) has pointed to an income gap between north and south that is much narrower than what had been assumed at the time of the Annan Plan talks. This is an important issue, since the perception of a massive inequality in living standards may have been an important element underlying the concerns on both sides in the negotiations, and also influencing the referenda outcomes.

The conventional wisdom at the time of the referenda was indeed that living standards in the north lagged very far behind standards in the south, and were not catching up with them. Ayres (2003), while warning of measurement hazards, cited EU per capita income data for 2000 that contrasted a level of US$6,000 in the north with US$13,000 in the south. The convergence projections of Mehmet (2004) started from a disparity of 60 per cent between income levels. The report on the Annan Plan by Eichengreen et al. (2004) similarly based its convergence projections on a 60 per cent wage gap. In sum, published estimates at the time of the negotiations were based on market exchange rates, and broadly suggested that incomes in the north were around *two-fifths* the level in the south. The authors of some studies thus foresaw very long catch-up periods. For example, Eichengreen et al. (2004) warned that, even in a benign scenario, incomes in the north might still be only 62 per cent of levels in the south by 2020. However, data available to the authors at that time did not allow for comparisons to be made on a purchasing power parity (PPP) basis, which explains the likely exaggeration in the estimates and projections (see table 14.2).

The World Bank (2006) instead has sought to adjust data roughly to a PPP basis, as shown in table 14.2. Its estimates suggest that the level of living standards in the north could be as much as *three-quarters* of that prevailing in the south. These estimates could perhaps be biased upwards, to the extent that the PPP adjusters used in these calculations are based on price levels in

Turkey, since data are not available for the north. Moreover, in assessing living standards, it should be borne in mind that the economy of the north benefits from very sizeable external assistance, mainly from Turkey – and in the event of reunification there would be a major adjustment to more open economic conditions. Nonetheless, it seems clear that earlier estimates seriously overestimated the gap in living standards between north and south, and this sheds new light on the context of a reunification settlement.

Table 14.2 Per capita income in the north and south of Cyprus, 2004 (US$1,000s)

	Nominal	World Bank Atlas[a]	PPP corrected[a]
North	8.1	7.2	14.8
North – revised base	9.2	8.2	16.9
South	19.4	17.6	22.3
Ratio (north/south, as percentage)	42	41	66
Ratio (north/south, as percentage) – revised base	48	47	76

[a] The World Bank Atlas method for correcting gross national income takes account of nominal exchange rate fluctuations; PPP (purchasing power parity) estimates corrected for differences in purchasing power. The revised database takes account of the input–output matrix developed to assess the adequacy of GDP data in the north by extending coverage of the formal private sector (but not the informal sector, which would add a further 20–35 per cent to estimates of economic activity).
Source: World Bank (2006).

Synergies in a converging intra-Cyprus economy

When we look for gains from economic integration, one of our first thoughts as economists is to exploit sectoral complementarities and benefits from comparative advantage. In Cyprus, however, the two economies are sectorally quite similar in structure and in comparative advantage. So sectoral synergies, rather than sectoral complementarities, are likely to be an important source of gains. These could be important in several areas.

There seem, first, to be major synergies available in tourism. Exploiting these now is rather difficult in terms of property rights. But it is easy to see how one-time visitors to the south could be tempted back by unexplored sites and the important and environmentally appealing areas in the north. Moreover, this is not a win–lose proposition. A night gained in the north may bring one more in the south along with it. In fact, convergence in tourism could help restyle the tourist-market image of the south by adding new cultural and eco-tourism destinations and beaches.

Education is another growth sector. Turkish-Cypriot academics rightly stress continuing challenges in relation to academic quality, but they have shed light on the way ahead. Cyprus has an exceptional position from which to deliver higher education to an eastern Mediterranean market, and indeed further afield, in the Middle East, the Caucasus and Central Asia. An island-wide education network – in an atmosphere of ethnic, linguistic and religious tolerance – is potentially a trump card in this service sector.

Business services represent a regional market of huge promise, and one where new and potential competitors are poised to expand their market shares. The years of early EU membership offer an unprecedented opportunity to build on existing success in the south. For the north, this is also a field in which important opportunities exist – but these opportunities are handicapped in a number of ways by the political status quo.

Manufacturing industry is not a sector of the future in Cyprus in terms of GDP share, but it remains important. Moreover, it seems to be underdeveloped in the north, where there is nonetheless a skilled labour force to make use of. Convergence could be seen as part of a broader philosophy of changing not just market access but also economic incentives in the north – which have not prevented economic development but which are public-sector oriented and very aid dependent. To the extent there is an anti-export bias in the north, this could be corrected. Nonetheless, it may be that full liberalisation and opening of the economy of the north trigger a major adjustment in the traded-goods sector, and it will be important to respond with actions that enhance flexibility and skills in the labour market – and not with a step up in subsidies.

These points may seem obvious. But they may not be the economics that the man and woman in the street in 2004 had at the back of their minds.

Over time, convergence through liberalised markets will tend to foster viable and outward-looking economic opportunities – although this will involve adjustment stresses. Divergence that routes the trade of the north through distorted channels will embed the vested interests which benefit from those channels; and such interests will suffer, inevitably, when those distortions are removed. It may be helpful at this stage to summarise schematically some of the actual and perceived economic influences that may be relevant to forward movement on reunification, and this has been done in table 14.3. Clearly, the points of view in this table should be viewed as stylised; in reality, there were many varying interests and no doubt a wide spectrum of opinion on each side.

Table 14.3 Selected factors that may have affected perceptions of the economic effects of reunification

	Perceptions in April 2004		Scope for perceptions to evolve	
	North	South	North	South
Perceived effect on living standards	Strong hopes of higher living standards	Concern that success may be eroded	More awareness of transition to prepare for change	Analysis may help highlight real synergies
Perceived effect on monetary stability	Would bring greater stability	Might weaken sound monetary regime	Euro adoption in south in 2008 to confirm this	Euro adoption removes this major concern
Perceived effect on fiscal management	Pain of fiscal reform underestimated	Strong concern about fiscal viability	Progress now would allow a transition period	Talks on fiscal federalism could reassure
Perceived effect on business interests	Hopes from direct trade and tourism	Concern about competition in, e.g., tourism	Must recognise extent of likely restructuring	Sectoral studies could reveal positive scope
Perceived effect on regional role	Scope to broaden regional trade	Settlement with Turkey positive potential	Must internalise need to upgrade competitiveness	Enhanced role as regional hub
Perceived effect on property settlement	Fear of disruption from movements	Negative view on credibility of proposed deal	Improved prospects with local remedy	This remains a major (and now tougher) hurdle

Economic reforms and the convergence challenge

The macro-economic and structural reforms in discussion or underway in both the north and the south have been conceived in terms of an accelerating sustainable growth and thus income convergence towards the EU average. In the case of the south, this implied an upgrading of the growth rate; in the north, by contrast, growth had risen to unsustainable levels, and a slowdown was underway. With sound policies, the two economies should settle on a path of stable 'internal' and 'external' convergence. The design and process of economic reform can help accelerate income convergence in both respects, and can also foster greater structural convergence in Cyprus.

First, in the north, the *acquis communautaire* represents a network of institutional and policy reforms that could accelerate economic integration of the north with the south and the rest of the EU. Presently the *acquis* is suspended in the north; but the scope exists to shadow it, and in a number of areas progress has already been achieved. Priority areas include those essential for a single market in goods and services – such as phyto-sanitary requirements, certification of origin of products or competition policy. Obviously, there is rich experience in the south with adopting the *acquis* in an economy similar in structure to that of the north. It would be perverse if problems with EU financing slowed the shadowing of the *acquis* in the north, still more so if problems concerning recognition that complicate the use of official offices or communications involving official job titles – or indeed just a negative psychology on either side – left the north without intra-Cyprus assistance with regard to adoption of the *acquis*. The agreement on the EU aid package can, *inter alia*, help catalyse progress on the *acquis*.

Second, public finance reform in the north can help address very positively a number of concerns that surfaced in the 2004 discussions on economic issues. Such reform should seek to achieve the following: shift resources from current to investment expenditure; cut the fiscal deficit; and deal with the issue of outstanding loans to publicly owned enterprises, which is important for incentives in the banking system. Placing public finances in the north on a viable basis, *inter alia* by clarifying public and external debt levels, represents both a key to improving the investment climate in the north and a major contribution to the reunification agenda.

The adoption of the euro by the Republic of Cyprus in January 2008 may also help to reduce fiscal and financial concerns in the south, to the extent that any risks to the exchange rate peg no longer apply, and the costs of reunification do not risk creating problems in observance of the Maastricht fiscal deficit reference value. In some ways, however, adoption of the euro will change rather than eliminate such concerns; and the absence of exchange-market discipline is not an unmitigated gain. The adoption of the euro removes the exchange rate as a source of flexibility and adjustment. In the south, of course, the longstanding nature of the peg for the Cyprus pound meant it had no role as an adjustment instrument. The north, however, has benefited periodically from a safety valve (i.e., the depreciation of the Turkish lira) when its competitiveness had become weak.

It is true that the membership of the monetary union has resolved some central banking issues. It has also brought strong fiscal commitments under the Stability and Growth Pact. Moreover, in both north and south the real sector will need to display flexibility in order to sustain growth, as relative resources are reallocated under reunification – particularly if neither side has the exchange rate available as a safety valve. It is important also to have some sense in advance of where there will be winners and losers, so as to identify skill needs and strengthen mechanisms to support adjustment.

Third, for the north and also the south, there is scope more generally for synergy in pursuing economic reforms. Several examples spring to mind. For instance, both north and south need to embark on social security reform to address the challenge of an ageing population. It would make great sense for the reforms to be designed in ways that have broad compatibility. More generally, the labour market is a key area in which convergence is taking place. It would be desirable to put in place a framework assuring the compatibility or portability of different types of benefits and regulations between north and south. At a more general level still, the EU's Lisbon agenda is clearly relevant to both parts of the island, where there will be a continuing need to move upmarket to meet competition from lower-wage economies. This process is crucial in unlocking more rapid growth, which in turn will ease concerns (in both north and south) about shocks and adjustments involved in economic convergence and reunification.

So there is scope to meet various economic reform challenges in Cyprus through a process of coordination between north and south – however informal – in the broad framework of the *acquis communautaire.* Unfortunately, in recent years, despite some progress regarding trade and movement across the Green Line, there seems to have been a gradual embedding of an uncoordinated approach to reform, but if insufficient regard is given to the challenges, the working of convergence mechanisms in the labour market or elsewhere will not be facilitated.

The risks that divergent forces dominate

An economic reform agenda is important for both economies not only in its own right: it can also enhance economic constituencies for reunification – indeed, it might serve as a form of high-level confidence-building approach. The alternative may be that opportunities to foster convergence begin to slip away. To make these opportunities and risks more concrete, it may help to think of them in terms of the different markets through which intra-Cyprus convergence could act as a mechanism of growth.

Economic links between north and south are developing through limited channels. Integration of the labour market and the tourist sector, through movement of persons across the Green Line, are the main elements. Trade volumes between north and south have been rising, but remain low, and there is little or no portfolio or direct investment across the Green Line. Overall, the partial opening of the divide since 2003 has added some €100 million (9 per cent) to the GDP of the north, mainly from labour income of workers from the north employed in tourism and construction in the south.

First, the labour market has begun to function substantially. We know relatively little about how it is affecting prices and wages, but a survey by Mehmet et al. (2007) explored the structural shifts going on in the labour market. This suggested that there has not necessarily been a net drain of skills from the economy of the north; it also drew attention to a set of integrated changes that included the flow of migrants from Turkey – and the need to think carefully about how to handle this situation. One aspect of the changes underway, in any event, must be to raise wage rates in the north (including migrant and other informal labour). This makes more urgent the pursuit of reforms to enhance productivity in the north. Moreover, the social security framework for those commuting across the Green Line appears to be in need of attention.

Second, in the service sector there is some synergy developing in tourism, but in a very informal manner. Both economies are probably gaining, but there is no synergy on the provider side. Some efforts have been made to explore joint projects, but barriers have surfaced – including property rights. And the dependency of the north on package tourism is troubling, since it encourages a pattern of development that is not particularly environmentally friendly. In the health-care sector, people in the north are now benefiting from facilities in the south.

Third, it is clear that the goods market is not working effectively. The volume of goods that crosses the Green Line has been rising, but very slowly in terms of the potential that is there. Trade with the south is equivalent to some 4 per cent of total exports of goods and services from the north. Flows of goods were some CYP275,000 in the last four months of 2004; CYP981,000 in 2005; and CYP142,000 in the first six weeks of 2006. Little trade passes from south to north. The main exports from the north have recently been agricultural products, followed by electrical goods and wood and stone products. While further studies on this issue need to be carried out, it is clear that a quantum change is needed for this channel to be truly substantive in terms of its effect on the pattern of economic growth. The problems are quite complex though – ranging from taxation to standards and certification, to marketing and design, and to consumer psychology as regards the acceptance of goods from across the Line.

Finally, an intra-island capital market is not there, and the capital market in the north is not yet fully supporting growth. An integrated capital market could, of course, play a key role in supporting economic expansion in the north – in combination with know-how and experience in the south in accessing other markets. Again, property rights are a major issue for capital market development in the north, affecting the scope for SMEs to be a source of dynamism, innovation and employment creation. Capital market segregation and distortion have costs. And, of course, developments in property ownership since 2004 have further complicated the issues to be resolved in future – whether through bilateral legal or broader settlements. In particular, a clause in the Annan Plan (version V) that took property improvements into account in determining the rights of a current occupant triggered further construction on disputed land and some improvement of properties since April 2004.

Anecdotal evidence suggests that economic links between the north and Turkey are also deepening. These links include sizeable financial flows to the north, technical assistance in approximating to the *acquis communautaire*, and help in designing and implementing public finance reforms. Available data suggest that airline flights between Turkey and the north have been rising at a pace exceeding 20 per cent per annum.

This is a mixed picture. It underscores, in several key respects, the costs to the economy of the north of the status quo. Even in narrow economic terms, a major drawback of the now traditional pattern of growth in the north is that it involves significant distortions. Those affecting trade are obvious, and include sizeable informal costs. Moreover, property rights are a major distortion, and their impact, as already noted, is rather pervasive – affecting the scope for bizonal tourist development and also the form and pace of financial development. In other words, economic incentives for the north strongly favour reunification. But, in the absence of progress on the economic front, the short-term incentive for firms and service institutions in the north can be to look for alternative strategies, in the long-standing setting of monetary union with Turkey. For the south, too, there are opportunity costs in continuing separation, as the economy adjusts to meeting the evolving challenges of an increasingly globalised service economy.

Conclusions: are there economic lessons for the future in Cyprus and other conflicts?

Looking at the Cyprus conflict from an economic perspective may seem a narrow focus, but it does highlight a major risk facing all parties. The passage of time could result in incentives and pressures that make any breakthrough progressively less likely. Economic interests can embed separation. Uncoordinated reforms can inhibit convergence. Unless other incentives are put in place – such as the EU aid package, initiatives that could flow from the Annan–Papadoloulos communiqué of March 2006, and the evolution of direct trade between north Cyprus and the EU – Cyprus could face creeping divergence.

In other words, if economic incentives were indeed to work perversely, they could jeopardise the path towards reunification. People would grow apart, not together. Reunification initiatives, as they affect the economic domain, could be like Gulliver tied down and immobilised by the Lilliputian threads of daily economic life.

This perspective also suggests a valuable way forward, which could contribute to catalysing a dialogue. Apparently foreshadowed in the Annan–Papadopoulos communiqué, this is to establish technical meetings between north and south that would provide a forum to study and report back, on a bicommunal basis, on key issues of mutual concern. While this may in part begin with modest and operational issues, it could also come to embrace some of the economic questions explored above. It could serve as a channel of communication on reform progress and compatibility. It could also call for submissions and contributions from other bodies. It could, for example, ask for an evaluation of EU experience with fiscal federalism and decentralisation in the context of the Stability and Growth Pact. Finally, it could explore areas in which economic elements of the reunification agenda could be put into place bilaterally, on a confidence-building basis.

This approach could help lead towards a path of convergence and reunification, which should be attractive to both sides, under the right conditions. There is no question that the role of a unified, multicultural Cyprus – an EU hub in the eastern Mediterranean, and a global exporter of high-quality business, tourism and education services – is an *image de marque* that could steeply enhance its citizens' prosperity and well-being. It could serve also as a pole of attraction, stability and security in the entire region. Good business and good politics seems a deeply attractive future – and one which, while perishable, is still open to Cyprus today.

The experience so far in Cyprus also suggests some wider lessons for other conflict zones and for the study of conflict and conflict resolution. First, it illustrates concretely the potential role of certain economic influences on progress in conflict resolution, especially in relation to issues such as property rights and the impact of a potential settlement on economic growth and stability.

Second, Cyprus is an unusual case in terms of progress in legalising trade. The Green Line regulation, in effect, works around the fundamental problem of recognition in the conflict, in that it allows legal bilateral trade to take place between the parties in dispute. As such, it has rightly attracted the attention of experts working on problems in the Caucasus (informal discussions on this have taken place during the past two years involving experts in Cyprus and the author of this chapter). In this respect, Cyprus may offer a model in other cases, though one that is dependent on three factors: an external actor (e.g., the EU) able to press through an agreement; a legal instrument that can be adopted externally (e.g., the Green Line regulation); and the identification of local agencies such as non-governmental organisations – in this case the Turkish Cypriot Chamber of Commerce – which can act as formal agents acceptable to both sides for the purposes of certification and other legal issues. From the point of view of some actors in northern Cyprus, the Green Line regulation has not lived up to all hopes; but for those who have no such legal trading regime it may be a promising avenue for progress.

Third, in the view of some commentators, there are lessons deriving from Cyprus about the way in which the EU's capacity to promote solutions to ethno-political conflicts evolves once it becomes itself a primary party to the conflict (insofar as one side is the legal representative of a member state), compared with the possible leverage the EU can exert during the accession process. It can be argued that the EU's influence post-accession is no longer on a level playing field, with one party having voting rights in the Council after accession. Alternatively, it could perhaps be argued that EU membership might actually facilitate the resolution of issues, because it offers the broad framework of the *acquis communautaire*, which helps foster deals and informal pressures that make a favourable outcome more likely. In any event, this issue deserves further study, since lessons here may be relevant in parts of south-eastern Europe.

Finally, informal organisations such as the Wolfson Cyprus Group have played a role in bringing together actors on both sides to debate macro- and micro-economic issues of mutual concern. Nonetheless, it has been difficult to secure substantive progress without the engagement of the two sides in direct talks. This underscores that, while economic analysis and perceptions can be important, they are at most co-drivers in what is, at heart, a deeply political process.

Notes

1 This paper is written in a personal capacity and in particular does not purport to present views of the European Commission (to which the author is an economic adviser).

2 One forum for such exchanges is the Wolfson Cyprus Group, founded by the author of this chapter.

15

The Cyprus problem at the European Court of Human Rights

Kudret Özersay and Ayla Gürel

Introduction

Human rights issues have almost constantly existed in Cyprus since the island's independence in 1960.[1] However, the 'protection of human rights' became a prominent concern in the efforts to find a settlement of the 'Cyprus problem' only after the dramatic turn of events in 1974, which led to the island's *de facto* division along ethnic lines. The resulting massive displacement of persons from both communities clearly entailed violations of fundamental individual rights and freedoms.

The issue of displaced persons' rights to their homes and properties has been a core item on the diplomatically delicate and tightly linked agenda of the inter-communal negotiations sponsored by the United Nations (UN) since 1974. However, irrespective of the negotiations, since the early 1990s this issue has also been a topic at the European Court of Human Rights (ECHR). This was because of cases resulting from Greek-Cypriot applications lodged against Turkey. To date, the ECHR has issued judgements on four individual applications (ECHR, 1995, 1996, 1998, 2003a,b, 2005a,b, 2006) and one inter-state application, by the Greek-Cypriot administration acting as the government of the Republic of Cyprus (RoC)[2] (ECHR, 2001).[3] In these judgements, Turkey has generally been found in breach of the European Convention on Human Rights with regard to the Greek-Cypriot displaced persons' rights to their homes and properties in northern Cyprus.

The Greek-Cypriot government was involved in these proceedings either directly as an applicant or by intervention as a third party in individual applications. Although, of course, this is a right possessed by any 'high contracting party' to the Convention, in the case of the Greek-Cypriot government it is significant that such involvement has been quite compatible with the latter's general strategy in the ongoing diplomatic battle over Cyprus. Generally put, this strategy consists in guarding the Greek-Cypriot government's – in fact, questionable – international status of being considered 'the sole legitimate government of the RoC', as well as in taking advantage of this status to promote its political goals *vis-à-vis* the Cyprus problem (see Coufoudakis, 2006: 25–6, 89–90). More specifically, by obtaining international support – in both moral and legal terms – for its own position, the Greek-Cypriot side has hoped to exert greater pressure on Turkey and to strengthen its hand against the Turkish-Cypriot side in inter-communal negotiations. Essentially, this position depends on two convictions: first, that the issue of displaced persons' rights to their homes and properties is not a matter for political negotiations but a question of human rights, as required by international law; and second, that this issue can be solved only by fully restoring these rights, irrespective of any other commitments made in the framework of a settlement, such as bizonality. These convictions run contrary to the general Turkish/Turkish-Cypriot[4] outlook that the issues involved in the Cyprus problem are not judicial but political. According to the Turkish side, this is particularly true in the question of rights to homes and properties, which, it claims, cannot be approached from a purely legal perspective. Nor can this question be treated in isolation from the other aspects of a political settlement, of which bizonality is the most crucial one. In the Turkish view, bizonality – a mutually agreed principle since the 1977 Makarios–Denktaş High Level Agreement – presupposes restrictions on the exercise of certain rights and freedoms, including the rights to pre-1974 homes and properties (Gürel & Özersay, 2006).

Seen from the Turkish perspective, the Greek-Cypriot recourse to the ECHR was not conducive to the progression of the inter-communal negotiations. These negotiations were based on a commitment from both sides to a comprehensive settlement of the Cyprus problem through compromise solutions reached by mutual agreement. Ignoring this important rule of negotiation, the Greek-Cypriot side in effect sought independently and unilaterally to achieve its desired outcomes elsewhere. Indeed, the Greek-Cypriot side could be said to have attempted to resolve a key issue on the tightly knit agenda of the UN-sponsored talks through third-party *adjudication* – a process in which the Turkish-Cypriot side could have no formal status – instead of *negotiation* aimed at mutual agreement. In other words, by trying ultimately to get a high-profile international court to support its positions and goals, the Greek-Cypriot side has attempted to score points against its Turkish-Cypriot interlocutors in the ongoing UN-sponsored negotiations. At any rate, the Turkish-Cypriot side has a natural tendency to see this move on the part of the Greek-Cypriot side as an instance of continuing 'war by other means' rather than their seeking an honest reconciliation.

Looking at the situation from a purely political angle, one could argue that the ECHR ought to have stayed clear of the Greek-Cypriot cases against Turkey, in order not to influence the UN-mediated negotiations through judicial intervention. The Court's acceptance of these cases had important implications with respect to both the procedure and the substance of those negotiations. Most crucially, the ECHR process implied debating certain core issues of the Cyprus problem within a framework that was fundamentally different from that of the UN. In the latter case, the two Cypriot sides were treated as equals in terms of their political status. This was evidently not so at the ECHR, where the Greek-Cypriot side was considered to be the legitimate government of the whole island and the Turkish-Cypriot side, at best, an unrecognised *de facto* authority, certainly lower in status than the Greek-Cypriot one. Notwithstanding the inherent danger of prejudicing the UN-sponsored negotiations, the ECHR was, from the outset, disinclined to refuse jurisdiction on these cases. This is because of the Court's self-perception as the most important organ within the human rights protection machinery created by the Convention. The ECHR sees itself as bound by a mandate that consists in upholding the 'object and purpose' of the Convention and its coherence as a system for the protection of individual human rights (Mowbray, 2005: 59–60; ECHR, 2001: para. 78). Thus, what tends to influence above all the decisions of the Court is the 'Convention's special and unique character as a human rights treaty, providing for application and enforcement of human rights', and the understanding of it as 'an instrument of international law' that 'is not concerned with the relations between states but with the rights of individuals, proclaiming solemn principles for the humane treatment of the inhabitants of the signatory states' (Mowbray, 2005: 60).

From the Court's point of view, the Convention applies to the entire territory of Cyprus, by virtue of the RoC's ratification of it in 1962. The *de facto* division of the island since 1974 does not alter this fact. Therefore, the ECHR considers northern Cyprus as a territory in which the individual rights and freedoms set out in the Convention must still be safeguarded (see the discussion on state responsibility in the next section). As demonstrated in its rulings, the Court's concern with the enforcement and protection of human rights in northern Cyprus has in fact been rather detached from either Cypriot party's own political agenda. Many observers of international affairs have noted that a clear division between politics and law is neither easy to draw nor particularly useful in understanding complex issues and developments (Reus-Smit, 2004). This is certainly true for the Cyprus problem, where the two sides have tried to sustain their essentially antagonistic policy objectives by casting key questions as either exclusively legal or exclusively political matters. Their performance before the ECHR has been the starkest manifestation of this attitude so far.

In this chapter, through an analysis of its judgements on property-related Greek-Cypriot cases against Turkey, we analyse how the ECHR became an arena for a complicated interplay of politics and law. We do this by examining the major recurring political elements in the positions and arguments of the parties involved in the proceedings, and the Court's handling of these. We also discuss the present – and quite possibly future – consequences of the Court's rulings for the Cyprus negotiations under UN auspices.

The Turkish attitude at the ECHR

As mentioned above, the Turkish side perceived the Greek-Cypriot applications at the ECHR first and foremost as a political attack. Consequently, the actual human rights aspect of the cases within the context of the Convention's protection mechanisms has been viewed as secondary in the Turkish side's approach. This is very much reflected in the way its defence before the Court has been largely devoted to the purpose of preventing loss of any diplomatic ground to the Greek-Cypriot side in connection with the Cyprus negotiations. Indeed, until 2003, the Turkish side appeared to have rarely tried to formulate its points within the framework of the Convention or the jurisprudence of the Court. What follows is an analysis of the main Turkish arguments that illustrate this characteristic aspect of its attitude at the ECHR. However, after 2003 – and triggered especially by the developments related to the creation of 'efficient domestic remedies' within the Turkish Republic of Northern Cyprus (TRNC) – a certain readjustment began to occur in the Turkish approach (discussed below).

The status of the TRNC was a major point in the Turkish defence in all the cases. It was raised to back the contention that Turkey did not have jurisdiction in northern Cyprus and that it could therefore not be held responsible for the alleged violations of the Convention. In *Loizidou* v. *Turkey* the Turkish side argued that the issues raised by the Greek-Cypriot side were in fact within the jurisdiction of the TRNC, which was portrayed as a sovereign and independent state established, not by Turkey, but by the Turkish-Cypriot people in exercising their right to self-determination. Accordingly, it was maintained that Turkish troops were present in northern Cyprus with the consent of the independent TRNC government and that neither Turkish soldiers nor the Turkish government exercised any form of governmental authority there (ECHR, 1995: paras 55–6; ECHR, 1996: para. 51). However, based on its observation of the 30,000 Turkish military personnel stationed throughout the area with checkpoints on all main lines of communication, the Court concluded that Turkey exercised 'effective overall control' in northern Cyprus (ECHR, 1996: paras 16, 56). It then ruled that, as a result of such control, Turkey was responsible for the policies and actions of the TRNC and therefore that those affected by these policies or actions came within Turkey's jurisdiction. In other words, Turkey's obligations under article 1 of the Convention were viewed as being extended to northern Cyprus.

In establishing state responsibility and jurisdiction regarding the Convention's obligations in northern Cyprus, the key factor which the Court relied on was Turkey's 'control' over that territory. According to the Court, the responsibility of a signatory state may arise:

> when as a consequence of military action – whether lawful or unlawful – it exercises effective control of an area outside its national territory. The obligation to secure the rights and freedoms set out in the Convention in this geographical area derives from the existence of such control, be this exercised directly, through armed forces, or through a subordinate local administration. (ECHR, 1995: para. 62)

It is important to note that the Court did not include in its considerations on state responsibility the alleged illegality of the TRNC, as asserted by the Greek-Cypriot side. What the Court did mention in this context, however, was its finding that:

> the international community considers that the Republic of Cyprus is the sole legitimate Government of the island and has consistently refused to accept the legitimacy of the 'TRNC' as a State within the meaning of international law. (ECHR, 1996: para. 56)

In view of the island's *de facto* division, the recognised RoC government could not exercise any authority in northern Cyprus. Therefore, as regards state responsibility under the Convention in northern Cyprus, the Court had to look elsewhere, and there is little doubt that this was an important factor behind the Court's verdict concerning Turkey's responsibilities. Indeed, in *Cyprus* v. *Turkey*, when reaffirming its ruling that Turkey had jurisdiction in northern Cyprus, the Court stated that, given 'the applicant Government's [that of the RoC] continuing inability to exercise their Convention obligations in northern Cyprus, any other finding would result in a regrettable vacuum' in human rights protection in that territory (ECHR, 2001: para. 78).

Notwithstanding these rulings and without any change occurring on the ground in terms of the presence of Turkish troops in northern Cyprus, the Turkish side reiterated its claim concerning the status of the TRNC in all the subsequent cases. In *Xenides-Arestis* v. *Turkey*, the Turkish side asked the

Court to deem the case inadmissible on the grounds that Turkey had no jurisdiction in northern Cyprus as the TRNC government was independent and therefore exercised exclusive authority there. It claimed that this was implicit in the Annan Plan and was acknowledged by the international community, as demonstrated by its endorsement of that very Plan. According to the Turkish side, the contents of the Plan as well as the process of its negotiation reflected the international acceptance of the Turkish-Cypriot people as an independent entity (ECHR, 2005a: 11–12).

The Turkish side also argued that the Greek-Cypriot government's campaign against the Annan Plan prevented a settlement that would have contributed to a better enjoyment of human rights throughout Cyprus, and asked the Court to attribute responsibility for this to that government and not to Turkey (ECHR, 2005a: 28). This was a non-consequential piece of reasoning as regards the need to address the applicant's complaints. It was probably aimed at getting the Court to reconsider its earlier opinions on the status of the TRNC under what were thought to be the new circumstances marked by the international community's more favourable disposition towards the Turkish Cypriots, due to their acceptance of the Annan Plan.

A standard point in the Turkish line of defence was that the question of rights and reciprocal compensation was the crux of the Cyprus problem and formed a core item in the inter-communal talks, which represented the only means to reach a solution. The Turkish side argued that because of this, the complaints regarding property were outside Turkey's jurisdiction (ECHR, 1995: para. 56). The point was advanced also to justify the Turkish-Cypriot side's interference with the full enjoyment of property rights; it was stated that, in the present political situation, allowing a displaced person to have full freedom of access to his/her property would undermine the inter-communal talks (ECHR, 1996: para. 59; ECHR, 2001: para. 29). Until 2003, the Turkish side utilised an augmented version of the same point also to argue against an award of compensation by the Court. Refusing to engage in any discussion concerning the amount of compensation, they insisted that such an award would undermine inter-communal negotiations and spoil the efforts for a settlement on 'the already agreed principles of bizonality and bicommunality', which, according to the Turkish side, entailed an exchange of properties and, if need be, payment of compensation for any difference in value (ECHR, 1998: para. 21; ECHR, 2003a: para. 22; ECHR, 2003b: para. 24).

An extensive reliance on 'global' or 'collective' arguments has been another chief weakness of the Turkish defence strategy. These arguments were generally incompatible with the Court's particular regard for the Convention's character, which elevates *individual* human rights as its core element, as manifested in the Court's interpretation of the Convention and its own 'object and purpose'. For example, the Turkish side attempted to justify interference with property rights – without reference to any permissible restriction in the Convention – through global claims, such as 'the ongoing inter-communal talks', or by arguing that 'taking of property in northern Cyprus arose from the need to re-house displaced Turkish Cypriots and was ultimately due to an irreversible expropriation by virtue of Article 159(1)(b) of the TRNC Constitution and was justified under the international-law doctrine of necessity'. The Court held that these reasons were unacceptable as a justification under the Convention, for they implied 'the complete negation of the applicant's property rights in the form of a total and continuous denial of access and a purported expropriation without compensation' (ECHR, 1996: paras 35, 64; ECHR, 2001: paras 187–8).

In *Xenides-Arestis* v. *Turkey*, the Turkish side argued in global terms for the inadmissibility of the case. It maintained that the Greek Cypriots should exhaust the remedies available in the TRNC, 'just as Turkish Cypriots who have property in southern Cyprus have to exhaust domestic remedies available therein' (ECHR, 2005a: 25). Then, they argued in favour of the appropriateness of the Turkish-Cypriot remedy in question at the time (under TRNC Law 49/2003). However, in doing so, the Turkish side did not demonstrate the proposed measure's accessibility and capability to address the applicant's complaints but, rather, it generally compared it to the Greek-Cypriot law for the regulation, control and compulsory acquisition of Turkish-Cypriot property in southern Cyprus (ECHR, 2005a: 27). This approach was problematic also because the Court had not previously examined the Greek-Cypriot law's compatibility with the Convention. Furthermore, the Turkish side claimed that the absence of any provision for property restitution in the TRNC law should not be viewed as a problem because of the acknowledgement in the Annan Plan that 'the physical restitution of property is likely to be limited and is only likely to be available as part of a wider political settlement and not by way of individual applications to the Court' (ECHR, 2005a: 21). None of these arguments were accepted by the Court.

Despite its lack of success before the Court, the Turkish side persisted in employing 'global' arguments in its defence. Particularly remarkable is its recurrent use of the point about 'the ongoing inter-communal talks' to fend off allegations of violations or demands for redress made on it during the proceedings. This attitude is probably linked to an unexamined Turkish assumption and expectation that there is ultimately a role to be played in these cases by the Committee of Ministers of the Council of Europe (CoE) – the body responsible for executing the Court's decisions, as well as those of the European Commission of Human Rights. In this context, it is useful to recall the Commission's handling of the first three Greek-Cypriot state applications against Turkey. The Commission assessed the initial two applications together (in 1974 and 1975), found Turkey in breach of the Convention and in 1976 submitted its report to the CoE Committee of Ministers. In 1979, the Committee approved the report but, more crucially, it announced that the enduring protection of human rights in Cyprus was possible only through the re-establishment of peace and inter-communal trust and that inter-communal talks were the appropriate framework to solve the dispute.[5] In 1983, the Commission produced its report on the third Greek-Cypriot state application against Turkey, with similar findings. In this case, the Committee, without endorsing the report, confined itself to adopting a resolution in 1992, to make the report 'open to public'.[6] Needless to say, the attitude of this basically political body of the CoE dismayed the Greek-Cypriot side at the time, while being highly appreciated by the Turkish side. In *Loizidou* v. *Turkey*, the Turkish side brought to the attention of the Court the Committee's previous stance, which, it maintained, was 'in line with the realities of the situation prevailing in Cyprus' (ECHR, 1995: para. 56).

One crucial point to bear in mind here is that, at the time of the above-mentioned three state applications, Turkey had not yet recognised the 'compulsory jurisdiction' of the Court. This meant that the ultimate decision concerning the conclusion of the applications was made by the Committee and not by the Court. However, in 1990 Turkey accepted the Court's competence, making it possible for individuals as well as states to appeal to the Court against Turkey, as indeed happened, starting with the *Loizidou* v. *Turkey* application. Once a case is presented to the Court, the Committee, as a political body, has no say over the final judgement, which is legally binding on all the parties involved. The Turkish side was slow in understanding the significance of this change in the process.

The Greek-Cypriot attitude at the ECHR

At first – as so often in its general approach to the Cyprus problem – the Greek-Cypriot side focused on what it took to be the relevant formal legalities. In other words, it was initially keen to argue essentially within the rules laid out in the Convention. This was natural, because these applications were not aimed simply to stir a Europe-wide debate on the situation in Cyprus. They were meant to succeed and lead to legal judgements and outcomes which, among other things, would both help to increase international pressure on Turkey (by highlighting Turkey's military presence and political influence in northern Cyprus) and have consequences for future negotiations on the question of displaced persons' rights to their pre-1974 homes and properties.

In addition, however, the Greek-Cypriot side's submissions to the Court also regularly included arguments that were directly related to overarching unresolved political controversies within the context of the Cyprus problem. This suggests that the Greek-Cypriot side hoped to get its own policies on wider political matters endorsed by the Court, as well as to ensure that its policies would not be undermined during the disputations before the Court. In this section we discuss these Greek-Cypriot arguments, which became increasingly persistent from 2001 onwards, especially after the developments related to the TRNC's establishment of a mechanism for a 'domestic remedy'.

In connection with the discussions on state responsibility, the Greek-Cypriot side repeatedly held that the TRNC was legally invalid. This was based on a claim which forms the core of the Greek-Cypriot position, namely that the 1974 Turkish military action, of which the TRNC is a consequence, was illegal (ECHR, 1996: para. 49; ECHR, 2001: para. 70; ECHR, 2005a: 29). Thus, the Court was called upon to decide on a highly sensitive political matter that was – and remains – unresolved. In its decisions, the ECHR generally relies on various rules or sources that are indisputably accepted in international law, such as rulings by the International Court of Justice (ICJ) or certain UN resolutions. However, on the question regarding the legality of the 1974 Turkish military intervention under international law, no such reference exists. Furthermore, the Court's area of competence is limited to interpreting the Convention. Hence, by pronouncing itself on such a matter, the Court would in effect go beyond its mandate. No doubt bearing all this in mind, the Court bypassed the question and stated that an enquiry concerning 'the alleged lawfulness or unlawfulness under international law' of Turkey's 1974 military operation was not required for the establishment of state responsibility (ECHR, 1996: paras 52, 56).

In *Xenides-Arestis* v. *Turkey*, the Greek-Cypriot side was plainly concerned that the Court process might have undesirable consequences for its strategic and political positions. This was evident particularly in its submissions concerning the Annan Plan. The individual applicant and the RoC government both maintained that the Plan was legally inconsequential and they dismissed the Turkish side's arguments based on the Plan as being purely 'political'. Oddly enough, however, the Greek-Cypriot side also made an elaborate attempt to justify the rejection of the Plan by their own community, which was indicative of their unease about a possibility of the Court's decision being negatively influenced by that referendum result. They averred that the Plan was rejected because it did not provide a just and reasonable solution to the Cyprus problem. They claimed, moreover, that certain provisions of the Plan, including those concerning rights to homes and properties, were not compatible with the Convention and therefore that the Plan's undertaking to provide 'domestic remedies for the claims against Turkey of the breaches of the Convention' was unsatisfactory (ECHR, 2005a: 4, 15–17). The Greek-Cypriot side's hope was probably twofold: to get the Court to pronounce the Annan Plan to be incompatible with the Convention; and to have the Plan's 'domestic remedies' rebuffed by the Court as inappropriate and thus to pre-empt any danger that might arise if the Court were to consider similar mechanisms in the future by the TRNC a 'domestic remedy'.

The Court refused to be dragged into an assessment of the Plan's compatibility with the Convention. This was because no part of the Plan was 'applicable law', meaning that such an assessment was outside the Court's mandate. However, one significant general remark by the Court – not calculated to please the Greek-Cypriot side – was that 'the Annan Plan would have been a significant development and break-through in inter-communal negotiations had it come into force' (ECHR, 2005a: 18).

A constant Greek-Cypriot contention has been that no act of the TRNC – including its 1985 constitution – could be allowed to have any legal effect, be it under the Convention or any other rule of international law (ECHR, 1996: para. 36; ECHR, 2001: para. 83; ECHR, 2005a: 29). This was an absolute claim and, as such, was not accepted by the Court. For example, in *Loizidou* v. *Turkey*, in its consideration as to whether the applicant could still be regarded as the legal owner of the property in question, the Court adopted a very specific approach. It stated that, in light of the international community's non-recognition of the TRNC as a state under international law, it 'cannot attribute legal validity *for purposes of the Convention* to *such* provisions as Article 159 [of the 1985 TRNC constitution]' (ECHR, 1996: para. 44, emphasis added).[7] Thus, it held that 'the applicant cannot be deemed to have lost title to her property'. One must bear in mind that article 159 basically stipulates an operation of expropriation without compensation, which could hardly be regarded as being respectful of international standards in the field of human rights. The implication thus seemed to be that, despite the TRNC's lack of recognition as a state, its acts could be considered valid by the Court if they conformed with and served to uphold the purposes of Convention. Confining itself to the above conclusion, the Court maintained that there was no need 'to elaborate a general theory concerning the lawfulness of legislative and administrative acts of the "TRNC"'. Moreover, it noted that:

> international law recognises the legitimacy of certain legal arrangements and transactions in such a situation, for instance as regards the registration of births, deaths and marriages, 'the effects of which can be ignored only to the detriment of the inhabitants of the Territory'. (ECHR, 1996: para. 45)[8]

With this reference to the Advisory Opinion of the ICJ in the Namibia case (the so-called Namibia principle), what the Court meant was that, notwithstanding the international community's position and the resolutions of the UN Security Council, certain legal transactions of the TRNC could be seen as valid, for instance in the context of 'purposes of the Convention'. In fact, this was a harbinger of the discussions to come in the subsequent cases in connection with the validity of the 'domestic remedy' measures created by the TRNC.

It must be noted that, regarding the question of validity of the TRNC's administrative and legislative acts, the Court's considerations were not based on the circumstances of Turkey's overall control in northern Cyprus – which was the case during its deliberations on 'state responsibility' (see above) – but on the standing of *de facto* political entities in international law. In the Court's view, certain acts of such entities can be accepted as having legal effect provided they conform to the principles of the Convention. As mentioned above, this was initially hinted at in *Loizidou* v. *Turkey*, and clarified later in *Cyprus* v. *Turkey*. The Court made no general statement on the validity under international law of the acts and transactions of the TRNC. Rather, it limited its thoughts to the Convention-specific matter at stake (e.g., the exhaustion of domestic remedies) and to the existing practice in international law regarding what unrecognised states can do.

In *Cyprus* v. *Turkey*, the Greek-Cypriot side criticised an opinion of the Commission reached on the basis of the Namibia principle (ECHR, 2001: para. 85). The Commission's conclusion was that, to the extent that they are accessible and effective, account must be taken of the remedies available in the TRNC for the purposes of the Convention rule requiring the exhaustion of all domestic remedies as a precondition to the admissibility of an application (ECHR, 2001: para. 86). The Court disagreed with the Greek-Cypriot objection and, concurring with the Commission, stated that:

> the Advisory Opinion [of the ICJ on the Namibia case] confirms that where it can be shown that remedies exist to the advantage of individuals and offer them reasonable prospects of success in preventing violations of the Convention, use should be made of such remedies.... this requirement, applied in the context of the 'TRNC', is consistent with ... the need to avoid in the territory of northern Cyprus the existence of a vacuum in the protection of the human rights guaranteed by the Convention.

The Court added, moreover, that recognition of such remedies did not legitimise the TRNC in any way (ECHR, 2001: paras 89–92, 96–8). It was thus made clear by the Court that, following the Namibia principle, it would attribute 'validity' to certain legal measures of the TRNC and consider these as 'domestic remedies', provided that they conformed with the purposes and requirements of the Convention.

Needless to say, the Greek-Cypriot side viewed the 'validity' issue from a very different perspective than the Court. This was clearly demonstrated in its submissions concerning 'the right to an effective domestic remedy'[9] and the TRNC's capacity to provide such remedies. The Greek-Cypriot side made the following pair of mutually exclusive claims:

- Turkey is in breach of the Convention to the extent that it does not create an effective domestic remedy regarding the violations of the Convention in the TRNC.
- As regards the domestic remedies within the TRNC, the issue is not their effectiveness but the 'context of total unlawfulness' in which they were created. The 'illegality' of the TRNC and Turkey's 'illegal presence and control' there imply that the TRNC's courts are 'illegal' and no 'legally valid' domestic remedy can be created in the TRNC (ECHR, 2001: para. 83). In fact, neither the courts nor any other legal measure of remedy in the TRNC could be considered to be 'provided by law' (ECHR, 2001: paras 84, 180).[10]

The Court explicitly criticised and rejected this approach. Stressing the inconsistency of the arguments, it remarked that 'it cannot be asserted, on the one hand, that there has been a violation of that Article because a State has not provided a remedy while asserting, on the other hand, that any such remedy, if provided, would be null and void' (ECHR, 2001: para. 101).

Despite the above opinions of the Court, in *Xenides-Arestis* v. *Turkey* the Greek-Cypriot side continued to raise similar objections to acceptance of the TRNC's legal measures (i.e., the 2003 Property Compensation Law) as a 'domestic remedy'. As before, it was claimed that this remedy could not be 'valid' since it arose from an illegal source. This was because, it was alleged, the TRNC is illegal, and the Turkish invasion and continuing occupation of northern Cyprus involved breaches of the rules of general international law and the UN Charter (ECHR, 2005a: 28–30).[11] More crucially, it was claimed that:

> given the history and environment of the 'TRNC' and the prevailing political circumstances, to require Greek Cypriots, such as the applicant, to exhaust this remedy, would in effect require them to seek a remedy in the hands of the occupying power and thus accord implicit recognition. (ECHR, 2005a: 40)

In fact, in its submission to the Court, the Greek-Cypriot government mentioned that, through public statements, it discouraged its citizens from applying to the TRNC property commission, because of what it saw as the 'danger … that the lodging of such applications … might seek to be exploited by Turkey as according some kind of recognition' (ECHR, 2005a: 42–3).

The Court refused to be dragged into discussing legality/legitimacy issues all over again, and confined itself to making references to its earlier rulings. In addition, it made the following point, which closed the discussion:

> international law recognises the legitimacy of legal arrangements and transactions in certain situations akin to those existing in the 'TRNC' and that the question of the effectiveness of these remedies provided therein had to be considered in the specific circumstances where it arose, on a case-by case basis. (ECHR, 2005a: 44)

Execution of judgements: efforts to create a domestic remedy mechanism

According to the Court's findings in the landmark cases of *Loizidou* v. *Turkey* and *Cyprus* v. *Turkey* – which were reaffirmed in subsequent cases – the situation regarding the Convention's application in northern Cyprus basically involves the following:

- Owing to its overall military control over northern Cyprus, Turkey has jurisdiction and responsibility for the acts of the TRNC, which exercises *de facto* authority there. Therefore any violation in northern Cyprus of human rights guaranteed by the Convention is imputable to Turkey.
- The Convention requirement of the exhaustion of domestic remedies covers legislative acts and judicial organs of the TRNC. Thus, a TRNC measure that can be shown to offer individuals reasonable prospects of success in preventing and/or redressing violations of the Convention should be regarded as an efficient domestic remedy that should be made use of.

As mentioned earlier, in establishing this situation, a primary consideration of the Court has been 'the need to avoid in the territory of northern Cyprus the existence of a vacuum in the protection of human rights guaranteed by the Convention' (ECHR, 2001: paras 78, 91). What is laid out in the first point above has, of course, been politically highly worrying for the Turkish side, if only because it repudiates its claim that the TRNC operates as an independent state. However, the situation outlined in the second point presents an opportunity to deal with the legal requirements imposed by the Court's judgements in ways that they could control and thus make more politically palatable. The reverse of all this is true for the Greek-Cypriot side. The Court's stance that the TRNC could, in principle, offer an 'efficient domestic remedy' is viewed by this side as extremely disconcerting. This is because, despite the reassurances of the Court to the contrary (ECHR, 2001: paras 90, 92), the

Greek-Cypriot side believes that such an acceptance carries a danger of giving 'implicit recognition' to the TRNC.

Especially after the *Cyprus* v. *Turkey* judgement, the Committee of Ministers of the CoE – the body responsible for the supervision of the judgement's execution – intensified its efforts to bring Turkey round to fulfil its obligation to abide by the Court's ruling. Such efforts included the Committee's constant communication with the Turkish side, in which it provided both encouragement and supervision. These exchanges played an important role in inducing subsequent developments, such as the TRNC's opening in April 2003 of the border crossings along the Green Line, the passing of the TRNC Property Compensation Law in June 2003 to deal with Greek-Cypriot property claims, and Turkey's payment in December 2003 of the compensation the Court ruled on in July 1998 in *Loizidou* v. *Turkey*. These were indeed remarkable adjustments in the Turkish side's attitude, given the earlier stance about the Court's rulings.[12] Of course, this transformation in the Turkish approach was closely linked with Turkey's determination to pursue its aspirations to join the European Union (EU), which had become the cornerstone goal of the Turkish government after the first election of the Justice and Development Party (AKP) in November 2002. What also cleared the way for and assisted in Turkish 'cooperation' with the CoE regarding the execution of the Court's rulings was the definite shift, after December 2003, in the Turkish-Cypriot political landscape and hence in the Turkish-Cypriot official policies concerning the Cyprus problem.

In *Xenides-Arestis* v. *Turkey*, the Turkish side's approach was noticeably more Convention-specific than in any of the previous cases, which suggests that the Turkish side was probably beginning to learn the rules of the game. Citing the above-mentioned 2003 Property Compensation Law, the Turkish side made a plea of inadmissibility on the grounds that domestic remedies had not been exhausted by the applicant. The Turkish side had apparently taken note of the Court's ruling in *Cyprus* v. *Turkey* concerning the domestic remedies available in the TRNC. However, the plea of inadmissibility was rejected based on the Court's assessment that the remedy proposed did not satisfy the Convention requirements and could not be considered an 'effective' or 'adequate' means of redressing the complaints in question. According to the Court, 'the purported remedy' had the following deficiencies. There was no provision for the possibility of restitution of property, nor for non-pecuniary damages or damages for movable properties. Complaints under article 8 (right to respect for private and family life) and article 14 (prohibition of discrimination) of the Convention were therefore not addressed. Furthermore, the Court also claimed that the TRNC law was not clear in its retrospective effects, that is, in relation to applications filed before its enactment. Finally, there were concerns regarding the composition of the Turkish-Cypriot Compensation Commission in light of the evidence that the majority of its members were living in houses owned or built on property owned by Greek Cypriots. On this, the Court further suggested that 'an international composition would enhance the commission's standing and credibility' (ECHR, 2005a: 44–5).

Subsequently, in its *Xenides-Arestis* v. *Turkey* judgement on merits, the Court described the violation of the applicant's rights in respect of her home and property as part of the larger problem of displaced Greek-Cypriot persons' rights in northern Cyprus, and mentioned 'the fact that there are already approximately 1,400 property cases pending before it brought primarily by Greek Cypriots against Turkey'. It then asked Turkey to 'introduce a remedy which secures genuinely effective redress for the Convention violations identified in the instant judgment in relation to the present applicant as well as in respect of all similar applications pending before it' (ECHR, 2005b: paras 38–40).

In response, and taking into account the Court's assessments and considerations of its initial reparation scheme, the TRNC enacted in December 2005 the Law for the Compensation, Exchange and Restitution of Immovable Properties (Law 67/2005). This legislation, which superseded the previous Law, provides for the establishment of an 'Immovable Property Commission', authorised to decide on three alternative forms of redress: restitution – under certain circumstances – of the immovable property; exchange of properties; or payment of compensation. Under the Law, compensation is available also for non-pecuniary damages, including those related to movable properties. As to the composition of the Commission, the Law does not permit the appointment of persons who directly or indirectly benefit from property owned by displaced Greek Cypriots. Indeed, the Commission currently has two foreign members.

About a year after the Commission began to operate, the Court announced that it 'welcomes the steps [thus taken] to provide redress for the violations of the applicant's Convention rights as well in respect of all similar applications pending before it' and noted that 'the new compensation and restitution mechanism, in principle, has taken care of the requirements of the decision of the Court on admissibility of 14 March 2005 and the judgment on the merits of 22 December 2005' (ECHR, 2006: para. 37). By that time, out of the numerous applications received from Greek-Cypriot claimants, the Commission had settled nine cases, in three of which properties were reinstated and in the rest of which financial compensation was paid to the owners.

As things stand at the time of writing, the Commission has received about 370 applications, of which fifty have been settled. Restitution was afforded in four cases, while in two of them the Greek-Cypriot claimants agreed to exchange properties between the north and the south.[13] The Court has yet to decide whether to accept the TRNC's redress mechanism as 'an efficient domestic remedy' under the Convention's requirements. Needless to say, a positive ruling about the Commission would have significant implications for the 1,400 Greek-Cypriot cases pending before the Court, which would have to be redirected to the TRNC's Commission.

Given its original expectations from these cases at the ECHR, the Greek-Cypriot side now finds the recognition of the Turkish-Cypriot Commission by the Court jeopardising its fundamental position and goals regarding the Cyprus problem. It fears that such a development would allow the Turkish side to present itself as upholding rather than violating human rights; it would also help to conceal the 'illegality' of the TRNC and thus avert international pressure on Turkey due to its military presence on the island (Palley, 2006). In the Greek-Cypriot view, attribution of validity of any kind to any law, court or other organ of the TRNC must be avoided in order to safeguard 'the state entity' and 'the international statehood of Cyprus [i.e., the RoC], on the basis of which we function as a member of the international community'.[14] Another serious concern is that, by approving the Turkish-Cypriot Commission, the Court would acknowledge methods other than restitution – namely payment of compensation and exchange of properties – as appropriate means for restoring property rights, a situation that is exactly the opposite of what the Greek-Cypriot side had originally aimed to achieve. Hence the unanimous condemnation and rejection of the TRNC Commission by the (Greek) Cypriot House of Representatives, and its call on Greek Cypriots to appreciate the consequences of their involvement in such procedures 'encumbering in this way the process of assertion of the rights of the refugees and the real interests of the Republic of Cyprus in international and legal fora'.[15]

Conclusions

We have tried to demonstrate in this chapter that the ECHR proceedings in the property-related Greek-Cypriot cases against Turkey have not been a purely legal affair. Nor have they ever been viewed by the parties concerned – except for the Court itself – as being solely about the legal protection of individual human rights. This was inevitable, given that the issues raised at the ECHR pertain to key items in the UN-sponsored peace process for a comprehensive settlement of the Cyprus problem. Indeed, the Greek-Cypriot side has pursued this course largely to obtain legally binding results that would favour its own bargaining position at the talks and weaken that of the Turkish side. The ECHR thus became another arena in which the two sides have continued their political battle, seeking international and local endorsement of their political arguments. The Court, however, has generally managed to manoeuvre its way around such extraneous disputations. It has confined itself to ruling to uphold the Convention's 'object and purpose', namely the protection of *individual* human rights, which crucially entails ensuring the provision of remedy and redress to stop any violation of the Convention rights.

Until *Xenides-Arestis* v. *Turkey*, the Turkish side viewed the ECHR judgements as negatively affecting its 'national' cause in Cyprus, while the Greek-Cypriot side considered these judgements to be important achievements in the advancement of its own 'national' struggle. However, this situation began to change as the Court proceeded with its rulings in *Xenides-Arestis* v. *Turkey*, reaffirming its stance on the question of the validity of the TRNC's legal remedies – expressed earlier in *Cyprus* v. *Turkey* – as well as instructing the creation of such remedies to provide redress 'in respect of all similar applications pending before it'. This was, of course, a 'pragmatic consideration' on the part of the Court (Hoffmeister, 2002). Given the lack of any imminent prospect of a solution, this pragmatic position understandably originates from the need to allow, under the existing circumstances, for the execution of the Court's judgements – a need which was undoubtedly made more urgent with the accumulation of over a thousand Greek-Cypriot applications waiting to be handled. The Turkish side's line so far has been to cooperate with the Court in this direction. However, it is now the Greek-Cypriot side that feels anxious about the developments on the ECHR front. It is particularly concerned that further progress in this direction may deal an irreparable blow to the basic premise of its political position, namely, that everything about what it calls 'the pseudo-state' – its original source as well as its continuing existence and actions – is 'null and void *ab initio*'.

The boundary between the 'political' and the 'legal' is extremely blurred in the Cyprus situation, as it is in many other international conflicts. The Turkish side, which seeks a new legitimate status quo after the 1974 *de facto* division of the island, tends to rely more on the 'political' than the 'legal', while the Greek-Cypriot side, given its present international recognition as 'the sole legitimate government in Cyprus', tends generally to appeal to the 'legal' for its political ends, as witnessed in its appeals against Turkey at the ECHR. Indeed, this fundamental difference between the two sides' approaches has been very much reflected in the ECHR proceedings. Submissions to the Court have often involved issues perceived by each Cypriot side as linked with its 'national interests'. The proceedings have thus become highly adversarial, with significant consequences for the UN-mediated peace process. In particular, this has meant projecting onto the conflict resolution process characteristics of adjudication – notably lack of flexibility for bargaining and compromise, and loss of control over the outcome. The Turkish side has understood this fact for some time. More recently, the Greek-Cypriot side seems to be close itself to making this discovery. Perhaps such a realisation by both sides will encourage them to start negotiating mutually acceptable solutions in earnest.

Notes

1 For example, between 1964 and 1974 Turkish Cypriots were deprived of political representation in their own parliament and confined to ghettos in 3 per cent of the island.

2 In the rest of the chapter, this administration is referred to as the 'Greek-Cypriot government'. Note that the RoC has been entirely administered by the Greek Cypriots since 1964, a situation that is plainly unconstitutional and in contravention of the Cyprus 1960 accords. However, we cannot discuss here either the origin or the continuing effects of this anomaly, which is a central feature of the Cyprus problem.

3 These ECHR documents are accessible through the ECHR portal search at http://cmiskp.echr.coe.int/tkp197/search.asp?skin=hudoc-en.

4 In the remainder of the chapter, the joint party of 'Turkey/Turkish Cypriots' is referred to as 'Turkish'.

5 The CoE Committee of Ministers' Resolution DH (79)1, adopted on 20 January 1979 (cited in ECHR, 2001: para. 17).

6 The CoE Committee of Ministers' Resolution DH (92)12, adopted on 2 April 1992 (cited in ECHR, 2001: para. 17).

7 The said article, entitled 'The Right of the State to Ownership', declares all the 'abandoned' Greek-Cypriot property in northern Cyprus to be state property.

8 Here the Court is quoting from: Advisory Opinion on Legal Consequences for States of the Continued Presence of South Africa in Namibia (South West Africa) Notwithstanding Security Council Resolution 276 (1970) [1971], *International Court of Justice Reports*, 16:56, para. 125.

9 Article 13 of the European Convention on Human Rights.

10 Note that, in the jurisprudence of the Court, 'provided by law' means that 'the legal basis for any interference with Convention rights must be adequately accessible and formulated with sufficient precision. The requirement for legality therefore not only requires a specific legal rule or regime authorising interference, but also relates to the quality of the particular domestic legal provision' (Leach, 2005: 162).

11 *Xenides-Arestis*, Admissibility Decision: 28–30.

12 The judgement was described by Şükrü Sina Gürel, then a state minister in the Turkish government, as representing a political attitude against Turkey 'submitted within the cover of principles of law', against which Turkey had no need to defend itself. The view of the then TRNC President, Rauf Denktaş, was that the ECHR decision was a great mistake and would not assist in resolving the Cyprus issue (Ankara Anatolia News Agency, 12 May 2001, cited in RoC Public Information Office, Turkish Cypriot Press and Other Media, 14 May 2001; available at www.hri.org/news/cyprus/tcpr/2001/01-05-14.tcpr.html).

13 Note that one of the claimants who agreed to have exchange of properties was an applicant in *Eugenia Michaelidou Developments Ltd and Michael Tymvios* v. *Turkey*,

a case already judged by the ECHR to involve violation by Turkey of the applicants' property rights (ECHR, 2003b).

14 See the statement by the Greek-Cypriot Attorney General, 7 April 2005, available at www.cyprusembassy.net/home/index.php?module=article&id=2410. See also statements by Demetris Christofias, President of the House of Representatives, Haravgi, 25 June 2006; and President Tassos Papadopoulos, Haravgi, 27 December 2006.

15 'Cyprus House Condemns "illegal exploitation" of G/C properties in "occupied areas"', Cyprus News Agency, 7 June 2007.

16

Conclusion

Thomas Diez and Nathalie Tocci

One picture, many pictures of the Cyprus conflict

The chapters in this book have painted a multifaceted picture of the Cyprus conflict. The authors have done so from a variety of perspectives, in terms of both ontological and methodological approaches, and from different disciplinary backgrounds. Yet does this picture amount to a whole? And is there anything we can learn for the study of conflicts in general? It is to these two questions that we would like to turn in these concluding remarks.

There is a tendency in relation to Cyprus as well as other conflicts to focus on a particular factor or actor in justifying a particular conflict position or in suggesting means of conflict resolution. In Cyprus, blame is often apportioned to external actors – if not Greece or Turkey, then the former colonial power, Britain, which sowed the seeds of conflict by pursuing a system of 'divide and rule' (Attalides, 1979; Stefanidis, 1999), or the neo-imperial United States, which betrayed Cyprus by letting the Turkish army invade (Hitchens, 1997; O'Malley and Craig, 1999; for a more nuanced picture see Nicolet, 2001). While outside actors certainly bear some responsibility for the perpetuation of the conflict, as Kaliber in chapter 6 has discussed for the case of Turkey, many of the contributions to this book make clear that the conflict is deeply engrained in various aspects of society on the island. To name but three: the logic according to which the media operate favours conflict over small and sometimes tedious-looking steps towards its resolution (Bailie and Azgin, chapter 4); gender stereotypes both grow on the fertile ground of and in turn reproduce conflict discourse (Hadjipavlou, chapter 13); and rather than being the objective force which they would like to invoke, international law is used by core Cypriot actors as a means to pursue their political struggle through unilateral and often antagonistic moves (Özersay and Gürel, chapter 15). Even if there were an agreement between the different sides on a new, common polity, these conflict discourses would still be present and pose a challenge to lasting conflict transformation.

Likewise, the rejection of the Annan Plan by the Greek-Cypriot majority in April 2004 is often put down to security concerns (Faustmann, 2006). The Annan Plan should have not allowed Turkish troops to remain on the island, people claim. Yet even though Lordos has shown in chapter 2 that security did feature as a core concern among Greek Cypriots, other factors, related to more tangible and immediate material benefits, need to be added, above all the vexed issue of property (Özersay and Gürel, chapter 15). More broadly, economic preoccupations (even if exaggerated or misplaced) represented an important factor underpinning the Greek-Cypriot reluctance to reunify with the more impoverished Turkish-Cypriot north (Watson, chapter 14). There are, indeed, two further complications when discussing specific factors 'causing' conflict or the failure of conflict resolution. Féron and Güven Lisaniler (chapter 11) point to the first, namely, the relationship between more immediate factors and what the authors call the 'salient dimensions' of conflict, which in the Cyprus case include a much longer list of cultural and socio-economic claims. Bailie and Azgin (chapter 4) as well as Hadjipavlou (chapter 13), in different ways, highlight the second complication, in that their chapters emphasise the socially constructed nature of the 'root causes' of conflict. In other words, what some represent as the inescapable nature of things in Cyprus may only be part of what Kaliber (chapter 6), following Wæver (1995), would call 'securitisation', that is, the representation of something as an existential threat, which from this perspective is one of the core forms of conflict communication (see Diez et al., 2006: 565–6).

The different accounts of the Cyprus conflict in this volume are not unrelated. Despite their different approaches, there are certain themes that run through many of them: that local and international actors are interconnected; that individual actors are located in particular contexts that shape their conflict behaviour, which they also reproduce; that local actors such as business (Balkır and Yalman, chapter 3) and elites (Kaymak and Vural, chapter 5), as well as individuals (Watson, chapter 14), often use conflict resolution initiatives for their own purposes, posing both opportunities and problems to any mediator, in that support for a solution may quickly falter if there are unintended consequences or if the benefits do not materialise quickly enough; that there are dissonances not immediately understood between the conflict constructions of conflict actors and the implications of a solution; and that there are alternatives promising a better return.

There is therefore an emerging picture of the Cyprus conflict but, with both the conflict being at a crossroads and the analysts finding themselves at a crossroads of different perspectives, this picture is a highly complex one – it is the picture of 'one Cyprus, many Cypruses', to paraphrase Rob Walker (1988). It may be likened to a cubist painting, in which the object is broken up into many different parts seen from different angles, or to a floor mosaic, in which millions of stones contribute to the emergence of a picture, which in itself though is so vast that it cannot be taken in with a single glance, and changes its appearance depending on the angle from which it is viewed (see also Diez and Wiener, 2004). Much as in a cubist painting, there are tensions between the different perspectives, often related to the ontology they build: should preference be given to the individual (Lordos, chapter 2), or should the analysis be conducted on the community level (Loizos and Kelly, chapter 12) or the discursive level (Kaliber, chapter 6; Verney, chapter 7)?

This does not, however, mean that we can easily generate from these different perspectives empirically testable competing hypotheses. This may of course partly be because the chapters were not written in a competitive spirit, but to illustrate the specific contribution a particular approach can make to the analysis of the conflict. Yet from our point of view, most of the time these tensions reflect different analytical purposes, in that the authors want to explain outcomes (Lordos), understand behaviour (Loizos and Kelly) or critically interrogate prevailing understandings (Hadjipavlou). These purposes require different methodologies, and they shed a different light on the conflict; yet they are not mutually incompatible. We can, therefore, explain why voters voted in the way they did in an explanatory approach and then investigate the discursive contexts in which they did so in a critical approach, without declaring one or the other to be false or misguided. In this spirit, we read in Lordos that Greek-Cypriot women voters were more likely to reject the Annan Plan than male ones, while Hadjipavlou reminds us that this may not be a consequence of their sex as much as of the dominant gender constructions in Cyprus that attribute to women a specific role in society and politics. This is not to say that we cannot derive competing hypotheses from the contributions to this volume, but more often than not they will come out of contestations of claims within individual chapters rather than from comparisons across chapters.

There is of course a trade-off between parsimony and complexity. For policy-makers in particular, this more complex and multifaceted picture of the Cyprus conflict may not be welcome – the more complicated the conflict, the more difficult it is to do something about it. Yet simple solutions often fail because they underestimate the complexity of the task at hand. The idea, for instance, that membership of the European Union (EU) could work as a catalyst to conflict resolution on the island, primarily because of the incentives it would provide to the Turkish Cypriots and the pressure it would put on Turkey, was a clear and reasonably straightforward policy. It failed, at least in the short run, above all because the international community had framed the conflict in a particular way (see Verney's chapter 7 for the case of the European Parliament before the Annan Plan) and did not fully appreciate that the catalytic function was part of the policy strategy of one of the conflict parties (i.e. the Greek-Cypriot government), which was seeking a solution on its own terms, and was not prepared to adjust to the expectations of, say, the European Commission, let alone the Turkish Cypriots or Turkey. Clearly, it would have helped if European policy-makers had treated the Greek-Cypriot rationale with more suspicion, as the contributors here would have advocated; one of the core messages of the chapters in this volume has been that local actors use conflict resolution schemes for their own purposes. Yet the EU itself was not involved in Cyprus in order to 'settle' the conflict. The nature of the Union's mandate was to pursue accession and not peace in Cyprus, and this partly explains why EU actors were blind to the multifaceted complexity of the conflict (Tocci, 2004b). Even where the EU catalyst seems to have worked, in the regime change in northern Cyprus, other factors (first and foremost, an economic and banking crisis) were the actual catalyst, and EU membership then provided the context in which the protest against the old regime could be articulated (Diez, 2005: 299; Tocci, 2007: 49).

Similarly, laying the blame for the perpetuation of the conflict squarely at the feet of the Turkish Cypriots was a simplistic analysis that dominated the international discourse until the Annan Plan, and backfired when it came to the referenda. There is no doubt that the behaviour of Rauf Denktaş, as Turkish-Cypriot leader, obstructed conflict resolution efforts for a long time, but this should have not detracted from a broader and critical analysis of the discourses, identities and interests of all parties involved. As Ker-Lindsay has shown in chapter 8, there had been enough indications in the past that the Greek-Cypriot side did not have an unqualified interest in a loose federal solution. Instead, most of the efforts of international actors to convince Cypriots in the run-up to the Annan Plan of its benefits were focused on the Turkish Cypriots, at a time when the regime had changed, when Turkey's Cyprus policy was changing and when it was already reasonably clear that it was the prevailing mood among Greek Cypriots that would be the real problem.

The one-sided analysis of the past shaped behaviour even then. On the one hand, funding streams are highly institutionalised, and the discourse on which these institutions relied identified the Turkish Cypriots as the main target of persuasion. Once the money was there, it could not easily be re-directed to organise workshops with Greek Cypriots instead. On the other hand, the decade-long, largely undisputed construction of the Greek Cypriots as victims meant that open interference in the Greek-Cypriot public debate would have come as a shock. It most likely would have been constructed and resisted as interference in domestic affairs, a questioning of the sovereignty of the Republic of Cyprus, and as an act of neo-imperialism, an accusation some domestic actors with links to international groups that spoke out in favour of the Annan Plan were only too familiar with (see Demetriou, 2008). Again, a more complex picture would have been an asset, not a problem to international policy-makers. True, by the time the Annan Plan was being finalised, the options in terms of whom one could talk to without further jeopardising the Plan were heavily reduced, but they would not have been had the international discourse not given in earlier to a one-sided narrative of the conflict.

Yet those engaged in supporting bicommunal activities between Greek Cypriots and Turkish Cypriots did not necessarily start from a more complex picture. There is a tendency to overestimate the societal reach of such activities. While they are important to build a base on which a new Cyprus can stand, they often rely on those already converted or, if held during the day, bring in people happy to engage in friendly talk for a few hours off. They normally engage with the same group of usual suspects, who are invited to engage in dialogue *qua* Greek Cypriots or Turkish Cypriots. By contrast, these initiatives often ignore the valuable peace work that could be carried out not only between communities but also within them and cutting across the bicommunal divide. They are thus not immune from the problem that internationally sponsored engagements can be and are used by local actors for their own purposes, sometimes in line with the aim of international actors, sometimes not.

International actors are, however, not only to be criticised for their too simplistic constructions of conflict (as Akçali has rightly done in chapter 10); they are also the victims of the constraints put on them by these discourses. Many have blamed, for instance, the EU for underestimating the problems with the Cyprus conflict and too easily agreeing to the accession of the Republic of Cyprus without demanding a solution in the first instance (e.g. Brewin, 2000; Tocci, 2007: 50–2). While it is true that member states' interests and political bargains at European Council meetings played a crucial role in this respect, it is also noteworthy that the options to articulate alternatives legitimately were at the time heavily circumscribed by the internationally 'valid' narrative, confirmed in judgements of the European Court of Human Rights and United Nations Security Council resolutions, that the Turkish-Cypriot regime, and in particular Turkey, were the perpetrators. This left little room for voicing concerns without being framed as wanting to go against international law and further punish the actual victim.

The complexity of 'one picture, many pictures' that this book provides may therefore make policy-making even more difficult than it already is but, given the past record, this may not be a disadvantage. Given the multiple facets of the conflict, the only viable strategy in any case seems to be a long-term one that focuses on dialogue with many different conflict actors in an effort to contribute to conflict transformation, in the sense of shifting the discourses on identity and interests on which conflict actors rely.

Cyprus as an instance of analysing conflict

What can this picture of Cyprus tell us about the analysis of conflict in general? First, it should be obvious that much of what we have discussed above regarding the 'one picture, many pictures' of Cyprus is applicable to the analysis of other conflicts as well. Like many other issues, conflict has in the past all too often been analysed from one perspective against others, realists making the case against liberals, rationalists against constructivists, those focusing on conflict management – appearing supposedly pragmatic and realist(ic) to one side, but as being in danger of reproducing conflictive identities to the other – against those emphasising conflict resolution, or transformation involving more structural change (removing the core of the conflict to some but remaining a utopian pipe dream to others). The message that comes out of the contributions in this volume, for scholars and practitioners alike, is that many of these studies should be read side by side, and that the preference given to one or the other is not a matter of true or false but of purpose and perspective.

This increased complexity can be as disturbing for analysts as it is for policy-makers, in that the analyst can never achieve a single and complete picture. There is a practical and a fundamental reason for this. On the practical front, we all operate with limited means, yet to conduct an analysis from all possible angles would require superhuman resources, not only in financial terms but also in the ability to put the different pieces of the puzzle together as a coherent picture. That the latter is so difficult has to do with the fundamental issue of thinking within different ontologies. Within a single approach, we find it difficult to combine different ontological perspectives without running into inconsistencies. The problem is evident, for instance, in the attempt of social constructivism to forge a 'middle ground' between individualism and holism, idealism and materialism, and structure and agency (see Adler, 1997). Methodologically, it has to bracket some factors because it cannot analyse everything at the same time and has to start from somewhere. Ontologically, it tends to give priority to either structure or agency, usually the one not bracketed. Epistemologically, it excludes its own undertaking from its 'structurationist' view of the world. Yet all of this does not make social constructivism a useless exercise. Many no doubt share its objections to one-sided views of the world.

It will, however, degenerate into such a view itself if it does not keep the space of the middle ground open for different perspectives – not a middle point, a middle ground. What applies to the social sciences in general also applies to the field of conflict studies. From such a perspective, the increased complexity is not something to worry about, but a necessary correction to the field, which in the case of the traditional literature on Cyprus all too often, and on both sides, has taken the form of simplistic analyses at best and outright propaganda at worst.

A second conclusion that can be drawn from the studies in this volume for conflict analysis in general is a reminder that, just as it takes two to tango, it takes at least two sides to engage in conflict. While there are cases in which one side clearly bears most or all responsibility, such instances are rare. This is part of the complexity argument above, but it is worth pointing out specifically. The easy condemnation of one side or another is an often-repeated mistake, performed against an existing prejudiced discourse and driven by media presentations that are, as Bailie and Azgin have shown in chapter 4, hugely problematic. We should further note the 'at least two sides' in the opening sentence of this paragraph. Cyprus is a case where it is often forgotten that there are more than Greek Cypriot and Turkish Cypriots, as Hadjipavlou has reminded us (see also Constantinou, 2007). The fate of such minorities as the Maronites, Latin Cypriots or immigrants from Asia in a conflict such as Cyprus is often illuminative of general problems in the way conflict societies operate. Yet appreciating that there are more sides to a conflict does not necessarily mean that proposed solutions must seek the perfect middle point between the parties' positions. Often international mediators, under the banner of objectivity, fairness and neutrality, present solutions which simply split the differences between the conflict parties. While in some cases there may be no alternative to this approach, in other cases alternative and more creative proposals may emerge if simple uni- or bidimensional views of the conflict are abandoned.

The chapters in this volume have not taken a clear line on the most desirable political organisation of conflict societies, not least because, as Berg has shown in chapter 9, constitutional arrangements need to be developed, on the one hand, in dialogue with the conflict parties while, on the other hand, not reinforcing antagonistic divides. Berg is critical of imposed federalist solutions in this respect, but it should also be noted that we do not have many alternatives to various degrees of federal arrangements in view of the resilience of the state-based system in international relations. Consociationalist solutions, not tying identities to territories, can run into the same problems as federalist ones, especially if the number of principal conflict parties is rather small, as the case of the 1960 Cyprus constitution shows. Ultimately, a lasting solution will therefore always rely on more fundamental transformations, as called for by Akçali in chapter 10. A transformative approach, however, is not necessarily opposed to a federalist solution, in which identities may initially seem to be reinforced. Indeed, it is one of the paradoxes of borders that their recognition (and therefore the recognition and at least initial reinforcement of the identities they contain) often leads to their reduced significance, and thus eventually to more possibilities to freely articulate a variety of identities than in situations where borders remain contested, in that they are both called for and disputed (see Diez, 2006). The challenge of federal solutions is thus that of setting in motion a process, through institutional, political, economic and social incentives, whereby the initially reaffirmed significance of communal identities and fixed territories may blur and change over time.

Following this line of reasoning, Berg and Akçali (chapters 9 and 10) but also Féron and Güven Lisaniler (chapter 11) point to the necessity of a shift in our conceptualisations of federalism not as a static institutional arrangement but as an ethos of continuous change, federalisation instead of federalism, following William Connolly's similar suggestion to think of an 'ethos of pluralization' instead of pluralism (Connolly, 1995). The challenge is therefore to think of constitutional rules that foster such an ethos rather than reinforcing existing antagonistic identities. In fact, the answer may not primarily lie with constitutional arrangements at all, but with a shift in the responsibility to work towards such an ethos back to the domestic and international actors discussed in parts I and II of this volume. Ultimately, conflict transformation takes place through the transformed interests and identities of the domestic and international actors involved in the process. Constitutional and institutional rules can only set the framework and provide the initial impetus for such a process of change to come about.

Above all, this book should be read as a plea to enrich our study of conflicts, including the one in Cyprus, with approaches from different disciplines and to engage in transdisciplinary work and interdisciplinary dialogue. This will automatically lead us to see the complexity of the conflicts that we study. In that sense, all conflicts are at a crossroads, and challenge us to engage with their richness in order to move them away from violence and to exploit rather than suppress this richness.

Bibliography

Aalberts, T. (2004) 'The Sovereignty Game(s) States Play: (Quasi)-States in the International Order', paper presented at the 5th Pan-European International Relations Conference 'Constructing World Orders', The Hague, 9–11 September.

Adamson, F. B. (2002) 'Democratisation in Turkey, EU Enlargement and the Regional Dynamics of the Cyprus Conflict: Past Lessons and Future Prospects', in Diez, T. (ed.), *The European Union and the Cyprus Conflict: Modern Conflict, Postmodern Union*, Manchester: Manchester University Press, 163–80.

ADEPT (Association for Participatory Democracy) (2003) 'Memorandum on Principles of Establishing a Unified State', 25 November, available at www.e-democracy.md/en/comments/political/20031125.

Adler, E. (1997) 'Seizing the Middle Ground: Constructivism in World Politics', *European Journal of International Relations*, 3(3): 319–63.

Allin, D. and Simon, S. (2003) 'The Moral Psychology of US Support for Israel', *Survival*, 45(3): 123–44.

Anderson, B. (1983) *Imagined Communities*, London: Verso.

Anthias, F. (1989) 'Women and Nationalism in Cyprus', in Yuval Davis, N. and Anthias, F. (eds), *Woman–Nation–State*, London: Macmillan, 114–32.

Anthias, F. and Yuval-Davis, N. (1992) *Racialised Boundaries: Race, Nation, Gender, Colour and Class and the Anti-racist Struggle*, London: Routledge.

Armaoğlu, F. (1963) *Kıbrıs Meselesi, 1954–1959* [The Cyprus Question, 1954–59], Ankara: Sevinç Matbaası.

Armaoğlu, F. (1974) '1974 Cyprus Crisis and the Soviets', *Foreign Policy*, 4(2–3): 177–83.

Ascher, C., DeSalvo, L. and Ruddick, S. (eds) (1984) *Between Women*, Boston, MA: Beacon Press.

Attalides, M. (1979) *Cyprus: Nationalism and International Politics*, London: Quartet.

Attalides, M. (2004) 'The Political Process in Cyprus and the Day After the Referendum', *Cyprus Review*, 16(1): 137–46

Avineri, S. (2004) 'Realities Behind the Failure of Cyprus', *Financial Times*, 27 April.

Avruch, K. (1998) *Culture and Conflict Resolution*, Washington, DC: United States Institute of Peace Press.

Aydın, M. (2004) *Turkish Foreign Policy: Framework and Analysis*, Ankara: Stratejik Araştırmalar Merkezi.

Ayres, R. (2003) 'The Economic Costs of Separation: The North–South Development Gap in Cyprus', *Ekonomia*, 6(1): 39–52.

Bahcheli, T. (1990) *Greek–Turkish Relations Since 1955*, London: Westview Press.

Bahcheli, T. (2004) 'Saying Yes to EU Accession: Explaining the Turkish Cypriot Referendum Outcome', *Cyprus Review*, 16(2): 55–65.

Bahcheli, T. (2006) 'Turkey's Quest for EU Membership and the Cyprus Problem', in Joseph, J. (ed.), *Turkey and the European Union: Internal Dynamics and External Challenges*, London: Palgrave Macmillan, 161–77.

Baker-Miller, J. (1976) *Toward a New Psychology of Women*, Boston, MA: Beacon.

Balancar, F. (2003) 'Last Tango in Cyprus', *Turkish Times*, issue 11, December.

Balkır, C. (2005) 'The Turkish Cypriot Business Community as a Politico-economic Actor Searching for a Solution', *Turkish Policy Quarterly*, 4(4): 127–46.

Banfield, J., Gündüz, C. and Killick, N. (2006) *Local Business, Local Peace: The Peacebuilding Potential of the Domestic Private Sector*, London: International Alert.

Barkey, H. and Gordon, P. H. (2002) 'Avoiding a Cyprus Crisis', *Policy Brief*, 102, June, Washington, DC: Brookings Institution, available at www.brookings.edu/papers/2002/07europe_barkey.aspx.

Bartmann, B. (2004) 'Political Realities and Legal Anomalies: Revisiting the Politics of International Recognition', in Bahcheli, T., Bartmann, B. and Srebrnik, H. (eds), *De Facto States: The Quest for Sovereignty*, London: Routledge, 12–31.

Belenky, M. F., Clinchy, B., Goldberger, N. and Tarule, J. (1986) *Women's Ways of Knowing: The Development of Self, Voice, and Mind*, New York: Basic Books.

Berg, E. (2006) 'Pooling Sovereignty, Losing Territoriality? Making Peace in Cyprus and Moldova', *Tijdschrift voor economische en sociale geografie*, 97(3): 222–36.

Berg, E. (2007) 'Examining Power-Sharing in Persistent Conflicts: De Facto Pseudo-statehood Versus De Jure Quasi-federalism', *Global Society*, 21(2): 199–217.

Bideleux, R. and Jeffries, I. (1998) *A History of Eastern Europe: Crisis and Change*, London: Routledge.

Bieber, F. (2002) 'Bosnia-Herzegovina: Developments Towards a More Integrated State', *Journal of Muslim Minority Affairs*, 22(1): 205–18.

Bieber, F. (2006a) 'After Dayton, Dayton? The Evolution of an Unpopular Peace', *Ethnopolitics*, 5(1): 15–31.

Bieber, F. (2006b) 'Bosnia-Herzegovina: Slow Progress Towards a Functional State', *Southeast European and Black Sea Studies*, 6(1): 43–64.

Bieber, F. (2006c) *Post-war Bosnia: Ethnicity, Inequality and Public Sector Governance*, Basingstoke: Palgrave Macmillan.

Bindebir, S., Handshin, M., Jovanovic, M. and Riek, C. (2003) *Federalism, Decentralization and Conflict Management in Multicultural Societies*, available at www.ecomod.net/conferences/ecomod2003/ecomod2003_papers/Bindebir.pdf.

Birand, M. A. (1985) *Thirty Hot Days*, Nicosia: Rustem.

Boedeltje, F., Plug, J., Kramsch, O. and Houtum, H. (2005) '*A Walk Along the Line of Recollection*': *Geopolitics of the Green Line in Cyprus*, Nijmegen: Nijmegen Center for Border Research, Radbound University.

Böröcz, J. (2001) 'Empire and Coloniality in the Eastern Enlargement of the EU', in

Böröcz, J. and Kovócs, M. (eds), *Empire's New Clothes: Unveiling EU Enlargement*, Telford: Central European Review, 4–50.
Bose, S. (2002) *Bosnia After Dayton: Nationalist Partition and International Intervention*, London: Hurst.
Brass, P. R. (1997) *Theft of an Idol: Text and Contact in the Representation of Collective Violence*, Princeton, NJ: Princeton University Press.
Brewin, C. (2000) *The European Union and Cyprus*, Huntingdon: Eothen Press.
Brock-Utne, B. (1985) *Educating for Peace: A Feminist Perspective*, New York: Pergamon.
Brock-Utne, B. (1989) *Feminist Perspectives on Peace and Peace Education*, New York: Pergamon.
Broome, B. J. (2005) *Yeşil Hat Üzerinde Kurulan Köprüler*, Nicosia: UN Development Programme.
Bruck, P. and Roach, C. (1993) 'Dealing with Reality: The News Media and the Promotion of Peace', in Roach, C. (ed.), *Communication and Culture in War and Peace*, London: Sage, 71–96.
Buchanan, A. (1991) *Secession: The Morality of Political Divorce from Fort Sumter to Lithuania and Quebec*, Oxford: Westview Press.
Buchanan, A. (2004) *Justice, Legitimacy, and Self-Determination: Moral Foundations for International Law*, Oxford: Oxford University Press.
Burton, J. (1990) *Conflict: Resolution and Prevention*, New York: St Martin's Press.
Buzan, B. and Wæver, O. (2003) *Regions and Powers: The Structure of International Security*, Cambridge: Cambridge University Press.
Buzan, B., Wæver, O. and de Wilde, J. (1998) *Security: A New Framework for Analysis*, Boulder, CO: Lynne Rienner.
Cantori, L. and Spiegel, S. (1973) 'The International Relations of Regions', in Falk, R. and Mendlovitz, S. (eds), *Regional Politics and World Order*, San Francisco: W. H. Freeman, 335–53.
Cem, İ. (2004) *Türkiye, Avrupa, Asya*, İstanbul: Bilgi Üniversitesi Yayınları.
Chace, R. S., Hill, E. and Kennedy, P. (1996) 'Pivotal States and U. S. Strategy', *Foreign Affairs*, 75(1), 33–51.
Champain, P. (2005) 'Introduction', in Champain, P., Klein, D. and Mirimanova, N. (eds), *From War Economics to Peace Economies in the South Caucasus*, London: International Alert, 18–26.
Christodoulou, D. (1992) *Inside the Cyprus Miracle: The Labours of an Embattled Mini-economy*, Minneapolis, MN: University of Minnesota.
Christophoros, C. (2004) 'The Vote for a United Cyprus Deepens Divisions: The 24 April 2004 Referenda in Cyprus', *South European Society and Politics*, 10(1): 85–104.
Christou, G. (2004) *The European Union and Enlargement: The Case of Cyprus*, Basingstoke: Palgrave Macmillan.
Christou, G. (2006) 'The Internalisation of Border Conflicts, Policy Change and the Case of Cyprus', paper presented at the ECPR workshop 'Cyprus – A Conflict at the Crossroads', Intercollege, Nicosia, 25–30 April.
Chrysostomides, K. (2000) *The Republic of Cyprus: A Study in International Law*, The Hague: M. Nijhoff.
CIVICUS (World Alliance for Citizen Participation) (2005) *An Assessment of Civil Society in Cyprus: A Map for the Future*, Johannesburg: CIVICUS, available at www.civicus.org/new/CSI_Cyprus.htm.

Clogg, R. (1979) *A Short History of Modern Greece*, Cambridge: Cambridge University Press.

Cockburn, C. (2004) *The Line: Women, Partition and the Gender Order in Cyprus*, London: Zed Books.

Collins, P. H. (1998) 'Finding a Voice: Coming to Terms with Contradictons', in Rogers, M. F. (ed.), *Contemporary Feminist Theory: A Text/Reader*, Boston, MA: McGraw-Hill, 379–93.

Commission of the European Communities (1993) *Commission Opinion on the Application by the Republic of Cyprus for Membership*, COM (93) 313 final, 30 June.

Commission of the European Communities (1998) 'Regular Report on Cyprus' Progress Towards Accession', available at http://ec.europa.eu/enlargement/archives/pdf/key_documents/1998/ cyprus_en.pdf.

Connolly, W. (1995) *The Ethos of Pluralization*, Minneapolis, MN: University of Minnesota Press.

Constantinou, C. (2007) 'Aporias of Identity: Bicommunalism, Hybridity and the "Cyprus Problem"', *Cooperation and Conflict*, 42(3): 247–70.

Coppieters, B., Emerson, M., Huysseune, M., Kovziridze, T., Tocci, N. and Vahl, M. (2004) *Europeanization and Conflict Resolution: Case Studies from the European Periperhy*, Gent: Academia Press.

Coufoudakis, V. (2004) 'Cyprus – The Referendum and Its Aftermath', *Cyprus Review*, 16(2): 67–82.

Coufoudakis, V. (2006) *Cyprus: A Contemporary Problem in Historical Perspective*, Minneapolis, MN: Minnesota University Press.

Council of Europe (2006) *Bosnia and Herzegovina: Compliance with Obligations and Commitments and Implementation of the Post-accession Co-operation Programme – Update on Developments (July–December 2006)*, SG/Inf (2006) 16 final, 7 February, available at https://wcd.coe.int/ViewDoc.jsp?id=1080039&BackColorInternet=9999CC&BackColorIntranet=FFBB55&BackColorLogged=FFAC75.

Crawford, B. (1998) 'The Causes of Cultural Conflict: An Institutional Approach', in Crawford, B. and Lipschutz, R. D. (eds), *The Myth of 'Ethnic Conflict': Politics, Economics, and 'Cultural' Violence*, Berkeley, CA: University of California Press.

Crettiez, X. (1999) *La Question Corse*, Brussels: Complexe.

Crocker, C. A., Hampson, F. O. and Aall, P. R. (2003) 'Introduction: Mapping the Nettle Field', in Crocker, C. A., Hampson, F. O. and Aall, P. R. (eds), *Grasping the Nettle: Analyzing Cases of Intractable Conflict*, Washington, DC: United States Institute of Peace Press, 3–30.

Cronin, C. (2002) 'The Politics of Ethnonational Identity', paper presented at the ECPR workshop 'Political Accommodation in Ethnonationally Divided Societies', Joint Sessions, Turin, 22–27 March.

CSCE Mission to Moldova (1994) 'Transdniestrian Conflict: Origins and Main Issues', 10 June, available at www.osce.org/documents/mm/1994/06/455_en.pdf.

Davutoğlu, A. (2001) *Stratejik Derinlik: Türkiye'nin Uluslararası Konumu* [Strategic Depth: Turkey's Role in International Politics], Istanbul: Küre Yayınları.

Davutoğlu, A. (2004) 'Türkiye Merkez Ülke Olmalı', *Radikal*, 26 February, available at www.radikal.com.tr/haber.php?haberno=107581.

Dayton Project (2006) 'EU Calls on Bosnia Ethnicities to Resume Talks on Constitution Reform', press release, 15 May, available at www.daytonproject.org/about/article.php?id=145.

Demetriou, O. (2008) 'Catalysis, Catachresis: The EU's Impact on the Cyprus Conflict', in Diez, T., Albert, M. and Stetter, S. (eds), *The European Union and Border Conflicts: The Power of Integration and Association*, Cambridge: Cambridge University Press, 64–93.

Denktaş, R. D. (1988) *The Cyprus Triangle*, London: Allen and Unwin.

Dent, M. J. (2004) *Identity Politics: Filling the Gap Between Federalism and Independence*, Aldershot: Ashgate.

Dervisbegovic, N. (2006) 'Serbs Do Not See Their Future in Bosnia – PM', press release, 12 September, available at www.daytonproject.org/about/article.php?id=162.

Deutsch, K. (1966) *Nationalism and Social Communication*, Cambridge, MA: MIT Press.

Diez, T. (2002a) 'Introduction: Cyprus and the EU as a Political and Theoretical Problem', in Diez, T. (ed.), *The European Union and the Cyprus Conflict: Modern Conflict, Postmodern Union*, Manchester: Manchester University Press, 1–13.

Diez, T. (2002b) 'Last Exit to Paradise? The EU, the Cyprus Conflict and the Problematic "Catalytic Effect"', in Diez, T. (ed.), *The European Union and the Cyprus Conflict: Modern Conflict, Postmodern Union*, Manchester: Manchester University Press, 136–62.

Diez, T. (2002c) 'Why the EU Can Nonetheless Be Good for Cyprus', *Journal of Ethnopolitics and Minority Issues in Europe*, 10(2): 1–18.

Diez, T. (ed.) (2002d) *The European Union and the Cyprus Conflict: Modern Conflict, Postmodern Union*, Manchester: Manchester University Press.

Diez, T. (2005) 'Eine doppelte Grenzproblematik: Zypern und die Europäische Union', in Huget, H., Kambas, C. and Klein, W. (eds), *Grenzüberschreitungen: Differenz und Identität im Europa der Gegenwart*, Wiesbaden: VS Verlag für Sozialwissenschaften, 289–306.

Diez, T. (2006) 'The Paradoxes of Europe's Borders', *Comparative European Politics*, 3(2): 235–52.

Diez, T. and Pace, M. (2007) 'Normative Power Europe and Conflict Transformation', paper presented at the UACES conference, Portsmouth, 3–5 September.

Diez, T. and Wiener, A. (2004) 'Introducing the Mosaic of Integration Theory', in Wiener, A. and Diez, T. (eds), *European Integration Theory*, Oxford: Oxford University Press, 1–21.

Diez, T., Stetter, S. and Albert, M. (2006) 'The European Union and Border Conflicts: The Transformative Power of Integration', *International Organization*, 60(3): 563–93.

Dodd, C. (ed.) (1993) *The Political, Social and Economic Development of Northern Cyprus*, Huntingdon: Eothen Press.

Dodd, C. (2000) 'Turkey and the Cyprus Question', in Makovsky, A. and Sayarı, S. (eds), *Turkey's New World: Changing Dynamics in Turkish Foreign Policy*, Washington, DC: Washington Institute for Near East Policy, 153–72.

Donovan, J. (1994) *Feminist Theory: The Intellectual Traditions of American Feminism* (new edition), New York: Continuum.

Duffy Toft, M. (2002) 'Indivisible Territory, Geographic Concentration, and Ethnic War', *Security Studies*, 12(2): 82–119.

ECHR (European Court of Human Rights) (1995) *Judgment: Loizidou* v. *Turkey (Preliminary Objections)*.

ECHR (1996) *Judgment: Loizidou* v. *Turkey (Merits and Just Satisfaction)*.

ECHR (1998) *Judgment: Loizidou* v. *Turkey (Article 50).*

ECHR (2001) *Judgment: Cyprus* v. *Turkey (Merits).*

ECHR (2003a) *Judgment: Demades* v. *Turkey (Merits and Just Satisfaction).*

ECHR (2003b) *Judgment: Eugenia Michaelidou Developments Ltd and Michael Tymvios* v. *Turkey (Merits and Just Satisfaction).*

ECHR (2005a) *Decision: Xenides-Arestis* v. *Turkey (Admissibility).*

ECHR (2005b) *Judgment: Xenides-Arestis* v. *Turkey (Merits and Just Satisfaction).*

ECHR (2006) *Judgment: Xenides-Arestis* v. *Turkey (Just Satisfaction).*

Economides, S. (2005) 'The Europeanisation of Greek Foreign Policy', *West European Politics*, 28(2): 471–91.

Eichengreen, B., Faini, R., von Hagen, J. and Wyplosz, C. (2004) *Economic Aspects of the Annan Plan for the Solution of the Cyprus Problem: Report to the Government of the Republic of Cyprus*, 17 February, Nicosia, available at www.mof.gov.cy.

Eisler, R. (1987) *The Chalice and the Blade: Our History, Our Future*, San Francisco, CA: Harper Row.

Elekdağ, Ş. (1996) '2½ War Strategy', *Perceptions: Journal of International Affairs*, 1(1): 33–57.

Emerson, M. and Tocci, N. (2002) *Cyprus as Lighthouse of the East Mediterranean: Shaping EU Accession and Re-unification Together*, Brussels: Centre for European Policy Studies.

Eralp, D. and Beriker, N. (2005) 'Assessing the Conflict Resolution Potential of the EU: The Cyprus Conflict and Accession Negotiations', *Security Dialogue*, 36(2): 175–92.

Ercakica, H. (2006) 'Resistance Against "Osmosis" Is a Right of Turkish Cypriots', *Cyprus Observer*, 13 April.

Eriksson, J. (1999) 'Observers or Advocates? On the Political Role of Security Analysts', *Cooperation and Conflict*, 34(3): 311–33.

European Council (1999) 'Presidency Conclusions: Helsinki European Council, 10 and 11 December', available at www.consilium.europa.eu/ueDocs/cms_Data/docs/pressData/en/ec/ACFA4C.htm.

Faludi, S. (1991) *Backlash: The Undeclared War Against American Women*, New York: Doubleday.

Farrell, M., Hettne, B. and Van Langenhove, L. (eds) (2005) *Global Politics of Regionalism: Theory and Practice*, London: Pluto Press.

Faustmann, H. (2006) 'Security Questions and the Search for a Cyprus Settlement', *International Spectator*, 41(2): 7–18.

Fearon, J. D. (1994) 'Ethnic War as a Commitment Problem', paper presented at the Annual Meeting of the American Political Science Association, New York, 30 August–2 September.

Féron, E. (2002) 'The Effects of Europeanisation on Community Conflicts: The Example of Northern Ireland', paper presented at the 35th EuroFor Conference, Burg Schlaining, Austria, 4–7 April.

Féron, E. (2008) 'Religions and Conflicts: Towards a Framework for Analysis', *Ares* 23(59): 37–55.

Fetherston, A. B. (2000) 'Peacekeeping, Conflict Resolution and Peacebuilding: A Reconsideration of Theoretical Frameworks', in Woodhouse, T. and Ramsbotham, O. (eds), *Peacekeeping and Conflict Resolution*, London: Frank Cass, 190–217.

Firestone, S. (1970) *The Dialectic of Sex: The Case of Feminist Revolution*, New York: Morrow.

First, A. and Avraham, E. (2003) 'Changes in the Political, Social, and Media Environments and Their Impact on the Coverage of Conflict: The Case of the Arab Citizens of Israel', *Conflict and Communication Online*, 2(1), available at www.cco.regener-online.de/2003_1/pdf_2003_1/first_avraham.pdf.

Gagnon, V. P. (1995) 'Ethnic Nationalism and International Conflict: The Case of Serbia', *International Security*, 19(3): 130–66.

Galtung, J. (1993) 'Preface', in Roach, C. (ed.), *Communication and Culture in War and Peace*, London: Sage, xi–xv.

Galtung, J. (2002) 'Peace Journalism – A Challenge', in Kempf, W. and Luostarinen, H. (eds), *Journalism and the New World Order, Vol. II: Studying War and the Media*, Gothenburg: Nordicom, 259–72.

Galtung, J. (2006) 'Peace Journalism as an Ethical Challenge', *Global Media Journal: Mediterranean Edition*, 1(2): 1–5, available at http://globalmedia.emu.edu.tr/fall2006/Fall_2006_Issue2/1Johan_Galtungpdf.pdf.

Galtung, J. and Ruge, M. H. (1965) 'The Structure of Foreign News: The Presentation of the Congo, Cuba, and Cyprus Crises in Four Norwegian Newspapers', *Journal of Peace Research*, 2(1): 64–91.

Geertz, C. (1973) *The Interpretation of Cultures*, New York: Basic Books.

Gellner, E. (1995) *Encounters with Nationalism*, Oxford: Blackwell.

Gilligan, C. (1982) *In a Different Voice*, Cambridge, MA: Harvard University Press.

Gramsci, A. (1971) *Selections from the Prison Notebooks*, London: Lawrence and Wishart.

Grant, T. D. (1999) *The Recognition of States: Law and Practice in Debate and Evolution*, London: Praeger.

Green, P. (with R. Collins) (2003) *Embracing Cyprus: The Path to Unity in the New Europe*, London: I. B. Tauris.

Groom, A. J. R. (1993) 'The Process of Negotiation 1974–1993', in Dodd, C. H. (ed.), *The Political, Social and Economic Development of Northern Cyprus*, Huntingdon: Eothen Press, 15–45.

Groom, A. J. R. and Webb, K. (2007) 'Settlements in Unended Conflicts: The Case of Cyprus', paper presented at the 6th Pan-European International Relations Conference, panel on European Integration and Conflict Transformation on the Edge: Cyprus and Turkey, Turin, 12–15 September.

Gürel, A. and Özersay, K. (2006) 'Cyprus and the Politics of Property', *Mediterranean Politics*, 11(3): 349–69.

Gurr, T. R. (1970) *Why Men Rebel*, Princeton, NJ: Princeton University Press.

Güven Lisaniler, F. and Rodriguez, L. (2002) 'The Social and Economic Impact of EU Membership on Northern Cyprus', in Diez, T. (ed.), *The European Union and the Cyprus Conflict: Modern Conflict, Postmodern Union*, Manchester: Manchester University Press, 181–202.

Habermas, J. (1984a) *The Theory of Communicative Action, Vol. I: Reason and the Rationalization of Society*, Cambridge: Polity.

Habermas, J. (1984b) *The Theory of Communicative Action, Vol. II: Lifeworld and System: A Critique of Functionalist Reason*, Cambridge: Polity.

Hackett, R. A. (2006) 'Is Peace Journalism Possible? Three Frameworks for Assessing Structure and Agency in News Media', *Conflict and Communication Online*, 5(2), available at www.cco.regener-online.de/2006_2/pdf/hackett.pdf.

Hadjipavlou, M. (2003) 'Inter-ethnic Stereotypes, Neighbourliness, Separation:

Paradoxes and Challenges in Cyprus', *Journal of Mediterranean Studies*, 13(2): 281–318.

Hadjipavlou, M. (2004) *Women in the Cypriot Communities*, Nicosia: PrintWays.

Hadjipavlou, M. (2006) 'No Permission to Cross: Cypriot Women's Dialogue Across the Divide', *Gender, Place and Culture*, 13(4): 329–51.

Hakki, M. M. (2007) *The Cyprus Issue: A Documentary History, 1878–2007*, London: I. B. Tauris.

Hannay, D. (2005) *Cyprus: The Search for a Solution*, London: I. B. Tauris.

Harding, S. (1986) *The Science Question of Feminism*, Ithaca, NY: Cornell University Press.

Haymes, T. (1997) 'What Is Nationalism Really? Understanding the Limitations of Rigid Theories in Dealing with the Problems of Nationalism and Ethnonationalism', *Nations and Nationalism*, 3(4): 541–57.

Hays, D. and Crosby, J. (2006) 'From Dayton to Brussels: Constitutional Preparations for Bosnia's EU Accession', Special Report 175, Washington, DC: United States Institute of Peace, available at www.usip.org/pubs/specialreports/sr175.pdf.

Hayward, K. (2004) 'Mediating the European Ideal: Cross-border Programmes and Conflict Transformation in Ireland', Working Papers Series in EU Border Conflicts Studies 11, Birmingham: University of Birmingham, available at www.euborderconf.bham.ac.uk/publications/files/NIWorkingPaperno11.pdf.

Hayward, K. (2006) 'Reiterating National Identities: The European Union Conception of Conflict Resolution in Northern Ireland', *Cooperation and Conflict*, 41(3): 261–84.

Hechter, M. (1995) 'Explaining Nationalist Violence', *Nations and Nationalism*, 1(1): 53–68.

Hemmer, C. and Katzenstein, P. (2002) 'Why Is There No NATO in Asia? Collective Identity, Regionalism, and the Origins of Multilateralism', *International Organization*, 56(4): 575–607.

Hentz, J. and Bøås, M. (eds) (2003) *New and Critical Security and Regionalism*, Burlington, VT: Ashgate.

Heraclides, A. (2004) 'The Cyprus Problem: An Open and Shut Case? Probing the Greek-Cypriot Rejection of the Annan Plan', *Cyprus Review*, 16(2): 37–54.

Hettne, B., Inotai, A. and Sunkel, O. (eds) (1999) *Globalism and the New Regionalism*, New York: St Martin's Press.

Hettne, B., Inotai, A. and Sunkel, O. (eds) (2000) *The New Regionalism and the Future of Security and Development*, New York: St Martin's Press.

Hill, C. and Wallace, W. (1996) 'Introduction: Actors and Actions', in Hill, C. (ed.), *The Actors in Europe's Foreign Policy*, London: Routledge, 1–18.

Hitchens, C. (1997) *Hostage to History: Cyprus from the Ottomans to Kissinger*, London: Verso.

Hitchner, R. B. (2006a) 'From Dayton to Brussels: The Story Behind the Constitutional and Governmental Reform Process in Bosnia and Herzegovina', *Fletcher Forum of World Affairs*, 30(1): 125–35.

Hitchner, R. B. (2006b) 'The Process and Future Prospects for Constitutional Reform in Bosnia and Herzegovina', presentation given at Woodrow Wilson International Center for Scholars forum 'Constitution Drafting in Bosnia and Herzegovina', 10 May, Washington, DC, available at www.daytonproject.org/publications/publication.php?id=143.

Hobsbawm, E. and Ranger, T. (eds) (1983) *The Invention of Tradition*, Cambridge: Cambridge University Press.

Hoffman, M. (1992) 'Third-Party Mediation and Conflict Resolution in the Post-world War World', in Baylis, J. and Rengger, N. J. (eds), *Dilemmas of World Politics: International Issues in a Changing World*, Oxford: Oxford University Press, 261–86.

Hoffmeister, F. (2002) 'Cyprus v. Turkey', *American Journal of International Law*, 96(2): 445–52.

Holland, R. and Markides, D. (2006) *The British and the Hellenes: Struggles for Mastery in the Eastern Mediterranean 1850–1960*, Oxford: Oxford University Press.

Hooks, B. (1981) *Ain't I a Woman: Black Women and Feminism*, Boston, MA: South End Press.

Hooks, B. (2000) *Feminist Theory: From Margins to Center*, Cambridge, MA: South End Press.

Horowitz, D. L. (1985) *Ethnic Groups in Conflict*, Berkeley, CA: University of California Press.

Huntington, S. P. (2002) *The Clash of Civilizations and the Remaking of World Order* (new edition), Washington, DC: Free Press.

Ifantis, C. and Aydın, M. (2004) 'Introduction', in Ifantis, C. and Aydın, M. (eds), *Turkish–Greek Relations: The Security Dilemma in the Aegean*, London: Routledge, 1–17.

Ignatieff, M. (1999) *The Warrior's Honour: Ethnic War and the Modern Conscience*, London: Vintage.

International Crisis Group (2008) *Cyprus: Reversing the Drift to Partition*, Europe Report 190, 10 January, Nicosia: International Crisis Group, available at www.crisisgroup.org/home/index.cfm?id=5255&l=1.

International Monetary Fund (2005) *World Economic Outlook: Building Institutions*, September 2005, available at www.imf.org/external/pubs/ft/weo/2005/02/index.htm.

Irwin, C. (2002) *The People's Peace Process in Northern Ireland*, London: Palgrave Macmillan.

Irwin, C. (2004) 'A People's Peace Process for BiH?', report from the result of a public opinion poll carried out in Bosnia and Herzegovina between 9 July and 23 July 2004.

Isaacs, H. R. (1975) *Idols of the Tribe: Group Identity and Political Change*, Cambridge, MA: Harvard University Press.

İsmail, S. (1989) *20th July Peace Operation: Reasons, Development and Consequences*, Istanbul: Kastaş.

Jackson, R. (1990) *Quasi-states: Sovereignty, International Relations and the Third World*, Cambridge: Cambridge University Press.

Jackson, R. (1999) 'Sovereignty in World Politics: A Glance at the Conceptual and Historical Landscape', in Jackson, R. (ed.), *Sovereignty at the Millennium*, Oxford: Blackwell, 9–34.

Jakobsson Hatay, A-S. (2004a) 'Popular Referenda and Peace Processes: The Twin Referenda on the Annan Plan for a Reunited Cyprus Put in Perspective', *Turkish Daily News*, 4 May, available at www.turkishdailynews.com.tr/archives.php?id=36300.

Jakobsson Hatay, A-S. (2004b) 'The People Deliver Their Verdict on the Annan Plan for a Re-united Cyprus', Lund: Transnational Foundation for Peace and Future

Research, available at http://transnational.org/SAJT/forum/meet/2004/Jak_Hatay_CyprusRef.html.

Jakobsson Hatay, A-S. (2005) *Peacebuilding and Reconciliation in BiH, Kosovo and Macedonia 1995–2004*, A Synthesis Report from the Project Democratization and Reconciliation in Post Intrastate Conflict Situations, Department of Peace and Conflict Resolution, Uppsala University, Uppsala.

James, A. (1999) 'The Practice of Sovereign Statehood in Contemporary International Society', in Jackson, R. (ed.), *Sovereignty at the Millennium*, Oxford: Blackwell, 35–51.

Janeway, E. (1971) *Man's World, Woman's Place: A Study in Social Mythology*, New York: Morrow.

Joseph, B. D., DeStefano, J., Jacobs, N. G. and Lehiste, I. (eds) (2006) *When Languages Collide: Perspectives on Language Conflict, Language Competition, and Language Coexistence*, Columbus, OH: Ohio State University Press.

Kaliber, A. (2003) *Rearticulation of Turkish Foreign Policy, Its Impacts on National State Identity and State Society Relations in Turkey: The Cyprus Case*, unpublished PhD thesis, Ankara: Bilkent University.

Kaliber, A. (2005) 'Securing the Ground Through Securitized "Foreign" Policy: The Cyprus Case Revisited', *Security Dialogue*, 36(3): 297–315.

Kanaaneh, R. A. (2002) *Birthing the Nation: Strategies of Palestinian Women in Israel*, Berkeley, CA: University of California Press.

Kandemir, N. (2004) Türkiyenin Ulusal Güvenlik ve Çıkarları Açısından Kıbrıs', speech delivered at the panel 17 Aralık Sonrası KKTC, Türkiye ve AB, 22 December, available at http://nuzhetkandemir.com/files/konusmalar_speeches/22122004.htm.

Katzenstein, P. (2005) *A World of Regions: Asia and Europe in the American Imperium*, Ithaca: Cornell University Press.

Kazan, I. (2002) 'Cyprus and the Eastern Mediterranean, Seen From Turkey', in Diez, T. (ed.), *The European Union and the Cyprus Conflict: Modern Conflict, Postmodern Union*, Manchester: Manchester University Press, 54–69.

Kazan, I. (2005) 'Turkey: Where Geopolitics Still Matters', *Contemporary Security Policy*, 26(3): 588–604.

Keane, R. (2002) *Reconstituting Sovereignty: Post-Dayton Bosnia Uncovered*, Aldershot: Ashgate.

Kelly, R. E. (2007) 'Security Theory in the "New Regionalism"', *International Studies Review*, 9(2): 197–229.

Kelman, H. C. (2004) 'Reconciliation as Identity Change: A Social–Psychological Perspective', in Bar-Siman-Tov, Y. (ed.), *From Conflict Resolution to Reconciliation*, Oxford: Oxford University Press, 111–24.

Kempf, W. (2003) 'Constructive Conflict Coverage: A Social–Psychological Research and Development Program', *Conflict and Communication Online*, 2(2), available at www.cco.regener-online.de/2003_2/pdf_2003_2/kempf_engl.pdf.

Keridis, D. (2001) 'Domestic Developments and Foreign Policy: Greek Policy Towards Turkey', in Keridis, D. and Triantaphyllou, D. (eds), *Greek–Turkish Relations in the Era of Globalization*, Dulles, VA: Brassey's, 2–18.

Ker-Lindsay, J. (2004) *Britain and the Cyprus Crisis, 1963–64*, Mannheim: Bibliopolis.

Ker-Lindsay, J. (2005) *EU Accession and UN Peacemaking in Cyprus*, Basingstoke: Palgrave Macmillan.

Khalidi, R. (1992) 'Observations on the Right of Return', *Journal of Palestine Studies*, 21(2): 29–40.
Kingston, P. and Spears, I. S. (eds) (2004) *States-Within-States: Incipient Political Entities in the Post-Cold War Era*, Basingstoke: Palgrave Macmillan.
Kışlalı, M. A. (2003) 'Irakta'ki Durum Sıkıntı Yaratıyor', interview with Hilmi Özkök, *Radikal*, 9 November, available at www.radikal.com.tr/haber.php?haberno=94844.
Kızılyürek, N. (2005) *Doğmamış bir Devletin Tarihi: Birleşik Kıbrıs Cumhuriyeti*, İstanbul: İletişim Yayınları.
Kızılyürek, N. (2006) 'Kıbrıs Cumhuriyeti Üstüne (2)', *Yeni Düzen*, 28 August.
Kleibor, M. (1996) 'Understanding the Success and Failure of International Mediation', *Journal of Conflict Resolution*, 40(2): 360–89.
Klein, E. (1984) *Gender Politics: From Consciousness to Mass Politics*, Cambridge, MA: Harvard University Press.
Kolstoe, P. (2006) 'The Sustainability and Future of Unrecognised Quasi-States', *Journal of Peace Research*, 43(6): 723–40.
Kurtulus, E. N. (2005) *State Sovereignty: Concept, Phenomenon and Ramifications*, Basingstoke: Palgrave Macmillan.
Kyle, K. (1997) *Cyprus: In Search of Peace*, London: Minority Rights Group International.
Kyriakides, S. (1968) *Cyprus Constitutionalism and Crisis Government*, Philadelphia, PA: University of Pennsylvania Press.
Lacher, H. and Kaymak, E. (2005) 'Transforming Identities: Beyond the Politics of Non-settlement in Cyprus?', *Mediterranean Politics*, 10(2): 147–66.
Lake, D. A. and Morgan, P. M. (eds) (1997) *Regional Orders: Building Security in a New World*, University Park, PA: Penn State University Press.
Larrabee, S. and Lesser, I. (2002) *Turkish Foreign Policy in an Age of Uncertainty*, Santa Monica, CA: RAND Corporation.
Leach, P. (2005) *Taking a Case to the European Court of Human Rights* (2nd edtion), Oxford: Oxford University Press.
Lederach, J. P. (2004) *Building Peace: Sustainable Reconciliation in Divided Societies*, Washington, DC: United States Institute of Peace Press.
Lesser, I. (2000) *NATO Looks South: New Challenges and New Strategies in the Mediterranean*, Santa Monica, CA: RAND Corporation.
Lesser, I. (2004) 'Energy and Middle Eastern Security: New Dimensions and Strategic Implications', in Bensahel, N. and Byman, D. L. (eds), *The Future Security Environment in the Middle East: Conflict, Stability, and Political Change*, Santa Monica, CA: RAND Corporation.
Loizos, P. (1976) 'Cyprus: An Alternative Analysis', in *Minority Rights Group Report*, No. 30, Part 2, London: Minority Rights Group.
Loizos, P. (1981) *The Heart Grown Bitter: A Chronicle of Cypriot War Refugees*, Cambridge: Cambridge University Press.
Lordos, A. (2004a) *Can the Cyprus Problem Be Solved? Understanding the Greek Cypriot Response to the UN Peace Plan for Cyprus*, available at www.cypruspolls.org/GreekCypriotsReport.pdf.
Lordos, A. (2004b) *Civil Society Diplomacy: A New Approach for Cyprus?*, available at www.cypruspolls.org/CivilSocietyDiplomacy.pdf.
Lordos, A. (2005) *Options for Peace: Mapping the Possibilities for a Comprehensive Settlement in Cyprus*, available at www.cypruspolls.org/OptionsForPeaceTextAndCharts.pdf.

Lynch, J. (2006) 'What's So Great About Peace Journalism?', *Global Media Journal: Mediterranean Edition*, 1(1): 74–87, available at http://globalmedia.emu.edu.tr/spring2006/7.%20Jake%20Lynch%20Whats%20so%20great%20about2.pdf.
Macris, N. D. (ed.) (2003) *The 1960 Treaties on Cyprus and Selected Subsequent Acts*, Mannheim: Bibliopolis.
Major, C. (2005) 'Europeanisation and Foreign and Security Policy – Undermining or Rescuing the Nation State?', *Politics*, 25(3): 175–90.
Manners, I. (2002) 'Normative Power Europe: A Contradiction in Terms?', *Journal of Common Market Studies*, 40(2): 235–58.
Marchetti, R. and Tocci, N. (2007) 'Conflict Society and Human Rights', SHUR Working Paper 3, Rome: LUISS, available at www.luiss.it/shur.
Markides, K. C. (1977) *The Rise and Fall of the Cyprus Republic*, London: Yale University Press.
Marko, J. (2006) 'Constitutional Reform in Bosnia and Herzegovina 2005–06', in *European Yearbook of Minority Issues* 5, Leiden: Brill, 207–18.
Marshment, M. (1997) 'The Picture Is Political: Representation of Women in Contemporary Popular Culture', in Robinson, V. and Richardson, D. (eds), *Introducing Women's Studies: Feminist Theory and Practice*, New York: New York University Press, 125–51.
Mayall, J. (1999) 'Sovereignty, Nationalism and Self-determination', in Jackson, R. (ed.), *Sovereignty at the Millennium*, Oxford: Blackwell, 52–80.
McGoldrick, A. (2006) 'War Journalism and "Objectivity"', *Conflict and Communication Online*, 5(2), available at www.cco.regener-online.de/2006_2/pdf/mcgoldrick.pdf.
Mehmet, Ö. (2004) *Required Investment for Convergence of Growth Rates and Incomes Per Capita in a Possible Federal Cyprus*, unpublished mimeo.
Mehmet, Ö., Tahiroğlu, M., Güven Lisaniler, F. and Katircioğlu, S. (2007) 'Labor Mobility and Labor Market Convergence in Cyprus', *Turkish Studies*, 8(1): 43–69.
Miall, H., Ramsbotham, O. and Woodhouse, T. (2005) *Contemporary Conflict Resolution*, Oxford: Polity.
Michas, T. (2002) *Unholy Alliance: Greece and Serbia in the Nineties*, College Station, TX: Texas A&M University Press.
Miller, L. (1973a) 'Prospects For Order Through Regional Security', in Falk, R. and Mendlovitz, S. (eds), *Regional Politics and World Order*, San Francisco, CA: W. H. Freeman.
Miller, L. (1973b) 'Regional Organizations and Subordinate Systems', in Falk, R. and Mendlovitz, S. (eds), *Regional Politics and World Order*, San Francisco, CA: W. H. Freeman.
Millett, K. (1970) *Sexual Politics*, New York: Doubleday.
Ministry of Foreign Affairs and Defence of the TRNC (2002) 'Statement by TRNC Ministry of Foreign Affairs and Defence on Visit of Armenian Defence Minister Mr. Serz Sargsyan to the Greek Cypriot Administration', 28 February, available at www.trncinfo.com/ENGLISH/pressrelease/010302.htm.
Mirbagheri, F. (1998) *Cyprus and International Peacekeeping*, London: Hurst.
Mitchell, C. R. (1981) *The Structure of International Conflict*, Basingstoke: Macmillan.
Morgan, P. M. (1997) 'Regional Security Complexes and Regional Orders', in Lake, D. A. and Morgan, P. M. (eds), *Regional Orders: Building Security in a New World*, University Park, PA: Penn State University Press, 20–44.

Morley, D. and Robins, K. (1995) *Spaces of Identity: Global Media, Electronic Landscapes and Cultural Boundaries*, New York: Routledge.

Mosco, V. (1993) 'Communication and Information Technology for War and Peace', in Roach, C. (ed.), *Communication and Culture in War and Peace*, London: Sage, 41–71.

Mowbray, A. (2005) 'The Creativity of the European Court of Human Rights', *Human Rights Law Review*, 5(1): 57–79.

Nantoi, O. (2005) 'The Plan for the Transnistrian Conflict Settlement Proposed by Ukraine: Pros and Cons', Chisinau: Institute for Public Policy, available at www.ipp.md/comentarii1.php?l=en&id=38.

National Security Council (2007) '2007 Yili MGK Toplantilarinin Basin Bildirileri', Press Releases of the NSC Meetings, 20 June, available at www.mgk.gov.tr/Turkce/Yazdirilabilir%20Surum/Basin%20Bildirileri/2007/20_Haziran_2007.pdf.

Naveh, C. (2002) 'The Role of the Media in Foreign Policy Decision-Making: A Theoretical Framework', *Conflict and Communication Online*, 1(2), available at www.cco.regener-online.de/2002_2/pdf_2002_2/naveh.pdf.

Neukirch, C. (2003) 'Coming Closer to a Solution in Moldova?', *Helsinki Monitor*, 14(4): 333–42.

Newman, E. (2001) 'The Secretary-General and Cyprus', in Richmond, O. and Ker-Lindsay, J. (eds), *The Work of the UN in Cyprus: Promoting Peace and Development*, Basingstoke: Palgrave Macmillan, 127–53.

Nicolet, C. (2001) *United States Policy Towards Cyprus, 1954–1974: Removing the Greek–Turkish Bone of Contention*, Mannheim: Bibliopolis.

Nugent, N. (2000) 'EU Enlargement and "the Cyprus Problem"', *Journal of Common Market Studies*, 38(1): 131–50.

Nye, J. (1968) 'Introduction', in Nye, J. (ed.), *International Regionalism: Readings*, Boston, MA: Little, Brown.

Olgun, M. E. (1999) 'Turkey's Tough Neighbourhood: Security Dimensions of the Cyprus Conflict', in Dodd, C. H. (ed.), *Cyprus: The Need for New Perspectives*, Huntingdon: Eothen Press, 231–59.

O'Malley, B. and Craig, I. (1999) *The Cyprus Conspiracy: America, Espionage and the Turkish Invasion*, London: I. B. Tauris.

Ortner, B. S. (1974) 'Is Female to Male as Nature Is to Culture?', in Rosaldo, M. Z. and Lamphere, L. (eds), *Woman, Culture and Society*, Stanford, CA: Stanford University Press, 67–86.

Ottosen, R. (2004) 'The Norwegian Media Image of the War in Afghanistan: Peacekeeping or Aggression?', *Conflict and Communication Online*, 3(1/2), available at www.cco.regener-online.de/2004/pdf_2004/ottosen.pdf.

Özcan, G. (2002) 'The Military and the Making of Foreign Policy in Turkey', in Rubin, B. and Kirişçi, K. (eds), *Turkey in World Politics: An Emerging Multiregional Power*, London: Lynne Rienner, 13–30.

Özcan, G. (2004) 'Turkey's Changing Neighbourhood Policy', *Turkish Yearbook of International Relations*, 35: 1–15.

Özersay K. (2005) 'Separate Simultaneous Referenda in Cyprus: Was It a "Fact" or an "Illusion"?', *Turkish Studies*, 6(3): 379–99.

Pace, M. (2006a) 'The Construction of EU Normative Power', paper presented at the International Studies Association Convention, San Diego, CA, 22–25 March.

Pace, M. (2006b) *The Politics of Regional Identity: Meddling with the Mediterranean*, London: Routledge.

Palestinian Center for Policy and Survey Research (2003) *Result of PSR Refugees' Polls in the West Bank/Gaza Strip, Jordan and Lebanon on Refugees' Preferences and Behavior in a Palestinian–Israeli Permanent Refugee Agreement, January–June 2003*, Ramallah: Palestinian Center for Policy and Survey Research, available at www.pcpsr.org/survey/polls/2003/refugeesjune03.html.

Palley, C. (2005) *An International Relations Debacle: The UN Secretary-General's Mission of Good Offices in Cyprus 1999–2004*, Oxford: Hart.

Palley, C. (2006) 'Turkish Tricks to Subvert Displaced Persons' Property Rights', *Cyprus Weekly*, 30 June–6 July: 4.

Panayiotou, A. (2006) 'The "Bias of Media Forms" and Prospects for Peace Journalism', *Global Media Journal: Mediterranean Edition*, 1(2): 25–33, available at http://globalmedia.emu.edu.tr/fall2006/Fall_2006_Issue2/6Andreas_Panayiotoupdf.pdf.

Panteli, S. (1990) *The Making of Modern Cyprus: From Obscurity to Statehood*, New Barnet: Interworld.

Papadopoulos, T. (2004) 'Declaration by the President of the Republic Mr Tassos Papadopoulos Regarding the Referendum of 24th April 2004', Press and Information Office, Republic of Cyprus, press release, 7 April 2004, available at www.moi.gov.cy/moi/pio/pio.nsf/All/B7CC10D781AC186AC2256E7000254D3E?OpenDocument.

Pegg, S. (1998) *International Society and the De Facto State*, Aldershot: Ashgate.

Personal Narratives Group (1989) *Interpreting Women's Lives: Feminist Theory and Personal Narratives*, Bloomington, IN: Indiana University Press.

Peterson, V. S. and Runyan, A. (eds) (1993) *Global Gender Issues*, Boulder, CO: Westview Press.

Platis, S., Orhanides, S. and Mullen, F. (2005) *The Property Regime and Property Markets under Annan V*, Nicosia: PRIO Cyprus Centre.

Polyviou, P. G. (1976) *Cyprus in Search of a Constitution*, Nicosia: Chr. Nicolaou and Sons.

Popescu, N. (2004) 'Europeanisation and Conflict Resolution: A View from Moldova', *Journal of Ethnopolitics and Minority Issues in Europe*, 1, available at www.ecmi.de/jemie/download/1-2004Comment02.pdf.

Posen, B. (1993) 'The Security Dilemma and Ethnic Conflict', in Brown, M. E. (ed.), *Ethnic Conflict and International Security*, Princeton, NJ: Princeton University Press.

Pressman, J. (2003) 'Visions in Collisions: What Happened at Camp David and Taba?', *International Security*, 28(2): 5–43.

Protsyk, O. (2005) 'Federalism and Democracy in Moldova', *Post-Soviet Affairs*, 21(1): 72–90.

Radaelli, C. (2000) 'Whither Europeanisation? Concept Stretching and Substantive Change', *European Integration Online Papers (EIoP)*, 4 (8), available at http://eiop.or.at/eiop/texte/2000-008a.htm.

Ramonet, I. (2004) 'Turkey, Welcome to Europe', *Le Monde Diplomatique*, November, available at http://mondediplo.com/2004/11/01Ramonet.

Republic of Cyprus (1998) *European Stand on the Cyprus Problem*, Nicosia: Republic of Cyprus Press and Information Office.

Reus-Smit, C. (ed.) (2004) *The Politics of International Law*, Cambridge: Cambridge University Press.

Reynal-Querol, M. (2002) 'Ethnicity, Political Systems, and Civil Wars', *Journal of Conflict Resolution*, 46(1): 29–54.

Richmond, O. P. (1998) *Mediating in Cyprus: The Cypriot Communities and the United Nations*, London: Frank Cass.

Roach, C. (ed.) (1993) *Communication and Culture in War and Peace*, London: Sage.

Robins, P. (2003) *Suits and Uniforms: Turkish Foreign Policy Since the Cold War*, Seattle, WA: University of Washington Press.

Robinson, G. (1997) *Building a Palestinian State: The Incomplete Revolution*, Bloomington, IN: Indiana University Press.

Rogers, M. F. (ed.) (1998) *Contemporary Feminist Theory: A Text/Reader*, Boston, MA: McGraw-Hill.

Rokkan, S. and Urwin, D. W. (1983) *Economy, Territory, Identity: Politics of West European Peripheries*, London: Sage.

Roper, S. (2004a) 'Federalization and Constitution-Making as an Instrument of Conflict Resolution', *Demokratizatsiya*, 12(4): 527–39.

Roper, S. (2004b) 'From Frozen Conflict to Frozen Agreement: The Unrecognised State of Transnistria', in Bahcheli, T., Bartmann, B. and Srebrnik, H. (eds), *De Facto States: The Quest for Sovereignty*, London: Routledge, 102–17.

Rosaldo, Z. M. (1980) 'The Use and Abuse of Anthropology: Reflections on Feminisms and Cross-cultural Understanding', *Signs*, 5(3): 389–417.

Ruggie, J. (1993) 'Territoriality and Beyond: Problematizing Modernity in International Relations', *International Organization*, 47(1): 89–125.

Russett, B. (1967) *International Regions and the International System*, Chicago, IL: Rand McNally.

Şafaklı, O. (2003) 'Basic Problems of the Banking Sector in the TRNC with Partial Emphasis on the Proactive and Reactive Strategies Applied', *Doğuş Üniversitesi Dergisi*, 4(2): 217–32.

Sant Cassia, P. (2004) *Bodies of Evidence: Burial, Memory and the Recovery of Missing Persons in Cyprus*, Oxford: Berghahn Books.

Sayarı, S. (2000) 'Turkish Foreign Policy in the Post-Cold War Era: The Challenges of Multi-Regionalism', *Journal of International Affairs*, 54(1): 169–82.

Sayigh, Y. (1997) *Armed Struggle and the Search for State: The Palestinian National Movement, 1949–1993*, Oxford: Oxford University Press.

Schneckener, U. (2002) 'Developing and Applying EU Crisis Management: Test Case Macedonia', ECMI Working Paper 14, Flensburg: European Centre for Minority Issues, available at www.ecmi.de/download/working_paper_14.pdf.

Schwarz-Schilling, C. (2006) '2006 is a Crucial Year for Bosnia and Herzegovina', Office of the High Representative, press release, 27 March, available at www.ohr.int/ohr-dept/presso/pressr/default.asp?content_id=36857.

Sezer, A. N. (2007) 'Cumhurbaşkanı Ahmet Necdet Sezer', opening speech delivered at the Military Academies Conference, Ankara, 13 April, available at http://jitem.wordpress.com/2007/07/21/cumhurbaskani-ahmet-necdet-sezerin-harp-akademileri-konferansinda-yaptiklari-konusma/.

Sharoni, S. (1995) *Gender and the Israeli–Palestinian Conflict*, Syracuse, NY: Syracuse University Press.

Shiblak, A. (1996) 'Residency Status and Civil Rights of Palestinian Refugees in Arab Countries', *Journal of Palestine Studies*, 25(3): 36–45.

Shinar, D. (2003) 'The Peace Process in Cultural Conflict: The Role of the Media', *Conflict and Communication Online*, 2(1), available atwww.cco.regener-online.de/2003_1/pdf_2003_1/shinar.pdf.

Skordas, A. (2007) 'Oil Exploitation in the Eastern Mediterranean: Cyprus, Turkey and International Law', presentation to Southeast Europe Project, Woodrow Wilson International Center for Scholars, Washington, DC, 29 March, available at www.wilsoncenter.org/index.cfm?topic_id=109941&fuseaction=topics.event_summary&event_id=225758.

Smith, D. (2005) 'Foreword', in Champain, P., Klein, D. and Mirimanova, N. (eds), *From War Economies to Peace Economies in the South Caucasus*, London: International Alert, 16–17.

Smith, K. (2004) *European Union Foreign Policy in a Changing World*, Oxford: Polity.

Smooha, S. (2002) 'Types of Democracy and Modes of Conflict Management in Ethnically Divided Societies', *Nations and Nationalism*, 8(4): 423–31.

Sokolović, D. (2005) 'Bosnia, the Balkans, Europe – and America, Politics and Society in the Modern Era in Balkans: Global and Regional Context', paper presented to the SRC international symposium 'Regions in Central and Eastern Europe: Past and Present', Sapporo, Japan, 14–16 December.

Solana, J. (2000) *Report on the Western Balkans Presented to the European Council by the Secretary General/High Representative Together with the Commission*, submitted to the Lisbon European Council, SN 2032/2/00 REV 2, 1 March.

Sommer, J. (2005) *Security in Cyprus: Threat Perceptions, Possible Compromises and the Role of the EU*, BICC Paper 44, Bonn: Bonn International Center for Conversion, available at http://se1.isn.ch/serviceengine/FileContent?serviceID=PublishingHouse&fileid=88D4AD9D-73E8-C8CD-3431-03DD6C53D78B&lng=en.

Spears, I. (2004) 'States-Within-States: An Introduction to Their Empirical Attributes', in Kingston, P. and Spears, I. S. (eds), *States-Within-States: Incipient Political Entities in the Post-Cold War Era*, Basingstoke: Palgrave Macmillan, 15–34.

Stacey, J. (1997) 'Feminist Theory: Capital F, Capital T', in Robinson, V. and Richardson, D. (eds), *Introducing Women's Studies: Feminist Theory and Practice*, New York: New York University Press, 54–77.

Stavrinides, Z. (2006) 'Is a Negotiated Settlement Possible in Cyprus?', paper presented at the ECPR Joint Session of Workshops, Nicosia, 24–28 April.

Stefanidis, I. D. (1999) *Isle of Discord: Nationalism, Imperialism and the Making of the Cyprus Problem*, London: Hurst.

Stephanou, C. and Tsardanidis, C. (1991) 'The EC factor in the Greece–Turkey–Cyprus Triangle', in Constas, D. (ed.), *The Greek–Turkish Conflict in the 1990s: Domestic and External Influences*, Basingstoke: Macmillan, 207–30.

Stephen, M. (2001) 'How the International Community Made a Cyprus Settlement Impossible', *Perceptions: Journal of International Affairs*, 6(1): 61–78.

Stephens, R. (1966) *Cyprus: A Place of Arms – Power Politics and Ethnic Conflict in the Eastern Mediterranean*, London: Pall Mall Press.

Stern, P. C. and Druckman, D. (2000) *International Conflict Resolution After the Cold War*, Washington, DC: National Academy Press.

Stivachtis, Y. A. (2002) 'Greece and the Eastern Mediterranean Region: Security Considerations, the Cyprus Imperative and the EU Option', in Diez, T. (ed.), *The European Union and the Cyprus Conflict: Modern Conflict, Postmodern Union*, Manchester: Manchester University Press, 163–80.

Stone, L. (2002) 'Critical International Theory, Theories of International Relations and the Cyprus Problem', in Efegil, E. and Kaya Ülger, İ. (eds), *AB ve Kıbrıs Bugünü ve Geleceği*, Ankara: Gündoğan Yayınları, 100–14.

Storey, D. (2001) *Territory: The Claiming of Space*, Harlow: Prentice Hall.
Strong, P. (1999) *The Economic Consequences of Ethno-national Conflict in Cyprus: The Development of Two Siege Economies After 1963, and 1974*, unpublished PhD thesis, London: London School of Economics and Political Science.
Tamari, S. (1999) 'Palestinian Refugees and the Palestinian–Israeli Negotiations', *Journal of Palestine Studies*, 29(1): 81–9.
Taşhan, S. (2003) 'Turkish Strategic Perspectives on Mediterranean Security', speech delivered at the Foreign Policy Institute, 18 March.
Tevetoğlu, F. (1966) *Kıbrıs ve Komünizm* [Cyprus and Communism], Ankara: Komünizmle Mücadele Yayınları.
Theophanous, A. (2004) *The Cyprus Question and the EU: The Challenge and the Promise*, Nicosia: Intercollege Press.
Threlfall, M. and Rowbotham, S. (eds) (1996) *Mapping the Women's Movement*, London: Verso.
Tickner, J. A. (2001) *Gendering World Politics*, New York: Columbia University Press.
Tocci, N. (2004a) 'EU Intervention in Ethno-political Conflicts: The Cases of Cyprus and Serbia-Montenegro', *European Foreign Affairs Review*, 9(4): 551–74.
Tocci, N. (2004b) *EU Accession Dynamics and Conflict Resolution: Catalyzing Peace or Consolidating Partition in Cyprus?*, Aldershot: Ashgate.
Tocci, N. (2007) *The EU and Conflict Resolution: Promoting Peace in the Backyard*, London: Routledge.
Tocci, N. and Kovziridze, T. (2004) 'Cyprus', in Coppieters, B., Emerson, M., Huysseune, M., Kovziridze, T., Noutcheva, G., Tocci, N. and Vahl, M. (eds), *Europeanisation and Conflict Resolution: Case Studies from the European Periphery*, Gent: Academia Press, 63–106.
Tonge, J. (2004) 'Resolving Conflict Through Functional Cooperation: The EU and Cross-border Activity in Ireland', paper presented at the ECPR Joint Sessions Workshop 19, 'The EU and Conflict Resolution', Uppsala, 14–18 April.
Touval, S. and Zartman, I. W. (eds) (1985) *International Mediation in Theory and Practice*, Boulder, CO: Westview Press.
Traynor, I. (2006) 'Serb Move May Trigger New War', *Guardian*, 6 September: 20, available at www.guardian.co.uk/international/story/0,,1865633,00.html.
Trimikliniotis, N. (2006) 'A Communist's Post-modern Power Dilemma: One Step Back, Two Steps Forward, "Soft No" and Hard Choices', *Cyprus Review*, 18(1): 37–86.
Tsakonas, P. and Dokos, T. (2003) 'Greek–Turkish Relations in the Early Twenty-First Century: A View from Athens', in Lenore, M. G. and Keridis, D. (eds), *The Future of Turkish Foreign Policy*, Cambridge, MA: MIT Press, 99–123.
Tsardanidis, C. (1984) 'The European Community and the Cyprus Crisis of 1974', *Revue Héllenique de Droit International*, 37(1): 185–207.
Türk, H. S. (1999) 'Turkish Defence Policy', speech at the Washington Institute for Near East Policy, Washington, DC, 3 March.
Turkish-Cypriot Chamber of Commerce (2004) 'İki toplumun yararına olacak, çalışabilir ve yaşanabilir bir çözümü destekliyoruz', Press Release, 15 March, Lefkoşa: Kıbrıs Türk Ticaret Odası.
Turkish Ministry of Foreign Affairs (1997) 'Joint Statement by the Republic of Turkey and the Turkish Republic of Northern Cyprus', 20 July, reprinted in *Perceptions: Journal of International Affairs*, 2(3): 195–8.

Turkish Ministry of Foreign Affairs (2007) 'Press Release Regarding the Efforts of the Greek Cypriot Administration of Southern Cyprus to Sign Bilateral Agreements Concerning Maritime Jurisdiction Areas with the Countries in the Eastern Mediterranean', press release, 30 January.

UNDP (United Nations Development Programme) (2003) *Early Warning Report, FYR Macedonia, No. 1 2003*, Skopje: UN Development Programme, available at http://unpan1.un.org/intradoc/groups/public/documents/UNTC/UNPAN016469.pdf.

UN Secretary-General (2003) *Report of the Secretary-General on His Mission of Good Offices in Cyprus*, 1 April, S/2003/398, New York: United Nations.

UN Secretary-General (2004) *Report of the Secretary-General on His Mission of Good Offices in Cyprus*, 28 May, S/2004/437, New York: United Nations.

Uzgel, I. (2003) 'Between Praetorianism and Democracy: The Role of the Military in Turkish Foreign Policy', *Turkish Yearbook of International Relations*, 34: 177–211.

Väyrynen, R. (2003) 'Regionalism: Old and New', *International Studies Review*, 5(1): 25–51.

Veremis, T. (2001), 'The Protracted Crisis', in Keridis, D. and Triantaphyllou, D. (eds), *Greek–Turkish Relations in the Era of Globalization*, Dulles, VA: Brassey's, 42–55.

Verney, S. (2002) 'Creating the Democratic Tradition of European Integration: The South European Catalyst', in H. Sjursen (ed.), *Enlargement and the Finality of the EU*, Arena Report 7, Oslo: Arena, 97–127.

Vural, Y. and Peristianis, N. (2008) 'Beyond Ethno-nationalism: Emerging Trends in Cypriot Politics After the Annan Plan', *Nations and Nationalism*, 14(1): 39–60.

Wæver, O. (1995) 'Securitization and Desecuritization', in Lipschutz, R. D. (ed.), *On Security*, New York: Columbia University Press, 46–86.

Wæver, O. (1998) 'Insecurity, Security and Asecurity in the West European Non-war Community', in Adler, E. and Barnett, M. (eds), *Security Communities*, Cambridge: Cambridge University Press, 69–118.

Wæver, O. (2000) 'The EU as a Security Actor: Reflections from a Pessimistic Constructivist on Post-sovereign Security Orders', in Kelstrup, M. and Williams, M. C. (eds), *International Relations Theory and the Politics of European Integration*, London: Routledge, 250–94.

Wagner, W. (2003) 'Why the EU's Common Foreign and Security Policy Will Remain Intergovernmental: A Rationalist Institutional Choice Analysis of European Crisis Management Policy', *Journal of European Public Policy*, 10(4): 576–95.

Walker, R. B. J. (1988) *One World, Many Worlds: Struggles for a Just World Peace*, London: Zed Books.

Wallace, W. (2002) *Reconciliation in Cyprus: The Window of Opportunity*, Florence: European University Institute, available at www.iue.it/RSCAS/WP-Texts/02_10p.pdf.

Watson, M. (2006) 'Growing Together? – Prospects for Economic Convergence and Reunification in Cyprus', paper presented at the ECPR workshop 'Cyprus – A Conflict at the Crossroads', Intercollege, Nicosia, 25–30 April.

Webster, C. (2005a) 'Greek Cypriot Perspectives on Interacting with Turkish Cypriots', *Cyprus Review*, 17(1): 123–32.

Webster, C. (2005b) 'Division or Unification in Cyprus? The Role of Demographics, Attitudes and Party Inclination on Greek Cypriot Preferences for a Solution to the Cyprus Problem', *Ethnopolitics*, 4(3): 299–309.

Weiner, M. and Teitelbaum, M. S. (2001) *Political Demography, Demographic Engineering*, Oxford: Berghahn Books.

Wolfsfeld, G. (2004) *Media and the Path to Peace,* Cambridge: Cambridge University Press.
Women's Organization of United Democrats (2006) *The Participation of Greek Cypriot Women in Politics and Public Life*, Nicosia: PrintWays.
Woodhouse, C. M. (1991) *Modern Greece*, London: Faber and Faber.
Woolf, V. (1938) *Three Guineas*, New York: Harcourt Brace Jovanovich.
World Bank (2003) *Bosnia and Herzegovina: Poverty Assessment*, Washington, DC: World Bank.
World Bank (2006) *Sustainability and Sources of Economic Growth in the Northern Part of Cyprus*, Washington, DC: World Bank.
Yaşin, M. (2000) 'Introducing Step-Mothertongue', in Yaşin, M. (ed.), *Step-Mothertongue – From Nationalism to Multiculturalism: Literatures of Cyprus, Greece and Turkey*, London: Middlesex University Press, 1–21.
Yeldan, E. and Cizre, Ü. (2002) *Turkey: Economy, Politics and Society in the Post-crisis Era*, Bilkent, Bilkent University, available at www.networkideas.org/feathm/jul2002/Turkey.pdf.
Yiangou, G. S. (2002) 'The Accession of Cyprus to the EU: Challenges and Opportunities for the New European Regional Order', *Journal of Ethnopolitics and Minority Issues in Europe*, 2, available at http://ecmi.de/jemie/download/Focus2-2002_Yiangou.pdf.
Yılmaz, I. (2002) 'Paper Presented to the Conference on Turkey and TRNC During the Process of EU Accession, Ankara, 8 December 2001, by the TRNC's Undersecretary for State Planning Organisation', *Mülkiye*, 232 (January–February).
Young, O. (1968) *The Politics of Force: Bargaining During International Crises*, Princeton, NJ: Princeton University Press.
Yuval-Davis, N. (1997) *Gender and Nation*, London: Sage.
Zahar, M. J. (2004) 'Republika Srpska', in Bahcheli, T., Bartmann, B. and Srebrnik, H. (eds), *De Facto States: The Quest for Sovereignty*, London: Routledge, 32–51.
Zetter, R. (1992) 'Refugees and Forced Migration as Development Resources', *Cyprus Review*, 4(1): 7–39.

Index

Note: 'n' after a page number indicates a note on that page.

CPSIA information can be obtained at www.ICGtesting.com
Printed in the USA
BVOW06s0443200816

459636BV00002B/20/P

9 780719 091162